FICTION

IN THE

QUANTUM

UNIVERSE

The
University
of
North Carolina
Press
Chapel Hill
and London

Fiction
in the
Quantum
Universe

Susan Strehle

© 1992 The University of
North Carolina Press
All rights reserved

Manufactured in the
United States of America

96   95   94   93   92

5   4   3   2   1

The paper in this book meets the guidelines
for permanence and durability of the
Committee on Production Guidelines for
Book Longevity of the Council on Library
Resources.

Library of Congress
Cataloging-in-Publication Data
Strehle, Susan.
    Fiction in the quantum universe / Susan
Strehle.
        p.   cm.
Includes bibliographical references and
index.
ISBN 0-8078-2024-5 (cloth : alk. paper). —
ISBN 0-8078-4365-2 (pbk. : alk. paper)
    1. American fiction—20th century—
History and criticism. 2. Physics in
literature. 3. Literature and science—
United States—History—20th century.
4. Postmodernism (Literature)—United
States. 5. Quantum theory in literature.
I. Title.
PS374.P45S77   1992
813'.5409356—dc20   91-36805
                    CIP

FOR ADAM AND MICHAEL

CONTENTS   Preface / ix

PREFACE

I began work on this book when a relatively simple problem turned
complex: I was exploring the influence that Vladimir Nabokov had on
Thomas Pynchon, who took a course from Nabokov at Cornell. But
historical reality—the world outside the text that alters the course of
fiction when two significant writers meet in a banked lecture hall—has
lost ground in the criticism of contemporary fiction. Postmodern narratives appear to many critics to be metafiction: a fiction designed to comment on its own textual and linguistic processes. More generally, critics
regard all contemporary writers who have abandoned realism as having
abandoned reality at the same stroke. In the prevailing metafictive climate, the world outside of fiction is assumed by some critics of postmodern fiction to be linguistic and textual, by others to be fictive or imaginary,
and by virtually all to be beside the point.

In exploring the connections between Nabokov and Pynchon, I found
that I needed to redefine the aims and interests of contemporary fiction
and to place it in a new context. I had to reconstruct the extraliterary,
historical dimension in which similar fictions can make kindred sense, and
I needed to supplement the metafictive model with another understanding of current fictional aesthetics. Once I had done so, I could not only
complete the project arguing for Pynchon's indebtedness to Nabokov (in a
study published in *Contemporary Literature* in 1983), I could also undertake
a meaningful study of a community of novelists.

My first premise is that contemporary fiction departs from realism without losing interest in reality. Reality itself is no longer realistic; it has more energy and mystery, rendering the observer's position more uncertain and more involved, than the solid and rocklike overlook from which the realist surveyed a stable world. In the quantum universe, space and time aren't separate, predictable, and absolute; narratives can't steer by the fixed poles that guided realistic fiction. While many living writers share a well-read fascination with the possibilities inherent in literary form, and while they make allied formal choices to displace realism, they do so in order to think more clearly about what we now understand as real. Their fiction considers twentieth-century history, politics, science, and discourse: in short, the actual world.

Instead of an exclusive focus on the writers' reflections on art, the criticism of contemporary fiction can only gain by recognizing these writers' mixed choices and plural aims: rather than choosing between art and actuality, contemporary novelists pursue both in fiction. A group of the most challenging and ambitious writers, like those collected in this book, can therefore resemble and influence each other in their parallel meditations, not only on the city of words, but also on the state of the nation and the quantum universe.

This book was long in the writing, in part because the novels I chose to discuss are themselves long, complex, and resistant to easy formulations. I'm grateful for various forms of assistance, all of them crucial, I had along the way. I would like to thank the National Endowment for the Humanities, the SUNY Research Foundation, and various deans of Arts and Sciences at Binghamton for granting me funding and time in which to write. Nathan W. Dean, vice provost for graduate studies and research, has consistently supported my need for time to complete the manuscript. A canny physicist, he has illuminated some of the scientific concepts on which I draw.

I owe a significant debt to John Kuehl, whose suggestions improved first the Gaddis chapter and then the whole book. Donald J. Greiner also made important contributions to the revision of the book. Astute and generous, both were ideal readers. Arnold Edelstein read and commented helpfully on the Pynchon chapter. My colleagues at Binghamton have offered illuminating suggestions, patient audiences at seminars, kindness, and wonderful collegiality. I'm especially grateful to William Spanos, whose profoundly original readings of postmodern critical theory and of postmodern fiction were liberating. Joe Church, Suzette Henke, Richard

McLain, Phil Rogers, Liz Rosenberg, Bernie Rosenthal, Albert Tricomi, Libby Tucker, and Grant Webster have given me specific advice, insightful readings, and interesting conversations about particular issues and collegial generosity. My students have also contributed meaningfully to this book; I'm especially thankful to Cristina Bacchilega, Giovanna Covi, Aliki Dragona, Anne Drolet, Anne Higginbottom, and Madeleine Sorapure, whose dissertations in this field have shown it in new light.

Thanks are also due to the University of North Carolina Press and its intelligent, attentive staff. Sandra Eisdorfer, senior editor and managing editor, has been wonderful to work with: clear, generous, and astute. Craig Noll is the most diligent and perceptive of copyeditors. Their careful reading and wise questions have improved the book.

The University Manuscript Center provided valuable help in preparing the manuscript. Its coordinator, Lisa Fegley-Schmidt, gave me unerring advice, various forms of help, and a new command of WordPerfect as I revised.

Charlotte Skuster created the index with skill and sensitivity, and Sue Rosenberg proofread the manuscript carefully.

My parents, Marie Bell, Shirley and Douglas Strehle, have offered encouragement and kindness, for which I'm grateful. Michael Conlon has been a perceptive reader and the best of friends. And, not least, my son Adam—whose eight-year-old life has been lived while I wrote—has kept me joyfully immersed in the actual world.

FICTION

IN THE

QUANTUM

UNIVERSE

ONE

ACTUALISM

FICTION IN THE

QUANTUM UNIVERSE

According to conventional aesthetics, fiction aims either at the realistic representation of life or at the antirealistic exploration of artistic processes. It selectively focuses either on the human reality that is its subject or on the linguistic and formal rendering that constitutes its art. Fictional choices work this way because, for traditional theorists, perception itself functions in either-or fashion; visual and literary readings must choose a single plane of orientation. Authors therefore direct readers to observe either the garden outside the window or the glass through which the garden appears, in the metaphor proposed by Ortega y Gasset.

> We have here a very simple optical problem. To see a thing we must adjust our visual apparatus in a certain way. . . . Looking at the garden we adjust our eyes in such a way that the ray of vision travels through the pane. . . . But we can also deliberately disregard the garden and, withdrawing the ray of vision, detain it at the window. We then lose

sight of the garden. . . . Hence to see the garden and to see the windowpane are two incompatible operations which exclude one another because they require different adjustments. Similarly a work of art vanishes from sight for a beholder who seeks in it nothing but the moving fate of [the characters]. . . . The portrayed person and his portrait are two entirely different things; we are interested in either one or the other.[1]

Following this binary logic, Ortega y Gasset sees nineteenth-century realistic fiction as pandering to the masses, by reducing the "strictly aesthetic elements to a minimum" and encouraging readers to "revel in the human reality with which the work deals." Modernism, by contrast, attempts a "purification of art" through the "progressive elimination of the human, all too human, elements."

We might begin by objecting in principle: surely this is too simple a model of perception. Surely vision can accommodate awareness of both garden and pane; surely reading encompasses interests in both portrayed life and the means of portrayal. Readers have always brought some awareness of aesthetic elements to the reading of fiction, and authors have devoted their own attention to artistic processes even (or perhaps especially) when they sought to make their art invisible. Since poststructuralist and deconstructive theory have sharpened the focus on textual and intertextual issues, postmodern readers can hardly see the most avowedly realistic fiction as a clear transparency through which to study human reality. Its textuality remains always an element of the text before us. At the same time, most fiction neither manages nor even attempts to eliminate the human element, the lived reality expressed in story. Where there is plot and character, even in the most self-consciously aesthetic of modernist and postmodernist texts, there is inevitably also some degree of worldliness to the text. The constricting binary logic of realism and antirealism has, however, reduced fiction's rich double interest in both art and life to a single dimension for many readers and critics.

The legacy of these assumptions becomes especially restrictive—even blinding, I would argue—for critics of postmodern fiction. While some writers appeal to realist assumptions about the world and the text (I think of Bellow, Fowles, Heller, Kesey, Oates, Morrison, Roth, Mailer, and Updike), others clearly and even explicitly refuse the realistic tradition in narrative, together with its vision of reality. Writers like Atwood, Barth, Pynchon, Gaddis, Coover, and Barthelme—as well as Hawkes, Didion,

Coetzee, Kundera, Eco, Calvino, Puig, and Nabokov, for example—cannot be described as realistic. They are, therefore, approached as antirealists. Limited to these two exclusive alternatives, critics who have appropriately identified the divergence from realism in postmodern fiction can only place it in the opposite camp, which flies most prominently the banner of metafiction. It has been called other things as well: irrealism, counterrealism, surfiction, disruptive fiction, and parafiction.

Logically, then, criticism has emphasized the antireferential nature of postmodern fiction. It has no relation to the external world, whose "reality" it sees as questionable; instead, it self-reflexively confronts its own status as language, performance, mental construct, city of words. According to this interpretation, postmodern fiction becomes a stained-glass window through which nothing is visible. "Clearly, then, the parafictionist seeks to vaporize our common universe . . . and replace it with another within whose verbal boundaries art would become but one more way to experience the fiction of life." For another critic, "If the world is absurd, if what passes for reality is distressingly unreal, why spend time representing it?" For another, surfiction "exposes the fictionality of reality."[2] Critics approach single authors with these assumptions—various essays place most of the writers I discuss in this book as metafictionists; equally, since Robert Scholes's definitive essay "Metafiction" (1970), critics bring the metafictive paradigm to bear on groups of contemporary novelists.

Its exclusive self-reflexivity has become, in fact, the most common starting point for critical discussion of contemporary fiction, both by critics who condemn its narcissism and by others who approve its artful stratagems. Even "neutral" reporters on the state of affairs in contemporary letters can by now assume its metafictiveness, so that a broadly introductory survey like Robert Kiernan's *American Writing since 1945* labels the texts I discuss here metafiction, which is the most "interesting fiction in the postwar period. . . . Stressing the *composed* aspect of fiction, it tends to put in the foreground both language and authorship in an attempt not simply to undercut the illusions of realism but to discover new modes of narrative gamesmanship. Essentially, it is a body of fiction about the making of fictions."[3] Since surveys like Kiernan's function in part to voice widely accepted premises, Kiernan's easy assimilation of metafictive assumptions illuminates the pervasive assent to arguments made with thoroughness and rigor by Scholes, McCaffery, Klinkowitz, Alter, Waugh, Christensen, Hutcheon, Imhof, and dozens more.

Metafiction does, of course, exist. It is practiced consciously and adeptly by Gilbert Sorrentino, Ronald Sukenick, and Raymond Federman. Some of William Gass's texts are explicitly metafictional; William Burroughs's theoretical emphasis on the arbitrariness of narrative ordering makes him describable as a metafictionist. Steve Katz, B. S. Johnson, Ishmael Reed, Russell Banks, and others write fiction of which critics like Jerome Klinkowitz can justly and satisfactorily say that it "does not represent reality. . . . it creates a whole life of its own."[4] John Barth's story "Autobiography" demonstrates the pure form of the metafictive impulse to foreground language, particularly through wordplay, and to explore theories of fiction-making. Philosophical, linguistic, theoretical in its interests and in its approach, and self-conscious to its core, metafiction is the educated offspring of modernist parents.

But what are we to make of the wealth of historically accurate detail in texts like Coover's *Public Burning* or Pynchon's *Gravity's Rainbow* or Barth's *LETTERS*? How are we to read the prominent commentary on Western culture, urban political economy, sexual and racial issues, and socially constituted forms of power and their abuse in texts like Gaddis's *J R*, Atwood's *Cat's Eye*, and Barthelme's *Paradise*? Far from excluding or "vaporizing" external reality, these texts, while patently not realistic, nonetheless seem impelled to explore, celebrate, criticize, and engage the outer world. These novels differ from the intentionally aesthetic narratives of metafiction.

The authors' statements about their fiction differ, too, from the positions taken by thoroughgoing metafictionists. Ronald Sukenick, for example, writes that "reality doesn't exist, time doesn't exist, personality doesn't exist"; and, "As artifice the work of art is a conscious tautology in which there is always an implicit (and sometimes explicit) reference to its own nature as artifact—self-reflexive, not self-reflective. It is not an imitation but a new thing in its own right, an invention."[5] To see the difference in emphasis, we can turn to Pynchon's introduction to his collection of early stories, *Slow Learner*. Pynchon finds his early work flawed, in part by its false assumption that "one's personal life had nothing to do with fiction, when the truth, as everyone knows, is nearly the direct opposite." The fiction he admires most engages both art and life and makes its artistry "luminous" by expressing human reality. "In fact the fiction . . . that moved and pleased me then as now was precisely that which had been made luminous, undeniably authentic by having been found and taken up, always at a cost, from deeper, more shared levels of the life we all really live."[6] The authors I discuss in this book have all made similar statements suggesting not only that reality *does* exist but that art's goal is to engage it.

These writers—Pynchon, Atwood, Barth, Coover, Gaddis, and Barthelme, as well as many others—cannot be described as metafictionists, however broadly one stretches the term, any more than they can be placed as neorealists.[7] In contrast to the theoreticians of self-reflexivity, they want fiction to comment on a lived reality through the pane of art. In contrast to the neorealists, they believe art cannot efface itself or become pure transparency, unconscious of its status as created language. They affirm *both* art (self-consciously aware of its processes and of aesthetic traditions) *and* the real world (specifically, the postmodern world, with a detailed awareness of its nature and history). Their fiction admits both the garden and the glass.

In the realm of aesthetic theory, the longstanding duality separating art and reality, or the perceiver and the world, has been exploded by modern discoveries about the nature of perception. Thus the argument I'm making about the effort among contemporary novelists to find a position blending some transformed assumptions from realism and antirealism, to create an art about both reality and artistic process, appears in persuasive theoretical terms in Raymond Williams's *The Long Revolution*.

> The new facts about perception make it impossible for us to assume that there is any reality experienced by man into which man's own observations and interpretations do not enter. Thus the assumptions of naive realism—seeing the things as they really are, quite apart from our reactions to them—become impossible. Yet equally, the facts of perception in no way lead us to a late form of idealism; they do not require us to suppose that there is no kind of reality outside the human mind; they point rather to the insistence that all human experience is an interpretation of the non-human reality. But this, again, is not the duality of subject and object—the assumption on which almost all theories of art are based. We have to think, rather, of human experience as both objective and subjective, in one inseparable process.[8]

Following Williams's logic, we can understand the group of writers I've identified as radically original: they form a challenging new fiction that is based on the awareness of interpretation as an interactive process. While the neorealists attempt, often in subtle and sophisticated ways, to see things as they really are, and while the metafictionists or neomodernists bring theoretical intelligence to the late idealism that spins reality out of the mind, these other writers engage the double but undivided nature of art as the human interpretation of a nonhuman reality. Their version of postmodernism does not emerge, as some critics suggest, as a late echo or higher amplification of literary modernism. Rather, their fiction creates its own different aesthetic stance through a process John Barth terms "the synthesis or transcension of these antitheses, which may be summed up as the premodernist and modernist modes of writing. My ideal postmodernist author neither merely repudiates nor merely imitates either his twentieth-century modernist parents or his nineteenth-century premodernist grandparents."[9] Breaking out of the false and restrictive duality between realism and antirealism, these postmodern authors manage an original fusion that transforms both strands of their literary heritage.

Because the language of realism and antirealism carries with it outmoded assumptions about reality and art, we need a new term or aesthetic category for these writers and their texts. As Alan Wilde points out in his important book *Middle Grounds*, "For want of an adequate designation," this "tertium quid of current literature" can only "languish in the outback of current criticism." Wilde proposes to call the "referential but nonmimetic literature" we both admire "midfiction." "Rejecting metafiction's pronounced tilt toward the reflexive . . . and rejecting as well realism's belief in the possibility of simple mimesis, midfiction is intended to suggest neither compromise nor mediation, and still less an inevitable or necessary moderation in its perceptions of the world and in the strategies that variously render them. What it does instead is to stake out a variety of middle grounds on which it tests the assumptions of other fictional forms and, more importantly, defines its own in opposition to them."[10] While I agree with many of Wilde's assumptions and much of his assessment of contemporary fiction, I would fault his term for suggesting a static resting place, a *ground* midway between the poles of the binary dualism we both find so damaging. Intended to suggest broad latitude, range, and what Wilde elegantly terms "the close interanimation of consciousness and world, of perception and creation," "midfiction" connotes too clearly the mean, or average, between extremes, where Wilde himself understands their transcension in a different mode of seeing and writing.

I propose, instead, to call the new mode of fiction *actualism*. I believe it emerges from a widespread change in the way reality is understood by the culture at large, and I see this shift localized usefully in the new physics. To anticipate a discussion I will complete after the necessary background in physical science, I derive the term "actualism" from a distinction Werner Heisenberg makes between the actual and the real.[11] At the subatomic level, he says, reality is not real, but it is active, dynamic, "actual." Actualistic fiction expresses, then, a literary version of the reality constituted by fundamentally new physical theories in the first half of the twentieth century. Departing from the stable material reality underpinning Newtonian science and realistic fiction, actualism abandons and even subverts the narrative conventions of realism. It does so, however, not to replace reality with the purified aesthetics of self-reflexivity, but rather, self-consciously and theoretically, to renew art's readiness for its perennial project: the human interpretation of a nonhuman reality.

Actualism and the New Physics

Actualism develops in postmodern fiction because reality has changed. It has changed for thinkers in every field, and the shift has been described and theorized variously in different disciplines. Physics, the science devoted to studying nonliving reality, provides an especially pronounced measure of the change in worldview. While the general importance of the new physics may be known by most of the educated public, the extent to which relativity theory, quantum theory, and wave mechanics revolutionized previous concepts of reality deserves emphasis. In *The Philosophical Impact of Contemporary Physics*, Milič Čapek defines in strong language the "astonishment" generated by the way modern concepts transform classical physics. "There is hardly any similarity between the 'matter' of modern physics and the traditional material substance of the classical period, and this is true in varying degrees of other concepts as well. . . . It is true that the effect of [relativity, quantum theory, and wave mechanics] on the imagination of physicists, philosophers, and even laymen was truly shattering; the contrast between the new theories and the appealing clarity of classical concepts was sharp and shocking."[12] Similar assessments, with a frequent invocation of the term "revolution," appear throughout studies of the new physics—one of them, revealingly, titled *Dismantling the Universe*.[13]

A skeptic might object here that, however radical the redefinition of reality in new physics, its impact on literature can hardly be immediate or direct—novelists surely don't read physics journals, nor could they follow the mathematical or theoretical subtleties if they did. Granted: of the novelists I discuss in this book, only Pynchon has a sound education, undergraduate at that, in physics. But changes in physical theories inspire changes in a culture's general attitudes, and art both responds to and shapes these assumptions. Physics and fiction inhabit the same planet, however divergent their discourses about it may be. Canadian fiction writer Alice Munro describes the way private individuals come to share the most progressive notions afloat in their culture: "It's as if tendencies that seem most deeply rooted in our minds, most private and singular, have come in as spores on the prevailing wind, looking for any likely place to land, any welcome."[14] Writers may, by nature, be a culture's most welcoming grounds for such spores.

Others have suggested that the new physics plays a significant role in changing concepts of the world for fiction. James Mellard, for example, argues that "the novel remained relatively stable through the trends in thought until the [new physics], for as long as it could count upon the changelessness of nature as viewed by empirical science, it had an authority that could counter any combination of the other modes of thought. But when the new science exploded the world, it exploded with it the novel as well."[15] Of growing importance in the study of contemporary fiction, the notion that physics has transformed twentieth-century thought, including philosophy, linguistics, and literature, appears in a number of recent books and essays.[16]

To characterize the way reality has changed at the intersection of physics and fiction is inevitably to select and to interpret. It is to construct a paradigm, invent a terminology and a focus. Actualistic fiction and contemporary physics join, I propose, in seeing the external world and the human relation to it as:

> discontinuous
> statistical
> energetic
> relative
> subjective
> uncertain

Each of these terms reflects a major transformation of the assumptions basic to the Newtonian/realistic paradigm. For a follower of Newton, reality was ordered by the presence of absolute space, time, and motion, and science proceeded through an objective methodology to determine the causal laws governing the continuous operations of an essentially material world. Science projected an attainable certainty in its attempts to uncover the deterministic and therefore clearly identifiable relations among the properties of nature. After the revolutionary new theories of relativity and quantum mechanics had been assimilated (between, roughly, 1905 and 1930), a changed understanding emerged. For a follower of Einstein, Planck, Heisenberg, and Bohr, space, time, and motion are relative and interrelated, and no privileged frame of reference remains to enable the determination of scientific results. At the subatomic level, reality is discontinuous or quantized; particles make quantum leaps from one energy state to another. Subatomic reality is energy, rather than matter, for particles whose position and velocity cannot be determined can't be said to "exist" as things. Their behavior is indeterminate, not predictable by causal laws, but only describable by the laws of statistics. Limited by the uncertainty principle to incomplete knowledge, science acknowledges the subjectivity generating its choice of focus and its inventions of theoretical models.

The complex story of the revolution in physics has been frequently told, with different emphases, by various historians and philosophers of science.[17] A condensed version of this story will place in sharp relief those assumptions of the new physics which have exerted a profound influence on contemporary culture and shaped the aesthetic mode of actualism.

The first disruption of the classical physicist's worldview occurred in 1905, when Albert Einstein published one paper advancing the special theory of relativity and another arguing that light sometimes behaves as particles—the assumption basic to quantum theory. The special theory of relativity assumes that the velocity of light is constant, regardless of whether its source is moving relative to the observer or not. Light does not propagate in waves through the ether envisioned by classical physics, and therefore the concept of this stationary medium could be abandoned. More important, Einstein theorizes that measurements are relative to their frames of reference, so that a measuring instrument changes depending on its motion. A clock on a speeding rocket runs more slowly than a clock on earth, and an accelerating measuring rod contracts to become shorter than an earthbound rod. This hypothesis explains why the speed of light remains the same for both the observer moving slowly through space on earth and the observer moving rapidly on a rocket. Each observer would see no change in the measuring instruments, which would appear entirely normal. In part, this is because the speeding observer too would contract and slow down.

Another implication of the special theory of relativity is that "simultaneity" does not exist for events separated in space. Simultaneity is relative to the observer's frame of reference; one observer might perceive events as happening simultaneously, but others in different states of motion could see either of the two as previous. None of these observers is right, because no absolute or privileged frame of reference exists.

An accelerating body increases in mass for an earthbound observer, though from the reference frame of the speeding body, earth also appears to be growing heavier. Einstein's famous equation describing this process, $E = mc^2$, suggests that mass or matter contains energy, while energy has mass. This idea radically alters the notion of matter in classical physics, creating a newly energized and dynamic version of the solid stuff basic to classical and common sense notions of reality. Seen in relation to the energy it contains, matter ceases to be distinct and absolute; matter itself becomes relative.

A similar transformation brings time and space, previously seen as separate and absolute, into relativistic relation. In order to posit a standard against which experimental results could be verified in classical physics, Newton defined an absolute time flowing equably, without relation to anything external. The mechanistic, or "clockwork," model of the universe that emerged inevitably from this hypothesis eliminated temporality, as Čapek points out. "Time in the sense of genuine succession has no place in the consistent necessitarian scheme."[18] Einstein reintroduces temporality by showing that it is relative to the observer's position and momentum in space—Einstein terms their relative relation a space-time continuum. Rather than spatializing time, Čapek argues, the notion of a continuum actually "dynamizes" space.[19] Time becomes a fourth dimension, a coordinate that joins the three spatial dimensions to form a mathematically definable continuum.

The general theory of relativity (1916) extends its inquiry from bodies in uniform motion to bodies in accelerating motion and thus defines the effects of gravitational fields. Gravity curves the space-time continuum, Einstein argues, and changes the geometry of space and time. Gravity itself is not the product of matter exerting its pull through empty space; rather, gravitational fields define space-time, and where they become intense, they constitute matter. Space, time, and matter are not discrete entities but rather interacting aspects of the curved gravitational field. Reality behaves as if its physical elements—space, time, matter, energy, gravitation, inertia—are not separate or isolated, as they were in Newtonian mechanics, but rather as if these elements function, and can be understood, only in a network of relational interdependence.

Einstein spent much of the rest of his life attempting to refute implications other physicists derived from his theories. A believer to the end, despite disturbing evidence to the contrary, that "God does not play dice with the world," Einstein retained his faith in a causal order existing in the objective world and in the possibility of a unified field theory that would establish universal scientific truth. Quantum theory led, however, in the opposite direction. Relying on Einstein's vision of interconnected phenomena, observed from involved, unprivileged, always relative frames of reference, drawing even on his 1905 argument for the emission of light in particular units, quantum theory grew to dismay, and finally to override the objections of, its reluctant sire.

Quantum theory originated with another unwilling revolutionary, Max Planck, who theorized in 1900 that light is emitted in packets, or quanta. Since light had been understood as waves for two centuries, and conclusive evidence had accumulated supporting its wavelike nature, Planck's quantum theory presented a major conceptual challenge to the framework of classical physics. But Planck could explain the phenomena of blackbody radiation in no other way: light is emitted in discrete whole units, never in the fractions wave theory would predict.

Einstein proposed in 1905 that light was made up of particles, thus explaining Planck's experimental results. Particles, emitted in wholes rather than fractions, make Planck's quantum theory logical. Arthur Compton's experiments with X rays confirmed Einstein's hypothesis in 1923, for Compton showed that X rays passed through paraffin not only scattered but changed their wavelengths, giving up energy in the collision of particles, as quantum theory predicts.

The problem remained, or rather became newly pressing, that light had been seen as waves because it behaves demonstrably in wavelike patterns. Paradoxically, light has a dual nature as both wave and particle. The attempt to resolve this paradox by bringing its two terms into alignment, or discovering some unifying relation between them, has occupied physicists ever since. One of the earliest of these attempts was Louis de Broglie's doctoral dissertation, submitted in 1924, suggesting that particles behave as waves. Responding to Niels Bohr's theory (1913) that electrons revolve around the nucleus of atoms in orbits or shells, jumping outward to another shell when energy is introduced and emitting this energy in the form of a quantity of light when it returns to the lower shell, de Broglie hypothesized that electrons behave as light does—as both particle and wave. Matter, he said, has waves that correspond to it; the greater a particle's momentum, the shorter its matter wave. Experiments with electron diffraction, passing a beam of electrons through a very small space, confirm de Broglie's theory: the beam diffracts just as light does. The paradox therefore expands: light, made of waves, behaves as particles, and electronic particles behave as waves.

In 1926 Erwin Schrödinger advanced the theory that electrons are not particles at all but standing waves, which are also quantized. Schrödinger developed a wave mechanics to describe mathematically the possible shapes of standing waves, and the mathematical values have been confirmed experimentally. At the same time, Werner Heisenberg advanced a matrix mechanics which, though it proceeds from different assumptions about subatomic processes, gives the same confirmable mathematical results. While Schrödinger envisioned electrons as spread out over their wave patterns in a cloud, Heisenberg assumed that physicists must abandon perceptual models of atomic processes and work with observable states at the beginning and end of experiments; these he correlated in mathematical tables of matrices. Continuous waves in Schrödinger's wave mechanics and discontinuous, unlocalized particles in Heisenberg's matrix mechanics, electrons appear democratically to confirm both irreconcilable theories.

Max Born suggested a way to resolve the paradox: he argued that electrons are particles whose wave function represents the probability that they are located at a particular place. Born assumes that the position and velocity of the subatomic particle cannot be defined; its behavior cannot be understood as causally determined, but only predicted by the laws of statistics.

Heisenberg's uncertainty principle (1927) posits a radical indeterminacy in scientific knowledge of the subatomic realm. Scientists cannot measure accurately both the position and the velocity of subatomic particles. Using light energy to measure position alters the velocity of particles; in measuring velocity, without altering the energy level of the system, one cannot determine position. No improved technology will ever remove this fundamental uncertainty from scientific knowledge, for basic to it is the recognition that the observer changes—disturbs—the system under study. While classical physics assumed that reality proceeds on its independent course, following immutable laws of causality, and objective scientists watch and predict its course, Heisenberg's principle recognizes that subatomic reality changes with observation—and, even more radically, is constituted by the choices the observer makes from an involved vantage. Heisenberg emphasizes the subjective interaction of the scientist with those aspects of nature he or she chooses to observe. "Science no longer confronts nature as an objective observer, but sees itself as an actor in this interplay between man and nature."[20] Physics meets philosophy and aesthetics here, for Heisenberg's "interplay" supplements Wilde's phenomenological "close interanimation of consciousness and world" and Raymond Williams's "inseparable process" through which objective and subjective meet in the human interpretation of nonhuman reality. When the scientist, for centuries a figure typifying neutrality, distance, and passive observation, becomes an actor in the interplay, the entire set of relations between mind and world has changed.

Heisenberg's principle has other implications that disrupt the Newtonian worldview. If scientists cannot determine position and velocity, they cannot apply Newton's laws of motion in the subatomic realm. They cannot predict the course of electrons they cannot measure, nor can they construct causal models explaining why reality behaves, at this minuscule level, as it does. According to Gary Zukav, "The whole idea of a causal universe is undermined by the uncertainty principle."[21] Moreover, a particle without a determinable position and velocity cannot be located as a "thing" in space or time, and the "reality" scientists study loses the solidity of matter (res) to take on the energetic quality of acts (acta).

The indeterminacy of the wave-particle duality of light generates Niels Bohr's principle of complementarity (1927). Known as the Copenhagen interpretation of quantum theory, complementarity sees irreconcilable and mutually exclusive concepts—both particle and wave—as necessary to understand subatomic reality, which behaves according to both opposite principles. In Bohr's view, "An independent reality in the ordinary physical sense can neither be ascribed to the phenomena nor to the agencies of observation."[22] Rather, the interactions between scientists and nature construct a necessarily double or complementary view of subatomic processes. Resolution of the paradox—or restoration of Newtonian clarity—cannot occur.

As this summary suggests, the new physics has reimagined reality. While other terms could be added, the new reality may be described as relative, discontinuous, energetic, statistical, subjective, and uncertain. The general conception of the change in reality implied by these terms extends beyond physics into psychology (where Lacan and others shift the emphasis from material causes of disorder to energetic processes of relation in language), philosophy (where Foucault and others replace absolutist concepts of people and events with relativistic notions of forms of representation and discourse), and literary theory (where Derrida and others see interpretation not as the penetration of certain truth but as an encounter with the duplicitous undecidability of texts). In short, like any significant change in reality, the latest one has rattled windows in every house on the block.

To express and address the new reality, postmodern fiction cannot be "realistic." One of Norman Mailer's characters puts it perfectly: he "does not want to write a realistic novel, because reality is no longer realistic."[23] I've called the new mode actualism to suggest both kinship with and difference from realism. My term derives from a distinction Heisenberg makes as he discusses the dubious reality of particles as mathematical forms. "Would you call such mathematical forms 'actual' or 'real'? If they express natural laws, that is the central order inherent in material processes, then you must also call them 'actual,' for they act, they produce tangible effects, but you cannot call them 'real,' because they cannot be described as *res*, as things."[24] With its roots not in things but in acts, relations, and motions, actualism describes a literature that abandons the old mechanistic reality without losing interest in the external world. Where "real" evokes the thing fixed in space, "actual" refers to the "action or existence" of phenomena in space-time; according to the OED, it implies action that is "present, current," not eternal or absolute. Indeed, with the notion that the laws of nature form an order "inherent in material processes," Heisenberg rejects a spatial, static idea of order for one oriented to time and interactive process. "Actual" is thus a relative term, linking time, space, and matter in Einsteinian fashion. Finally, the dual meaning of "to act" as both "to make" and "to fake" gives "actualism" special relevance for a fiction that describes and embodies both sorts of acts.

Actualism and the Form of Fiction

As Erich Auerbach demonstrates in *Mimesis*, cultural beliefs about reality affect profoundly the matter and the manner of artistic representations. A changed perception of reality therefore invalidates some previous conventions by which fiction refers outward and calls for the invention of new ones. Actualism differs from previous modes of fiction not only in the vastly altered reality emerging at the level of content, or theme, but also in the renewal it accomplishes at the level of fictive form. Not least, actualism revises the conception of artistic activity itself.

Realistic fiction represented the Newtonian cosmos, in all its causal continuity. Examining the novel's origins in the eighteenth century, Ian Watt underscores its rejection of the classical and medieval heritage of universals in favor of the position of philosophical realism, "that truth can be discovered by the individual through his senses." This assumption belongs, of course, as much to Newton as it does to Descartes and Locke; it has disappeared from the conception of reality in recent physics. Describing the analogies between philosophical realism and prose fiction, Watt sketches a ground mapped powerfully in classical physics. "The methods of investigation" used in philosophical realism and the novel, Watt says, emphasize "the study of the particulars of experience by the individual investigator, who, ideally at least, is free from the body of past assumptions and traditional beliefs."[25] This "scientific method" of observation and analysis, carried out by a detached observer who imagines that investigation can occur in the absence of assumptions and beliefs, defined the ideal mode of vision in Newton's cosmos and became the *only* means of vision for scientists during the next two hundred years. While early novelists liberated themselves from allegorical projections in the Slough of Despond to undertake a joyful immersion in the particulars of experience, they nonetheless remained bound to Newtonian understandings of reality and investigation. And, from a post-Einsteinian perspective, we can see that while they did away with universals in a theological sense, they simply replaced those with scientific universals. The faith in absolute mathematical time and space, in causality, in objectivity and certainty— these became the new universal principles relied on unawares by realistic fiction.

Logically, then, realistic novelists of both the eighteenth and the nineteenth centuries came to model their own imaginative activity on the pattern of the Newtonian scientist's detached observation of nature. In a persuasive argument for the realistic novel's basis in Newtonian assumptions, Robert Nadeau writes: "The novelist was confident in his ability to depict the objectively real in fiction because he implicitly assumed, as Newton did, that its essential structures were known to him. Since the conceptual forms inherent in the construction of the fictive landscape were presumed to have actual existence in the life of nature, the objective space of the novel, to use the eighteenth-century metaphor, was regarded as the mirror held up to objective space itself."[26] Because the truth about reality exists in an absolute objective space external to consciousness, the student of nature—the novelist, like the scientist—casts an impersonal gaze across empty space toward atoms of discrete materiality, whether characters or things, and traces the effects of linear, causal time in producing coherent, predictable, explicable, and final results. And the writer, far from inventing language or creating fiction, simply holds a mirror up to nature, as in a Newtonian optical experiment, or takes a tissue sample from society's vitals to produce a "slice of life."

The scientific model of artistic activity reached its height in nineteenth-century realism, at the same time the natural and physical sciences were reveling in their power to solve nature's last mysteries. Flaubert articulates the vision of art as the observation of a Newtonian reality perhaps more clearly and powerfully than any other nineteenth-century writer, though the rhetoric and assumptions of classical science run through all the variations on realist aesthetics George Becker collects in *Documents of Modern Literary Realism* and shape Becker's introduction as well. The discourse of mathematics and science permeates Flaubert's descriptions of his artistic goals and practices, as the following glimpses from letters written between 1852 and 1866 suggest.

> I am trying . . . to follow a geometrically straight line. No lyricism, no comments, the author's personality absent. . . . That's what is so fine about the natural sciences: they don't wish to prove anything. Therefore what breadth of fact and what an immensity for thought! We must treat men like mastodons and crocodiles. . . . When literature has the precision of results of an exact science, that's going some. . . . Art ought, moreover, to rise above personal feelings and nervous susceptibilities! It is time to give it the precision of the physical sciences, by means of a pitiless method! . . . I believe that Great Art is scientific and impersonal.[27]

The version of scientific activity implied in these comments is as illuminating as their construction of artistic activity. The sciences have no assumptions or points to prove, but only subject broadly collected facts to dispassionate thought. Their pitiless (uninvolved, detached) method leads to precise results, ones corresponding exactly to the truth of nature. Art, then, emulates the great method of scientific inquiry, effacing subjectivity and personality, pinching out lyricism and evaluative comment, rendering style transparent so that readers can secure an unmediated vision of external reality.

While its premodernist grandparents pursued a version of artistic activity as the scientific study of reality, actualism's modernist parents (and metafictive cousins) celebrate instead art's inventive role in making alternative realms. Responding to the loss of faith in external order that occurred in history, philosophy, theology, and science in the first decades of the twentieth century, modernism conceives its charge as replacing reality's chaos with the orderly truth of art. Art can construct Byzantium, Xanadu, the crystal land, the verbal icon, the well-wrought urn. Armed with the romantic belief that truth lies not in detailed observation of the external world but in the imagination's power to structure (and perfect) aesthetic alternatives, modernism turns away from representation and toward what Robert Scholes terms fabulation. In doing so, the modernist recalls, appropriately, that art differs from reality; fiction is language, form, and imagined events, characters, and places.

But modernism remains, in its way, faithful to Newton's vision. The spatial form conceived as basic to modern literature by Joseph Frank relies on an absolute frame of reference—an inertial, self-enclosed frame, like the locus of Newton's absolute time and space. While the modernist text eliminates linear, causal development, as Frank observes, in favor of simultaneity, reflexive reference, and juxtaposed motionless glimpses fit into a formal unity, these spatial strategies in no way displace the classical cosmos or suggest the relativistic, indeterminate reality of the new physics. Rather, the modernist artist rises above the fluctuating phenomena of natural reality to the eternal, static reference frame that Newton posited as validating earthly experiments. The aesthetic structure revealed in (or imposed on) mundane experience from this omniscient vantage is as fully and finally determinate as that in realistic fiction: nothing is left to chance, left unassimilated, or left uncertain. The picture of reality emphasizes its own composed nature, to be sure, but it composes according to Newtonian principles.

No longer a mere observer of reality, the modernist becomes the maker of a clockwork universe. Empowered by the ordering activity of mind, the artist takes a position of absolute authority over the text: she or he becomes the mystified and absent presence, the *deus artifex*, or godly maker.[28] Stephen Dedalus, we recall, believed that "the artist, like the God of the creation, remains within or behind or beyond or above his handiwork, invisible, refined out of existence, indifferent, paring his fingernails."[29] All particular subjectivity or personality refined away, the artist becomes as objective and impersonal for Joyce and Eliot as for Flaubert—and as pitiless of method. In the stance of aloof indifference to the created world, the modernist maker emulates not only the Old Testament God but also that allied figure, the great machinist who crafted the clockwork universe and left it running on its own. This artist functions, then, with many of the same assumptions as realism's scientific observer; modernism's artist does not watch but less humbly decrees an essentially Newtonian cosmos.

Actualism does have its precursors, to be sure, and my quick sketch of these narrative traditions has left out the dozens of figures at odds with the Newtonian vision underlying both realist and modernist fiction. The world didn't change in December 1910, as Virginia Woolf suggested; rather, its actualistic qualities became increasingly visible after 1910, as physicists joined with others in changing the way we understand and talk about reality. But before that, even under Newton's very nose and prism, reality was relative, discontinuous, and accidental. Some early writers saw this way and, as a result, wrote a fiction significantly allied to actualism. Among the early novelists, those Robert Alter identifies with the "self-conscious" tradition (Cervantes, Sterne, Fielding, and Diderot) are important ancestors for contemporary actualists, primarily because they focus on the problematic nature of representation. Like the actualists, they question the process by which narratives, made of words, reflect on realities not clear or predictable but contingent, shaped in part by the subjective consciousness brought to bear on them. As Alter puts it, "The hallmark of the true self-conscious novelist is a keen perception of paradox in the relationship between fiction and reality."[30] Another group of writers in the nineteenth century shares that perception; influenced by the romantic reaction against materialist conceptions of reality, these writers of what Hawthorne calls Romance (including Hawthorne and Melville) explore the problematic nature of consciousness. Their fiction suggests, as actualism does, that reality is not "realistic." Common to the fictional antecedents for actualism is a skeptical response to prevailing Newtonian assumptions about art, reality, and their relation.

The actualist, by extension, not only displaces Newton's absolute space with the interactive field theorized by Einstein, Heisenberg, and Bohr but, at the same time, necessarily reconceives art's relation to actuality. In the field model, art can no longer be the transparent glass or reflective mirror, and fiction cannot simply represent external reality; neither, in contrast, can art replace reality with an orderly self-reflexive word-world. Instead, art participates, as an energetic force, in the interconnected field of culture. Fictional constructions refer to actuality, taking part in a large web of related discourses, including those of physics, psychology, linguistics, philosophy, mathematics, and sociology (among many others), all conjoined in meditating, from different directions, on an external world that limits, even while it responds to, the inventive power of human discourse. Neither the invisible observer of nature nor the indifferent maker of a stable narrative picture, the actualist takes a subjective, involved position in the text and destabilizes it in the process. Since actualistic subjectivity opens out on the indeterminate contingency of the external world, the author's relation to the text both enables and provides a metaphor for its relation to reality.

Like actualistic fiction, this study also has its vigorous and interesting precursors. Much of the critical work done on contemporary fiction over the past twenty years falls in the general category of descriptive poetics: whether they see it as fabulation or literary disruption or antirealistic fiction, critics of very different persuasions agree that describing the poetics of recent literature is a requisite first step and, in its own right, an important critical activity. In general, too, these studies have agreed that contemporary fiction is *not* realistic; its departure from the conventions of realism explains why readers, students, and scholars need some reorientation in their sense of what this fiction is and seeks to accomplish.

While the largest number of these studies choose to focus on the "self-referential" artistic strategies that place contemporary fiction—mistakenly, in my view—as a late form of modernism, many also acknowledge that these artistic strategies respond to an understanding of external reality as fundamentally changed. They therefore suggest a view I've made central: that contemporary fiction is referential without being realistic, that it subverts the conventions of realism without abandoning reality. In an influential study, *The Exploded Form* (1980), James Mellard argues that the paradigm shifts of modern philosophy, aided by those in recent science, have "exploded" the assumptions of realistic fiction, while posing the question of an "adequate new realism" which would acknowledge consciousness as an aspect of reality, and reality itself as "provisional and, finally, indeterminate."[31] From a position further removed from my own, Brian McHale writes in *Postmodernist Fiction* (1987) that this writing "turns out to be mimetic after all, but this imitation of reality is accomplished not so much at the level of its content, which is often manifestly un- or anti-realistic, as at the level of form. . . . [it imitates] the pluralistic and anarchistic ontological landscape of advanced industrial cultures."[32] Still further removed, one of the most judicious students of metafiction, Patricia Waugh, argues that it "does not abandon 'the real world' for the narcissistic pleasures of the imagination"; in fact, "there are two poles of metafiction: one that finally accepts a substantial real world whose significance is not entirely composed of relationships within language; and one that suggests there can never be an escape from the prisonhouse of language and either delights or despairs in this."[33] For each of these critics, contemporary fiction's inquiry into its own practice and assumptions occurs in a broader climate of social, philosophical, and sometimes scientific change.

Among the most adept discussions of contemporary fiction's antirealistic poetics are those by John Kuehl and Robert Siegle. Both critics invent flexible terms and adopt inclusive strategies for describing the goals, patterns, and underlying assumptions of a fiction that turns away from realism. Kuehl's *Alternate Worlds: A Study of Postmodern Antirealistic American Fiction* (1989) traces eleven patterns, including reflexivity, the ludic impulse to play, absurd quests, fictitious history, and entropy, through a large number of contemporary texts. Kuehl sees different varieties of antirealism; some writers practice self-referential metafiction, he observes, but several do not. Most writers "try to capture the contemporary reality lying beneath phenomena, and so they could be considered 'actualists' or 'superrealists' who . . . discern a world no less vivid than the one we perceive through our eyes."[34] Like Kuehl, Siegle uses the term "reflexive"—which, he says, has been misread as simply in-turned, or turned "away from what is represented" into "a safe but frivolous project" about only art. Siegle argues that "far from being a single focus chosen from one of two options (reality or itself), reflexivity focuses on all possible topics and their potentially simultaneous achievement." From this assumption, *The Politics of Reflexivity: Narrative and the Constitutive Poetics of Culture* (1986) argues that reflexivity "is everywhere in narrative, in all periods and forms, sometimes explicit and sometimes implicit, always revealing the conceptual puddle over which fiction gallantly casts its narrative cloak so we can cross untroubled by the fluidity of our footing."[35] Like Kuehl—and like Alan Wilde, whose important study *Middle Grounds* I have cited earlier—Siegle rejects the binary division of art into representational realism and "self-conscious" metafiction.[36] Fiction's reflexivity, for Siegle, turns outward: it exposes the naturalization of social categories and therefore enables a highly political focus on the constitutive poetics of culture.

Recognizing the importance of what Thomas Kuhn calls the "paradigm shift" in modern understandings of reality, two book-length studies (as well as a great many essays, the largest number of them on Pynchon) have developed the importance of the new physics for contemporary fiction. I find much to admire in the books by Robert Nadeau and N. Katherine Hayles; yet, I would argue, they leave wide latitude for a study like this one to interpret the connections between new physical concepts and recent fiction. Robert Nadeau's *Readings from the New Book on Nature: Physics and Metaphysics in the Modern Novel* (1981) builds on extensive discussion of classical and new physics an argument that writers like Fowles, Barth, Pynchon, and DeLillo reflect "the metaphysical implications" of concepts from the new physics. Nadeau's readings come unfortunately loose from their moorings in physics and turn to other, more directly philosophical sources of the "metaphysical assumptions" that are Nadeau's real interest. Writing on John Fowles, for example, Nadeau turns to existential philosophy for a thematic reading of choice, freedom, and responsibility in *The Magus* which, though relevant to Fowles's text, has virtually no connection to physics. Leaving aside the problematic nature of "metaphysics" for poststructuralist theory, Nadeau's perceptions of fictional themes remain troubling for their traditional language and focus, over which relativity, complementarity, or uncertainty do not cast a shadow.

A theoretically sophisticated book, Hayles's *Cosmic Web: Scientific Field Models and Literary Strategies in the Twentieth Century* (1984) argues the centrality of the field concept of interconnectedness. Hayles brings an unusually rich scientific background to the study, which begins with an excellent chapter discussing mathematical and physical models of the field. But Hayles gives up the unique position and the variable possibilities generated by the interconnected field to focus instead on the well-tilled ground of linguistic self-referentiality. The shift to the "field concept had the effect of bringing the self-referentiality of language into focus," she argues, and this quality "is virtually the defining characteristic of postmodern criticism and texts, [as it is] also of post-Newtonian science."[37] Hayles grounds a "field view of language" on Saussure (22), and while she makes a sound case for self-referentiality extending into the language of physics, she has left the dynamic field of physics for the "linear, fragmented, and unidirectional" medium of language (59). Rather than metaphysics, "the problem of articulation" is what connects physics and fiction in Hayles's view. "The novelist's concern with language will have much in common with these scientific concerns" (59). Again, physics disappears into the background in readings that focus on aesthetic issues (the rhetorical strategies foregrounding the fictionality of the text) very similar to those addressed in essays on metafiction.

Two other recent studies place contemporary fiction in the context of shifts in twentieth-century scientific assumptions. In *The Soft Machine* (1985), David Porush discusses a range of scientific developments, including those in physics as well as cybernetics, that lead machines to have metaphoric power for contemporary writers. He discusses references to computer intelligence, to mathematical concepts, and to physical theories, within fictions that "appear to be machines but foil the simple production of sense, the blueprinting, that mechanism promises."[38] Porush supplies useful glosses of scientific and cybernetic concepts, though he does not read texts or their relations to these concepts in detail. Tom LeClair turns to the systems theory developed by biologist Ludwig von Bertalanffy to provide the basis for his new conceptual paradigm in *The Art of Excess: Mastery in Contemporary American Fiction* (1989). LeClair's paradigm of "epistemological redirections" uses terms congruent with my own.[39] LeClair understands contemporary fiction, as I do, as extending beyond metafictional self-reference to commentary on external reality. "Systems novels deform the conventions of the realistic novel in order to defamiliarize the world, not just to defamiliarize the text" (21). But my assumptions differ vastly from those suggested in LeClair's subtitle. He sees the novels' excess of length and scale in light of their—and their authors'—mastery: of narrative methods, of the world, of power systems, of the reader. The novels he describes are "works of mastery, novels that represent and intellectually master the power systems they exist within and are about" (6), and systems theory "is a master code" (13) through which the "masterwork" can be read.

Though LeClair erases with one hand what he sketches with the other ("no writer masters the world" but only synecdoche, the illusion [18]; "authors do not . . . actually master the reader" [27–28]), and though he disarmingly recognizes that "my criteria for mastery have allowed into *The Art of Excess* only one woman and no Afro-American writers" (29), he appears to the end unaware of the political (sexist, racist) as of the philosophical and scientific implications of his choice to honor mastery. In scolding reviewers and academic critics for their "failure to identify and encourage mastery" (26), and in displaying his own mastery over the unified "systext" he invents from the seven novels he has chosen, LeClair endorses an authoritarian and elitist mode of reading, one which seizes power over the subjugated other (including critics like Alan Wilde [3] and novelists like Toni Morrison [30]). In a scientific context where relativity and uncertainty limit the scientist's "knowledge" to interactive speculation and where theory can never master reality, LeClair's choice seems very odd. In philosophical and literary contexts where the signifier has indeterminate relation to the signified and where meaning can never be mastered, where the "self" that might "master" anything cannot be identified, the choice might seem naive, despite LeClair's invocation of a wide variety of theorists. In a cultural context where mastery has been exposed as a virulent fantasy of (white, civilized, male) conquest over a (dark, barbarian, female) victim—whether nature, the truth, the other, or the text—LeClair's choice comes to seem dangerous.[40]

The six writers I discuss in the following chapters are by no means the only actualists—others, to whom I return in the concluding chapter, include Didion, Calvino, Coetzee, Kundera, Puig, Hawkes, Gardner, Eco, and Nabokov. Nor are all the texts produced by any of these writers equally or definitively actualistic; some of Coover's, Gardner's, and Barth's, for example, strike me as more "realistic," while some of Barth's, Nabokov's, Hawkes's, and Barthelme's seem like late "modernist" or even "metafictional" narratives. The texts at the ends of the spectrum are often fascinating, however, in their subtle divergence from the standard forms of realism and modernism. In the chapters that follow, I focus on texts ranging from Atwood's, which has been read as flawed realism, to Barth's, which has been read as exhausted modernism. The variety among these texts enables me to define actualism from multiple vantage points; I don't envision one quintessential actualistic text. Nor do I imagine an actualist's club or propose to debate in John Barth's wry terms "who should be admitted to the club—or clubbed into admission."[41] Rather, the chapters that follow attempt to define an actualist aesthetic as it emerges variously in contemporary novels and to read these texts in the light of their different expressions of a similar view of reality.

Among the writers I've chosen to discuss, Thomas Pynchon stands out as the most obvious example of an artist influenced by the new physics, and therefore I begin with him. He studied engineering physics at Cornell,[42] and he makes specific and sophisticated references to new physical theories in his fiction. Beginning with his early story "Entropy," Pynchon writes about a world defined, not by the stability of matter, but by the way energy transforms matter and shapes an interconnected field. Critics have commonly recognized the referential nature of Pynchon's fiction; especially since 1980, some have objected to earlier attempts to identify Pynchon as a metafictionist. Thomas Moore, for example, notes that "a common mistaken critical practice has been to group Pynchon with those 'reflexivist' contemporary novelists whose chief concern is with what is felt to be the inherently involuted, self-referential nature of language itself."[43] Recent criticism acknowledges, for the most part, that Pynchon addresses *both* the realm of language, consciousness, and art *and* the larger external world of history, society, nature, and science. The voluminous set of approaches to Pynchon's fiction includes, as a result, a provocative mixture of those beginning with Pynchon's relation to language (Ames and Russell), interpretation (Quilligan), myth (Hume), fantasy (Clark), the literary strategies of realism and modernism (Cooper, Van Delden, and McHale), and various traditions and genres in the realm of art (Morgan, Seidel, and Mendelson);[44] and, in contrast, those beginning with Pynchon's relation to the external world.

Most remarkable among this latter group is the widespread perception that Pynchon reflects on the developments in contemporary physics. In fact, Pynchon's use of quantum theory as imaginative ground for his fiction has become virtually commonplace: essays focused on Pynchon and physics appear everywhere (Cooper, Moore, Schwartz, Hayles, Friedman, Friedman and Puetz, Pearce), but even essays focused elsewhere, like Henkle's approach to comedy, Schaub's to ambiguity, and Hume's to myth, also acknowledge in more than passing reference the centrality of scientific metaphors and ideas to Pynchon's texts.[45] One can read more general discussions of relativity theory and quantum mechanics in the criticism of Pynchon's fiction than anywhere else in the literature section of the library.

The essays discussing Pynchon's use of physics emphasize precisely those qualities I've identified as constituting an actualistic view of reality. These essays anticipate, with remarkable frequency, not only the terms I understand as most definitive of the shift in contemporary perceptions of the universe, but also the parallels I sketch between concepts in recent physics and narrative strategies in recent fiction. Pynchon's rejection of Newtonian causality, absolute frames of reference, continuity, materiality, objectivity, and certainty has been amply remarked. More broadly, too, some essays distinguish Pynchon's aesthetic from realism (Schwartz calls it "irrealism" and Cooper "counterrealism") and from modernism (McHale argues that *Gravity's Rainbow* "sets itself against this Modernist mind-set, chiefly by luring the paranoid reader—the Modernist reader—into interpretive dark alleys").[46] Clearly, then, my reading of Pynchon as an actualist takes its place in a well-defined landscape of criticism interpreting his nonrealistic references to the new physical reality.

Pynchon's critics tend, however, to see his texts as fundamentally different from those of other postmodern writers and to agree with the predominant critical mode in defining these other writers as metafictionists. Pynchon is not self-reflexive, but Barth, Coover, and Barthelme are, according to critics who place Pynchon in opposition to the reigning fictional aesthetic.[47] This argument has the unfortunate consequence of detaching Pynchon's achievements from the larger cultural and literary contexts that inform his discourse and, furthermore, of making the very reference to reality these critics find in his fiction the expression of a single private vision, rather than a uniquely focused response to contemporary thinking about the world.

Assuming that writers must choose between the garden and the glass— that no new choices are possible for art, which must either represent reality according to the old rules of realism or explore its own language and process by the old rules of modernism—some of the most influential critics of contemporary or postmodern fiction have seen it as a belated, derivative echo of either realism or modernism. Critics of Coover, Barth, Gaddis, and Barthelme discover in the self-reflexivity of their texts a postmodernism harking back to the aesthetic self-consciousness of modernism. Critics of Atwood find in the plausibility of her characters and plots a conservative representational strategy that resurrects realism. In chapters discussing these writers, I am therefore concerned to show why their novels cannot be understood as realism or as metafiction—how, in fact, the garden/glass, realism/modernism paradigm distorts readings of these texts. By assimilating into antiquated and oversimple aesthetic categories the newest qualities of contemporary texts, the qualities that make them strange and different, such a criticism can only erase the distinguishing features of actualistic fiction. To identify these features, I appeal in part to the authors' statements about fiction and its relation to reality, though my case for a new, actualistic vision rests primarily on readings of major novels. The following chapters attempt both to interpret texts and to explore the nature of actualism; each chapter therefore begins with a different term ("relativity," "uncertainty," etc.) from the model I've constructed in this introduction and uses it to gain access to the text's complex relation to new physical reality. Each chapter addresses both the content through which the novel meditates on relativity or uncertainty and the formal strategies through which it becomes, itself, relative or uncertain, thereby creating a place for literature in the field model of the universe. Together, the chapters argue that actualism lifts Newton's absolute and singular gravity from atop contemporary narratives and sets them loose to play in an energized, interconnected field.

This book is intended to redress an imbalance. In the latter half of the twentieth century, literary texts always address their own processes and reflect on the nature of art; after modernism, writers cannot ignore the artful and constructed status of novels or the deliberate choices they make in writing. Similarly, the nature of its interest in plot and character keeps fiction always addressed, in some degree and from some angle of vision, to a world external to art. Contemporary novelists do not respond to the same external conditions as their realistic ancestors did; they write in reference to a changed external world. They choose to write as they do because of events and ideas occurring in the larger field of discourse. Emerging from interrelated thinking about reality in physics and in fiction, actualism constitutes a literature open to the dynamic and multiple relations that make up the quantum universe.

TWO

THOMAS PYNCHON

GRAVITY'S RAINBOW AND

THE FICTION OF QUANTUM

CONTINUITY

Nowhere in contemporary fiction is modern historical reality more carefully presented, or recent science more prominently explored, than in Pynchon's *Gravity's Rainbow*. Pynchon shares with other actualists an understanding of the new physical reality and a delight in exploring it in his fiction; his third and most complex novel is an important, perhaps even quintessential actualistic text. While some critics read it as a late-modernist exploration of self-reflexivity, most of the voluminous critical writing about this novel recognizes, as I've said in chapter 1, not only the worldliness of Pynchon's text but also its use of a metaphorics based on the new physics.[1]

Gravity's Rainbow constitutes a massive, detailed, and encyclopedic portrait set in the historical, scientific, economic, and political context of Europe during nine months of 1944–45. Like other actualists, Pynchon also sketches the rough beast our age has inherited from that tense gestation: the rockets rising near the end of World War II eventually fall on the Western theater in which we sit, suggesting, among other things, that our postwar technologies and bureaucracies somehow "rose" at the end of the war with a promise to return and crush us. Pynchon chooses his historical setting, moreover, for its scientific significance: like *Public Burning, Gravity's Rainbow* chronicles a period near the beginning of the atomic age, when scientific discoveries began to invalidate traditional assumptions about reality. The novel refers frequently to the new science, quantum leaps, cloud chambers, and Heisenberg's uncertainty principle. "Right now," says zootster-anarchist Blodgett Waxwing, "all the hepcats are going goofy over something called 'nuclear physics.' "[2]

The "un-hep," meanwhile, persist in imagining Newtonian levers beneath experience, in Pynchon's version of the clash between old and new realities. Like other actualists, Pynchon writes a large and public novel, with a huge cast of characters, many of whom are "public servants." Like Gaddis and Coover, he locates the most conservative dedication to Newton's principles in the public sector—in various governments and corporations, in the firm and the cartel. These institutions encourage and exploit popular beliefs in stability, continuity, causality, objectivity, and certainty, because Newtonian beliefs make citizens and soldiers more docile and more useful for institutional work. An assumption that phenomena are causally linked, for example, can be channeled into dutiful productivity for "the war effort" or "the nation," but a notion that things are accidental and mysterious creates an undependable worker. The very principle of linear, rational problem-solving, or "the scientific method" (Blicero will call it "the order of Analysis and Death" [722]), emerges from and depends on a Newtonian cosmos.

In private, Pynchon's men and women are confused, like those in Gaddis and Coover, as they experience the new reality and try to make sense of it with old concepts. Failing to discover lines of continuity or causality in their lives, they fall back on invention: paranoia, so prevalent among Pynchon's characters, constitutes their imagination of a traditional realistic plot focused on the heroic self. The paranoid plot occurs, in various forms, to Tyrone Slothrop, Edward Pointsman, Franz Pökler, Duane Marvy, Byron the Bulb, Richard M. Zhlubb, and dozens more. As these characters experience relativity, accident, and the radical uncertainty of the world, they understand all this opacity as a challenge to their sanity: they must "solve" apparent mysteries by constructing causal continuities.

While Pynchon explores various implications of the new physics in *GR*, he devotes special attention to its invention of non-Newtonian continuities. Discussing the shift from classical to quantum physics, historian of science Daniel Kevles writes:

> Classical physics assumed natural phenomena to be continuous, describable in space and time, causally predictable, and, as such, mathematically expressible in differential equations. Quantum theory could describe atomic behavior only as a series of discontinuous transitions between states, could not locate atomic electrons in space and time when they leaped from one orbit to another, and could not predict when such leaps would occur. To theorists who appreciated these divergences, a genuine quantum mechanics might possibly be a mechanics of discontinuity, mathematically expressed in equations of differences rather than in differential equations.[3]

Recent physics supposes that reality, at least at the subatomic level, has gaps which electrons leap in nonlinear fashion and for no evident cause. Phenomena remain "connected," in a sense: electrons do not leap out of the nuclear orbit. But the connections are looser and more discontinuous than a classical physicist could have imagined.

For a writer like Pynchon, the new mechanics suggests a vision of identity, history, and fictional plotting arranged in some nonlinear order that suspends causal links. Episodes in *GR* cannot be said to "produce" or "cause" others, but rather to parallel each other, metaphorically. In a resonant passage, Leni Pökler tries to explain such a possibility to her husband, the "cause-and-effect man": " 'Not produce,' she tried, 'not cause. It all goes along together. Parallel, not series. Metaphors. Signs and symptoms. Mapping onto different coordinate systems, I don't know' " (159). While serial connections imply the rigid and explicable orderings of Newton, parallels suggest the relative and mysterious form of the new physical world.[4] To inhabit this richer and more dangerous terrain, actualists like Fausto Maijstral will sell their souls to history. "It isn't so much to pay for eyes clear enough to see past the fiction of continuity, the fiction of cause and effect, the fiction of a humanized history endowed with 'reason.' "[5]

While most of his characters devote their lives to inventing paranoid continuities in their own and the world's history, Pynchon imagines their parallel efforts in a narrative form full of leaps, digressions, gaps, and anticlimaxes. This chapter begins with a thematic analysis of Newtonian expectations of end-ordered linearity preserved in the public understanding—in politics, business, family structures, science, and the arts—and, disastrously, in the private hopes of Westerners like Tyrone Slothrop. Slothrop, I argue in a second section, enacts the Western view of history as realistic narrative. Slothrop begins as a realist, chasing a deterministic version of the past, and ends as a surrealist, renouncing connections and forgetting the past: he never achieves an actualistic perception of the mysterious, metaphoric links between events. Others do, however; a third section of this chapter explores the open forms of continuity imagined by characters like Tchitcherine, Mexico, Geli Tripping, and Leni Pökler. These and other characters manage, without abandoning history, to imagine it as loose and accidental. Pynchon, too, invents open, energetic, random continuities, as the last section of this chapter explains. Setting chaotic disconnectedness against rigid, imposed, serial connections, Pynchon's novel occupies the middle ground between; GR maintains the temporal continuity without which narratives cannot reflect the external world but denies the linear, causal, and unbroken nature of time. Plots break off, characters disperse, suspense trails off into anticlimax, and allusions provide fragmentary glimpses of vast and dissimilar realms of knowledge. Connections do not disappear in the richness of Pynchon's text; rather, they proliferate to the point of resonant uncertainty. Unlike the narrative continuity of realism, Pynchon's continuity does not render multiplicity into graspable unity; rather, it reveals behind every seeming unity an intricate and endless tangle. GR introduces a new, actualistic fiction of quantum continuity.

Antiquated Continuities

In the first of four epigraphs, all ironic, beginning the four sections of GR, Wernher von Braun voices the commitment to a Newtonian, linear, teleological continuity that pervades the novel. "Nature does not know extinction; all it knows is transformation. Everything science has taught me, and continues to teach me, strengthens my belief in the continuity of our spiritual existence after death" (1). Since life is ordered from the end, this transforming death, human beings should read experience in end-ordered lines, study the causal links between successive events, and impose a clearer, more useful order on the "messy" changes of nature. For the good public servant like Teddy Bloat or Pirate Prentice, such a view encourages submission to duty and dedication to higher causes—like Nazism, for example, which von Braun served during the war. The faith in causal continuity, which is inscribed in the public consciousness in scientific/Newtonian, religious/Calvinistic, and aesthetic/realistic forms, carries with it a sinister belief that the *dis*continuous, the arbitrary, the aberrant, and the preterite should be either assimilated to the meaningful series—colonized, as it were—or eradicated. A seemingly innocuous notion that the world obeys Newton's laws thus becomes, for Pynchon, a commitment to the imperialist politics through which the West has fought to control life.

Colonialist expansions of political and economic power preoccupy most public institutions and their servants in *GR*. Every Western nation characterized in the novel has a similar colonialist history. Each encloses its open, natural spaces, each attempts to assimilate other races, and each has exterminated some "unassimilable" populations: Hereros, Jews, American Indians, and Russian, Argentine, and Indian natives. The various forms of colonialistic conquest aim to establish global political continuities so that civilization—the government, religion, and cultural customs of the West—might be continuous worldwide, and so that Western technologies might profit from these links. Above all, Pynchon suggests, European colonizers teach their linear and teleological view of time, their rational systems of "death and repression," to tropical natives who have believed in natural cycles (317). In this way, Western history becomes a single "mission to propagate death" (722).

While colonialist policies make eco-political power continuous through space, the bureaucratic systems supporting every Western organization in the novel ensure the continuity of power through time. The war, Pynchon reminds us, "was never political at all, the politics was all theatre, all just to keep the people distracted" while various bureaucracies and technologies compete for funding (521). Individuals become bureaucrats to partake in the sheltered continuity of the firm. "We're all going to fail," says Sir Marcus, "but the Operation won't" (616). This illusion of temporal continuity serves death just as surely as imperialism does: like colonizers, bureaucrats eliminate what they can't use. In their bored, routine, and apparently insignificant service to organizations whose policies they often distrust, "a million bureaucrats are diligently plotting death and some of them even know it" (17).

At the domestic level, Pynchon's families enforce the continuation of social values (obedience, duty, work) supported by the teleological basis of Western culture. In fact, the parents of GR become colonizers, regarding their children as recalcitrant natives to be conquered in the name of decency and submissiveness. At the same time, these parents also function as bureaucrats, serving authority in menial, routine gestures. " 'Mother,' that's a civil-service category, Mothers work for them: They're the policemen of the soul," says Leni Pökler (219), and Otto identifies a "Mother conspiracy" to destroy children with guilt and casseroles (505). Two women, Katje and Greta, play "Mother Night" in the novel, destroying sons in the process; all mothers, including Nalline Slothrop, hope their sons will die heroically, so they may hang the Gold Star (134, 682).[6] Like their partners, fathers also perpetuate the joyless and deadly codes they have inherited. "The fathers have no power today and never did, but because 40 years ago we could not kill them, we are condemned now to the same passivity, the same masochist fantasies *they* cherished in secret, and worse, we are condemned in our weakness to impersonate men of power our own infant children must hate, and wish to usurp the place of, and fail. . . . So generation after generation of men in love with pain and passivity serve out their time in the Zone [. . .] willing to have life defined for them by men whose only talent is for death" (747). By accepting the continuity of "pain and passivity," fathers sacrifice their children to death or death-in-life, as surely as Abraham, passive before God the father, was ready to kill his son—followed in Pynchon's text by Blicero, Broderick Slothrop, and Franz Pökler, among many others.

Scientists, too, pursue dual roles as bureaucrats and colonizers in feeding the world's illusion of Newtonian continuity. As bureaucrats, they offer routine services to armies and nations, in exchange for funding that allows them only to go on providing the same dubious services. Like Pointsman and the scientists of PISCES, Franz Pökler and others of the VfR, founded to build interplanetary rockets, agree to serve the army in exchange for money (400–401). Worse, the scientists of GR also serve as colonizers: nature itself appears in the role of the undisciplined savage committed to superstitious organic cycles, and Western science comes to tame this native vitality. To the chaotic accidents of nature, Pointsman hopes to bring an absolute causality that will show "the stone determinacy of everything, of every soul" (86). Jamf exhorts students to "move beyond life, toward the inorganic. Here is no frailty, no mortality—here is Strength, and the Timeless" (580). Just as German colonizers exterminated the less "useful" or docile Hereros and converted the others to a Christian faith in death, scientists in GR attempt to eliminate the faces of nature they cannot control, while changing the teeming, time-bound world into enduring, synthetic forms of death.

The great lie of continuity has, in *GR*, its artistic form and medium as well: film, which Pynchon presents as the most Newtonian of arts. Popular films (Westerns, musicals, situation comedies, gothic horror and adventure movies) invariably rely on linear continuity in structuring experience. In the interest of plausibility, they use seemingly arbitrary details, but like other forms of realistic fiction, including the *Time* magazine story discussed in the chapter on Coover and the "tubal" clichés in *Vineland*, they begin from the end of the adventure and so exclude chance. Every detail can, by the end, be fit together by the detective-viewer, for apparent mysteries have underlying causes. The Argentine epic *Martín Fierro* might be filmed with this beginning: "A shadowed plain at sundown. An enormous flatness. Camera angle is kept low. People coming in, slowly, singly or in small groups, working their way across the plain, in to a settlement at the edge of a little river. Horses, cattle, fires against the growing darkness. Far away, at the horizon, a solitary figure on horseback appears, and rides in, all the way in, as the credits come on" (386). In this scene, dispersed elements slowly gather together into a single unity, as they are supposed to do in teleologically ordered narratives—and as, in the projected film, the Gaucho and Indian populations will be united by the "solitary" hero. The camera angle is low, of course, to encourage viewer identification with the "lowly" Indians, but behind that deceptive angle, cameraman and director really see the whole plot from high above.

That *GR* makes frequent references to film has been commonly noted; that these allusions indict popular movies for their dangerous ordering and false simplifying of reality has, however, not often been understood.[7] John Stark, for example, suggests that Pynchon presents film as an innocuous, often powerful art form that "reproduces bits of objective reality more accurately than any other artistic medium."[8] David Cowart goes further: "Pynchon uses film as a critique of life, insisting that the one is not more or less real than the other," so references to film challenge readers' conventional views of reality.[9] On the contrary, I believe that film seems to Pynchon to uphold precisely those conventional views, which, like any form of realistic narrative, it does by "finagling" so that reality appears coherent. Pynchon insists that we must distinguish reality from film. His own fiction does not at the end transform itself into the "show" for which we "old fans who've always been at the movies" clamor but rather resembles the "darkening and awful expanse of screen," the "film we have not learned to see" (760). *GR* does not pretend to be the entertaining film we came to watch, but rather the break in that film, when the darkness, the falling rocket, and the reality of death intrude.

Repeatedly, Pynchon emphasizes the disjunction between reality and film—or, more simply, the lying nature of popular film. Whatever Pynchon's views of artistic films (to which he seldom refers), he clearly regards the Hollywood/German/international "industry" as part of the cartel's effort to "colonize" film viewers and render them docile. Quite plainly, he finds popular films simplistic and sentimental, especially in their politics. They give us, for instance, the Irish, "those million virtuous and adjusted city poor you know from the movies—you've seen them dancing, singing, hanging out the washing on the lines, getting drunk at wakes, worrying about their children going bad [. . .] on through every wretched Hollywood lie" (641). Such films tend to glamorize war, like "the lads in Hollywood telling us how grand it all is over here, how much fun"; on the other side, it "looks like German movies have warped other outlooks around here too" (135, 474). The movies also endorse colonialism, making tropical hierarchies seem jolly and predictable; in India in 1935 Pirate Prentice is surprised to find "no Cary Grant larking in and out slipping elephant medicine in the punchbowls out here" (13). In short, the film industry reaffirms all of the old assumptions about social and cosmic order that support conventional, repressive power structures.

By no accident, then, such powers (cartels, firms, and nations) not only influence but also directly employ filmmakers and thus buy into their falsifications of reality. The Germans hire Morituri to watch "Allied footage for what could be pulled and worked into newsreels to make the Axis look good" (473). The British hire von Göll, a German with "sinister connections" to the IG cartel, to fake a film sequence showing black rocket troops in Germany (387). As *GR*'s main filmmaker, von Göll deserves a closer look, for Pynchon locates in this egomaniacal character some reasons why film is so pliant to various political uses.[10] Like filmmaker-agent Hector Zuñiga of *Vineland*, von Göll finds film attractive for its glamour and for its "exorbitant profits" (386). From *Alpdrücken*, made for the prewar Germans, to *New Dope*, made for postwar drug fans, von Göll's films show a sensitivity to commercial interests that almost matches their insensitivity to art, morality, or taste. Politically neutral in a text where one's political stance is one's morality, von Göll betrays his friends for profit: he brings the police to close Säure Bummer's counterfeiting operation, turns Klaus Närrisch, who is ready to die for him, over to the Russians, fails in his promise to deliver Slothrop a discharge, and even, it seems, betrays Slothrop's location to Pointsman and his castration team. In von Göll, Pynchon shows that the director of popular films—and by extension the medium itself—has only the most tenuous commitment to reality and therefore accedes readily to a variety of uses.

Film's primary use in *GR* is to condition and manipulate. In our first glimpse of moviemaking, a cameraman shoots footage that Pointsman will use to train octopus Grigori to attack Katje on a Riviera beach. The secrecy of this conditioning process, from Katje, Slothrop, and the dumb beast Grigori; its results, creating a violence unknown in the nature of crab-eating Grigori; and the layers of illusion involved, as film, itself stills counterfeiting movement, serves the larger "filmic" pretense that Slothrop rescues Katje from danger—all these elements of the novel's first film introduce the sinister potential that characterizes later movies. Grigori, who watches the film uncritically and responds to it instinctively, figures all of Pynchon's subsequent film fans. Slothrop, for example, an ardent Western-watcher, not only quotes "Saturday-afternoon western movies dedicated to Property if anything is" (264) but also shows, in the narcosis episode at PISCES, that the Western's violence, racism, and simplistic continuities have formed his perception of reality. Greta Erdmann expects the world to conform to the "vaguely pornographic horror movies" in which she has acted (393); Pökler and, he implies, a generation of Nazis envisioned the world in the decadent romantic forms of German movies between the wars (577), and Osbie Feel thinks he lives amid the simple fantasies and fears of *White Zombie* and *Dumbo* (106). In these and other characters, Pynchon suggests that movie audiences happily consume bad movies and then, without reflection, behave like Western heroes, German supermen, or zombies, as if they lived in a film reality.

Eventually, devoted moviegoers lose their ability to see a reality unmediated by the standard scenes of popular film, and they expect to achieve the easy resolutions of the typical movie plot. Pynchon's readers are not exempt from this movie conditioning. He accuses us of being loners, "slouched alone in your own seat" watching *Alpdrücken* (472), and he describes us at the end as "old fans who've always been at the movies" (760). While Pynchon provides readers with standard filmic fare, he twists typical film elements into ironic and unfulfilled forms. So, for example, groups of extras break into the song and dance routines of musicals (12, 15, 22, 593, 657), suffer the physical gags of situation comedies—including the inevitable pie throwing (334)—and escape the near-brushes with tame death of adventure movies (186, 248). Above all, there are chase scenes (198, 308, 334, 637, etc.), every one of them peculiar in its mixture of comedy and terror (as when Slothrop, wearing only a purple bedsheet, chases the unknown thief of his American identity—which he never recovers), and every one, also, unsuccessful: no chaser ever catches what he or she pursues. Pynchon ridicules the set of expectations behind the chase scene, especially the assumption that chases, movies, and lives must always end in fulfillment. He scoffs at "aficionados of the chase scene, those who cannot look at the Taj Majal, the Uffizi, the Statue of Liberty without thinking chase scene, chase scene, wow yeah Douglas Fairbanks scampering across that moon minaret there" (637).[11]

In all of *GR*, no fan follows movies more ardently than Tyrone Slothrop—who is, by no accident, the most conditioned and conditionable of men. While characters who perceive the world as actualists rarely see movies—Enzian, Tchitcherine, and Geli never mention films, and Roger Mexico finds the popular *Going My Way* "awful" (38)—others couple enthusiasm for film with a belief that life shares the order shown on screen. "Slothrop's been to enough movies," the narrator comments (114); the American lieutenant has absorbed the moving picture of reality. As though his life were a series of plotted scenes, he imitates his favorite actors: Errol Flynn (248, 381), Cary Grant (292), Fred Astaire (561), and the fictitious Max Schlepzig, among others. He awaits the happy end, the "Shirley Temple smile" from a little girl trapped for hours in the rubble (24). When, much later, he finds that smile in Bianca's elaborate imitation of Shirley Temple, Slothrop responds enthusiastically—in the limited way film has taught: he acts a passionate scene with Bianca and then leaves her as nonchalantly as he might leave a theater.

Slothrop's Story

Slothrop embodies Pynchon's troubled assessment of modern Western man. Men control history in *GR*: they exert power in making the political and economic decisions that shape and express the West. To be sure, women may collude with the system that perpetuates men's control, and women characters are as manipulative and damaging in this novel as in *V.* Greta Erdmann, Nalline Slothrop, and Katje Borgesius are, for example, as vain, controlling, and emotionally dead as lady V. They lack her status as an organizing and powerful symbol, however, and the novel implies that the worst acts perpetrated by these women are invented and choreographed by hidden men. So Pointsman entirely controls Katje's degradation of Brigadier Pudding. Pynchon's protagonist is, by a logic important to the novel, a young man seeking to understand his relationship to the male configuration of power that Pynchon calls the elect. Tyrone Slothrop's earliest infancy was given over to men of power; in the virtual absence of his mother, he was traded and used by men. Slothrop's manhood, his penis, is Their object: it has made him first useful, then threatening, to various men. Ironically, even its heterosexual drive does not lead Slothrop to intimacy with women. His business is with men: Slothrop is the young man who must first read, and then choose a relationship to, the network of power termed, after Derrida, "phallogocentrism," and summed up in *GR*'s abiding image: the rocket.

Various critical approaches to Slothrop's character have yielded divergent readings of his fate and of the novel describing it; his dispersal has often, surprisingly, been regarded as an achievement of pre-Westernized natural peace. Mark Siegel, for example, writes that "Slothrop fails to fulfill his destiny but seems to succeed, through the loss of the self that causes man to be egocentrically irresponsible to nature, to find harmony with the world."[12] Similarly, Douglas Fowler believes "Slothrop's fate may not be *quite* as terrible as death, and although he has been lost as an 'integral creature,' as an identity with a service number and a personal history, Slothrop's scattering may have been a transformation into another, humbler form of life."[13] William Plater suggests that Slothrop achieves "Dionysian charisma" and "may have found the preterite's form of grace. . . . There is no evidence of Slothrop's death in the novel, only his disintegration. One of the last to see him is Pig Bodine when he gives Tyrone the symbol of grace."[14] My own understanding is closer to that of Edward Mendelson, who argues that Slothrop, a "mock-charismatic figure," "progressively forgets the particularity of his past, and replaces his memory of past events with garish and crude comic-book versions of them. His disintegration of memory is not the work of those who oppose or betray him, but is the consequence of his own betrayals, his own loss of interest in the world, his own failures to relate and connect."[15] The end of *GR* does not, in my view, constitute Slothrop's recovery of the pastoral garden, but rather his progressive loss of memory in the despoiled urban Zone, accomplished not by shedding the Western analytic ego but rather by succumbing to what Pynchon considers the quintessential Western disease, the failure of will (472). Slothrop is never more fully the modern

American than when, playing his harmonica amid European natural beauty, he forgets the war, the rocket, and his own humanity.

Reading Slothrop at some length is necessary for several reasons, despite the connections sketched in GR between interpretation and the repressive, death-oriented face of modern culture. Molly Hite puts it well: "All such attempts to enclose Slothrop in an explanatory structure (which tacitly affirm Pointsman's working premises by making Slothrop an object of study) fail to comprehend him, 'even as a concept.' Slothrop's conceptual fragmentation becomes an emblem for the impossibility of explaining him."[16] More starkly, Katherine Hayles argues that, for Pynchon, inevitable destruction follows from structures of organization and control that are basic to consciousness: "As long as we remain cognitively conscious, the holocaust is inevitable."[17] Yet, at the same time, Pynchon's fiction *also* suggests that consciousness, rationality, and reading are inescapable for human beings—his characters constantly engage in acts of interpretation, and his readers can do nothing else.[18] Surely there are more (as well as less) valid, viable, open, nonlinear, acausal, noncontrolling modes of reading.

In reading Slothrop, we read Pynchon's text. As the novel's "central character" who moves to the periphery, he demonstrates Pynchon's egalitarian impulse to mingle the narrative elect and preterite. More important, he points both to the external world and to the realm of art—to Pynchon's meditations on culture, history, science, and technology and to his reflections on narrative and interpretation. Slothrop is, on the one hand, connected intimately with the rocket, and as Hite points out, this affinity "promises to make him a mirror of all the forces at work in the cosmos."[19] On the other hand, since so much of the text occupies itself with his own and others' readings of his story, he serves as a focal point for Pynchon's exploration of acts of interpretation. His story requires readers to choose a position reflecting on Slothrop's own hermeneutics, as Maureen Quilligan insists. "We must judge Slothrop's reading to have been at one point surely very trivial. But his persistent concern with texts, along with all the other characters' obsessions with reading, makes us judge his success or failure in terms of how well he reads the signs about him."[20]

Slothrop's story comments directly on my concerns in this book: he is, I believe, a realistic reader in an actualistic text. He brings Newtonian assumptions to his reading of reality until his experience forces him to abandon them; then, unable to imagine other alternatives, he simply turns Newton's cosmos on its head and envisions its binary opposite. He begins with expectations of linear continuity in his own and the world's history, with the realist's anticipation of causal connections. He pursues his identity as though self and world were simple and graspable. Gradually, however, after Tantivy's disappearance and various frustrations of his pursuit of linear order, Slothrop abandons realism for surrealism.[21] He "flips" from causality and "flops" for chaos, in *V.*'s terms; like Herbert Stencil, he seeks to unravel a singularly determined past, and then, like Benny Profane, he obliterates all memory of the past. From paranoia, "the discovery that *everything is connected*" (703), he turns to "anti-paranoia, where nothing is connected to anything, a condition not many of us can bear for long" (434). Unlike Oedipa Maas, who "had heard all about excluded middles; they were bad shit, to be avoided,"[22] Slothrop unreflectively ignores a range of middle possibilities, that *some* things might be connected, loosely and mysteriously. Slothrop's story, or Pynchon's story of the modern West, thus resembles other actualistic texts in which the realistic/Newtonian heritage continues to baffle people's understanding of actuality.

The famous office scene in which Slothrop's goods provide a first glimpse of his character anticipates both the realist and the surrealist positions he will later take. His map of London constitutes a realist's effort to fix, sort out, and memorialize his experience; his desk, in contrast, displays a surrealist's capitulation to disorder, flux, and unconnectedness. On the map, Slothrop plots events; on the desk, he allows them to scatter and disperse. The same impulse that leads him to record his conquests on the map's grid makes him "a faithful reader" of *News of the World*, where events are detailed in realistic narrative, and a student of "Weekly Intelligence Summaries from G-2," and the "F.O. *Special Handbook* or *Town Plan*" (18). That commitment to ordering disparate phenomena also accounts for Slothrop's interest in jigsaw puzzles, for the puzzle solver, like the detective, uses careful observation of detail to recover the intended unity, or "big picture," beneath apparently discontinuous fragments. But Slothrop's desk contains "lost pieces to different jigsaw puzzles," which, like the "forgotten memoranda" and "busted corkscrewing ukulele string," serve as monuments to lost, even irrecoverable connections—to a Dali-like surrealism where the disembodied "amber left eye of a Weimaraner" floats above a wasteland.

The scene also introduces Pynchon's actualistic parody of realistic narrative conventions. Slothrop first appears through a catalog of his goods, a standard literary device in which the external, material objects a character collects manifest his internal nature. This device rests on the assumptions, implicit in realistic representation, that identity is material and materially expressible and that the life story of an individual may be invoked through a chain of physical symbols. But in parodying the realistic catalog, Pynchon rejects these assumptions.[23] He includes, first, several nonsignificant items that do not reveal character: "bits of tape, string, chalk," and other debris that challenges the realistic detective to make something of average bureaucratic waste. Second, he describes several items with multiple links and with indeterminate or polyvalent significance to the rest of the novel. These things do not solve Slothrop's identity for the reader, nor does the aggregate collection on his desk; rather, they provide a mysterious and disunified glimpse of some of his interests. And the realistic reader, determined to carry away a clear picture of Slothrop? Pynchon mocks this sneaking, voyeuristic detective in the figure of Teddy Bloat, who threads his linear way through the maze of office/prose/life, who seizes the picture he wants from the welter of Slothropian detail, and who delivers Slothrop up to a mode of interpretation that will grasp and use him as an object.

Though the office scene indicates conflicting impulses in Slothrop, his principal role in part 1 of *GR* is that of realistic plotter. He acquires importance in the novel for his mapmaking: he pastes colored stars, labeled with the names of girls he has met, lusted after, conquered, or simply imagined, all over the map of London. The narrator suggests, "At its best, it does celebrate a flow, a passing from which—among the sudden demolitions from the sky [. . .]—he can save a moment here or there" (23). Slothrop's map attempts, in other words, to fix pleasant moments and to track in a series of times and places a multitude of girls. By plotting these conquests in a sequential order of dated stars on the grid of London, Slothrop reveals his Western, analytical understanding of the world, in which the map—the two-dimensional survey from a God's-eye view *above* experience—becomes an acceptable symbol for experience itself. If his map tries to counter his own tendency to lose and forget (girls, memories, paper clips) and to save meaning from the world's "sudden demolitions," it remains, perversely, a dead memorial and a mockery of meaning, precisely because it valorizes material quantity and external setting.

Slothrop's map attracts the attention of other cartographers, with their inevitable realistic expectations. Because Slothrop's map is identical to Roger Mexico's map of rocket strikes, "It's the map that spooks them all" (85). Those who study Slothrop misinterpret the correlation of the two maps when, unable to envision the two as *parallel*, the result of a purely mysterious coincidence, they try instead to imagine causal connections linking them in *series*. While Roger Mexico, alone, argues that the correlation is "a statistical oddity," "Rollo Groast thinks it's precognition," Edwin Treacle imagines "psychokinesis," and Pointsman believes Slothrop responds to a stimulus in the rocket (and in Jamf's early conditioning) which Slothrop somehow feels before the rocket strikes (85–87). These psychoscientists attempt, in short, to invent reasons, whether mechanical or extrasensory, determining the peculiar correlation; as arch-Newtonian Pointsman says, "No effect without cause, and a clear train of linkages" (89). But the curiously matching maps, whose mystery generates Pynchon's plot, derail causality and deconstruct the very notion of the map as a fixed and accurate representation of the world.[24]

In part because of the scientists' obsession to explain Slothrop's sexuality and its connection with the rocket, readers have also tried to solve what Pynchon intends as inexplicable mystery. Jamf's conditioning leads Slothrop to have erections in anticipation of the rockets, critics suggest;[25] perhaps "his penis has been replaced or grafted with Imipolex G."[26] But Pynchon provides no such reassuring cause, psychological or mechanical, for Slothrop's erections. In fact, he undermines the likelihood of any direct link—especially Imipolex G—between Jamf's experiments and Slothrop's later behavior. The plastic, Jamf's supposed stimulus, may not have been invented until well after the experiments (249, 286); moreover, the V-2 rockets fired at London did not contain Imipolex G, for Slothrop finds reference to it only in the materials list for the Schwarzgerät, the single rocket 00000 modified by Blicero (242). Furthermore, Slothrop receives, and carries in his pocket for several days, a white chess knight supposedly made of Imipolex G—to which he does not respond with an erection (436). Any connection between whatever Jamf used to cause the infant's erections and the rockets, which seem to arouse the adult, becomes impossible to forge from the evidence. And, to expand the ambiguities, Slothrop later reveals that his map and his stories were partly fictionalized (302). The perfect correlation of maps was based, then, on a mixture of real and invented data.

Other moments in Pynchon's text suggest that the correlation happens by purest chance. By chance, Tantivy proposes that Slothrop investigate bomb strikes: "It's the best chance we'll have to one-up that lot over in T.I." (234). By accident, then, Slothrop's job makes him follow the bombs, which strike in a Poisson distribution all over London; Slothrop meets girls in that same pattern. The episodes marked by stars on his map occur by chance and by the woman's desire: Slothrop is, if anything, a passive but willing follower in the meetings we see with Cynthia (26) and Darlene (114), both of which begin with coincidental contacts in accidental places. Instead of the realist's causal link between serial events, sought so desperately by Pointsman and his mad scientific crew, Pynchon rests his plot on the actualist's metaphoric parallel between various eruptions of chance.

True, Slothrop does respond to rocket falls with erections (26, 120), and to the study of rocket technology with lust for Katje (224); but his sexuality is neither simpler nor more determined than that of other characters. Does his sexual response to rocketry confirm analyst Mickey Wuxtry-Wuxtry's hypothesis that Slothrop is "in love, in sexual love, with his, and his race's, death" (738)? Or does it amount to a more life-affirming quest for pleasure and warmth in the face of a terrifying death-technology, as Darlene suspects (120)? We cannot be sure, and so the rocket-erection link remains ambiguous in nature as well as in cause and extent. Parallels with other characters stir the same muddy waters: Pudding's coprophilia, Pirate's fetishism, and Blicero's or Sir Marcus's sadomasochism all reveal Western society's death instinct, as Lawrence Wolfley observes,[27] but all, simultaneously, attempt to reject the deadened sexlessness the West encourages. "Just a neuter, just a recording eye" is what "They" want, according to Sir Stephen Dodson-Truck: "They aren't even sadists. . . . There's just *no passion at all*" (216). It is not, then, Slothrop's sexuality but rather his impulse to grid his conquests on a map that demonstrates his Western, realistic consciousness in part 1 of the novel.

These mental traits reach full bloom in part 2, where Slothrop's definitive role changes from plotter to reader: he becomes the realistic exegete. Sent to the Riviera to read, he spends most of his time studying voluminous documents on rocketry, plastics, propulsion, and marketing. When he is not reading printed words and figures, Slothrop occupies himself with compulsive interpretations of the minute details of his surroundings. On the first morning, he reads Katje's ID bracelet, then her face, and "the conniving around him now he feels instantly, in his heart" (188). He learns to interpret dialogue by the books: "He will learn to hear quote marks in the speech of others. It is a bookish kind of reflex" (241). He sees raindrops as asterisks, "inviting him to look down at the bottom of the text of the day, where footnotes will explain all" (204). Not only does Slothrop interpret everything, major or minor, plotted or accidental, as though it all bore directly on him, but he also applies a particularly paranoid mode of reading, in which everything connects to everything else in one grand design revealing the careful hand of the creator.

In part 2, Slothrop allows chance no role at all in his own or the world's affairs; for every effect, he posits a cause. Most of part 2 is set in the Casino Hermann Goering, whose ornate game room makes Slothrop prickle repeatedly with a sense of hidden design. Though Pynchon never provides any basis for Slothrop's hunches, Slothrop resolutely reads the game room as a sinister locus intended, like the realistic narrative, to invoke the appearance of chance while excluding the reality. "These are no longer quite outward and visible signs of a game of chance. There is another enterprise here, more real than that, less merciful, and systematically hidden from the likes of Slothrop" (202). His own pursuits at the casino are not, in his view, accidental: "Slothrop has been playing against the invisible House, perhaps after all for his soul, all day" (205). Finally, inevitably, the same logic extends backward to include his entire life story in one rigidly determined realistic plot. "All in his life of what has looked free or random, is discovered to've been under some Control, all the time, the same as a fixed roulette wheel" (209). Slothrop eventually interprets all phenomena—Tantivy's death, the bomb patterns destroying railroad tracks—as causally ordered results of hidden designs.

Slothrop's readings also rely on the realistic assumption that all phenomena, however apparently discontinuous, actually cohere in a single unified design: not only are all accidents linked by plots, but all plots are connected by an Overplot. Amassing information from various documents on rocketry at the beginning of part 2, and a history of Jamf and Imipolex G at the end, Slothrop assimilates all the data into a continuous story, all the corporations into a single cartel, and all the villains into one simple They. His own education at Harvard, the heterocyclic polymer, a Swiss chemical cartel, and the gathering of rocket intelligence in the office of Duncan Sandys—these and other apparently disparate phenomena conceal an all-inclusive order, a continuous global conspiracy focused on Slothrop. Pynchon places Slothrop at Jamf's grave as part 2 ends and shows him that "Jamf is only dead," but Slothrop will not be deterred from his obsessive continuities. "The absence of Jamf surrounds him like an odor, one he knows but can't quite name, an aura that threatens to go epileptic any second" (268–69).

In part 3, Slothrop shifts from questing to drifting and from paranoia to antiparanoia. He stops forging the linear continuities of realism and abandons detective rationality. "Rain drips, soaking into the floor, and Slothrop perceives that he is losing his mind. If there is something comforting—religious, if you want—about paranoia, there is still also anti-paranoia, where nothing is connected to anything, a condition not many of us can bear for long. Well right now Slothrop feels himself sliding onto the anti-paranoid part of his cycle, feels the whole city around him going back roofless, vulnerable, uncentered as he is [. . .] Either They have put him here for a reason, or he's just here. He isn't sure that he wouldn't, actually, rather have that *reason*" (434). In the antiparanoid state he inhabits through the later episodes of part 3, mindless and antirationalistic pleasures, including sex, drugs, and food, gain the upper hand over Slothrop's urge to map or to read them. Indeed, Slothrop increasingly cultivates mindlessness, imagining himself in a surreal, disconnected environment where he can become a "glozing neuter." He forgets continuities of mind, will, and heart in the act of shedding rigid Western causality. Caught in the either/or, reason/reasonlessness, garden/glass binary logic that Pynchon presents as a central problem in Western thought, Slothrop stops being a Western man, but he also ceases to be human. This change, which occupies him throughout part 3, can be measured through Slothrop's encounters with other characters, especially as they increasingly supply his motivation.

Geli Tripping, Slothrop's first companion in part 3, displays mental powers different from the linear, rational, analytical ones synonymous with the West and thus suggests alternatives to Slothrop. Like other benign figures Slothrop meets near the end of part 2, Geli stimulates Slothrop's mind, providing him with information as well as food and safety. She awakens his memory and intelligence, and she challenges his habitual modes of perception: "Forget frontiers now. Forget subdivisions. There aren't any" (294). When she takes Slothrop to the Brocken to make God-shadows at dawn, she demonstrates a natural vitality that does not exclude mind, but rather draws on intuitive and alogical mental powers the West has suppressed, and these enable a united celebration of mind and body. Like the good witch in *The Wizard of Oz*, Tripping gives Slothrop magical shoes (Tchitcherine's boots), furthers his travels (in the Oz-like balloon), and liberates him from some misconceptions. Shortly after he leaves her, he comes to the realization that "the Schwarzgerät is no Grail, Ace, that's not what the G in Imipolex G stands for. And you are no knightly hero" (364).

Emil ("Säure") Bummer, Slothrop's next important companion, helps both to free Slothrop from social rules and linear logic and to strip him of mind and identity. A one-man sedition act, cat burglar, counterfeiter, doper, and "depraved old man" (365), Bummer provides a model of counterculture resistance to Western social norms and thus encourages Slothrop's readiness to drop out of that particular game. Bummer quickly drafts him for a different game, however; he projects superhuman powers onto Slothrop (now Rocketman) as surely as Pointsman and the Home Office did, reclothes him as they did, and sends him out into the Zone for his own purposes, as they did. Slothrop is willing enough to forget his own identity and quest, put on Rocketman's cape, and go to Potsdam for hashish. Under the influence of drugs, Slothrop suspends connections and loses contact with people and memories. Hence Bummer, suggestively named for a bad encounter with drugs, and the life-style of mindless pleasures he represents, actually hasten Slothrop's disintegration.

Dissolution guides Slothrop's alliance with Margherita (Greta) Erdmann. Slothrop plays another temporary role with her, suspending pursuit of his own history in order to follow her quest for her daughter Bianca. Acting the part of Max Schlepzig, whip wielder, he becomes a meek appendage to Erdmann's masochism. Their couplings parody human connection, as do their conversations, all filmic, false, and self-absorbed. Since Slothrop feels his isolation more acutely in these mock contacts, he naturally slips into antiparanoia, "where nothing is connected to anything," while lying in bed beside Greta (434). Worse, he also slides into a willingness to cause pain, to which Pynchon suggests all Western men are prone; "their" punishments become "his own cruelty," and Erdmann "his victim" (396–97).

The ease, then, with which Slothrop turns from whipping the mother to using eleven-year-old Bianca suggests that links of moral accountability remain operative in Pynchon's world, if not in Slothrop's. Bianca provides an alternative to disconnectedness in the possibility of a loving union. "He knows. Right here, right now, under the make-up and the fancy underwear, she *exists*, love, invisibility. . . . for Slothrop this is some discovery" (470). Like Geli Tripping, who fulfills a similar promise with Slothrop's double, Tchitcherine, Bianca is very young, innocent despite her sexual precociousness, natural despite her affectations (Bianca tells time by the sun, not clocks [468]), vulnerable, and lonely. But Slothrop refuses to risk being transformed by union: "for this he is to be counted, after all, among the Zone's lost. The Pope's staff is always going to remain barren, like Slothrop's own unflowering cock" (470). He not only resists the magical connection of love, but he even rejects the links of memory: he forgets Bianca as his eyes turn away.

From the beginning, Slothrop uses Bianca as an object and thus repeats the sins of the fathers: his contact with her marks his transition from sinned-against-son to sinning father. On first sight of Bianca, he reacts with instant lust (463). He joins the decadent partiers on the *Anubis* in a voyeuristic mass orgy, replete with couplings of every variety except those capable of producing life, as Greta spanks Bianca's naked bottom. When she comes to his bed, Slothrop explodes like the rocket that can only bring death. While the narrator emphasizes her childishness throughout this scene—her smallness, "presubdeb breasts," "little feet," "the little girl," "slender child," face "round with baby-fat," and while Bianca herself reminds him, "I'm a child," Slothrop treats her like any other adult female object (469–70). Though the narrator pleads, "she must be more than an image, a product, a promise to pay," Slothrop takes his mindless pleasure with her as though she were a futureless thing, which she soon becomes. Like Blicero, who uses his "children" Gottfried and Katje, or even more like his own father, who has sold him as a commodity for sexual use, Slothrop doubly betrays the child Bianca. Framed on the one side by the story of Achtfaden's betrayal of his friend Klaus Närrisch (456), and on the other side by the account of Greta Erdmann's murder of Jewish children (478), Slothrop's encounter with Bianca constitutes both a betrayal of friendship and a sacrifice of innocence.

Appropriately, then, Slothrop next takes up with Gerhardt von Göll (der Springer), manipulator, profiteer, father figure, and betrayer. Slothrop serves von Göll unquestioningly; after failing to rescue Bianca, he succeeds in saving von Göll from the Russians and then in recovering a package for him—one planted, ironically, beneath the dead Bianca's feet. Von Göll, meanwhile, virtually reenacts Broderick's original betrayal: he evidently sells Tyrone out to Pointsman, who, like Jamf, has evil designs on Slothrop's penis. His alliance with von Göll comments on Slothrop's assumption of the father-user's role. It also reveals his growing indifference to actuality, his diminishing awareness of a consequential world outside the one he "frames" in any instant. On the *Anubis*, the narrator has pointed out Slothrop's "general loss of emotion, a numbness he ought to be alarmed at, but can't quite" (490–91). Later, the narrator adds that Slothrop "has begun to thin, to scatter. [. . .] the narrower your sense of Now, the more tenuous you are. It may get to where you're having trouble remembering what you were doing five minutes ago, or even, as Slothrop now—what you're doing *here* [. . .] So here passes for him one more negligence . . . and likewise groweth his Preterition sure. . . . There is no good reason to hope for any turn, any surprise *I-see-it*, not from Slothrop" (509). Slothrop sheds the pernicious Western determination to forge linear, causal chains of time—only to explode time's continuity into small, unmemorable fragments of "now."

After von Göll, Slothrop's companions mean less to him and to his story as, increasingly isolated, he shuns close contacts and forgets the people he meets. He tries to become less visible and to see others as little as possible. He avoids involvement, learns few names, keeps moving, and becomes "intensely alert to trees," grass, and inanimate things (552). To evade the burden of his memory, he "won't interpret, not any more" (567). His associations during this period are brief, and he prefers the company of children. For a time Slothrop follows a "fat kid of eight or nine" named Ludwig, whose plumpness, doomed innocence, and unlikely quest (for a lost lemming) make him a young double for Slothrop. Soon, though, Slothrop leaves Ludwig in dangerous company and never thinks of him again (559). Slothrop plays games with groups of nameless children, one of which drafts him as Pig-Hero Plechazunga (567). He loses the "tiny girl" who clutches his leg in the riot; he leaves the girl of seventeen who helps him escape without asking her name (570–71).

Toward the end of part 3, Slothrop willingly sheds adulthood, reason, and human identity. He wears the pig suit for weeks, rather than changing to human attire. While he has previously fit into various borrowed suits, uniforms, and evening clothes, now, with his humanity become tenuous, the pig costume "seems to fit perfectly. Hmm" (568). Frieda the pig adopts him as kindred flesh, and even the narrator seems to forget Slothrop's name and race: he calls him "the pig" ten times as the sequence in Cuxhaven begins (595–96). Others have, of course, failed to recognize Slothrop in different clothes, as if only his inanimate and always borrowed apparel gave him identity at all. David Seed argues that Slothrop's disguises suggest a "ubiquitous stage-director choosing these costumes for him," and his resemblances to others "undermine his individuality."[28] As he renounces more and more of his adult humanity, Slothrop fittingly appears for the last time in part 3 naked, curled, asleep, his regression to mindless and irresponsible babyhood complete. He dreams of Zwölf-kinder, the city of falsely preserved, illusory childhood, "and Bianca smiling, he and she riding on the wheel" (609).

Slothrop virtually disappears from part 4: he does little but think, and his mind becomes increasingly confused and chaotic. Having rid himself of the sense of continuity in his own and the world's history, he has lost any recognizable identity. "He has become one plucked albatross. Plucked, hell—*stripped*. Scattered all over the Zone. It's doubtful if he can ever be 'found' again, in the conventional sense of 'positively identified and de-tained'" (712). Invisible, then, to others, he has eventually no human contacts; even the narrator turns away from Slothrop, as he ceases to be involved in events in time, and focuses instead on other characters who still have stories.

In his last appearance as an active character, Slothrop appears to merge with nature. All his renunciations of mind and identity, begun in part 3, reach full expression here: he recalls less and less, eventually forgetting the rain by the time the rainbow appears (626); he lives naked and alone and does not speak to anyone (623). In his advanced antiparanoia, even his past selves appear disconnected—all "ten thousand of them" (624). His last two gestures, however, suggest to some critics that Slothrop achieves grace, transcendence, or Rilkean salvation. First, Slothrop lies "spread-eagled at his ease in the sun . . . he becomes a cross himself, a crossroads, a living intersection where the judges have come to set up a gibbet" (625). Critics often quote from Rilke's *Sonnets to Orpheus*:

> Be, in this immeasurable night,
> magic power at your senses' crossroad,
> be the meaning of their strange encounter.

Pynchon refers to Rilke here and elsewhere far more ironically than critics suppose.[29] Pynchon sees Rilke as part of a decadent Germanic romanti-cism which contributed to Nazi power. Like his references to Wagner, who is played on the Nazi toiletship (450), his allusions to Rilke actually parody the Austrian's mysticism. In the crossroads passage of *GR*, Slothrop does not attain magic power or feel his senses converge. Rather, he lies, obliv-ious, at an intersection *once* charged with magic power that has since dispersed: ages before, a hanged man ejaculates as his neck breaks, and one drop of his sperm changes to a mandrake root. This power is imme-diately exploited for profit by a magician who carries the root home to multiply his cash. The mandrake's magic is further routinized when a bureaucrat arrives to discuss the long-range fiscal implications of the uprooting, with a "fraternal business smile" (625). If the sexual response to death, as old as European civilization and still shared by Slothrop, as well as virtually every character in *GR*, once contained possibilities for magic, those were at once seized by bourgeois professionals and turned to profit. Does Slothrop become "the meaning of his strange encounter" with this resonant crossroads? Hardly. He lies "spread-eagled at his ease."

Once, the narrator reminds us, Slothrop had "days when in superstition and fright he could *make it all fit*," when he forcibly read all phenomena as entries "in a record, a history." Now, instead, he sees "a very thick rainbow here, a stout rainbow cock driven down out of pubic clouds into Earth, green wet valleyed Earth, and his chest fills and he stands crying, not a thing in his head, just feeling natural" (626). This gesture suggests that Slothrop achieves emotional and physical peace—and indeed he does, but at the cost of the mental qualities that have made him a human being as opposed to a rock or a tree. The "stout rainbow cock" promises fertility for Earth, but not for Slothrop, whose "unflowering cock" "is always going to remain barren" (470). That he must empty his head to feel natural suggests that Slothrop has defined his alternatives too narrowly—early on, when he was still able to define alternatives, he might have saved both head and heart, civilized reason and natural feeling.

The rest is anticlimax: later glimpses present Slothrop's inevitable fritterings away of self. Significantly, the last depictions of Slothrop seem intended deliberately to undermine whatever peace or transcendence he might have achieved in the rainbow vision. Rather than leaving Slothrop "feeling natural," we see him subsequently engaged in the same old Oedipal conflicts, the same movie and comic-book simplifications, and the same regressive nostalgia for childhood. In one episode, Slothrop inhabits a comic-book Raketen-Stadt where, as part of the Floundering Four, he battles the ever-murderous father (674). In another, he becomes the "Sentimental Surrealist," obsessed with paranoid plots like the vacuum of "sun-silence." This last picture emphasizes his isolation from external reality (he hears only his own heart), from humanity (he becomes "the stranger"), from the past (he does not remember "how he got to the white tiled room half an hour before hose-out time"), and especially from nature: he sits inside a greasy spoon, under "bulb-shine," at a "riveted table" (696–97). Later, he returns to the father theme he can neither resolve nor outgrow; young Tyrone instructs his father in the mechanical means to immortality: "*We* can live forever, in a clean, honest, purified Electroworld" (699). Speaking for this vision, as *un*natural and oversimplified as any in the novel, Slothrop's voice takes on the vocabulary and the stammer of the perennial ten-year-old, suggesting once again that he has regressed rather than transcended.

An understanding of the end of the novel depends, I believe, on an awareness that Weissmann/Blicero's sacrifice of Gottfried in the rocket not only bears on Slothrop's story but logically completes it. First, though, I want to examine an alternative approach, one advanced in rather extreme form by Douglas Fowler in *A Reader's Guide to GR*. Interpreting *GR* as "romantic art," the rocket as "a graceful piece of romantic death-machinery," and Gottfried as motivated by a "romantic impulse to *die beautifully*," Fowler sees the ending as a satisfying culmination for the "acetylene intensity of Weissmann's and Gottfried's hopeless love."[30] This ending also provides a tragic catharsis for the reader, according to Fowler. "Life is obvious and tiresome; it is repetitious, inconclusive, utterly anticlimactic. We do our best not to admit to this fact, but our most impressive responses to it are fantasies of escape—of death. The confinement from which so much of our great artistic achievement releases us is probably nothing more glamorous than boredom with the continuity of instinctual life. Whatever its ethical claims, tragic literature is immensely satisfactory because our participation in it brings us to an *ending*, a way out, an escape from continuity."[31]

One must, I think, object: surely Blicero embodies romantic ideals in a perverse and decadent form; surely Pynchon suggests neither boredom with life, whose rich variety interests his narrator, nor longing for death; and surely no text can intend so climactic "an *ending*" when it has, as Fowler himself ably explains, continually withheld resolutions, suspended subplots, and celebrated a "pattern of inconclusiveness and anticlimax."[32] A better approach must allow the ending its continuity with the rest of Pynchon's text and Blicero his relationship to Slothrop.

These two have, first, a schematic relationship as antithetical doubles: they can be imagined as zero and one, where both points represent different forms of death, and life occupies the excluded middle ground. While Slothrop abandons connections, including those linking his various selves, and thus loses human identity, Blicero pursues linear connections to their inevitable end in death and thus loses human identity. Slothrop ceases to make fictions about his own role, and Blicero constructs a perfect, closed fiction; both thereby deny themselves living roles. Slothrop, the realist-turned-surrealist, abandons the quest for coherence at the cost of life; Blicero, the romantic, pursues an exclusive, even monomaniacal coherence at the cost of life. Blicero, the anti-Slothrop, achieves prominence in *GR*'s last movement partly because his yearning for a climactic, ego-affirming end at once parallels and opposes—and both ways illuminates—Slothrop's own anticlimactic and ego-dissolving end.

Slothrop's scattering has, more importantly, a dynamic and enabling relationship to Blicero's rocket firing: Slothrop, the sacrificed son, fails to break out of the disastrous cycle of filial passivity and paternal ruthlessness, thus empowering Blicero's murder of his "beloved son," Gottfried. Slothrop never outgrows his adolescent resentment of the father, or his alternating wish for revenge on and atonement with this figure; Slothrop reenacts the sins for which he blames his father, especially in his use of Bianca. Slothrop thus legitimates Blicero, who "is the father you will never quite manage to kill," and helps to perpetuate the Oedipal cycle (747). Granted power by the son's meekness, Blicero fires the phallic rocket that signifies Western man's age-old lust for conquest, while Gottfried—a clear analogue for Slothrop—climbs inside the father's system and rides it passively to his death. Like Slothrop, Gottfried chooses his own annihilation at the father's hands. "He knows, somehow, incompletely, that he has a decision to make . . . that Blicero expects something from him . . . but Blicero has always made the decisions" (724). Like Slothrop, Gottfried simply fails to choose and thereby obeys the father's will, while the narrator ironically comments: "If there is still hope for Gottfried here in this wind-beat moment, then there is hope elsewhere. The scene itself must be read as a card: what is to come" (724)—which is, as we soon learn: the sons, Gottfrieds and Slothrops, betray their potential to create "God's peace."

Pynchon, meanwhile, has plucked the rocket firing out of its sequence (it supposedly occurred in the last days of the war, otherwise presented in part 2 of GR) and placed it at the very end: this disruption of chronology emphasizes the connection between these sons' submission to the father and the apocalypse descending on the Western world. In the final pages of Pynchon's text, Blicero takes on a larger meaning than the unkillable father. As his tarot unfolds, he becomes the intellectual authority sustaining political and corporate powers. "The King of Cups, crowning his hopes, is the fair intellectual-king. If you're wondering where he's gone, look among the successful academics, the Presidential advisers, the token intellectuals who sit on boards of directors. He is almost surely there. Look high, not low. His future card, the card of what will come, is The World" (740). Blicero stands behind "Richard M. Zhlubb" (Nixon), who manages the theater in which we sit, absorbing images of reality and waiting to be destroyed. Thus, in its fullest implication, Slothrop's capitulation to a past that he only imagines has conditioned his responses authorizes powers that promise to devastate the future. A victim of authority like all Western sons, Slothrop nonetheless spends his life affirming traditions—especially the realistic vision of linear continuity—whose inadequacy eventually shuffles him, and may explode the rest of us, into oblivion.

Parallel, Not Series

Against Slothrop, the primary—though certainly not the only—realist of *GR*, Pynchon contrasts several secondary and inevitably preterite characters who see the world as actualists. These characters do not occupy elect roles in Pynchon's narrative, but rather minor ones commenting, through parallel and metaphoric resemblances, on Slothrop's problems and choices. Unlike the Mossmoons, the Pointsmans, or the Bliceros, they have little power within the various systems they serve and from which they are always partly alienated. Given the wartime setting, most of them work for a government and therefore come under the direct influence of the elect, with Their assertion that life is realistic; typically, then, the actualists only gradually trust their own intuitions of contingency. Although magic often follows when chance brings two of them together, they do not form a systematized group. They are not all members of the Counterforce, which becomes in its later days another colonizing elect. Who, then, are the actualists? They include Tchitcherine, Geli Tripping, Roger Mexico, Enzian, Leni Pökler, Pig Bodine—and among the yet more minor, Tantivy, Bianca, Darlene, Trudi, Webley Silvernail, Squalidozzi, Graciela Imago Portales, and Beláustegui.

The actualists envision a form of continuity that is, to return to Leni Pökler's formulation, "parallel, not series": links are neither obliterated nor imagined in rigid, causal lines. Events and phenomena remain connected, but by loose, conditional bonds like those metaphor sketches between entities whose difference it openly acknowledges. While stories of the past may be constructed (for events are not simply a chaotic jumble), the actualist genealogy posits an intricacy to the plot, grants accident a major role, and assumes that motives, origins, and causes are not solvable. Actualists neither forget the past, public or personal, nor dedicate their lives to perpetuating it. For this reason, they use drugs more sparingly than, say, Osbie Feel or Säure Bummer: actualists avoid the loss of memory as emphatically as they reject its overzealous reconstructions.

Very near the start of *GR*, two different images of continuity juxtapose linear against metaphoric links and, not coincidentally, deadliness against vitality. In the first, a train moves. "They pass in line, out of the main station, out of downtown, and begin pushing into older and more desolate parts of the city. Is this the way out? [. . .] No, this is not a disentanglement from, but a progressive *knotting into* [. . .] much too soon, they are under the final arch: brakes grab and spring terribly. It is a judgment from which there is no appeal. [. . .] It is the end of the line" (3–4). Like the rocket's linear motion from point *A* to point *B*, the train's journey suggests the realist's conception of one-directional time, moving toward "the final arch," or last judgment, or death. The second image, appearing a few pages later, follows the nonlinear spread of banana odor. "Now there grows among all the rooms [. . .] the fragile, musaceous odor of Breakfast: flowery, permeating, surprising [. . .] taking over not so much through any brute pungency or volume as by the high intricacy to the weaving of its molecules, sharing the conjuror's secret by which—though it is not often Death is told so clearly to fuck off—the living genetic chains prove even labyrinthine enough to preserve some human face down ten or twenty generations" (10). Woven, highly intricate, labyrinthine, and unpredictable, this molecular continuity serves the multiple needs of life, with its linked helical "chains" that preserve without imprisoning. Nonlinear as this meandering growth is, it constitutes a form of continuity for our organic lineage; the train, by contrast, can only follow its tracks to "the end of the line."

With linear continuity, actualists also reject the colonialistic conquest of the "out-of-line." They refuse to assimilate or convert the other but rather allow it to remain alien, accidental, and free. Politically, they oppose imperialism—whether they fight it in the streets, like Leni Pökler; or lead anti-imperialist groups, like Enzian; or subvert the power of imperialist systems, like Pig Bodine and Roger Mexico. Personally, they try to achieve relationships based not on dominance and submission but on equality. Typically, they do not fix, control, or keep the other but rather encourage change and freedom, as Geli Tripping permits Tchitcherine to roam. Pynchon's actualists do not passively efface themselves, like Katje, Gottfried, Franz Pökler, and the later Slothrop; they do not submit any more than they seek to dominate, but they manage to insist actively on their own voice and values without imposing any system forcefully on others. Rather than colonialist hierarchies, then, their relationships are characterized by fluidity, openness, and tolerance for eccentricity.

Pynchon's actualists resist teleologies; they do not allow life to be shaped by its end. For these actualists, time is not a causal chain directed at death, transcendence, or salvation but a succession of coincidental moments to be celebrated for their own sake. "There is the moment, and its possibilities," thinks Leni Pökler (159); the Argentinian Beláustegui "knows his odds, the shapes of risk are intimate to him as loved bodies. Each moment has its value, its probable success against other moments in other hands, and the shuffle for him is always moment-to-moment" (613). This metaphor of time as a game of chance suggests both the risks actualists perceive in momentary time and the playful attitude with which they accept the odds. Their perception of time liberates actualists from the debilitating earnestness of those like Jeremy, Pointsman, and Blicero; though they work, actualists always have time for play, jokes, song, dance, and fantasy. So Roger Mexico clowns during Pointsman's dog hunt, Webley Silvernail imagines a comic dance routine with the rats and mice from the lab, and Darlene plays her elaborate "English candy drill" on Slothrop; none sees their work, their company, or its products as ends worthy of their entire attention.

As actualists, these characters affirm accident and multiplicity in place of causality and unity; hence they understand even their own paranoid suspicions as possible metaphors, not certain truths. While others imagine a single, causally unified plot, Bodine and Leni/Solange envision many plots, and looser ones.

> "This is some kind of a plot, right?" Slothrop sucking saliva from velvet pile.
>
> "*Everything* is some kind of a plot, man," Bodine laughing. "And yes but, the arrows are pointing all different ways," Solange illustrating with a dance of hands, red-pointed finger-vectors. Which is Slothrop's first news, out loud, that the Zone can sustain many other plots besides those polarized upon himself. (603)

If actualists remain paranoid, in other words, they do not understand events as simply "caused" by other plotters, and they insist on a relative freedom to elude Their clumsy stratagems. The subject, envisioned by actualists as contingent rather than necessary, may not finally be so important in Their plans: Slothrop, for example, turns out to be a trivial tool in the eyes of Sir Marcus and the Home Office, while the blacks and their rocket are the real, short-term objective (615). Early on, Enzian tries to suggest to Slothrop such a statistical view; the Hereros, he says, have "a sense for the statistics of our being. One reason we grew so close to the Rocket, I think, was this sharp awareness of how contingent, like ourselves, the Aggregat 4 could be—how at the mercy of small things" (362). While actualists continue to invent coherent fictions about their experience, they do not forge the linear, necessary, and unified plots of realism: they tell themselves the plural and indeterminate stories of actualism.

As a final expression of their openness to chance, Pynchon's actualists are inveterate risk-takers and, therefore, lovers: of individuals, races, humanity, life. Where realists like Teddy Bloat and Pointsman try to minimize risk, establishing bureaucratic systems for self-preservation and avoiding the dangers of close contact with others, actualists like Geli Tripping accept their own vulnerability, "not holding a thing back," taking the world in "bare and open arms" (294–95). Unlike Slothrop, actualists refuse numbness; they risk losing those they love, but they remain emotionally vital. Slothrop's friend Bodine, for example, undergoes "a transvestism of caring, and the first time in his life it's happened" when he takes on Magda's mannerisms after her arrest (742). Long after he and Blicero part, Enzian "risks what former lovers risk whenever the Beloved is present" (659). By itself, caring is not enough in *GR*; no character says, with *V.*'s McClintic Sphere, "Keep cool but care." Indeed, as if in answer to Sphere's too-simple formula, several characters in *GR* care while remaining icy. Pirate Prentice cares for Roger and Jessica (35); Franz Pökler adores Leni (162); Pointsman cares about Gwenhidwy (170–71); and Dodson-Truck feels fond of Slothrop and Katje: "I care about you, both of you. I do care, believe me, Slothrop. . . . I *care!*" (216). In addition to caring, the actualists of *GR* also refuse to use, sacrifice, dominate, or control. Their caring does not constitute a passive yearning to escape the confines of self, but rather an active, responsible, and generous creation of continuities between subject and other.

While film is *GR's* realistic art, with its emphasis on linear narrative, plausible detail, and causal continuity, actualistic art has its particular representative in music, especially song. Relying as it does on parallels, counterpoints, harmonies, and repeated motifs, as well as a series of notes and words, song is ideally suited to express the actualist's sense of multiplicity, accident, and quantum continuity. Song reflects the playful, momentary temporal faith of the preterite, as opposed to the end-ordered earnestness of the elect. "While nobles are crying in their nights' chains, the squires sing. The terrible politics of the Grail can never touch them. Song is the magic cape" (701). While film serves the colonialist ends of those in power, song—even the traditional religious lyrics of the compline service, and even sung by a choir of soldiers—retains a subversive, system-disrupting and life-affirming potential. Celebrating as it does the possibility that *"love occurs"* (440), song enables one's furthest reach beyond rationality, materialism, and causality, toward intangible and unpredictable magic. In the evensong, with "the tired men and their black bellwether reaching as far as they can, as far from their sheeps' clothing as the year will let them stray," listeners suddenly arrive in Bethlehem, "for the one night, leaving only the clear way home and the memory of the infant you saw" (134–35). Song does not dispel time or darkness or uncertainty; song frees people from the determinacy of their own rational systems. That *GR* ends by granting us time, despite the darkness and the falling rocket, to sing a hymn invoking alternatives to our imminent ruin ("there is a Hand to turn the time") surely signals Pynchon's hope that we might yet lift the repressive burden of Western linear reason.

Of those who come to actualistic perceptions of reality in *GR*, Tchitcherine particularly merits a closer look for the parallels between his and Slothrop's stories. The Russian bears a signal resemblance to his American counterpart: "When you came in I almost thought you were Tchitcherine," Geli says to Slothrop (290). Both men are pattern seekers and paranoids; both intuit a multinational cartel; and both chase the rocket through the Zone. Both go east in the service of their governments—Slothrop to Europe, Tchitcherine to Central Asia. Both encounter revelations at "Holy Centers" (the Kirghiz Light and Peenemünde), but both fail to recognize their meaning, doomed "always to be held at the edges of revelations" (566). Both enjoy drugs and costumes; both share an obsession with blackness; both feel betrayed by their fathers; both undertake personal quests in the Zone—quests for origins, for causality, and for their own lineage, which become perverse quests for annihilation. Quickly suspected by their governments, both men are isolated and exiled in the Zone. Such resemblances, central (as Molly Hite argues) to Pynchon's narrative strategy, function to multiply loose, parallel connections;[33] they also invite readers to explore questions of difference.

Tchitcherine's fate, unpredictably, differs sharply from Slothrop's. Near the end, Tchitcherine becomes a willing accomplice of Geli Tripping's benevolent magic. He abandons the pursuit of a closed and causal history—of his father, his brother, and his own past; but Tchitcherine does not, like Slothrop, give up continuity altogether. Rather, he chooses local and momentary continuities with Geli, whose important role in his recent past demonstrates that Tchitcherine has not simply forgotten or abolished history. His last appearance, camping by a stream with Geli in the open air, marks a departure from the linear pursuit of quests. Similarly, his attitude to the Enzian he meets in the middle of the bridge does not fulfill his previous anticipation that one or both would not survive the meeting. "The two men nod, not quite formally, not quite smiling, Enzian puts his bike in gear and returns to his journey. Tchitcherine lights a cigarette, watching them down the road, shivering in the dusk. Then he goes back to his young girl beside the stream" (734–35). This meeting occurs, not as the end of a line, but as the middle of various continuities: midbridge, midjourney, middusk, mid-Zone, and, above all, since he takes food rather than death from Enzian, midlife.

Given the similarities between Slothrop and Tchitcherine, we must wonder why they adopt such different positions as the novel ends. Predictably, Pynchon admits no one cause. In part, Tchitcherine is simply lucky, for by good chance he has won the love of a powerful and determined, as well as playful and open, young witch. A believer in nonrational magic, Geli enters the text singing about the continuity of love through memory. By no more predictable accident, Slothrop has not formed such an attachment. But Tchitcherine has consistently displayed an openness to magic and to love, especially in his repeated returns to Geli, while Slothrop habitually avoids returning to any woman. In one nightmare, he admits, "Jenny, I heard your block was hit [. . .] and I meant to go back and see if you were all right, but . . . I just *didn't*" (256). The two men diverge definitively in their willingness to return in memory: Tchitcherine recalls much more than Slothrop does. When in the Zone he sees a duel between black and white singers, he remembers the same structure signaling his approach to the Light a decade before (610–11). Later, Tchitcherine cultivates memories for company; he welcomes "an albatross with no curse attached: an amiable memory" (701). Unlike Slothrop, who plucks away the albatross of past selves, Tchitcherine remembers and thereby remains continuous: he can, at the end, return to Geli. This makes his story one of "magic. Sure—but not necessarily fantasy" (735).

Quantum Continuity: The Form of Gravity's Rainbow

Avoiding in its own larger motions the "zero" of discontinuity and the "one" of serial causality, Pynchon's story resembles neither the fragments into which Slothrop disperses nor the monomyth Blicero creates as he fires his rocket. *GR* occupies the actualistic space between, where narrative elements, like historical events or subatomic particles, remain loosely bonded but unsolvable. "It all goes along together. Parallel, not series. Metaphors." The very density of Pynchon's novel, where Slothrop, Blicero, Tchitcherine, Enzian, and Mexico enact permutations of similar responses to reality, doubling and diverging in a Western "League of Nations," and where dozens of other characters reflect different facets of their overlapping struggles, enforces a parallel, not serial, mode of understanding. Phenomena as related as Pudding's coprophilia, Slothrop's rocket-erections, Greta Erdmann's sadomasochism, and Pirate Prentice's fetishism do not have one identical underlying cause, nor do they follow one another with any serial clarity in the text. Where serial order exists, as in Slothrop's story, the content of the story militates against the assumptions traditionally attached to its form: Slothrop's linear progress takes him out of line, off the Western time-line, away from a linear identity altogether. As if in answer to Forster's too-simple "only connect," *everything* connects in Pynchon's text, and the mysteries proliferate.

One feature of Pynchon's quantum continuity is an unpredictable motion from subject to subject: the narrative eye leaps surprising gaps, which the narrative voice does not fill in or justify through any retrospective reasoning. In a traditional realistic narrative, changes of temporal or spatial plane tend to follow the blocks of chapter divisions and to be "mapped" for the reader with clear transitions. After Isabel Archer's engagement, for example, James skips four years, beginning chapter 36 of *The Portrait of a Lady*: "One afternoon of the autumn of 1876, toward dusk, a young man of pleasing appearance rang at the door of a small apartment on the third floor of an old Roman house," and right away readers know where they are. Within the chapter, all the significant events of Isabel's experience during the temporal gap have been retrospectively extracted and summarized. The gap becomes, not a void, but a sketchy line: Isabel married, settled in Rome, had a son, who died six months later, and she learned to disagree with her husband.

Pynchon's quantum leaps differ in several ways. First, because he does not envision his narrative as embellishments around a single line, he does not supply missing segments but rather leaves narrative threads truly broken. What happens to Roger, Jessica, and Jeremy between II, 8, when Pointsman decides to send Jess away, and IV, 2, when she appears engaged to Jeremy? How does Katje come to leave Slothrop on the Riviera in

II, 3, and why does she agree to act her sinister role with Pudding in II, 4? What does Franz Pökler do between leaving Dora in III, 1 and playing chess with Slothrop in Zwölfkinder in III, 28? Pynchon does not fill in the blanks. He does not place the reader securely or map relations between disconnected events. In three consecutive sections of part 1, Roger and Jessica spend a night together, Slothrop follows his harp down the toilet under narcosis, and Pirate receives a coded message: no narrative guide provides dates, locations, or transitions among these events. As his text progressively dissolves spatialized time-lines, Pynchon's leaps of focus occur more frequently within, as well as between, chapter units. No rationale appears for the ordering or the breaks in continuity between segments: Pynchon's narrative does not invoke causal reasoning to account for its fluctuations but rather makes of accident and uncertainty sufficient structural principles. Those empty squares between narrative sections, so frequently explicated as film-sprocket holes, also figure the gaps left by Pynchon's quantum leaps.

Pynchon similarly dismisses the stable, spatializing binary divisions on which many characters and institutions rely. Categories like war and peace disintegrate in a novel where the war's nominal end arrives unannounced, and where, as several characters perceive, the "real" wars have only begun. Distinctions like black and white, male and female, we and they, or hero and villain may indeed obsess Pynchon's characters, seeking a static order and a balanced clarity in experience; Pynchon undermines these flimsy constructions to demonstrate the fluidity and shapelessness of real time. For every opposition his characters imagine, he interjects contradictions, qualifications, confusing third and fourth terms, and webs of complication: black and white lose meaning when one central black character, named for a yellow and blue flower, is half white, and another is nicknamed "Red"; the white Russian is part silver and part gold—and there are "Norwegian mulattos." Force and counterforce, assumed to be viable alternatives by some characters, emerge as similar entities serving the same firms, especially after the Counterforce becomes, inevitably, routinized. Pynchon's narrative refuses to balance itself on these traditional pilings: it does not alternate between "hero" and "villain," it does not set dark lady against fair, it does not juxtapose civilized interiors against natural gardens. To balance pairs is to stabilize reality and to stop time; Pynchon disrupts his characters' binary assumptions and immerses them in an unbalanced, unpredictable temporal flow. His novel's four parts do not form pairs; in length, they do not balance; although numbered, titled, and provided with epigraphs, they do not impose or expose a meaningful order patterning events.

With binary oppositions, Pynchon rejects an insidious corollary: namely, the hierarchical categories erected to preserve systems in power. Not only does he interrogate colonialism in all its various guises, as it privileges "civilized" over "savage," Western over non-Western, elect over preterite; he also undermines the hierarchies of narrative form that tacitly support colonialism in traditional narratives. Divisions like "major" and "minor" characters, significant and insignificant information, or dominant and subordinate motifs appear in texts reaffirming ontological and political hierarchies, whether explicitly or implicitly. Even the structural paradigm calling, after Aristotle, for a crisis and denouement implies a hierarchical arrangement of experience in which narratives valorize one event over all others. Pynchon begins with a major character, convinced of his own major status in the plot, but as Slothrop's sense of living in a realistic novel wanes, he turns to a minor character in his own mind and in *GR*. When the category of "minor" characters broadens to include over two hundred figures, the novel has not simply inverted, but exploded this hierarchy. Similarly, information—about the past, the rocket, the tribal customs of Hereros, or the migratory habits of lemmings—fills the novel, to such an extent that none of it can matter, but with such insistent connections that it *all* matters. The novel's "crisis" cannot be pinpointed, especially since so many of the figures who expected crises (Slothrop, Tchitcherine, Enzian, for example) do not encounter them, and those who arguably do (Blicero and Gottfried) do not experience them as epiphanic moments: rising in the rocket, Gottfried thinks of the red setter who bade him good-bye and of other minute phenomena, rather than of the meaning of life and death. No one event determines Slothrop's scattering; no single crisis precipitates the rocket hanging over the West at the novel's end. Since hierarchies such as these are necessarily retrospective and detached, selected from an exterior and final view of what mattered "in the end," an actualist like Pynchon must inevitably dismiss them in favor of the uncertain, inconclusive view of one involved in time.[34]

Like other actualists, Pynchon rejects a disciplined novelistic economy to produce in *GR* a large, sprawling, inclusive "baggy monster." Since the diffuse energies of an actualistic reality do not lend themselves readily to condensation or miniaturization, none of Pynchon's texts constitutes a synecdoche for the world it represents; even *Crying*, Pynchon's "smallest" novel, figures the artist's task not as reproducing the world in little but as "embroidering a kind of tapestry which spilled out the slit windows and into a void, seeking hopelessly to fill the void."[35] *GR*, too, spills out: without seeming edited from a foreknowledge of the end, it includes in its selected version of reality events that impend but do not fulfill their adventurous promise, acts that lead nowhere, things with no significance beyond themselves. In fact, it focuses squarely on the coincidental, the digressive, and the "finally" insignificant: Prentice picks bananas; Pointsman steps into a toilet bowl; Katje wanders around a house; Pökler plays chess. While events that would be highlighted in traditional narratives (Bianca's death, von Göll's betrayal of Slothrop, or Blicero's reaction to Gottfried's death) happen offstage in *GR*, so that their reality and import are never fully established, the events making up *GR* are comical, accidental, and, from a traditional perspective, unimportant. A novel celebrating the narrative preterite, as *GR* and other actualist texts do, commits itself to be all "middle," loose, prodigal, lengthy—anything but economical.

For related reasons, *GR* does not aspire to unity, as that has been understood and honored in the Western literary tradition. Pynchon's text emphasizes its plural focus, expanded beyond the main plot and subplot which still coalesce in a unified whole. *GR* ramifies subplots and characters past any possibility of fusion into oneness; while its multiple strands relate to each other in multiple ways, their density mocks any simple unity. Where traditional narratives devote their conclusions to a gathering together of loose ends and an integration of figures or events that have seemed (but never really been) eccentric, *GR* spins characters and actions off into more and more widely separated orbits. The novel is nowhere less single or more fractured than near its end, as Pynchon dissolves whatever illusory unity he has preserved to that point.

Allusive patterns, too, function in *GR* to suggest the dispersion of knowledge, rather than the essential unity of the world. David Cowart reads Pynchon as a traditional novelist when he asserts that "all of Pynchon's allusions—scientific and artistic—form patterns that lend unity not only to the individual stories and novels, but to the author's work as a whole."[36] On the contrary, Pynchon's allusions seem precisely intended to abolish the unities of traditional reference. As Cowart, Stark, Fowler, Ozier, and others have indicated, Pynchon alludes to worlds of information so diverse as to be unassimilable by any one reader or even—until the annotated edition, perhaps—by any one reader's guide: from calculus to King Kong, tarot to Tannhauser, Poisson to Pabst, fragments of data baffle the reader who pursues wholeness and harmony beneath this encyclopedic debris. The very nature of early criticism of *GR*, so much of which has "tracked down" references and allusive patterns without "solving" the novel's mysteries, attests the problematic disunity generated by Pynchon's allusions.

Pynchon rejects the various forms of closure through which conventional novels present reality as a stable and determined thing. From brief individual sequences to the novel at large, he substitutes anticlimax and irresolution for the cathartic end. On the last page of *V.*, "Nothing was settled"; on the last page of *GR*, the fate of the West hangs in midair, while the novel culminates, not in a definitive period, but in a dash: "Now everybody—" (760). In the meantime, Slothrop has never located the rocket or the cause of his own erections in response to it; Tchitcherine and Enzian have met without recognizing each other, and Pointsman has neither died from the "Book's curse" nor won the Nobel Prize. Peripheral sequences, too, come to nothing: Närrisch does not die, the torpedo misses the USS *Badass*, and Tantivy's death is never confirmed or explained. By refusing to bring these plots to a "satisfactory" conclusion and by repeatedly invoking readers' expectations of climactic outcomes that he suspends or denies, Pynchon makes of endlessness an epistemological strategy. With the "sense of an ending" conditioned in readers, he exposes the consequent assumptions that history itself has an end in which all loose threads will be knotted and all puzzling phenomena explained and that individuals' experience properly follows the same course of return after errancy to atonement with the Father and alignment with the past.

As closure vanquishes time by turning it to a spatial object, epiphany too constitutes a static, permanent illumination in which mind conquers time; Pynchon denies his characters that inward conclusiveness so favored by modernist writers. Unable to get out of time or to achieve a final perspective on temporal events, because their reality *is* time-bound acts rather than spatial things, these characters cannot achieve revelation. Every time one of them credits a vision of truth, the vision explodes and the "truth" turns useless or wrong. Pointsman has a repeated vision of a face turning to meet his eyes and confirm his destiny; no face turns. Närrisch envisions his imminent end "about to burn through the last whispering veil" (518), but no end, burning, or vision beneath the veil occurs. Tchitcherine encounters the Kirghiz Light, "but not his birth" (359). Even Gottfried, the only character given accurate knowledge that he is about to die, does not thereby see conclusively. "Where did he—it's already *gone*, no . . . they're beginning to slide away now faster than he can hold, it's like falling to sleep—they begin to blur" (759). Like these characters, the novel itself does not move toward revelation; if it concludes by warning that Western civilization may be rushing toward a self-destructive end, it never pretends to forecast anything beyond the realm of time.

Because actualists can only see subjectively and from the uncertain midst, Pynchon avoids the favorite realistic illusion of authorial detachment. The narrative perspective in *GR* is neither objective nor omniscient; while the narrator adopts a personal stance within the novel, he does not try to seem unbiased or unlimited in his knowledge. He offers no smug hints at outcomes, at Jessica's eventual choice of Jeremy or Geli's success with Tchitcherine. Knowing no more of the future than the characters themselves, he cannot write from the end. He displays his biases openly, setting the "mean heart" of Pointsman against "rough love in the minor gestures" of Gwenhidwy (171, 170), the destructive "claw" of Greta against the vulnerable "baby rodent hands" of Bianca (478, 469). He chides readers who bring the wrong expectations to his text, in direct addresses emphasizing their personal origin. "You will want cause and effect. All right," he says, and proceeds with a farcical burlesque (663). "You used to know what these words [perception and will] mean," he complains, but now "somebody has to tell you" (472). Losing Jessica forever, Roger suffers: "Sure. You would too. You might even question the worth of your cause" (716). In these and other asides to the reader, Pynchon disbands the old narrative conspiracy allowing readers to share in an authorial wisdom superior to the characters' limited understanding. Pynchon's implied reader, by contrast, is as subjective, limited, and involved as characters and author, but even more liable to misjudgment because of the conditioning of earlier texts. For character, narrator, author, or reader, no vantage point remains but the actualistic one: involved, uncertain, personal and temporal.[37]

In various related ways, Pynchon rejects the teleological forms traditional among Western narratives. The four large sections of *GR* have mock-titles and ironic epigraphs, parodying the habit of labeling experience from the end, as Fielding and others did. The seventy-three smaller divisions have no titles, numbers, or epigraphs, showing that one cannot extract spatial form from temporal flow. The novel occupies the present tense: "A screaming comes across the sky," plunging readers and characters into time, rather than lifting them above or after events. The preterite, in which a screaming came across the sky once and for all, allows elect readers to see the past from its end and thus creates a class of blindly preterite characters; actualistic writers like Pynchon more often choose the present. Although *GR* does, like conventional novels, cycle back, repeat itself, and develop echoes among scenes, characters, and motifs, it creates an *open* cycle that never closes or stabilizes. The novel arches from one Western city to another, from a rocket ascent to a descent, from blackout to burnout, from a sense that "it's all theatre" to a seat in "this old theatre," from one nightmare of annihilation to another. *GR* does not, however, arrive back at its point of origin but rather celebrates change and difference in a network of similar phenomena. Its repetitions do not therefore nullify energy but, instead, increase it; its echoes do not result in stasis but in motion.

Given all these related commitments to a narrative form capable of reflecting actualistic reality, it must come as no surprise that *GR* occupies itself in large part with an intertextual response to *the* realistic novel form par excellence, the bildungsroman. Its very name designates a certain end-shaped plot, dependent on linear continuity, on causal stability in the world, on epiphanic insights in an educable hero, on hierarchy, unity, and objective certainty in the account of his progress. The one miniaturized man of his times, the bildungsroman's protagonist always reveals the properly traditional order in the world, whether by religious atonement with the father in *Robinson Crusoe* or by aesthetic alignment with the "old Artificer" in *Portrait of the Artist*. As the protagonist achieves an identity, he comes to oneness with himself and reality—to unity and certainty, not to multiplicity and indeterminacy. How inevitable, then, that Pynchon elects to invoke this narrative form for his story of Infant Tyrone's growth to manhood and then inverts and subverts its every premise. To be sure, Tyrone receives his education, so that he and his story and its underlying conventions scatter beyond retrieval. Slothrop's story brings one sort of education to its end.

And inaugurates a different sort: just as James's protagonists learn through their experience the "realistic" nature of reality, Pynchon's characters confront the less graspable, actualistic nature of theirs. This latter education is complicated, on the one hand, by the uncertainty of all knowledge in the new physical reality; at best, Pynchon's figures are liberated by knowing how little, and how subjectively, they know. On the other hand, education in the new reality is also constrained by the powerful conservative force of Newtonian assumptions; at worst, like Slothrop, characters either fall into old habits of thinking or fall out of the habit of coherent thought altogether. Actualistic texts attempt to dispel the outmoded and pernicious Newtonian/realistic system and to deconstruct the literary forms it has authorized; *GR* interrogates virtually every assumption underlying the Western traditions in science, philosophy, and narrative art. But it does so without being merely negative or simply revisionary. Hence, *GR* also educates its readers: it teaches us a massive new song—"one They never taught anyone to sing"—for our actualistic occasion.

THREE

ROBERT COOVER

THE PUBLIC BURNING

AND THE ACCIDENTS OF

HISTORY

Robert Coover has been accused, like most of the novelists I consider actualists, of "a headlong and idiosyncratic betrothal of unreality."[1] Consistently grouped with other writers of self-reflexive fiction, he has been frequently praised and occasionally condemned as a metafiction- ist. His most important and ambitious novel, *The Public Burning* (1977)—ten years in the writing, two years and several rejections in the publishing— has been found flawed by a "historical incoherence" deriving from its metafictive approach. "The difficulty with *The Public Burning* remains the collision between its metafictional technique and its political content. . . . The more specific the political impulse of the text, the more difficult the dramatization of that purpose through metafiction—otherwise, politics becomes reduced to the celebration of liberation in the 'openness' of the text, in the act of writing itself."[2] Indeed, to interpret this densely historical novel as metafiction, as the most vocal and sophisticated critics of Coover suggest we should, is to find its factual detail excessive, its approach to history and politics baffling, and its self-reflexivity marred in peculiar ways by an inconsistent focus on the actual world.

If we consult instead Coover's own statements about the nature of fiction and about his goals in writing, we discover the actualist's engagement with reality in its normal, inevitable conjunction with an awareness that art can't naively mirror or simply represent, because it also knows itself as language, construction, fiction. Coover understands the novel as born of, and directed to, the marriage of art and actuality. Emerging from Cervantes's "synthesis between poetic analogy and literal history (not to mention reality and illusion . . .)," the novel serves "as a mythic reinforcement of our tenuous grip on reality. The novelist uses familiar mythic or historical forms to combat the content of those forms and to conduct the reader . . . to the real, away from mystification to clarification, away from magic to maturity, away from mystery to revelation."[3] Coover acknowledges the self-conscious treatment of language and form as "necessary but secondary. I know there's a way of looking at fiction as being made up of words and that therefore what you do with words becomes the central concern, but I'm much more interested in the way that fiction, for all its weaknesses, reflects something else—gesture, connections, paradox, story."[4] Responding to interviewer Larry McCaffery's impulse to see metafictional elements in his writing, Coover places himself instead in the realistic tradition. "Maybe I think that all my fiction is realistic and that so far it has simply been misunderstood as otherwise." Yet, as suggested by his choice of Cervantes (rather than Fielding or Richardson or Dickens) as the significant ancestor to whom he dedicates his fiction, Coover does not see the novel's commitment to actuality as originating in, or as fulfilled by, the conventions of realistic fiction. If he sees "the overview" of his novels as "wholly realistic," he sees their design—the formal qualities that distinguish them as art—as "born of, well, something else. That vibrant space between the poles of a paradox: that's where all the exciting art happens, I think."[5] Coover voices here the paradoxical will of actualism to bring the awareness of language and fictive traditions and forms, as well as a sense of fiction-making as basic to human consciousness, into dialogue with art's ancient imperative to speak of and to external reality. Neither the terra firma of realism nor the airy habitat of metafiction, Coover's "vibrant space" between art and actuality is the realm sought after in actualistic fiction.

Coover approaches reality, not as the stable, material *res* of realism, but as the energetic, uncertain *acta* of actualism. Throughout his fiction and his statements in interviews, he reveals a perception that reality has shifted in the twentieth century. He says in one interview (1973), "Our ways of looking at the world and of adjusting to it through fictions are changing. . . . our basic assumptions about the universe have been altered, and so change has occurred in the broad base of metaphor through which the universe is comprehended."[6] In another interview (1979), Coover adds that "all the disciplines were affected, not just writing. Physics, for example, had long since been leading the way."[7] That Coover regards the new physics as an important agent transforming our assumptions about reality is suggested by prominent references in his fiction. In *Public Burning*, for example, he mentions relativity theory (217), black holes (224), and the random universe (328); Einstein appears briefly with the less-well-known physicist Harold Urey (494).[8] More generally, Coover's third-person narrator in this novel sees through an actualistic lens; at one point he watches a crowd of people in the dark who resemble "atoms let loose in a walled void" (520). This "atomic vision" of the masses attending the Rosenberg executions ironically emphasizes their accidental motions in the midst of a ritual designed to restore the illusion of causality.

Coover's fiction specifically engages the shift, crucial to recent scientific understandings of the way events occur, from causality to probability. One of the major revisions quantum theory brings to our concept of reality is its rejection of a determinate chain of causal levers beneath events, in favor of the admission of chance or accident. Because it saw occurrences as necessarily connected by causal laws, Newtonian science assumed that, with enough information, any physical event could in theory be predicted. But for quantum mechanics, science can predict only the probability of events; the laws of statistics replace those of causality. Why? Because of chance: which electrons leap to which orbit around the nucleus of an atom, or which atoms disintegrate in the process of radioactive decay, is purely accidental. As a result, quantum theory provides a statistical description of the probability of group behavior but denies that individual events can be predicted. This is, in part, because of the uncertainty principle, which defines a radical indeterminacy in scientific knowledge of subatomic phenomena and thereby suggests not only that scientists cannot determine causes but also that reality includes accidents. Einstein saw this implication at once, and his passionate rejoinder to Heisenberg objects precisely to the newly central role of chance: "God does not play dice with the world."[9]

But despite Einstein's resistance, contemporary physics posits a reality in which, since God *does* play dice, its own inquiry amounts to defining the probabilities for any given throw. Max Born thus writes that "physics is in the nature of the case indeterminate, and therefore the affair of statistics."[10]

For an actualist like Coover, "the broad base of metaphor through which the universe is comprehended" in fiction shifts to disrupt causality with the acknowledged force of accident. Coover's second novel, *The Universal Baseball Association* (1968), reads as a Heisenbergian refutation of Einstein's famous statement, for the creator named J. Waugh (an inversion of Jahweh) runs his baseball-league world with three dice. Accident intrudes disastrously to kill a favored player, whose success also results from statistical oddities, when the dice stretch probability and come up triple ones three times in a row. As the statistician and the physicist know, however, probability includes a range from very low (but not impossible) occurrences to very high (because more average) ones. The dice-run world has no underlying causal order; both success and death arrive by the statistical "turns of the mindless and unpredictable—one might even say, irresponsible—dice."[11]

Coover's other fictive worlds are similarly probabilistic. His plots often address the irruption of chance in the lives of characters who have believed in causality: a mining accident sets off *The Origin of the Brunists* (1966), and "A Pedestrian Accident" (1969) begins, "Paul stepped off the curb and got hit by a truck."[12] More important, much of Coover's fiction develops multiple repetitions or complementary variations of episodes, suggesting a probabilistic rather than causally necessary approach to narrative form. In *Spanking the Maid* (1982), the maid and the master perform ritual variations on the theme of her (accidental) inability to keep order in his room and his (unwilled) inability to impose a restorative discipline on his maid, his dreams, his sexuality, and his life. As this paradigmatic relationship repeatedly rebegins, the novella plays out several of the possibilities inherent in it, replacing the single chain of cause-and-consequence that unifies traditional narrative with pluralistic variations on the probabilities. The multiple filmic tales of *A Night at the Movies* (1987) explore alternative possibilities for plot developments in classic movie genres (the Western, the gothic horror, the Chaplin comedy, the Bogart adventure), each of which loses its ground in safe causality and catapults into the world of the authentically strange. In *Gerald's Party* (1986), death, chaos, and absurdity invade a party (reminiscent of Pynchon's "Entropy" on a much larger scale), and the narrative itself suffers similar interruptions and invasions.[13]

While Coover's texts consistently interrogate, from an actualistic perspective, the human rage to construct causal, coherent myths out of the accidents that make up experience, Coover's third novel, *The Public Burning*, occupies itself directly with the fictionalization of actual, historical reality. President Eisenhower, Richard Nixon, J. Edgar Hoover, Justice Douglas and others become characters involved in a great national purgation ritual, the electrocution of Julius and Ethel Rosenberg on June 19, 1953. Coover has obviously done extensive research on the period, the events, and the people he presents, for other sources confirm the accuracy of even minor details (Nixon took his family to the beach on the day he was elected to the Senate) and of broad characterizations (Eisenhower distrusted Nixon, who alternately fawned on and resented Eisenhower) that appear in *Public Burning*.[14] The novel does not direct its energies to a "realistic" representation of facts or to an investigative reporter's objective account of the cultural milieu behind events; hence, it differs profoundly from the Capote-esque "nonfiction novel" to which one otherwise perceptive reviewer connects it.[15] It also differs from E. L. Doctorow's realistic (and carefully researched) novel about the Rosenbergs, *The Book of Daniel*. John Kuehl has shown that "the realist [Doctorow] then tends to put disguised principal figures in more or less authentic situations, where they encounter actual people, but the antirealist [Coover] reverses this, placing his undisguised, historically verifiable cast in more or less inauthentic situations, where they may encounter fabulous characters."[16] Coover's focus remains, as in his other fiction, on the mythic, dramatic, and fabulous structures with which individuals and cultures recall Newtonian stabilities amid Heisenbergian uncertainties. Its remarkable impulse to make fiction out of reality—possible because Coover does not see reality as realistic—makes *Public Burning* an unusual actualistic text.

Coover does not randomly select the Rosenberg case as material for fiction: he chooses a significant moment near the beginning of the atomic age, which created the *new* scientific reality, when Americans' horrified but naive and nostalgic reactions to the spread of nuclear power led them to infer causal continuities, to "detect" a spy ring, after the assumptions of the *old* scientific reality. Convicted as hostages to Newtonian absolutes, the Rosenbergs die as scapegoats for popular fears of relativity and indeterminacy. Coover chooses, then, a moment of maximum conflict between old reality and new.

Like other novels explored in this book, *Public Burning* relies on contrasts between old and new modes of representation, realism and actualism—the muses demanded by Newton and Heisenberg. It locates these contrasts, not between different characters (as Gaddis and Barth will do), but rather, and perhaps more provocatively, *within* each character. As befitting its concerns with American culture and with communal fictionalizations of history, *Public Burning* traces a schism between public and private versions of actuality—what is said and done on record and what is felt, intuited, and feared by isolated individuals. Committed to a public assurance that masks private doubts, all of the characters play two contradictory roles. The public America of 1953 enforces an outdated, realistic view of reality; American identity and domestic and foreign policies rest on assumptions that truth is absolute, history continuous and causally coherent, the universe material and mechanistic, observers (including news reporters, presidents, prosecutors, judges, and above all FBI sleuths) objective, reliable, and certain. The public statements of officials, like the actions of government agencies, reveal a realistic metaphysics of Presence: the world is causally ordered and thus understandable and representable. These public certainties are fed by and in turn foster popular forms of realistic representation. In contrast, characters privately intuit an actualistic reality, expressed in subjective musings which are relative, discontinuous and accidental, "grounded" in a physics of absence. Reinforcing these private glimpses of contingency, Coover's ironic inversions of realistic forms of representation make *Public Burning* an actualistic alternative to the public and popular modes it parodies.

Since actualism and realism embody contrasting views of reality and representation, they also include, to come to Coover's more specific concerns, divergent understandings of history and historiography. In *Public Burning*, actualism and realism imply attitudes toward past events corresponding to what Michel Foucault terms, after Nietzsche, genealogy and history. Genealogy, writes Foucault, approaches the past without trying "to restore an unbroken continuity that operates beyond the dispersion of forgotten things," but rather identifies "the accidents, the minute deviations—or conversely, the complete reversals—the errors, the false appraisals, and the faulty calculations that gave birth to those things that continue to exist and have value for us; it is to discover that truth or being do not lie at the root of what we know and what we are, but the exteriority of accidents." Genealogy offers a more statistical means of understanding and describing the past than the form of history. History assumes "a suprahistorical perspective: a history whose function is to compose the finally reduced diversity of time into a totality fully closed upon itself. . . . The historian's history finds its support outside of time and pretends to base its judgments on an apocalyptic objectivity. This is only possible, however, because of its belief in eternal truth."[17] Like actualism, then, genealogy reads events as part of an open temporal process whose acausal, probabilistic nature it affirms. History, on the other hand, sees events spatially, from the end, "objectively," and as causally connected by an "eternal truth."

Besides its useful reminder that the actualistic view of reality, now common among physicists, was intuited by philosophers like Nietzsche or Heraclitus long before atomic study began, Foucault's genealogical project also provides rich ground for an approach to *Public Burning*. From this perspective, its plot concerns a public effort to construct History (capitalized throughout the novel to suggest its metaphysical status in characters' minds) out of accident, dispersion, and flux. As Uncle Sam says to Nixon, "It ain't easy holdin' a community together, order ain't what comes natural, you know that, boy, and a lotta people gotta get killt tryin't to pretend it is" (559). When the USSR exploded an atomic bomb in 1949, a witch-hunt ensued for the spies who had sold Russia the secret—despite the testimony of physicists that "there was no 'secret' of the bomb," and despite the report in 1945 by an American scientist who visited Russia that "within a very few years" the Russians would explode atomic bombs.[18] The notion of a spy ring passing secrets amounted, then, to an invented History: beginning from the end, the FBI, called in as an agent of "apocalyptic objectivity," does indeed restore an "unbroken continuity." It coerces diversity (many scientists can invent atomic bombs) into unity (only U.S. scientists invent; Russians have to steal), because scientific invention, as the penetration of eternal truth, is single and only happens once. The spy ring, itself a perfect image for the "totality fully closed upon itself," provides both temporal and causal links that convert exterior accident into essential truth.

Coover, however, writes a genealogy of this History. He presents events in all their singularity, while exposing the multiple accidents that shape them. He writes of "the unreliability of history," according to Vincent Balitas.[19] Taking what Foucault calls the "dissociating view" that liberates "divergence and marginal elements," he emphasizes characters (a cabdriver, an old panhandler) and events (Ethel Rosenberg at age sixteen acting in melodrama) that have no place in a single, composed History. Coover's text is long, uneconomical; it "tells a thousand researched and courageous truths, uses its excess as both emotionally affecting rhetoric and imitative form," and "presents a distinctly postmodern politics: power as the electronic display of information and symbols," according to Tom LeClair.[20] Public Burning includes so many details, so seemingly gratuitous ("Mrs. Sarah Brock Dodge, U.S. Army nurse in the Spanish-American war . . . drops dead as a doornail" [45]), precisely because, as Foucault says (and demonstrates in his own writing), genealogy "requires patience and a knowledge of details and it depends on a vast accumulation of source material."[21] Rather than locating an underlying unity and completeness in this material, as his characters strive to do, Coover allows a finished historical episode to decompose, to disperse into multiple complexities, and finally, far from producing a catharsis, as it does for witnesses of the sacrifice ritual, to explode readers' belief in this—or any—History. Régis Durand has commented that Coover "plays with the codes, disorients, produces a text which escapes the logic of causation, of origin, continuation, and closure . . . negates, opens the safe reservation of past narrative to the thrust and threat of the present."[22]

Constructing a Causal History

Most of Coover's characters commit themselves to the public version of History as a realistic text or coherent story plotted along one continuous, end-ordered, causal line. Whether personal or national, the story has no random details or divagations, but only significant minor motifs designed by destiny. Nothing is accidental; paranoia runs as wild in Public Burning as in Gravity's Rainbow. For Judge Kaufman, the Rosenbergs cause the Korean War and all its deaths, while even the protests over their execution are "not a mere accident . . . I think it has been by design!" (26, 295). Nixon also denies the play of chance in "my guided life." Conceiving of "History working things out for me in its inexorable but friendly way," he is not worried by apparent setbacks. "It wasn't necessary, I knew. I'd read the ending" (186, 149). Since the preordained end shapes all events from the beginning in realistic narratives, interpreters can work backward, assimilating diversity into unity and constructing History recollectively, as in this public reading of America's role in global History. "Throughout the

solemn unfolding of the American miracle, men have noticed this remarkable phenomenon: what at the moment seems to be nothing more than the
random rise and fall of men and ideas . . . is later discovered to be—in the
light of America's gradual unveiling as the New Athens, New Rome, and
New Jerusalem all in one—a necessary and inevitable sequence of interlocking events, a divine code" (9). In the end, even momentary readings,
as of the Rosenberg case, turn sequential, necessary, and even divine, so
that no excess or deviation occurs, and no data exudes outside the system.

As part of the divine plan, History and politics are governed by an
absolutist conception of reality, seen in Newtonian fashion as spatial,
symmetrical, and static. For the public sector, well trained in realistic
assumptions in Coover's novel, the world balances binary pairs that reflect
its absolute, unchanging, and causal order: God and the devil, truth and
falsehood, freedom and Communism, light and darkness, Uncle Sam and
the Phantom—all reflect the unity beneath apparent diversity and the
certainty one gains in the absence of any penumbral middle ground. The
"eye for an eye" nature of the Rosenberg executions (they are "thieves of
light to be burned by light" [3]) reveals one sinister face of the public drive
for symmetry in the novel, as a club of circus fans, called "Saints and
Sinners," reflects a more benign aspect. Because these symmetries resolve
into absolute unities, into one truth separate from all falsehood, they do
not lead dialectically toward motion or synthesis; they imply a preexisting
stasis. So Eisenhower's inaugural prayer reads, "Give us, we pray, the
power to discern clearly right from wrong" (195), and Nixon rightly concludes, "I'm no believer in dialectics, material or otherwise, let me be
absolutely clear about that, I wouldn't be Vice President of the United
States of America if I was, it's either/or as far as I'm concerned" (51). Later,
he exposes the function of these binary oppositions, to simplify and
structure, to eliminate ambiguity: "I loved to debate both sides of any
issue, but thinking about that strange space in between made me sweat.
Paradox was the one thing I hated more than psychiatrists and lady
journalists" (142).

For the public agencies and personages constructing a realistic version
of History, events must disclose some clear and meaningful form; even
Uncle Sam is "still hungering after some kind of shape to things" (359).
Coover's Americans impose two complementary structures on History.
The first, linear one expresses itself equally in the beginning-middle-end
form of realistic fiction and the temporal line of Judeo-Christian history, in
both of which time appears as continuous and material. But linear prog-

ress turns circular in response to the imperative pull of the end: for the reader or the human soul, seemingly gratuitous details, narrative digressions, accidents, and eccentricities turn out to be necessary to the outcome or causally linked to ends immanent from the beginning. Sartre's Roquentin remarks on this narrative process of catching "time by the tail."

> Everything changes when you tell about life. . . . You seem to start at the beginning: "It was a fine autumn evening in 1922. I was a notary's clerk in Marommes." And in reality you have started at the end. . . . the story goes on in the reverse: instants have stopped piling themselves in a lighthearted way one on top of the other, they are snapped up by the end of the story which draws them. . . . And we feel that the hero has lived all the details of this night like annunciations, promises, or even that he lived only those that were promises, blind and deaf to all that did not herald adventure. We forget that the future was not yet there.[23]

Between the beginning which contains the ending, and the end that points to its origin, all experience revolves in the mythic, ritual cycle of heroism, sacrifice, catharsis, and renewal. Emerging logically from the circular line, the second—the polar or binary—shape reflects the absolute spatial and moral order beneath cyclic time. The two shapes join in essential harmony, as the conflict between polar opposites like good and evil leads, in linear sequence, to the outcome promised by the original nature of the conflict. Both imposed structures assimilate accidents into a causal order.

Musing on public records that invoke these shapes to present the Rosenberg case as a battle between evil Russian spies and good American detectives, Nixon thinks, "If you walked forward through all this data, like the journalists, like the FBI invited everybody to do, the story was cohesive and seemed as simple and true as an epigram" (137). Nixon links journalists with FBI agents appropriately in this context, for both dedicate their energies to the fabrication of realistic narrative. The detective emerges from, and addresses his objectivity to unraveling the secrets of, a Newtonian, causal reality, as suggested in Pynchon's Stencil, Pointsman, and Slothrop. That the journalist serves this same nostalgic vision, producing falsely coherent representations, is among Coover's most original perceptions in *Public Burning*. Like FBI detectives, journalists work backward from catastrophe to cause, positing the power of objective reason to discover continuities between apparently disparate facts; then, like detectives solving mysteries, journalists present their readers with linear, cohesive, and Historically composed versions of the evidence. As Raymond Mazurek puts it, the news industry, with its "objectification" of reality, "creates a monolithic version of history which has a hegemonic function, regardless of the intentions of those who write the news."[24]

Coover's interest in the news industry as a producer of Historical fictions supporting American ideology is established from the novel's first chapter, titled "President Eisenhower's News Conference." The president and his advisers do not intend to announce new facts, events, or positions, but rather to "confirm the details" of the execution and to "remind the nation" of the president's implacable opposition to Communism (31). The conference is not about news; the president's advisers suppress the only real news to arrive during it, that Douglas has issued a stay of execution. Instead, both president and journalists engage in a reaffirmation of America's heroic role in the coherent story unfolding through current events as an epic battle against Communism. Disparate issues— the Rosenberg executions and the book-burning scandal involving Roy Cohn and David Schine—reduce to simple exempla of this one unified theme, just as texts by Stalin, Marx, and Al Capone level into oneness under Eisenhower's blurring gaze.

Because journalism creates Historical fictions rather than reporting genealogical details, Coover's journals take on mythic roles. The *New York Times* appears as a shrine or monument, to which readers make holy pilgrimages; *Time* magazine becomes the national poet laureate, whose "news" Coover prints as free verse. These two journals shape History as religion and as art, Coover suggests; interchangeably, both transform accidental processes into linear, causal stories. The daily litanies of the *Times*, where readers commune with "the Spirit of History" (200), resemble in function the weekly poetic revelations of *Time*, who "is also a prophet of religious truth, the recreator of deep tribal realities" (346). Indeed, one of *Time*'s reports is printed as a balanced, diamond-shaped poem in the manner of religious poet George Herbert (25). Both journals strive for a similar aesthetic and metaphysical distance from time itself, so ironically invoked in their names.

Using binary and linear shapes to structure individual stories and whole issues, both organs construct meaningful, causally complete, realistic representations of events. One typical *Time* story echoes Roquentin's hypothetical, end-directed beginning.

it was a quiet rainy night in
   prisoner of war camp number nine
under the brow of a green hill in
   pusan
     at 2:30 a.m.
pfc willie buhan was reading . . .
   he wasn't
worried much though vaguely aware
   that his two rok buddies on guard
duty had been acting sort of
   "funny."

(41–42)

The details of this opening establish its affiliation with realistic fiction, where minor and random data turn necessary, "snapped up by the end of the story," and where exact times, places, names, and actions help readers grasp an essentially material reality. The linear narration ("it was," "buhan was," "the next thing he knew he was looking down the barrels") actually returns full circle to fulfill the promise made in the opening lines, where the quiet and the private's subdued worry guarantee an adventure that will justify his vague awareness of trouble. Within the ritual circle of one soldier's adventure, made interesting as it reflects on the Korean War and, more broadly, the war between freedom and Communism, the superficial lines between North Koreans and ROK-American allies break down to reveal the even-deeper binary division between Americans and Asiatics, between West and East. As Coover's quotations from actual stories indicate, these publications do not simply report information but also and more subtly construct realistic tales that assimilate random data into a causally coherent worldview.

Trying to provide "a talisman against the terrible flux" (200), both *Time* and the *Times* resurrect the Newtonian universe in their representations. Both invoke absolutes, unify discontinuities, and account logically for accidents. The *Times* creates a "fragile episodic continuity" out of experience; *Time*, "an effective mosaic" out of fragmentation (200, 337). Beyond wholeness out of dispersion, both journals aim at recovering meaningful Historical patterns out of random accidents. Echoing Fausto Maijstral, who learns in Pynchon's *V.* "life's single lesson: that there is more accident to it than a man can ever admit to in a lifetime and stay sane," *Time* considers, "Raw data is paralyzing, a nightmare, there's too much of it and man's mind is quickly engulfed by it. Poetry is the art of subordinating facts to the imagination, of giving them shape and visibility" (337). Similarly, the *Times* was founded on "the tenacious faith in the residual magic of language" to name and evoke Presence; thus it tries "to reconstruct . . . each fleeting day in the hope of discovering some pattern, some coherence, some meaningful dialogue with time" (203). Appealing to an absolute and unwavering Truth, the *Times* preserves a "static tableau" "within which a reasonable and orderly picture of life can unfold," while *Time* dedicates its art to a "real grasp" of "Ultimate Truth" (205, 337).

Both journals, in sum, write History by negating time and in order to negate time—or in Foucault's terms, from a perspective that implies the end of time. "The great experience of the twentieth century," writes Coover's narrator, "has been to accept the objective reality of time and thus of process—history does not repeat, the universe is not changeless," and time is not space. But the *Times* makes it spatial, he continues: the paper "transforms this time process into something hard and—momentarily anyway—durable" (207). Their freezing of flux does not occur without slippage, however; residual hints remain of the time process and its terrible outcome, death. *Time* tries to avoid "confrontations with the Shape-Shifting Absolute," the real time that changes life to death (345). Yet, as *Time*'s fears for its own mortality indicate, it cannot ignore "the world's entropic attack" (338). The *Times* also seeks escape from "the terrible center, the edgeless edge," distancing death in routine stories and obituaries, but some readers remain "disturbed by these litanies, discovering in them hints of the terrible abysses beyond the tablets" (207–8). To insist on the reality of the time process against the futile impulse to solidify it, Coover opens those abysses for his readers. The last paragraph of his "Pilgrimage to *The New York Times*" chapter, conjoining fragments of ads and stories in a mockery of linear sense, degenerates into the meaningful chaos that it is the paper's purpose to preclude: "*The Goddess Strapless in fine white* Push-Button Loading. DULLES' REMARKS SHARP: Don't Neglect Slipping FALSE liquid will help you to handle expanding demands" (209).

As a result of the realistic representation of reality by the news industry—and also, of course, by the entertainment industry that produces movies like *House of Wax* and *High Noon* and plays like *The Valiant*, in which hero and villain are clearly opposed in linear, causally controlled adventures that take on the circularity of myth—all Americans who read newspapers, see movies, or watch television inherit a public faith in reality as

Historical Presence. They adopt, above all, a belief in objective omniscience, in deities, sacred or profane, with the assimilative vision of the realistic narrator. As one chapter puts it, they admire "the Eye in the Sky" (Foucault calls it the panoptic eye) that sees everything from outside time. For Eisenhower, the Eye belongs to "Almighty Gawt"; for Nixon, it peers from the news media: "I determined to face the Eye in its nakedest form: the television camera" (325). For all Americans, the Eye symbolizes the omniscience of Uncle Sam, a secular deity who flies like Superman. For the Rosenbergs, pathetically, the Eye is the finalizing—and vindicating—perspective of History. Although, as Marxists, they reject other forms of omniscience, they nonetheless turn the impersonal forces of time into a "superhuman presence" watching them. Nixon suggests that they have been seduced by the human need "for pattern. For story. . . . If they could say to hell with History, they'd be home free. The poor damned fools" (321–22). Their jailer agrees, remarking on the oddity of their symbolic behavior, "acting like they're establishing historical models or precedents" (429). Thus the Rosenbergs ironically fail prey to another secular variant of the same mythic Seeing Eye that supports the FBI, the judges, and the president who condemn them.

Complementing their faith in an external, objective witness to human affairs, Coover's characters also see in the detached overview their own best access to Truth. They strive to become realistic narrators or Eyes themselves, to separate themselves from what they see, and to gain certainty by looking backward or down on the world. Charged by Uncle Sam to study the Rosenberg case, Nixon spreads the papers around his office floor, then "stood and gazed down on all the documents and records scattered about the room, trying to get an overview" (319). At another point, he says he must "reach a panoramic view of the event" (247). Nixon struggles for objectivity: he tries to wrench himself out of a subjective identification with Ethel, flees in horror from an imagined perception of her past; finally, he literally backs out of a personal involvement with her. Like most other characters in the novel, he believes that Truth, in the form of causal coherence, answers the call of the scientific, rational, impartial observer.

Witnesses to Contingency

Coover's characters fail, however, to achieve objective detachment—or to penetrate Truth—because their author invents them in an actualistic novel. Privately, many of them perceive reality as absence and accident, their own knowledge as, at best, uncertain. For all the public affirmation of the Eye in the Sky, they see from the ground and in the dark. Judge Kaufman projects an "enlightened" certainty onto the anonymous public, from which he feels isolated in his private doubt: "If he were just a common citizen out there in the faceless crowd, he might have a better overview of the whole, but—" (451). Underscoring the futility with which they pursue clear, scientific observation, much of the novel occurs at night and emphasizes visual distortions or blocks. On Thursday night, "the children of Uncle Sam" have "nightmare visions" of chaos around the world; they cry out, "The Angel of Darkness is loose in the world . . . Confusion and panic beset us" (113–14). On Friday night, a total blackout interrupts the executions, confronting spectators with their uncertainty. "In the nighttime of the people, everything is moving and there is nothing to grab hold of," and eventually truth and perversity become indistinguishable (515, 519).

Coover's invocation of darkness, blindness, and "the nighttime of the people" is part of his actualistic rejection of the Enlightenment tradition, which—as Derrida and Foucault have argued—constitutes the dominant institutions and discourses of the West. Expressing the binary logic of realism and its basis in Enlightened rationalism, light/clarity and darkness/confusion form the stable poles of conventional fictive optics: darkness makes its chaotic appearance only to be dispelled by a privileged and final Light. For Coover, in contrast, not only is the light extinguished and characters repeatedly confused by an inability to see clearly, but their very drive for clarity takes its place in the crippling logic that leads to public burnings, both electrocutions and, as LeClair observes, "nuclear holocaust, the ultimate public burning and final sub-text of Coover's title metaphor."[25] Light—the will to fix life, especially to determine clear causes for seeming accidents—generates a politics and a metaphysics that lead inevitably to death. Uncle Sam, then, springs "fully constituted from the shattered seed-poll of the very Enlightenment" (7–8), spreading death with an ideology of global domination in the war between "the Sons of Light" and "the Sons of Darkness."

While Coover's public remains committed to light, reason, causality, and History, private individuals in *Public Burning* often intuit the actualistic nature of reality. The experience of "being in the dark" is more common than any other in the novel; allied with Barthelme's "not-knowing," it leads characters to feel, however tentatively and privately, that History is a lie constructed by reason to explain away the real accidents of experience. Coover's choice of subject ensures that public voices, with their affirmations of public values, must dominate the novel; his choice of "public servant" Richard Nixon to narrate the "private" half of the novel makes vivid the community's power in the lives, assumptions, and stories of private citizens. Yet his genealogical approach to the narrative of the Rosenberg executions leads Coover to introduce alternative voices—insignificant in History, unassimilated to the reigning ideology, marginalized by the culture, economics, and politics of Uncle Sam, deviant from Enlightened norms. These voices appear scattered through the text, powerless to change its outcome.

Quirky and isolated, the witnesses to contingency object to the Historical plot constructed by the government in its persecution of the Rosenbergs. Justice Douglas, to whom the novel is dedicated, tells Uncle Sam that the trial and sentencing violated the law and then remarks, "Don't you think it's about time you got down off this Sons of Light and Darkness kick? I've about had it with all this—" (82). A remarkable cabbie, whom Nixon mistakes for the Phantom, later amplifies a similar sense that binary shapes and expulsion rituals violate life's complexity. "They got nothin' to do with life, you know that, life's always new and changing, so why fuck it up with all this shit about scapegoats, sacrifices, initiation, saturnalias—?" Openly admitting the limits of his own subjective understanding ("I'm only a lousy cabdriver. Shit, I don't know everything"), he nonetheless insists to Nixon that "life's too big, you can't wrap it up like that" (288). To demonstrate that "truth" and "identity" are relative and confusable, he tells Nixon a long, salacious story that seems to be about Ethel Rosenberg but turns out to concern Julie Rosenblatt. To suggest the government's persecution of two innocent human animals, the cabbie races across traffic to hit a pair of copulating dogs. Though Nixon is blind to his point, the cabbie tells him that the evening's ritual murder will fail to reconstruct a realistic, causal, safe version of time and events.

Two other characters, victims of prophetic misperceptions of reality, stumble out of Historical systems and into accident and confusion. One man emerges from *House of Wax* still wearing his 3-D glasses, to stagger around the city seeing "two separate and unassimilable pictures, each curiously colored" (299). From seeming sanely unified and causally coherent, as the movie implied, the world turns multiple, fragmented, and mad. After a series of accidents and injuries, he decides that "sanity is murder": that the rational, linear, Western mode of vision has brought about the atomic holocaust and that, as a formerly sane man, he is the guilty scapegoat, the Rosenberg. Liberated from a plausible, Enlightened, realistic perspective, he perceives the deadliness in just that socially privileged perspective.[26] Another bewildered character, an old panhandler, undergoes a similar loss of bearings with a temporal, rather than spatial, distortion. Finding a "gathering of millions" in Times Square, "he blinks, casts a bleary eye at the clock over the Square, and mops his brow in disbelief," and then goes to get an overcoat, believing it New Year's Eve (369). To this panhandler, time has seemed knowable, predictable, and material; on New Year's Eve he gathers money and free liquor, as well as the occasional tourist's watch. Now, however, he enters the real time-process, as "he's beginning to wonder if somebody is finally out to get him for good, cutting the years in half" (373). His confusion appropriately identifies the occasion as an attempt at ritual rebirth, mistimed and unseasonal, and initiating only death.

Coover's most complex study of the clash between old and new visions, History and genealogy, realism and actualism, occurs in his portrait of Richard Nixon. An exploiter of, but not a believer in, realistic systems, Uncle Sam tells Nixon early on (with a reference to Henry Ford) that all testimony about the past is "a baldface lie" and "history itself—all more or less bunk . . . the fatal slantindicular futility of Fact! Appearances, my boy, appearances!" (90). Nixon resists this lesson, continuing sporadically to assert that History has an ordered design. Yet, as divided as his constituents, Nixon also perceives randomness and relativity. His experiences as a private citizen have led Nixon to the same intuitions of accident and uncertainty that others have; he is isolated, disappointed in his marriage, uneasy in his political career. Indeed, one critic offers a psychological reading of Nixon in which he detects "the causes of his isolation" in Nixon's relationship with Pat, the "cause of Nixon's separation from others" in his masking of himself, and, in the end, "a cause for the failure of the 'Schizophrenic Experience': fear."[27] But Nixon's private experience leads away from causality as definitively as do the public events of the novel: he suffers accident upon accident through the course of his life, and he can neither discover nor invent an adequate cause.

His exploration of the Rosenberg case leads Nixon to speculate, "watching truths blow by like shifting clouds," that History, for all its impact, "was nothing but words. Accidental accretions for the most part, leaving most of the story out. . . . What if we broke all the rules, played games with the evidence, manipulated language itself, made History a partisan ally?"

(142). If truth is plural, relative, and volatile, and History an order surviving accidentally in words, then, Nixon realizes, the whole system can be twisted and used. But he resists this understanding; he consoles himself that he will "fortunately" forget: "these errant insights always fled and something more solid, more *legal*" replaces them (142). In rejecting the errant or deviant, whatever strays outside the system of laws or norms, Nixon promises to repress his emergent understanding of the new, accidental world and dooms himself to betray his incipient sympathy for Ethel Rosenberg.

On his way to see Ethel, he has another significant intuition, that History is an *invented* order which does not really exist in random, discontinuous, shapeless events.

> There were no scripts, no necessary patterns, no final scenes, there was just *action*. . . . This, then, was my crisis: to accept what I already knew. That there was no author, no director, and the audience had no memories . . . perhaps there is not even a War between the Sons of Light and the Sons of Darkness! Perhaps we are all pretending! I'd been rather amazed at myself, having thoughts like these. Years of debate and adversary politics had schooled me toward a faith in denouement, and so in cause and consequence. The case history, the unfolding pattern, the rewards and punishments, the directed life. Yet what was History to me? (380–81)

As he demonstrates in the novel's climactic interview with Ethel, however, Nixon cannot accept an open, undirected reality. Soon after dismissing the well-made-play metaphor as an inadequate image of life, he acts a scene with Ethel; he follows old scripts, using (and muffing) lines and gestures from old plays. John Kuehl has pointed out that "theater represents the main parallel uniting Nixon and Ethel," defining the staged quality of Nixon's focus on her in a larger context where "Americans are histrionic, if not historical."[28] Nixon continues to play to History: he goes to the prison to win the public audience, the presidential role, the "statues of myself in Berlin, in Seoul, in Prague, Peking, and Peoria" (390), and so, appropriately, he backs out of the interview onto the stage in Times Square.

Moreover, the expected denouement directs his actions throughout the scene. First, he is powerfully aware of Ethel's impending death as an immediate end; though he begs her to save her life by lying, he knows she is beyond help, even if she would lie (468). In fact, his perception of her doom charges him sexually: he has envisioned her nude, masturbated to a fantasy of her in wet clothes, and awakened, like the other male leaders of the nation, sexually aroused on the day of her death. He intends to kiss and conquer her: "This *was* what I'd been planning to do all along! Fuck all the phony excuses I'd made to myself, *this* was what I'd come all the way up here for" (461). Second, Nixon also keeps his own, more distant end in view—the expected denouement of his success story, in which he becomes president. While kissing Ethel, he keeps "my eye on the door at the far end" and reflects that he "was fighting for my political life" (460). He thinks about escaping without damaging exposure throughout the scene, and at the end begs Ethel to help him get out: "it is important for the nation" (470). Indeed, far from accepting the open-ended actualistic universe, with its genealogical imperatives, Nixon retreats into realistic History: "I am making history this evening, not for myself alone, but for all the ages!" (463).

Ethel Rosenberg appears to understand her role as a victim sacrificed to Historical coherence. She sees that Nixon reflects the country he leads in using her as an object. His urge to conquer the weak, errant female resembles the court's, for both sexual conquest and political execution reaffirm the potency of the phallic, patriarchal absolute. Throughout the scene, she twists to her own ironic purposes the clichés with which stage and screen versions of women have traditionally inflated masculine self-esteem. "Oh, Richard! . . . You're so strong, so powerful! . . . I feel so weak!" (464). Accurately sensing that prurience and lust, an urge to violate rather than love her alienness, motivate Nixon, she concludes the scene with devastating irony directed at his end-ordered, self-centered success story. "Above all they shall say of you: Richard Nixon was a great lover!" (470). Finally, to expose the corruptness of the leaders and the system that condemn her, she sends him, literally exposed and with "I am a scamp" lipsticked on his bare behind, before the American public.

Nixon's effectiveness as a first-person narrator derives in part from his dual status as public figure and private citizen. As the child of immigrants who feels alien himself, he identifies and sympathizes with Ethel; as the vice-president courting a presidency, he pulls the switch that finishes her off. His schizophrenic alternations between public, Historical, realistic visions and private, genealogical, actualistic intuitions dramatize the plight of other Americans, who publicly affirm absolutes they profoundly doubt in private. The disjunction between public dogma and private uncertainty leads, for Nixon and his peers, to a sense of isolation, paranoia, and inadequacy; alone with a private terror, each character feels condemned to confusion and blindness in a land of clarity and light, the only errant, godless doubter in One Nation under God. Dread therefore dominates the novel, from Nixon's constant sense of persecution to the poet laureate's paranoia to the crowd terror in the blackout. "Your country is sick with fear!" cries Sartre (493), and it is the dread of death, difference, aliens, poverty, uncertainty, and accident that leads to the executions. Nixon stands, then, as both product and producer of the failures of his culture and his times: as a representative, flawed, frightened, two-faced American, and as a failed leader-hero, whose inability to overcome his egoism or to accept his intuitions of accident breeds further doom for his land.

Genealogical Form in The Public Burning

Coover's novel constitutes a private and actualistic vision of the public antics, figures, and values it presents. Its sustained ironies in content and in form explode the realistic view of reality and affirm contingency. In its treatment of the executions, Coover's text withholds the completion, the ordering catharsis, the aesthetic distancing which the executions are staged, precisely, to provide. The last chapter (preceding an epilogue) ends with Ethel flying, endlessly, in the electric current: "Her body, sizzling and popping like firecrackers, lights up with the force of the current, casting a flickering radiance on all those around her, and so she burns— and burns—and burns—as though held aloft by her own incandescent will and haloed about by all the gleaming great of the nation—" (546). Concluding with a dash suggests the unending, ongoing, inescapable terror in this event, from which readers are not rescued by a period or by a home-going, rounding-off sequence. Rather, the image of Ethel grotesquely sizzling, her body become the sinister and deadly fulfillment of the promise of light, illuminating the powerful survivors who have condemned and killed her with the radiant reflection of death: this disruptive image hangs, suspended in motion, mocking the redemptive closure that would allow readers to distance and bury the terror in relief at the end of realistic fiction.

To explore the accidental nature of the past in his genealogical novel, Coover invokes, and ironically inverts, the linear/cyclic and binary teleological models of History. He uses a linear chronology that seems destined to come full circle, because he writes about a completed episode with a foregone conclusion that his readers know. The novel ends, however, by deconstructing the notion of foregone conclusions, even of conclusion itself as "ending" or "deduction": the conclusion of the book and our conclusion about what we "know" become more complex and less certain as we read. Rather than the straight causal line that bends back to its origins in a circle, Coover sends his readers into the pathlessness of an open-ended time process. He also invokes the polar symmetries that his characters admire, countering prologue with epilogue, balancing four seven-chaptered parts, divided by three "intermezzo" sections. For even the amateur numerologist, the divine trinities meeting the earthly quaternions balance this dualistic universe in the "perfect number" seven. But Coover's parodic revelation actually dismisses the binary order, or as LeClair says, "The characters continually set up dualisms—up and down, center and periphery, end and beginning, sacred and profane—that generate metaphors, but these metaphors deconstruct the binary oppositions, make them fuzzy, show how they are reciprocally created figures of huge cultural and religious systems."[29] Not only does he expose the simplistic viciousness attending popular symmetries like hero and villain or Uncle Sam and the Phantom but Coover also admits and even emphasizes what they close out: that "strange space in between," of undecidable ambiguity, which makes Nixon sweat. Nixon himself is neither hero nor villain but a complex, self-conscious, skeptical intelligence with traits of the clown and fool.[30] Coover's elaborate structures emerge, like those of Barth or Nabokov, from "a delight with the rich ironic possibilities that the use of structure affords."[31]

Coover's narrative perspective also invites rich ironies. Invoking binary symmetries in another way, the point of view alternates regularly between Nixon's first-person accounts and a third-person narrator's. Observing the intertextual echoes of Dickens's *Bleak House* in this novel about the social and human damage inflicted by a corrupt legal system, we anticipate the traditional division between the involved account of a participant in the fictive world and the detached recollective vision of a judge of that world. Nixon's sections, then, should be personal, subjective, private, and limited, and the third-person narrator's impersonal, objective, public, and omniscient. But neither account matches those expectations. While Coover certainly encourages readers to consider the differences implied by public and private angles of vision, he more importantly suggests that public angles are themselves slanted, private angles resisting their own subjectivity: " 'Objectivity' is in spite of itself a willful program for the stacking of perceptions," his third-person narrator writes (203). As a result, the apparent binary opposition between points of view breaks down, leaving a first-person narrator who strains for omniscience while caught in a particularly egoistic subjectivity, and a third-person narrator whose most journalistic accounts disclose a personal bias, often ironically ("Rhee, the obstreperous old bastard, has pulled the straw mat out from under Uncle Sam's feet and let his prisoners go" [42]), and whose interest focuses on limited private individuals, from the panhandler to the poet laureate.

Readers, then, resemble the character in 3-D glasses, who "seems to see two separate and unassimilable pictures, each curiously colored" (299). Coover's two lenses provide different angles of vision, variously colored by their subjective origins. While the two narrators see differently, write in different styles and tenses (as in *Bleak House*, the first-person narrator writes in the past tense, while the third-person narrator uses the present), and even assume different values, their pictures do finally join in producing depth and complexity. Coover's picture does not, like the 3-D movie, level the two into one continuous, unified, simply coherent version; rather, it shows discontinuity and difference as irresolvably the nature of vision, fiction, and reality.

Public Burning also relies on an ironic appropriation of cyclic, mythic archetypes. In his well-known essay "*Ulysses*, Order, and Myth," T. S. Eliot posits a radical difference between the linear (realistic) novel and the cyclic, mythic (modernist) one: "Instead of narrative method, we may now use the mythical method," which manipulates "a continuous parallel between contemporaneity and antiquity. . . . It is simply a way of controlling, of ordering, of giving a shape and a significance to the immense panorama of futility and anarchy which is contemporary history."[32] But despite their obvious surface differences, narrative/linear and mythic/cyclic methods meet in harmony, because linear narrative actually cycles back to fulfill the promise of its origins. As the realistic line comes to resemble the mythic circle, realism discloses its affiliation with symbolist modernism, and both reveal their basis in a metaphysics of Presence. Supposing that time is ordered from the end and that experience has some underlying unity and coherence, both of these systems invite parody from a novelist who believes that "all good narrative art" struggles "against the unconscious mythic residue in human life . . . against adolescent thought-modes and exhausted art forms."[33] To be sure, Coover sees mythmaking, much as Eliot does, as a necessary human activity. "The crucial beliefs of people are mythic in nature . . . we invent constellations that permit an illusion of order to enable us to get from here to there." Discussing Christianity, newspapers and television, "the American civil religion," and communal rituals as forms of myth, Coover points out that eventually these rigidify, become impotent, or even "disturb life in some unnecessary way," and so artists must "break them up and perhaps change their force."[34] *Public Burning* thus parodies the outworn American and Western myths (with their underlying assumption of the closed mythic circle) that impede the invention of actualistic fictions for a postmodern community.

On the simplest level, Coover's mythic inversions generate some of the novel's black humor. Coover credits a "profound influence" in Emile Durkheim's discussion of communal meetings; among other insights relevant to *Public Burning*, Durkheim points out that sacrificial rituals are acts of alimentary communion, always involving worshipers in sharing food with the divinity.[35] As a result, Coover has Betty Crocker, "America's matron saint of the kitchen," preside with soup ladle over the preliminary rituals for the execution, in a chapter titled "Spreading the Table of Glory" (479). In the preceding chapter, "A Taste of the City," Nixon has taken communion by nibbling at Ethel. As the spies are cooked, "the odor of burning meat" leaves Hoover and others looking sick from "a case of severe heartburn" (544, 539). These and other grotesque jokes about the eating of the sacrificed spies also enforce the serious point that outworn mythic forms, adhered to rigidly, become barbaric and deadly.

To structure his most important insights into Nixon's failure to redeem himself or the nation he leads, Coover makes extended ironic use of the archetypal patterns of heroism described by Lord Raglan, Joseph Campbell, and Mircea Eliade.[36] Campbell's scheme is especially suggestive, for many of Nixon's experiences form ironic echoes of the first large stage of heroic adventure, the separation or departure, as Campbell describes it. Nixon's call to adventure, for example, occurs on the seventh tee of the Burning Tree Golf Club, an appropriately modernized "dark forest" with its "great tree" and "babbling spring"—where Uncle Sam, as herald, washes his golf balls.[37] Though Nixon studies the Rosenberg case and even proceeds to further stages of departure, he remains caught in the wasteland-producing "refusal of the call," "essentially a refusal to give up what one takes to be one's own interest."[38] He has, in fact, refused the real adventure even before he arrives at "the crossing of the first threshold," or entry to the unknown—Sing Sing Prison, appropriately guarded by dreadful ogres (police, guards, and reporters) and haunted by "sirens of mysteriously seductive, nostalgic beauty" (Ethel, "become extraordinarily beautiful, a vision almost medieval in its wholeness").[39] Nixon continues to resist the call even inside "the belly of the whale," traditionally the "worldwide womb" for the hero's rebirth, after a descent into his unknown self.[40] Designed by Disney and placed in the square to entertain the crowd, Nixon's whale contains the image of his dead Grandma Milhous, who, acting as his own, projected conscience, accuses him of a series of moral failures. A sham like Disney's whale and Nixon's conscience, she turns out to be J. Edgar Hoover in drag (558).

After Campbell's departure stage, the hero undergoes two more large phases of adventure, which are encountered by and forecast for Nixon in parodic form: the initiation or enlightenment, and the return and reintegration with society. In the epilogue, Nixon suffers a perverse form of the ultimate initiation adventure, the mystical marriage with the Queen Goddess of the World. When Uncle Sam (homosexual Queen Goddess, as well as herald and "protective figure" to Nixon) rapes him, wedding him to a future presidency, Nixon has a grotesque illumination in which, smitten by Sam's beauty, he falls in love with him. The mystical marriage normally "represents the hero's total mastery of life";[41] although Nixon is more mastered than master in the sequence, Sam's action confers a future power on him. The conclusion, then, predicts a horrifying return to society as the incarnation of Uncle Sam, teaching Americans what he has learned of rapaciousness.

The goal of the heroic journey, a personal maturation that symbolically redeems the hero's culture as well, cannot be accomplished by Coover's antiheroic Nixon. Far from advancing in maturity and wisdom, Nixon actually regresses toward infancy as the novel unfolds. He dwells more frequently on nostalgic and self-pitying memories of his childhood, from Thursday night, when he confuses his youth and Ethel's (151), to Friday night, when he wails to her, "*My* mother sent me away to live with my aunt!" (466). His gestures and emotions become more childish: "I pricked my thumb on the safety pin and was almost pleased. I sucked my thumb and demanded to know: How much must I give? . . . I was bawling my goddamn eyes out" (358). Ethel terms Nixon a "scamp" (a mischievous youngster, as well as a rogue); Uncle Sam urges, "Don't be a baby, baby! . . . so there, little boy, don't—don't cry" (561); and Pat snaps in irritation, "Oh, Dick, grow up" (551). Instead, as the novel ends, Nixon lies "scrunched up around my throbbing pain and bawling like a baby" (563);

his assumption of the fetal position suggests the ultimate regression and, at the same time, promises his ominous rebirth in the image of Uncle Sam. For his culture, the symbolic flow of new life into the World Navel at the center of the universe dries up. Times Square, Coover's World Navel, "ritual center of the Western World" and site of the annual New Year's Eve celebrations that affirm dreamtime (176–77), becomes instead a place of death.

From general mythic patterns like those identified by Campbell, Coover's parody extends also to one specific myth, the fairy tale "Beauty and the Beast." Not only does this tale concern a transformation analogous to the initiation/return cycles of Campbell, but it especially interests Coover for its exploration of the heroic conversion as an act affirming public, civilized values at the expense of private, natural ones. As the feminine, cultured beauty seeks to domesticate the rough male beast, she disciplines him to civilized norms, then loves her own tamed creature and transforms him to a prince with a chaste kiss. In Coover's ironic version, a repressive society can only project Beauty in habits of obsessive cleanliness and frigidity, as suggested in Nixon's descriptions of Pat. Nixon himself has "played" Beast all his life, writing his mother a letter from the perspective of "Your good dog Richard" (328), inventing a "patron beast" for his fraternity, and acting the "good dog" in an ongoing game of "Beauty and the Beast" with Pat. For all his games, however, Nixon admires cleanliness as much as Pat and secretly believes that, while evil forces like the Phantom and the Rosenbergs are bestial, he is not: his higher nature transcends the "dying animal." During the course of the novel, Nixon must increasingly confront his own inescapable beastliness, as he suffers hunger, grows dirty and smelly, steps in horseshit, tears his clothes, exposes himself in public, and finally endures Sam's rape. In the epilogue, titled "Beauty and the Beast," Nixon finally admits that the game has taken over his perceptions: "I'd wanted to tell Pat that she was the only one who could free me from this terrible enchantment, but all I could think of were arf and whine and snarl" (552).

Read in light of this fairy tale, Nixon's experiences in the epilogue become a devastating commentary on American public values. Pat, of course, must fail to transform Nixon, for she represents the American civilizing force in an enervated, sterile, deadened condition. With even her magic power to love dissipated, she abandons Nixon to Sam's lust. Sam accomplishes the transformation by taking on the role of Beast himself, thus converting Nixon to Beauty. Sam first appears with "eyes glittering with animal menace," "with a wolfish grin" and "a heavy doggy stink": "You're a . . . a beast!" gasps Nixon (559), and the rape, "dog-style" among Checkers's blankets and biscuits, confirms Sam's bestiality. Nixon, then, becomes "my beauty," blushing with submissive love at last (560). This transformation is doubly grotesque: first, Nixon becomes not human male or prince but rather princess; second, his transformation is achieved, not by any conversion magic involving genuine growth and love, but rather by Sam's simple act of unveiling a far worse brutishness in himself, making Nixon Beauty in name only. Sam, of course, embodies both the rapacious beast *and* the American civilized norm; with the helpless Nixon in the role of Beauty before the untamed Sam, Coover's ending forecasts more beastliness unleashed around the world.

In his ironic use of myth, whether the general motifs from Campbell or the specific pattern of this tale, Coover identifies a dual lack: he exposes the failure of America's leaders to be heroic or princely—from one per-spective, even human—with the consequent impossibility of redemption for their culture; he also reveals the insufficiency of these very myths and fictions to generate understanding of or action in the world. Coover uses these antique mythic patterns to measure the community, found wanting, and then to measure themselves: found doubly wanting, because their misleading affirmation of the closed, causal, and certain world not only fails to provide an accurate (let alone redemptive) model of reality but also breeds paranoia, witch-hunts, murder, and brutality in the name of mak-ing a contingent reality *appear* necessary and absolute. Thus mythic fic-tions—and by extension, modernist ones—and realistic fictions appear to Coover exhausted, oversimple, and damaging.

Public Burning provides an alternative, actualistic fiction addressed to and expressing a postmodern reality. The novel does not try to vindicate the Rosenbergs; it does not revise one absolute verdict, through Historical hindsight, for another. Rather, Coover's fiction addresses the American culture that condemns the Rosenbergs to die. Without pretending to locate an unbroken series of causal links, the text explores the unchained collection of accidents, the discontinuous movements of masses and leaders, the random processes that lead to the executions. Above all, *Public Burning* distinguishes a cultural faith in the archaic cosmos, whose absolute, causal continuities echo not only those of nineteenth-century realism but also those of the medieval Inquisition. Besieged as it is by private doubters, Coover's American theocracy reasserts official dogma with an auto-da-fé, a public burning of two heretics whose Marxist dissent symbolizes a range of challenges to unity and certainty. So, indeed, does Coover's mode of reference: a mixing of genres and modes of discourse,[42] providing discontinuous glimpses of several faces of the culture, seen from more different angles of vision than two perspectives need imply, and from perspectives in motion, as both narrators go from place to place and from hypothesis to hypothesis about what they see—these subjective fragments form a genealogy of events. In the multiple indeterminacies of an open temporal process, Coover's *Public Burning* portrays the accidents of history.

FOUR

WILLIAM GADDIS

J R AND THE MATTER OF ENERGY

L ike other actualists, William Gaddis engages contemporary reality in
his fictions. In *The Recognitions* (1955), *J R* (1975), and *Carpenter's
Gothic* (1985), Gaddis presents satiric portraits of the postwar
wasteland. Deeply immersed in the details of contemporary culture, all
three novels satirize its deadly materialism. An abiding concern with the
power of Mammon shapes Gaddis's fiction; his sense that the lust for
money and material goods defines postmodern culture—and in the process deadens spiritual energies that would create art, love, and generosity—accounts for Gaddis's insistent satiric tone. Posed variously by critics
as the battle between strife and love or money and art,[1] this opposition
appears in actualistic terms as the conflict between matter, which made up
reality in Newtonian physics, and energy, which constitutes actuality for
quantum theorists. While all of Gaddis's novels bring an actualistic emphasis on energy to bear in disrupting the cultural privilege granted to
matter, *J R* is my focus here for its unique approach to the thematics of
energy in an original energetic form.

The antirealistic nature of Gaddis's discourse has led some critics to
place him, with other actualists, as a writer of self-reflexive metafictions.

One critic terms *J R* "a paper empire," a work of "unintelligible surrealism" that compels readers "to acknowledge further that all empirical reality is no less a fiction."[2] Another finds that "within the text, the world consists only in a 'thin' acoustic surface, without materiality," to which the reader gives substance "by reading through the blizzard of noise to the fictional reality which generates the noise."[3] For still another, *J R* "suggests that we are continually victimized by such linguistic fictions and that our ideational constructions have no relevance to the world we hypothesize as real."[4] More persuasively, Tom LeClair finds *J R* and other "novels of excess" "referential, if not exactly realistic,"[5] and Steven Weisenburger argues that "Gaddis rejects a literature that refers only to itself; yet the admiration of self-reflexivity in fiction, and of texts as 'performances,' are *the* critical standards of our time. But a Gaddis novel has a way of returning powerful echoes to this noisy, dissembling culture."[6]

In a rare interview, Gaddis himself identifies *J R*'s grounding in reality. While he rejects "the question of autobiographical sources in fiction" as "one of the more tiresome going," Gaddis reveals that *J R* was inspired "by the postwar desecration of the Long Island village of Massapequa where my family had had property since around 1910, take a look at it now and you'll see all the book's worst hopes realized."[7] As John Kuehl and Steven Moore suggest, in the only biographical glimpse of Gaddis published to date, the author's experiences writing about school television for the Ford Foundation and working in public relations for Pfizer International, a maker of pharmaceutical drugs, also turn up in the novel, together with pieces of writing projects Gaddis abandoned.[8]

More revealing than his use of actual places, people, and experiences as the basis for fiction is the commitment these fictions express to art's necessary relation to reality. Through contrasts between creators who succumb to and serve the decadent material culture around them and those who resist it, while still addressing it in art, Gaddis's novels suggest that artistic energies play an active role in shaping reality. Gaddis's worthy artists (who are not, of course, his overtly successful ones) must be wrenched away from self-imposed isolation and immersed in the real world; Edward Bast must give up his father's studio, where he "shut it all out so I could work,"[9] for an apartment whose chaos, entropy, noise, and daily-increasing clutter of useless material goods reflect the external world. Gaddis's satire simultaneously reflects the world—the things and forces that waste modern men and women—and reshapes it through art. As Rhoda says, "You forget, you know? I mean like really how to hate?"

(609). By reminding readers how to hate a ruined and ruinous social world, Gaddis's fiction intervenes in reality.

Gaddis's sense of the external world is shaped by his awareness of physics; like Pynchon, he knows the importance of entropy both to thermodynamics and to information theory. "Entropy rears as a central preoccupation of our time," Gaddis writes in "The Rush for Second Place," an essay weaving its sustained criticism of modern America out of a genealogical gathering of multiple details in a manner strongly reminiscent of Coover's *Public Burning*.[10] That Gaddis finds the terms and concepts of contemporary physics useful for the artistic expression of reality is amply demonstrated in his fiction, especially in the entropy-ridden *J R*. He names a physics teacher Jack Gibbs, after one of the founders of thermodynamics, Josiah Willard Gibbs, who developed a geometric model of its second law. While his contemporary James Clerk Maxwell immediately recognized the significance of Gibbs's work, Maxwell's early death and Gibbs's own retiring nature left his theories in obscurity until 1920. But according to Norbert Wiener, in *The Human Use of Human Beings*, "it is, I am convinced, Gibbs rather than Einstein or Heisenberg or Planck to whom we must attribute the first great revolution of twentieth century physics."[11] Jack Gibbs serves throughout *J R* as a spokesman for the importance of entropy. In his first, resonant appearance in the novel, Gibbs turns off a televised lesson clearly based on Newtonian physics. "Energy may be changed but not destroyed [. . .] Scientists believe that the total amount of energy in the world today is the same as it was at the beginning of time," and then he interrupts the student who recites Newton's laws of motion: "The tendency of a body which when it is at rest to [. . .] and which when it is in motion to re . . ." (20–21). He urges his class to reject the Newtonian assumption, inscribed in the film, the textbook, and the entire educational system, "that organization is an inherent property of the knowledge itself, and that disorder and chaos are simply irrelevant forces that threaten it from outside. In fact it's exactly the opposite. Order is simply a thin, perilous condition we try to impose on the basic reality of chaos" (20). Gibbs tries to introduce his students to the new physical world, grounded in energy which dissipates rather than in enduring, stable, and predictable matter. Gibbs voices Gaddis's awareness of the pernicious hold the old, Newtonian physics continues to retain in the public curriculum and in the popular imagination.

J R addresses the deadening implications of antiquated Newtonian habits of perception in the energetic world of quantum physics. For a

Newtonian, we recall, reality is matter obeying inexorable laws, by which nature expresses its ordered regularity; through objective observation and reason, scientists can determine material causes behind events and thus solve the apparent mysteries of being. To experience reality in this way, for Gaddis's twentieth-century Americans, is to see very little and to ignore most of what they see in the Heisenbergian, actualistic cosmos. But the Newtonian worldview derives its honorific status in Gaddis's text from precisely this mode of overlooking flux, chaos, random energies, and uncertain motions. From a Newtonian perspective, temporal flow is stilled, chance explained away, death organically regulated, and life rationalized into graspable material forms. Above all, and in Gaddis's view, most deadly of all, value is considered to inhere in tangible goods, not in being and doing, but in owning, conserving, and controlling *things*. Arising from and expressing generally shared Newtonian assumptions about reality, materialism takes over everywhere in the novel, with devastating human consequences—or as Gibbs puts it, after Emerson, "God damned things [are] in the saddle and ride mankind" (400).

While most of his characters pursue goods and money, Gaddis himself explores the energies of their pursuit, using an actualistic narrative form that admits waste, flux, and chaos. Gaddis's text criticizes the Newtonian physics perpetuated in it by individuals and by institutions as well as the materialism that physics authorizes. From an actualistic perspective, of course, reality is not stable matter, motion cannot be plotted by causal laws, and human observers cannot know with objective confidence the behavior of systems they study. While contemporary physicists do not deny the reality of matter, they suggest that matter is more energetic and mysterious than Newton supposed and modified by its surrounding *field* (rather than empty space or "ether"), which cannot be distinguished qualitatively from matter. As Einstein puts it, "Classical physics introduced two substances: matter and energy. The first had weight, but the second was weightless. In classical physics we had two conservation laws, one for matter, the other for energy. We have already asked whether modern physics still holds this view of two substances and the two conservation laws. The answer is: 'No.' According to the theory of relativity, there is no essential distinction between mass and energy. Energy has mass and mass represents energy."[12] Similarly, quantum physics begins with the odd behavior of quanta as both particles of matter and waves of energy, and Heisenberg's uncertainty principle asserts that one cannot know both the position (matter) and velocity (energy) of the atomic fragments of actuality which he refuses to call *res*.

To collect and control things in an effort to create a solid, stable identity (as his characters do) becomes, for an actualist like Gaddis, not only a losing proposition but a ludicrous one; a more satisfying alternative is to seek meaningful activity, some means of directing one's energies into labor that, whatever it produces, forms its own reward. Since both pursuits activate Gaddis's characters, this chapter focuses, first, on the forms of materialism in which many characters escape their own energies; then it examines the efforts of others to locate intangible fulfillment through worthy action. The chapter concludes by exploring Gaddis's formal enactment of these thematics, and the physics on which they are grounded, in a narrative that refuses to be a well-made thing, resists closure, ignores visual surfaces, rejects unity, economy, and artificially imposed order, and celebrates multiplicity, prodigality, and randomness. The matter of *J R* is energy, imagined in energetic form.

Clinging to the Material World

If the world of *J R* at first appears static, and if most of its characters undergo no transformation, it is because these characters cultivate the stasis of objects. Resisting the imperatives of time, several characters with almost interchangeable voices (Davidoff, Whiteback, Hyde, Cates, Flesch, Zona, Eigen, Stella, and others) flee change in various forms of materialism. Gaddis's dynamics calls into question their assumption of stasis, for in fact these characters change and exchange clothes, jobs, houses, marriage partners, and money. More important, they are subject to the changes of time: they age, get sick, have accidents, and die. Their resistance, then, is only to the mental, moral, and spiritual changes which their experience in time would urge, but which would compel them to recognize the radical temporality of their lives. This section explores the materialistic steady state they cultivate, its implications and its sources in Gaddis's version of the American past, and his own thematic disruptions of stasis in and through time.

"Money . . . ?" provides the starting point for *J R*, as well as the end pursued by many of its characters. "God damn it can't, why can't people just shut up and do what they're paid for!" is nearly the last sentence in the novel. Between those two points, stealing, earning, investing, controlling, winning, spending, borrowing, and endlessly amassing more money preoccupies every character.[13] In the realistic fictions which have shaped the social milieu and the philosophical assumptions of Gaddis's characters, money provides an index of how the inner, moral, and spiritual self relates to the outer, social, and commercial world, with all its potential for fraud and deception. Heirs to the belief that money offers a stable, objective, and reliable measure of worth, characters readily take it for worth itself and for all other, less tangible forms of value. Asked by his mother how much he loves her, David Eigen replies, "Some money" (267). School officials conceive of education in terms of budget, businessmen understand their work in terms of tax deductions and their lives as entries in expense accounts, and chemists, as Mr. Duncan points out, evaluate human worth at $3.50 (685). Even Edward Bast pursues money throughout the novel; "It's not that it's the money, it's the money," he insists (37).

By emphasizing the purely representational nature of money, Gaddis dissolves his characters' equation of cash and worth. Money is an agency of exchange, a power to buy survival while one pursues worthy action and relationships; it has value only for the immaterial and energetic possibilities it signals. Gaddis, then, stresses its nature as a sign, interchangeable with other representations of worth, but never worth itself. On the first page, the Bast sisters recall the silver coins of their youth, now replaced by paper bills that stand for gold. "You couldn't believe it was worth a thing." Junior-high school Rhinemaidens use a paper sack full of coins to represent gold in rehearsal for a perverse production of Wagner's *Ring;* outside, a young girl collects the greenest fall leaves, twice removed from the gold they stand for, to fold and put in her purse (36, 32). In the corporate boardroom, the drapes contain a "gold-on-blue arrangement of denarii, ducats, shekels, and similar bright testaments to long submerged mercantile struggles" (92). Gaddis focuses on this represented gold as itself a representation of energies, "struggles," rather than matter or worth. For all the characters' obsession with it, money lacks primary reality in the novel, in part because Gaddis introduces so many other things that stand for it: leaves, drapes, stolen goods, tax deductions, and a multimillion-dollar "paper empire." By divorcing money from active purchasing power, Gaddis strips it of even representative worth: multimillionaire J R, for example, never buys new sneakers.

Unlike J R, most of the other characters do purchase, own, and reverence things. They value objects that are costly, manufactured, and—

especially—mechanical. Machines—cars, appliances, saws, clocks, televisions, and computers—fill all the spaces in the novel. Computer testing equipment and home appliances (both unused) crowd the school, forcing the elimination of the kindergarten and classes for retarded children. Each day's mail brings a deluge of new machines to the East Ninety-sixth Street apartment, already packed to the rafters with books, papers, and mementos. Bast receives an electric letter opener that tears the mail to pieces and a "solid state computer programmed for broiling steaks and chops to perfection" (555). Gaddis underscores the worthlessness of these mechanical objects: when they are used, they usually destroy (like the saws and letter opener), and when they sit unused, they turn to clutter, crowding out the people they supposedly serve.

Committed to amassing a static group of material goods, characters typically hoard objects. Though a certain amount of trading occurs, and though a great deal of breakage and loss disrupts their gatherings of goods, most characters nevertheless collect compulsively. Gibbs saves paper bags, and Eigen preserves newspapers and the hopelessly broken fragments of his son's toys. The Bast sisters keep mementos—playbills, notices of performances, photographs, postcards; Davidoff collects cuff links, and Crawley, stuffed trophies of his hunting expeditions. These and other characters try to bring things together into a mass that might define meaning, as if a static collection of goods could bring stability, coherence, and wholeness to the collector. Between the emptiness of what they collect and their inability either to keep their collections intact or to derive satisfaction from them, Gaddis indicates the futility of this hoarding impulse.

Several characters devote their energies to conserving things, in gestures that appear at first counterentropic and potentially saving. The Bast sisters sew on a button for attorney Coen, using carpet thread that "will probably outlast the suit itself" (8). Bast, Eigen, and Gibbs sort the mail; Eigen tries to fix a marionette, and Gibbs attempts to tune Al's guitar. Bast makes repeated efforts to repair, order, and save material goods: he fixes things for his aunts, uses teabags three times, and even tries, during a passionate encounter with Rhoda, to protect an Indian headdress that J R has rented. These various efforts to prevent the decay and loss of goods are not, however, redemptive: they arise from a sense of responsibility in and for the material world—in other words, from precisely the veneration for things that leads to the decadent materialism pervading Gaddis's text. Too, these conservative gestures express a naive and damaging faith in the potential permanence of things: naive, because things only break again, or the button remains on the fraying suit; and damaging, because energy serves matter rather than worth.

Out of a related belief in the submissive manageability of things, characters work at controlling the material world. They try to maintain order among their possessions, to use them without accident, and to dispose of them promptly and efficiently when they are used up. These characters thus imagine they can master a safe, objective world and eliminate the prodigal waste that would remind them that all matter is subject to time, decay, and death. Gaddis, of course, deconstructs their artificial orderings: as the pages of Miss Flesch's script fall and scatter, Amy Joubert drops her sack of coins, and J R spills his stacks of mail, which get mixed up with the Hyde boy's, none of these characters can keep the walls intact.[14] Larger and more life-destroying accidents occur throughout the novel to demonstrate that the objective world is far less safe, and human control of objects far less secure, than the characters would believe. Nor can they keep waste at bay: candy wrappers blow energetically down the streets, beer cans surface to trip them, used prophylactics dangle obscenely from the stairways, and a whole pailful of "what was stopping up the plumbing in the junior high" erupts in the principal's office (50).

Gaddis's characters end by imitating the things they value, as if identity were material. Not only do they cultivate a sense of self in and through their clothes, rings, cars, and other goods, but they also aspire to the "thingly" status of these goods. In a seedy automat, J R and young Hyde admire a woman who performs with mechanical efficiency (113); Donny DiCephalis wraps himself in cords and plugs into outlets throughout the novel (56). A shift from himness to itness occupies John Cates, who, like Pynchon's lady V., undergoes a series of bodily transplants. His companion Zona Selk considers having Cates declared nonexistent. "He's nobody, he's a lot of old parts stuck together he doesn't even exist he started losing things eighty years ago [. . .] now look at him, he's listening through somebody else's inner ears those corneal transplants God knows whose eyes he's looking through, windup toy with a tin heart" (708). The pursuit of mechanical thinghood is really a pursuit of immortality; while Cates implants a "tin heart," other characters emulate automata in a futile effort to evade time: their repetitions of words, phrases, conversations, gestures, and actions suggest the automatic responses of atemporal machines.[15] Like Pynchon, Gaddis examines the impulse to defy death by denying life.

One immediate consequence of their intimacy with the material and the mechanical is to deaden characters' sexual energies. Reified, fetishized, stolen, bought, and traded throughout the novel, sexuality mostly occurs as a commodity like any other. It is sold by the burgeoning pornography industry in the novel, including mail-order catalogs in which young Hyde studies coitus splints. Sexuality is also used as barter; Stella tries to seduce Bast to secure his cooperation in settling the family estate. After they are interrupted by her husband, Norman Angel, the episode ends with an appropriate inversion: on her doorstep, Stella is herself used by a flasher who finishes Bast's coitus against her skirt, in an act as impersonal and exploitative as her own (146). Rhoda, who rejects more obvious forms of materialism, appraises herself as a sexual object. Rhoda covets the perfect body: "Like how her cheeks hang where they part how high and round, you know? [. . .] Like I'd give anything for her ass, you know?" (366). For Rhoda, as for almost every other woman in the novel, sexuality confers the right to ask for money from her partners; but unlike many others, Rhoda does not sell sex, she only uses it to kill time. Since it is, in economic terms, such a waste of time, the sexual urge is eliminated altogether by the novel's two best businessmen, J R and Cates.

In similar ways, the larger natural world of the novel is ignored and neglected by some, tamed and destroyed by others. Since their materialism leads characters to covet the made and costly, they inevitably discount the natural and free. In fact, as the Protestant ethic teaches, they try to civilize nature, turning it to useful and productive ends. The novel opens on the shriek of saws trimming trees near the Bast property; these reared "their splintered amputations in all directions, an atmosphere of calamity tempered, to the south, by a brooding bank of oak" (17). By the end of the novel, all the trees have been cut down, and the hedges surrounding the house; the lot of flowers opposite has been paved over, and the Bast house itself condemned. But perhaps even more insidious than the outright destruction of nature is the simple obliviousness which passively allows its decimation: not only do the Bast sisters not tend their garden, but they do not quite notice when it disappears. J R has no overt hostility to nature; he merely ignores what fails to fit into his materialist system, where "everything you see someplace there's this millionaire for it." Amy Joubert and Edward Bast make separate attempts to show him the natural world, but J R cannot see the moon for the top of a "Carvel icecream cone stand" and the profit it represents (661).[16]

The reasons for which Gaddis's characters eliminate or ignore nature extend beyond their Protestant will to turn everything to account; the natural world provides explicit reminders of the temporal flux they try so determinedly to forget. Since real plants die, attorney Coen explains, most businesses have given them up for plastic varieties that conceal matter's liabilities in and to the process of time (360). Gaddis's narrator studies this process behind the characters' backs, presenting natural forces energetically at war with each other and with the relics of humanity's puny and passing civilization. The town "gave way to depths of locust long stunted in internecine struggle now grappling with woodbine, and the sidewalk itself finally disappeared under grass at the designated site by God's grace of an edifice for worship by the people of Primitive Baptist Church on a sign about to be reclaimed by the undergrowth" (57). In this and other visions of the natural world, the narrator emphasizes its endless, if slow, motion toward obliterating all that humankind constructs (sidewalks, signs, churches) to hold off precisely this eventuality of being "reclaimed by the undergrowth." If sinister notes echo in the background, as in "the prospect of roses run riot only to be strangled by the honeysuckle which had long since overwhelmed the grape arbor at the back" (4), the narrator nonetheless locates in this battle a flowing, energetic force, compared to which the human efforts to prune and deaden are still more sinister.

The characters' materialism extends into every phase of their lives, devastating their ability to use energy in any worthwhile pursuits. Action itself ceases to have any value; work, in particular, is degraded to a mechanical production of things, which may have worth, in a process which does not. As a result, all the workers Gaddis depicts feel alienated and profoundly bored with their jobs. Bored telephone installers, secretaries, delivery boys, nurses, mailmen, ticket agents, and teachers all try to kill time on the job; they stare out windows, file their nails, watch clocks and members of the opposite sex, prepare for lunch or quitting time, and chat together about anything except their work. When they do work, Norman Angel complains, they "turn something out they don't care what the hell it is, there's no pride in their work because what you've got them turning out nobody could be proud of in the first place" (359). In pursuing money through labor that is stripped of value, characters turn their lives into empty conduits between the salaries they earn and the products, made by others like themselves, they buy.

Like other labor, art is defined by these characters as the production of things, or "pieces," for money and awards. Whiteback puts it baldly, "We can make this cultural drive pay off" (19). Many other characters express a similar faith that the worth of art, like anything else, is defined by the money paid for it. You get art, Major Hyde opines, "where you get any-thing you buy it" (48). In higher-income brackets, art is a means to tax deductions, so Zona Selk locks all of Schepperman's paintings up for depreciation. For Crawley, who commissions a musical score from Bast, art is a consumable product; Crawley rejects the completed score and demands a symphonic recording: "I meant music, and to me Mister Bast music is *something I hear*" (439, 447, my emphasis). Even in the Bast family, genuine musical talent conflicts with materialistic assumptions about art. The family company makes player-piano rolls, cut by famous pianists. Central to Gibbs's book discussing mechanization and the arts, and also to Edward Bast's ambiguous heritage, the player piano epitomizes a variety of ideas about art in the novel: that it is a product, mass-produced and mechanized, salable for profit, and, of course, timeless—Paderewski may die, but his piano roll endures eternally.[17]

Education, then, in this ironic postmodern bildungsroman, trains young people to be docile wage earners and enthusiastic consumers. At the Long Island school, of which J R is one inevitable product, children are taught various forms of the will to buy. Whiteback orders the showing of drivers' ed films to the elementary classes, to "motivate the elementary youngsters' potential carwise," and when Hyde, for his own profit, do-nates several home appliances to the school, Whiteback lists them in the "motivational resources area" (175). Amy Joubert teaches sixth graders how to invest in the stock market, together with assumptions about money that she has learned from her father and uncle; though she is one of the most sensitive and sympathetic teachers at the school, her teaching (together with bits and pieces picked up from Cates and others) enables J R's disastrous rise into the world of high finance. All of the officially sanctioned lessons at the school, including the Newtonian physics piped into Gibbs's class, suggest that the world is static and consumable. Even the materialistic form of teaching, with television monitors, films, tapes, and follow-up computer-graded tests, removes what Whiteback calls "the offensive human element" in learning (174).

Language itself is turned to a currency serving the manipulation of things. On the simplest level, characters talk about goods and money, rather than ideas, feelings, or even real events. Their habitual conversa-tion is objective, informational, and factual. Beneath it, moreover, lies an assumption that language names and fixes reality, allowing speakers and listeners to grasp static objects and manipulate them. This understanding of language and its "economic" uses encourages characters to violate the mysterious energies of their own subjective being and the outer temporal world. Talk becomes an agency of routinization, in which reality is taken hold of and fit into the prevailing materialistic system. So, for example, when a teacher named Glancy commits suicide in a brand new Cadillac, Whiteback, Hyde, and Dan DiCephalis discuss the event in terms of the car (which Hyde wants to buy) and the suit (Dan's, which he wants to recover) that Glancy was wearing when he died. Vern Teakel, the superintendent and one of Gaddis's demonic voices, provides the only reminders of the reality—death and decomposition—which the others use language to conceal.

> that was Gottlieb down to the Cadillac agency, he thinks he can put the financing on the car right into your name without repossessing it from Glancy's estate to handle it like ahm, like a used car sale that is to . . .
>
> —What was that about a smell.
>
> —No well of course it was used since Glancy did use it to ahm, I think the Cadillac people prefer to say previously owned yes and he'd only driven it seven miles but of course he'd been in it for a week when they found him down in the woods there and apparently they've been unable to remove the, to restore the smell of a new car interior that is to . . .
>
> —Won't mind a whiff now and then will you Major, be like driving Glancy around in the back seat where you can't see his . . .
>
> —Look Vern I don't have time to . . .
>
> —Yes well I think Vern just means the back seat would have been more ahm [. . .] sitting behind the wheel yes even though he wasn't going, wasn't dressed to go anywhere that is to say, he . . .
>
> —Yes what about his suit, I meant to. . . . (452)

Every time Whiteback veers away from things and their fiscal implications and toward the real catastrophe that involves them, he halts and tacks away. Hyde, of course, has no time for Vern's bleak jokes, not because he perceives that time is the real subject of Glancy's story, but because he wants to finalize the details of the Cadillac transaction. Even more appallingly oblivious to the process of decomposition, DiCephalis can only reiterate his desire to repossess his suit.

One effect of the characters' use of language is, paradoxically, to open up the ambiguities they would avoid and therefore to isolate them from each other as they converse. Stephen Matanle usefully observes that since the world of *J R* is ruled by "strife, whose function is to separate," "language is separated into different forms of discourse, and signs are separated from their referents."[18] Suits, for example: Whiteback considers suits from his perspective as head of the bank; Hyde worries over his liability in an earlier automobile accident with Dan; Dan, whose daughter gave away all his clothes to a thrift shop, see suits as things to wear. If they cannot communicate about things, still less can they share responses to or feelings about the less tangible "matter" at hand, to the point where, unable to express it, they lose access to the world of thought and feeling.

At the source and end of the vicious circle in which they trap themselves is the reification of time. Gaddis's characters envision time as a spatial object, measurable, divisible, and above all usable. In a process I have discussed elsewhere at greater length, these characters close off and forget the open flow of time by cutting it into pie-shaped units on their ubiquitous, and often malfunctioning, clocks and watches.[19] Describing the actions of these timepieces, Gaddis emphasizes their spatialization of time: "The clock severed another of the minutes that lacked the hour" and, distinguishing between the characters' and the narrator's view of time: "For time unbroken by looks to the clock the only sound was the chafing of an emery board, and the clock itself, as though seizing the advantage, seemed to accomplish its round with surreptitious leaps forward, knocking whole wedges at once from what remained of the hour" (51, 256). Refusing to specify how much time has passed, or what time it is, Gaddis presents time flowing in "unbroken" round. The secretaries filing their nails, however, eagerly count the wedges that lead to quitting time. Perceiving time as a thing, characters typically assume—as the Protestant ethic dictates—that it should be turned to account: "time is money," says Crawley, as elsewhere do Gibbs and Rhoda (85, 115, 552). Characters therefore "invest" the present in fiscal pursuits, forget the past, and ignore the process of time's (and life's) passing. Time is, precisely, what they flee in material goods and materialist systems; time does, gently and inexorably, destroy their goods and invalidate their systems.

As my references to the Protestant ethic indicate, I believe Gaddis identifies it as one significant source for the decadent materialism that pervades American culture. Indeed, the Protestant ethic figures prominently in Gaddis's "Rush for Second Place," his analysis of Americans' drive to acquire wealth and property while abandoning moral accountability.[20] The Puritan will to demonstrate election by good (industrious, serious, disciplined, frugal, and methodical) works in the world, with their elimination of bad (playful, spontaneous, and prodigal) impulses, appears to Gaddis to have shaped Lyndon Johnson, Dean Rusk, and America's presence in Vietnam; it clearly guides most characters in *J R*. In a text Gaddis cites, *The Protestant Ethic and the Spirit of Capitalism*, Max Weber traces the "work ethic" to its culmination in an "iron cage."[21] As Weber explains, this ethic valorizes order, economy, and a disciplined "worldly asceticism" and castigates the waste of goods, money, and time. Exemplified in the following passage Weber summarizes from Richard Baxter, the Puritan view of wasted time informs the secularized desire of characters in *J R* to turn each minute to profit. "Waste of time is thus the first and in principle the deadliest of sins. . . . Loss of time through sociability, idle talk, luxury, even more sleep than is necessary for health . . . is worthy of absolute moral condemnation. It does not yet hold, with [Benjamin] Franklin, that time is money, but the proposition is true in a certain spiritual sense. It is infinitely valuable because every hour lost is lost to labor for the glory of God."[22] As Weber and Gaddis both demonstrate, however, this Protestant drive to invest time economically in the production of saving works has ironically damned its modern heirs to prodigious wastes of energy, time, and life itself.

Gaddis refers to the Protestant ethic and its economic assumptions several times in *J R*. Most explicitly, Jack Gibbs indulges in a long, drunken, demonic, funny near-monologue with Amy Joubert, in which he traces Americans' malaise to their inability to forget, replace, or live satisfactorily with the Protestant ethic. "First time in history so many opportunities to do so God damn many things not worth doing [. . .] went to the woods to live deliberately Thoreau says couldn't escape from the Protestant ethic, be the first ones to redeem it Amy make monogrammed doormats deliberately [. . .] God damned Protestant ethic can't escape it have to redeem it, have a kid right from the start wants to be a dry cleaner when he grows up how's that [. . .] problem now's to justify the Protestant ethic" (477). If one approaches work as the single definitive sign of election (or source of worth) and then finds only trivial and degrading work to do, the only way to justify one's existence is, indeed, to "make a million dollars"; this is, in brief, the story of J R, whose compulsion "to find out what I'm suppose to do" leads to his ruthless pursuit of money (661). With Ben Franklin's worldly suggestions as his subtext (like Gatsby, J R keeps a list of rules for success [647]) and with Horatio Alger as his model, J R reenacts the American rags-to-riches myth. But, as J R's initials suggest, he only emulates his elders, and virtually every character in the novel is, like J R, caught up in some form of the virulent Protestant economy. Cates, for example, believes that "waste shows an undisciplined strain of mind" (110).

In the Bast family, Gaddis exposes the Protestant heritage which the others have assimilated beyond recollection. The Bast sisters tell of their grandfather (Edward's great-grandfather) who rejected music as an end in itself. "Father was just sixteen years old. As I say, Ira Cobb owed him some money. [. . .] instead of paying Father Ira gave him an old violin and he took it down to the barn to try to learn to play it. Well his father heard it and went right down, and broke the violin over Father's head. We were a Quaker family, after all, where you just didn't do things that didn't pay" (4). This anecdote suggests that the musical impulse in the family may have begun out of a desire to turn a bad debt to profit: having received the violin, the boy has to learn to use it in order to get his money's worth. His father, interpreting all "play" as wasteful idleness, breaks the instrument to teach his son to pursue better profits. Indeed, the boy does; almost every other remembrance his daughters have of their father involves the jingling, earning, and spending of coins.

Each of the patriarch's children takes on an identity blending artistry with avarice, a veneration for music and material goods.[23] Thomas founds General Roll, a corporation mass-producing piano rolls, in part for the considerable money to be made, in part to preserve the genius of contemporary virtuosos (63). James expresses contempt for his brother's mechanization of music and devotes his own life to composing, with evident success; he wins not only a number of awards but also Gibbs's high praise for his opera *Philoctetes*: "that whining tenor part he gives Ulysses real stroke of genius, comes off as a real sneak the only man who's ever seen Ulysses clear whole opera's the God damndest thing I ever" (117). If he has presented Ulysses—by some accounts a protobourgeois, shrewd, enterprising figure—as a sneak, James must feel at least suspicious of his own American and familial heritage.[24] But James, too, hated waste; he worked compulsively, sacrificed his family to his work, and "just wouldn't waste time on people without talent" (66). James also indulged his own greed. He joined in a scheme to sell "waterfront" lots to poor immigrants, telling them the Long Island town would be turned to a new Venice, with docks and canals; by his sister's account, "James took it all as rather a lark" (60). The Bast sisters display similar mixtures of artistic talent with the Protestant interest in works and the capitalist yearning for wealth: they hope to live in "a white Victorian with a tower and a porte cochere along one side" (15).[25] Since Julia and Anne have raised Edward, in view of his father's disinterest, their inept efforts at shrewdness, conservative materialism, and romantic leaning toward the past have influenced the boy.

Although fathers are, like James Bast, almost invariably dead or absent in *J R*, leaving their children potentially free of the past, their influence persists in the lives of their heirs. The large cast of technically fatherless characters includes Edward Bast, J R, Gibbs, Reuben, and eventually the children of Eigen, Hyde, DiCephalis, Joubert, and Gibbs. But these characters typically adopt foster fathers with the same coercive authority, exerted in favor of the same conservative materialistic values, as their own parent's. Like Barthelme's Dead Father, Gaddis's defunct sires make their absence present in their children's lives. On the first page of the novel, Anne Bast recalls a story about "Father's dying wish to have his bust sunk in Vancouver harbor, and his ashes sprinkled on the water there, about James and Thomas out in the rowboat, and both of them hitting at the bust with their oars because it was hollow and wouldn't go down, and the storm coming up while they were out there, blowing his ashes back into their beards" (3). Indeed, this hollow figure who cannot be buried, whose remains cling to his sons, might stand for all of Gaddis's fathers—as, in a grotesque communion near the end of *The Recognitions*, Wyatt Gwyon eats bread baked with his father's ashes. Rather than trying to sink their father's memory, in fact, most characters perpetuate it: J R finds a surrogate father in Cates; Edward Bast in Crawley and Duncan; Reuben in James Bast; Gibbs in Schramm, and so on. Ann and Dan DiCephalis make a comically revealing error: when an elderly drifter moves in with them, telling them to call him "Dad," each assumes he is the other's father (685). Neither questions the rights of this difficult old man, who eats the dog's food, makes rude noises, and insults both DiCephalises, to invade their lives. Similarly, neither interrogates the authority of the past. This veneration for the father and for the past expresses, once more, these characters' longing to escape time and change: all become good "juniors" in Gaddis's text.

Investing Energy

Against the background of materialistic stasis, authorized by a Newtonian physics and a Protestant metaphysics, and constituting the world perceived by most of Gaddis's characters, some try to derive satisfaction from the worthy use of their own energies. These characters struggle to find meaningful action in the world through the *process* of laboring, rather than its products. For the most part, their efforts are as confused as their understanding of what constitutes worth, but, however dimly and erratically, they seek a sense of dignity. As Duncan says to Bast shortly before he dies, "Just get a good opinion of yourself that's all you need, reach the end of the line waiting for God to drop the other shoe that's all you've got" (686). These efforts are made far more difficult—in most cases, even doomed—by their environment, with its pervasive assumption that value inheres in products and fees. But by the process of directing narrative interest to the activities, struggles, and changes of these characters who pursue worth, rather than to the collections and self-objectifications of those who pursue money, Gaddis reasserts his own actualistic belief that energy and process constitute reality, as well as the proper "matter" for literary texts.

Both J R and Dan DiCephalis try to find out "what you do." J R's invasion of the stock market and his policy of constant reinvestment of capital constitute an effort to find an activity or process more meaningful than his schoolwork. Likewise, DiCephalis's energetic pursuit of a rewarding job emerges from a desire for worthy action: after he fails in his efforts to make teaching worthwhile, he moves to a job with J R's corporation and eventually to a subsidiary trying to telegraph human beings. The two characters are similarly childlike. J R's actual youth is matched by DiCephalis's naïveté—he first appears carrying a child's umbrella and moving "at home" among the children (21). Both have an almost-engaging innocence, a hopefulness about the possibilities for fulfillment within the corporate world that is not mitigated by any of their experience.

Both characters doom their searches for worthy labor, however, by conceiving worth as an end, an objectified and external *image* of success, rather than as a process generated out of internal self-respect. Like most other characters in the novel, each has what Rhoda calls "this lousy opinion of himself" (616). Both are unloved, powerless, and, at beginning and ending, poor. DiCephalis and J R are the two most ragged and scruffy-looking characters in a novel where others measure human worth through clothes. To remedy their sense of worthlessness, both covet the image of the socially respected, prosperous, and vigorous corporate executive. Attaining this image becomes an absolute end, while the processes involved, seen as unimportant, do not and cannot provide fulfillment for their own sake. Because they seek to escape a deep-rooted worthlessness, both are drawn to glamorous mail-order promises—they can apply without being seen and evaluated. While J R sends away for picnic forks and stocks, hiding his youth in postal transactions, DiCephalis mails off for "coded anonymity" in a computerized employment office where names are replaced by numbers (55). Both cultivate the facial expressions, the mask, accompanying the image; both study their reflections in the mirror while practicing their parts (166, 652).

J R and DiCephalis find the business of business unrewarding in itself, important only as a means to the end of wealth, power, and security. Neither expresses satisfaction with any given transaction or job. J R's hopes, shared by Dan, are directed at ineffable glamour and success. "I always thought this is what it will be like you and, and me riding in this here big limousine down, down this, this here big street" (636). Though he is in fact riding in a limousine with Bast as he makes the statement, J R is actually in tears; far from enjoying the process, he can only weep for the failure of his larger ends. Just as ends take precedence over processes in the Protestant, teleological worldview and in Newtonian, action-reaction physics, the ends pursued by DiCephalis and J R form a coherent part of the antiquated vision of reality so common in their society. Both eager young men fail, in other words, to imagine anything better than the vision, created by PR-men like Davidoff, of materialistic success, reflected in material wealth. Dan's eventual fate—he is telegraphed from one point, turned from matter to energy, but lost in transmission and never "received" *at the end*, because the process has not been worked out—forms an ironic commentary on the futile pursuit of material ends. Metaphorically, J R is also "lost in transit" at the end, when his voice on the phone, unheard by anyone, projects another fresh start in politics.

In a different way, Norman Angel also pursues worthy action through work. Angel takes pride in the company for which he has worked since his youth and which he now heads. He has for years channeled all profits back into the business. Like J R, he takes nothing for himself, buys no briefcase but rather uses old envelopes to carry papers, and gives little thought to his clothes. Though his wife, Stella, accuses him with some justice of being unable to "understand anything you can't get your hands on, anything you can't feel or see or, or count" (144), his materialism takes less selfish and acquisitive forms than her own, for example. He wants control of the company resolved, he explains, only so he can guard its commitment to quality, "to keep it doing something that's, that's worth doing" (359).

Yet Angel frustrates his search for worthy action and eventually destroys himself. Like J R and DiCephalis, he understands worth in objectified and external terms. To improve the company, he tries to increase its productivity; he redecorates to raise the company's sales. Even in his fumbling eagerness to keep the company doing something worth doing, he understands "doing" purely through the things produced. That his company actually produces holes in paper suggests Gaddis's ironic view of the emptiness and banality of corporate "ends." Since he sees himself as an object producing objects, Angel cannot survive the loss of his corporate function. While Duncan goes out of the wallpaper business with his self-esteem intact, mocking those who "think winning's what it's all about" (672–73), Angel is reduced to despair when he loses control of his company. He shoots himself in the head and lies comatose in the hospital— having become, ironically, a mindless thing produced by his own labor.

With even more promise than these others, Amy Joubert and Jack Gibbs explore the possibilities of finding worth through work and love. Because they are less overtly materialistic than most other characters, their efforts to find and create intangible forms of worth become more plausible. Amy is freed by her immense inherited wealth from some of the other characters' concern with money and goods; she is the only character in the novel capable of saying, as she does in her first appearance, "This? No, it's just money" (18). While Jack perpetually needs money, he is also freed, by his education and intelligence, from the others' perception of the world as consumable matter. As a physics teacher, he understands reality in energetic terms; not only does he teach his class about entropy in his first appearance, but he also points out the entropy in the Ninety-sixth Street apartment to Bast (287) and later sees his own difficulty there as "problem just no God damned energy" (585). Both Amy and Jack seek worth in being and acting. Amy teaches "to have something to do, something alive to do" (211), and Jack works on an ambitious essay. Their passionate relationship confers on each a renewed sense of self-worth: Amy rejoices that Jack desires her for herself, not her wealth; Jack delights in believing that Amy cares for him despite his poverty and his previous failures.

Like Gaddis's other doomed Americans, however, Amy and Jack remain committed to products and ends and to the view, mocked by Duncan, that "winning's what it's all about." Strikingly similar to Elizabeth and Mc-Candless in *Carpenter's Gothic*, they reflect the problems in their culture without being able to find alternatives.[26] Amy believes in winning, and she does eventually win her battles for control of her son and of her family's company; she describes her relationship with her former husband as "playing against him and helping him win" (488). She plays a similar game with Jack, attempting to transform him with a new suit into the very image of her father, uncle, and former husband—all products and producers of American materialism. Jack also believes in winning, especially after he wins a large sum at the races. Above all, Jack believes he must produce the book he has begun and given up on: not simply that he must "work on" it, which is all Amy asks, but rather complete it, and he feels this imperative as an increasing burden. He snaps, "I don't know when I'll finish it no!" and later rationalizes that there is no real reason to finish it: "God damned pianist already shot . . . nobody give a God damn book everything's happened book about everybody knows hate it!" (605).

Their faith in products is doubly damaging to Amy and Jack because, unlike Angel and even J R, they do not produce anything. Gibbs, especially, believes that the creation of art is the single most worthy activity available to human beings, and for this reason he adopts artistic friends like Schramm, Bast, and Schepperman. But he himself cannot do what he defines as worthy, so he turns instead to a project which rationalizes his failure: his essay argues that mechanization has eliminated the possibility for art. Then, of course, he cannot even finish the essay, so, both before and after his romance with Amy, he invests his time in trivia, like "somebody afraid of failing at something worth doing" (491). Because he doubts his own worth, Jack doubts the worth of everything else; he finally doubts not only that Amy loves him but even that it matters. He sacrifices her, hiding behind one of his frequent personae: "he pretended he was an old black retainer yas'm, yas'm, dat ole Mistah Gibbs he a genuine rascal to play de ladies so" (725). Both his desertion and the manner of it, in which Jack suggests the affair was merely another sexual fling, play on Amy's self-doubts and contribute to her despair. Like Jack, she has reasons for her lousy opinion of herself: after being manipulated for her money by most men in her life, including her father, she is told she has been used as a sexual object. Like Jack, Amy gives up on herself by the end of the novel; seeming "frozen inside," she marries one of her father's business associates, Dick Cutler, of whom she has said, "that would be like, like marrying your issue of six percent preferreds" (707, 214). Both Amy and Jack have, in opposite ways, destroyed their chances for finding worthy action: Jack condemns himself to futile inaction, and Amy acts, for the first time, in ways she knows are wrong and worthless.

Of all Gaddis's major characters, only Edward Bast may achieve worthy action. Bast has not accomplished anything by the novel's end, but unlike the others, he has discovered that worth inheres in the actor and the process of action rather than in the completed product.[27] He turns, then, from the service of others' material goods (which, true heir of the Basts, he responsibly protects through most of the novel) to the proper use of his own energies. Since the process of his "education" leads Bast away from goods and money, from the Protestant ethic, from fathers and traditions, and from a Newtonian perception of reality as causal and material, this process merits a detailed examination.

In his first appearance in *J R*, Bast displays a naive and self-effacing passivity. He says nothing while Whiteback babbles on with clichés ("what America is all about") and materialistic ideas ("we can make this cultural drive pay off") he knows are false and harmful (19). When Amy drops her sack of coins, Bast kneels to pick them up: gallant, courteous, and romantic, he is not aware enough of the actual world to protect himself. He is willing to be used and even damaged (Amy steps on his hand with her sharp high heel) in the interest of conserving property in the material world. As he silently allows his own exploitation by the rich and the manipulative in this scene, he will later permit J R to abuse him repeatedly. Not only is he young (between eighteen and twenty years old) and timid, Bast also has a low opinion of his own worth: with a mother who died shortly after his birth and a father who ignored him, Bast feels unproved, unloved, and unworthy.

In another early appearance on television, however, Bast also displays honesty and courage. Asked to fill in for Miss Flesch on a televised lesson about Mozart's life, he agrees; he meekly follows her script until, its pages mixed, it degenerates into chaos. When he throws out the script, he discards its falsifying optimism and its romantic vision of the composer's "fairy tale life" (40). In Bast's more honest version, he describes Mozart's poverty, exhaustion, illness, and abuse by the rich—foreshadowing similar events in Bast's own life and his eventual ability to understand them. His ability to know reality without romantic coloring and his willingness to express it, even though it costs him his job at the school, eventually liberate him.

A first step in his education occurs when his studio is invaded and its sanctuary destroyed. The studio is important to Bast as a place to "shut it all out," to work on "the wildest secret fantasy" without intrusion (69–70). There he pursues dreams of Stella and works at setting the sentimental and optimistic "Locksley Hall" to music.[28] That his father, James, used this studio increases its significance for Bast, especially since he fantasizes that his music will win his father's notice and approval. In the studio, Bast has dismissed present for past, actuality for a nostalgic romanticism. His education begins, then, when he is jolted out of this sanctuary, pried out from under his father's influence, and immersed in a reality whose energy he cannot ignore. He loses his job on the first day of the narrative and his studio on the second; he then moves to the East Ninety-sixth Street apartment whose clutter, entropy, chaos, and openness to invasion make it an apt microcosm for the larger world.

Through the middle of the novel, Bast serves J R and, more generally, material ends; in return, he learns the materialistic system that occupies Americans and its ability to destroy worthwhile energies of various kinds. At the beginning, he knows almost nothing about money—his own need for it, his ability to earn it, the rules and customs (like unionization) regarding it. He first regards music as ineffably beyond the material sphere; rejecting J R's crassness and revealing his own innocence, he says, "Look I'm not trying to write tunes for money" (134). As a result, he does other things for money, and they take up all his time. The only progress he seems to make with the music he wants to write (as opposed to deliberately imitative music others commission) is to scale it down and to revise away its romantic grandeur, taking a tone more suited to the actual world. He changes the form of this composition from an opera to a cantata, to an oratorio, to a suite for small orchestra—none of which he begins after the first, which he quickly sees as awful. All of his experience in the business world amounts, then, to a preparation for writing worthy music, addressed not to a Tennysonian reality but to his own, actualistic one.

When J R's financial empire collapses, Bast finally refuses to follow him further, thus liberating himself from the pursuit of material ends. In the significant last conversation between Bast and J R, set in the same place as their first, Bast tries to show J R the omissions and lies in his vision of reality. While J R believes the world is pure matter, Bast forces him to listen to a cantata by Bach, to "show you there's such a thing as, as, as intangible assets," and "things only music can say, things that can't be written down or hung on a clothes-line" (655). When J R appeals to news accounts labeling him a man of vision who caused his own success, Bast points out that accident, rather than causality, guided J R's ventures, and that the news accounts have been written by men in J R's own employ. Bast tries to make J R see that he lives in an actualistic world rather than a Newtonian one. He fails, of course, and at that point he rejects J R. In a last temptation, J R asks if he needs any money; Bast has only a few cents and has accepted "loans" and "advances" from J R before. This time, however, Bast answers, "No . . . !" in what turns out, appropriately, to be his last word to J R in the novel (663).

In the hospital, Bast undergoes a purgation (he repeatedly vomits during this period) and an ironic resurrection; he emerges reborn in a new image, with the help of a new spiritual father, Mr. Duncan.[29] Bast has written music to win attention and approval from a father who ignored him; he has tried hard to be a good "junior." But he is both Bast and bastard, loosely related to the coercive father he remembers, for the real one is, like the *Deus absconditus*, absent throughout the novel. Duncan absolves Bast of failure; he says that "winning" doesn't matter and finally tells Bast to believe in his own dignity: "just get a good opinion of yourself that's all you need" (686). Then Duncan dies, freeing Bast of all fathers, genetic and spiritual. Bast first responds with a half-terrified recognition that he does not have to achieve anything or to write music at all. "I always thought I had to write music all of a sudden I thought what if I don't, maybe I don't have to I'd never thought of that maybe I don't! I mean maybe that's what's been wrong with everything maybe that's why I've made such a, why I've been thinking of things you've said as though just, just doing what's there to be done as though it's worth doing or you never would have done anything you wouldn't be anybody would you" (687). In pursuit of the time to write music, his unquestioned "end," Bast has ignored the means he used and caused harm to others in the process. Now he realizes there are no valid ends, but that worth arises in processes based on the assumption of human dignity.

As part of Duncan's legacy, Bast comes to understand process, to see music as a process of conception rather than a product for consumption. He has worried compulsively about producing a finished piece of music: "he has to finish something before he dies" (675). But Duncan tells him that worth does not inhere in products or in specific kinds of labor, but rather in striving with dignity. Bast sees music, at the end, as one of several possible ways to enact his own worth. "Nothing's worth doing he told me nothing's worth doing till you've done it and then it was worth doing even if it wasn't because that's all you . . ." (715). With this unexalted view of art, Bast also assumes—unlike other, more egoistical artists in the novel who see their work as divine and necessary—that he must not violate others in creating art. Near the end, Bast learns that his father, the driven, productive, Protestant-ethic-ridden musician, destroyed his mother. He refused to marry her or to raise his son because "he was afraid for anything to come between him and his work," and she committed suicide (716). With this discovery, Bast is truly on his own, detached from his father and able, finally, to see composing as his own work. Unlike his father and unlike Schepperman, who seizes an old man and forces him to sit for days for a portrait, though the old man's bedridden wife dies during the sitting (724), Bast will not use people as means to the end of artistic production.

In his last appearance in the novel, Bast reveals a new assurance.[30] Where he never managed to get enough money for food or travel from J R, he gets the cash he needs from Eigen, suggesting that he can now survive in the material world. He eludes J R's last phone call, which arrives too late. Insisting on his own dignity under Eigen's self-important assault, he mocks the conception, common among the failed artists (Schramm, Gibbs, and Eigen) of art as product. When Eigen rants about the cost of artistic vision, Bast interrupts him. His music, he says, looks like "a lot of chickentracks don't they, look. . . . I mean until a performer hears what I hear and can make other people hear what he hears it's just trash isn't it Mister Eigen, it's just trash like everything in this place everything you and Mister Gibbs and Mister Schramm all of you saw here it's just trash!" (725). Bast's sarcasm, itself a new and more assured tone than he has previously mustered, dismisses Eigen's smugness and suggests that his own work, in the process of becoming, may achieve something more. Finally, when Eigen tries to send Bast away, asking, "Will you just go do what you have to," Bast replies, with significant, and highly promising, certainty, "That's what I'm doing yes!" (725). And while Eigen envisions the accomplished action in his "go do," Bast encompasses the active, ongoing temporal process in his "doing."

Energetic Form in J R

While Gaddis explores in *J R* the thematic matter of energy, the novel becomes a highly significant actualistic text for its original energetic form. Gaddis rejects the beginning-middle-end structure that confers aesthetic unity on the work of art as well-made thing. He denies his narrative status as an object, shaped to static wholeness by a design that begins from the end. Rather, Gaddis begins and ends in the middle: midsentence, midconversation, midday, midaction. He resolves few of the complications he has introduced; instead, most characters simply continue, unchanged, to respond to new forms of the same old problems in the same old ways. There is little suspense in Gaddis's narrative, no important secrets withheld for a climax, no detective hunt in which the reader can "figure out" the trick pattern the author has planted, no revelation for readers or epiphany for characters, and no hidden keys to motives or behavior. Gaddis's text is far looser, far baggier, and far more monstrous than James or even Tolstoy could have imagined possible. It flaunts its own monstrosity, playing with readers' expectations of order, center, and design.

The point requires some insistence, because critics often come to Gaddis's texts with the modernist assumption that art resolves contradictions. Johan Thielemans, for example, assimilates Gaddis into Joyce's modernist aesthetics and, in the process, misses the unique and deliberate disruptiveness Gaddis brings to that tradition. "The text is, rather, a veil behind which he hides . . . the text exhibits an organization that the chaotic surface of the text tries to eradicate or obscure. There every accident of the text signifies irony, discrepancy, contrast, and contradiction. The fragmentation is only apparent and articulates itself in a complex argument on the level of the grammar of the novelistic form. . . . On this level the felicities of invention are plenty, and it is by bringing these devices into play that the novel as a whole may claim a place in the pantheon of Perfection."[31] I would say, rather, that Gaddis invokes Perfection ironically and chooses imperfection (disorganization, accident, fragmentation) with full knowledge and deliberate care. While aesthetic Perfection symbolized the modernists' will to raise the work of art above reality's own chaotic temporality, imperfection and monstrosity suggest the actualist's commitment to immerse the text in time.

All of the artificial forms imposed on time in conventional narratives disintegrate in *J R*, leaving time flowing.[32] Gaddis does not divide his narrative: without chapters, sections, or even open spaces in the text, time passes unclassified, unorganized, and unspatialized. The narrator does not "edit" time, presenting heightened moments and summarizing uneventful ones; rather, he includes both more and less significant times. His descriptions of time's passing emphasize its continuous unfolding: "the morning still lingering outside appeared to have decided to stay there, dwindling to the gray of afternoon," as the categories of "morning" and "afternoon" appear tentative and arbitrary (316). Similarly, hours, days, and months, the artificial divisions of clocks and calendars with which the characters reify time, do not fix narrative time. Gaddis does not place events in a certain year or named months, and for all the clock watching that goes on in the novel, readers never know what time it is. Ian Watt reminds us that, in writing *Tom Jones*, Fielding used an almanac, "that symbol of the diffusion of an objective sense of time by the printing press: with slight exceptions, nearly all the events of his novel are chronologically consistent, not only in relation to each other, and to the time that each stage of the journey of the various characters from the West Country to London would actually have taken, but also in relation to such external considerations as the proper phases of the moon and the time-table of the Jacobite rebellion in 1745, the supposed year of the action."[33]

Gaddis dispenses with that "objective sense of time." As Steven Moore has shown, Gaddis's first two novels are riddled with chronological inconsistencies, whether as a test of their readers or as an oversight: "more probably, Gaddis did not feel that a painstakingly accurate chronology was really important to either novel."[34] One can, I believe, further suppose that Gaddis deliberately made it impossible to "plot" his actions in chronological/objective/almanac time in order to emphasize instead the subjective, open, and "plotless" nature of lived time. By thus insisting on the radical temporality of time, lives, and processes, Gaddis provides an implicit formal critique of his characters' materialism: the very flux they would rationalize away into material shapes is, in Gaddis's account, the moving energy of their lives.

J R is not, like Newton's universe, causally constructed; actions and reactions do not follow each other in well-linked chains. Rather, as in the Heisenbergian universe and in Coover's *Public Burning*, statistical accumulations of events can precipitate others, but underneath each "effect" one finds chance and accident, rather than causality. Many of the meetings and conversations leading to important events occur by accident, like the chance meeting of Amy and Jack on the train at the start of their affair. Most of the deaths and injuries (perhaps all of the ones not self-inflicted) are accidental, like the shooting of the little retarded boy who carries a cap gun. The very texture of Gaddis's plot is compounded of accident on accident. Why, for instance, does Bast work for J R? By accident, Miss Flesch's script is dropped and scrambled; she is hurt in a car accident; by chance, Dan DiCephalis finds Bast and asks him to take her place; Bast gets fired and then, by accident, J R walks home with him and suggests an alliance. Unlike the accidents and coincidences of well-made novels, where chance always serves meaning and aesthetic unity, the accidents in *J R* lead only to pain and frustration, never to epiphany. Amy Joubert steps on Bast's hand, and it means nothing—except that the world is accidental.

How different when, by chance, Strether takes a trip to the country, stops at a randomly chosen inn, strolls to the river, and learns the truth about Mme. de Vionnet and Chad Newsome: coincidence inevitably illuminates the ends of the realistic novelist because it is never really chance, but artfully concealed intention. In Gaddis's text, by contrast, *nothing* hides behind chance.

J R refuses to be, like the industrious Protestant or the well-made novel, economical. In criticizing Tolstoy's "large loose, baggy monsters," James continues, "There is life and life, and as waste is only life sacrificed and thereby prevented from 'counting,' I delight in a deep-breathing economy and an organic form."[35] After James, most novelists and critics concur in preferring method and order to unruliness and waste in fiction. Yet, like other actualists, Gaddis violates this sober and constricting economy: a proliferation of characters and events with no bearing on the "central" plots or figures marks Gaddis's commitment to "waste" his artistic material.[36] Gaddis presents characters whose devotion to virulent forms of the Protestant economy leads them to waste time and lives. Hence, prodigality, spontaneity, and play—all that the Western economy suppresses, including waste itself—have their place in J R. Like Sterne, Gaddis includes odd, nonnarrative pages: one of J R's compositions (438), a page of fragmentary quotations written in calligraphy by Gibbs (486), designs for the logo of J R's company (536), a page of business opportunities torn from the newspaper (126), and so on. These pages are "filler"—or as Gibbs says, "More trash" (487).

Similarly, one of the most unique and original features of Gaddis's style is its daring inclusion of linguistic "trash." Barthelme's dwarves, who like "books that have a lot of *dreck* in them" and who "pay particular attention, too, to those aspects of language that may be seen as a model of the trash phenomenon," would surely admire J R.[37] Not only does Gaddis depict the typically banal language most Americans speak, he includes the misstatements, hesitations, reversals, and fillers normally left out of the heightened discourse of fiction. Whiteback, for example, issues this statement to the newspaper over the phone: "Yes well of course implementing the new drug detection program is providing a meaningful insight into the students ahm, body, the student body's ahm . . . urine yes, urine tests under the school nurse who, yes no by the school nurse that is to . . . yes yes very successful, no cases have been reported at all since the detection program went into ahm" (340). Whiteback wants to fill space in a newspaper innocuously, so he tries to keep his language bland and abstract.

The referential nature of language keeps undermining his intention to make the entire statement "filler"—it sneaks in "body" and "urine" and the visual image of urine tests under the nurse. Every time his language threatens to lose its "sludge" quality, Whiteback tacks away, first with literal fillers ("ahm," "yes," "no," "that is to") and then with more abstract "stuffing," like the notion that the detection program is successful because it has not detected anything. This same willingness to include conversational "waste" occurs on a larger level, too, where whole dialogues and monologues that do not advance the action or characterization nonetheless appear. Some conversations between the Bast sisters, between Ann and Dan DiCephalis, between Whiteback and various teachers or Davidoff and various secretaries, for example, make no contribution to a linear progress in the novel; they are excessive, loose, and wasteful.

Gaddis thus turns the premises of realistic dialogue on their head, ironically producing a spoken language far more accurate, more actualistic, than any in realistic fiction. John Kuehl calls the novel an "acoustical masterpiece" for its innovative rendering of jumbled voices.[38] Gaddis's characters speak in fragments, not the complete sentences of realistic dialogue which promise that syntax and meaning are stable and whole. They interrupt each other, trail off, and rarely pursue their own or others' ideas to a conclusion: for Gaddis, thought is not matter but energy, developed in processes that do not have proper "ends." Nor is spoken language rhetorically heightened in *J R*, as in most realistic novels, where the author's power to deploy a language gracefully shaped by a knowledge of the outcome extends into the characters' own speech. In *J R*, characters cannot polish their speech because they have no foresight. With only a dim sense of what they themselves will say and no way to predict what others will say to interrupt them, their thinking presents its own formation as they speak. To take an extreme example, Bast's realization that one must act, "as though just, just doing what's there to be done as though it's worth doing" (687), would constitute an epiphany, presented in elevated language, if it occurred to a Strether or a Stephen Dedalus. But here, what may be a crucial moment and a life-changing recognition for Bast stumbles out without grace, without exalted diction, and without even forming its own conclusive climax—Bast trails off and asks for the nurse when Duncan does not reply.

By focusing on energy rather than matter, Gaddis also fractures the spatial logic of traditional novels. He does not set scenes spatially; in fact the narrator does not *see* as often or as fully as he *hears*. With a scarcity of seen things, he rejects the realistic novel's emphasis on the plastic image and its concern to fix characters and events materially. Gaddis does not fix even those images he sees: rather, he catches fragmentary glimpses of *moving* objects because his narrative eye does not pause to look at static things. So, for instance, the narrator sees parts of moving characters— "Mrs. Joubert's expensively shod instep," Pecci's "pinstripe presence," Gibbs's "hole in the trouser seat" (19, 24, 21)—but the lack of a description, especially of eyes, hair, and faces, functions to strip the characters of a plastic or material identity and, rather, to highlight the identities they create with their own energies, in words and actions. Similarly, the narrator sees some things in the various settings—pails, boxes, chairs, desks, rugs—but he sees them only when they move or when characters, smoke, light, or wind move against them. A chair at the Bast house attracts his attention when Coen moves, "seating himself in the Queen Anne chair whose arm came off in his hand" (6). By ignoring the static material world his characters only think they inhabit, Gaddis places them amid the moving energies of an actualistic universe.

Gaddis's narrative eye and ear follow motions both between and within scenes. Locations, speakers, and topics of conversation may change radically from one page to the next, without the conventional narrative guidance that places the next action in space. These transitions typically occur not at the ends of conversations or interviews but midsentence. Nor do scene changes arrive when the narrator, seeing his plot from the end, detaches his attention from immediate things shown inside the text to summarize what lies outside: Gaddis never detaches himself from these immediate words and actions. Transitions occur, rather, when the narrator follows motion and energy inside the text; he observes a character moving from one location to another, leaps through television lines, or jumps telephone wires. Even within scenes, the sections of narrative typically observe forms of energy—sunlight, mechanical and natural motions, fast and slow changes—and underscore the ongoing, processual nature of these energies with gerundive verbs: "Whiteback's car *shearing* from the curb, *rounding* the corner into Burgoyne Street to course through the shrieks of saws and limbs *dangling* in unanesthetized aerial surgery, *turning* at last into the faculty parking lot and into Gibbs' limited vista from a second floor classroom window *watching* Mrs. Joubert alight" (19). Like this example, itself only part of a much longer chain of actions, the narrator's sentences suspend their information about various motions in mobile fashion, with part descending from part and the whole having its own unpredictable motion. Gaddis's narrative thus insists on the primary reality of energy, not matter.

Gaddis's focus on the characters' energies also functions to reveal their misuse. The narrator does not directly present the significant events that shape traditional narratives. Such events—Schramm's suicide; the accidents of Flesch, Hyde, and DiCephalis; the stealing of Francis Joubert from his school; the shooting of the retarded boy; the deaths of Hyde, Glancy, and Vern Teakel—occur in plenty in *J R*, but readers never see them. Rather, we hear other characters talking about them later, fitting these events into materialist systems and thus rationalizing away their emotional force. In other words, Gaddis shows his characters using their energies precisely to neutralize the legitimate energy arising from a recognition of time and death. As in the account of Glancy's death, characters like Whiteback, Hyde, and DiCephalis try to routinize despair and suicide into a simple question of things: debts, cars, and suits. But while his characters fit destructive energies into comforting and static forms, Gaddis himself refuses to formalize death. He does not highlight any death as a dramatic climax; he does not suspend his narrative from the skeleton of these traditionally significant actions; rather, he lets deaths occur casually, accidentally, and formlessly. By making these events happen offstage, he allows them their full, unpurged, irrational energy.

Gaddis also makes his novel actualistic by affirming the subjective limits of his own single narrative view. The authorial presence, expressing itself in a third-person narrator, remains engaged in time and events throughout *J R* and never departs to pare its nails above the action.[39] This authorial/narrative voice renounces the omniscience traditionally associated with the third person, pursuing a single view of events in one place, without departing to summarize other actions in other places. Gaddis rejects the objectivity common to third-person witnesses in realistic novels. He admits his own subjective opinions in openly biased, often satiric narrative; he describes, for example, a student's "face where mascara awash in perspiration descended a bad complexion to streak the imbrications of silvered cardboard covering the padded bosom below" (33–34). Gaddis emphasizes his own presence with self-conscious language play: "Davidoff veered full throttle cutting across vagaries of wind and sail and the dictates of labored metaphor, threatening capsize on all hands" (90). By thus calling attention to the narrative language, and by expressing in it clear attitudes toward characters and events, Gaddis celebrates the subjective vision which is, for an actualist, the only available point of view.

Bast's music provides an analogue for Gaddis's novel. Both try to represent heard energies rather than plastic images; both explore motion and change rather than static material. Both consciously reject the traditions that have "fathered" their art. Both may be unheard, unread, or misinterpreted by an audience trained to measure worth in products, awards, and public recognition; still, Bast and Gaddis insist the worth of their compositions lies in the fluid energy of their conceptions of actuality. Both compose from life—it takes Bast's immersion in and near destruction by reality to enable him to create a worthy art. But finally, both adapt to and express the exigencies of our time: Bast's last piece (and first worthy one), written in the hospital with a purple crayon which is "all they'll give him" to work with, resembles Gaddis's own texts, written in difficult times with the materials at hand. By meditating on the actual world, understood and expressed in all its accidental energy, both pieces become actualistic creations.

FIVE

JOHN BARTH

LETTERS AND THE

RELATIVE FRAME

Like the Author in *LETTERS* (1979), John Barth "had long since turned his professional back on literary realism in favor of the fabulous irreal, and only in this latest enterprise had projected, not without misgiving, a detente with the realistic tradition. It is as if Reality, a mistress too long ignored, must now settle scores with her errant lover."[1] If his attentions have strayed in previous works, Barth returns in *LETTERS* to an affectionate dalliance with this mistress. Like Coover's *Public Burning* or Pynchon's *Gravity's Rainbow*, Barth's text incorporates a wealth of factually accurate detail about the various "nows" of its composition, from 1812 to 1978. Like other actualistic texts (and unlike some of Barth's earlier fictions), *LETTERS* also concerns itself with contemporary women and men, characters with detailed and more or less believable families, histories, jobs, and crises, who live in "more or less actual places" like Cambridge, Maryland, and Buffalo, New York, and who remark on news events actually occurring in the novel's present, 1969 (190). Discussing the novel in an interview, Barth emphasizes his conscious choice to reflect reality. "I wanted to return in some way to the 'Old Turf,' the Maryland Tidewater country. I even wanted, God help me, to deal with something like contemporary problems among contemporary people—people whom I wished to be believable."[2]

But errant he has indeed been. After writing two novels he considered realistic (*The Floating Opera* [1956] and *The End of the Road* [1958]), Barth turned to the mythic, the classical, and the "fabulous irreal." In a 1964 interview, he repudiates realistic fiction and dismisses concrete reality.

> I didn't think after *The End of the Road* that I was interested in writing any more realistic fiction—fiction that deals with Characters From Our Time, who speak real dialogue. I never could write realistic dialogue very well anyhow, and so I decided it was a bad idea for writers to write realistic dialogue. One ought to know a lot about Reality before one writes realistic novels. Since I don't know much about Reality, it will have to be abolished. What the hell, reality is a nice place to visit but you wouldn't want to live there, and literature never did, very long. . . . Reality is a drag.[3]

Similarly, in his famous 1967 essay "The Literature of Exhaustion," Barth observes that the conventional devices of realistic fiction—"cause and effect, linear anecdote, characterization, authorial selection, arrangement, and interpretation—can be and have long since been objected to as obsolete notions, or metaphors for obsolete notions."[4] To be sure, in statements like these Barth advances the objections to conventional realism shared by all actualists. But the fiction of what we may now see as his "middle period"—*The Sot-Weed Factor* (1960), *Giles Goat-Boy* (1966), *Lost in the Funhouse* (1968), and *Chimera* (1972)—also suggests, for reasons I will return to, that "Reality is a drag."

It is therefore not surprising that, like other novelists treated in this book, Barth has been widely praised for or convicted of espousing a nonreferential art. Whether derided as a shallow parodist who ignores human values[5] or admired as a "fabulist" who "invents forms according to the logic of his own genius, not according to conventional ideas of 'reality'";[6] whether listed as an exemplary "Anti-Realist"[7] or writer of "self-conscious fiction"[8] or more puzzlingly described as a self-consciously antirealistic social satirist,[9] Barth is commonly understood to refer in his texts to his own and other writers' imaginations, but not to external reality. Edward Said puts it clearly: for Barth, "Fiction is viewed not as an intervention into reality, nor as an addition to it—as was the case with classic realist fiction—but rather as an intervention in other fiction, or in other writing."[10] From a different critical perspective, Campbell Tatham agrees: "The essence of Barth's aesthetic is the assertion that even as vision is personal, potentially arbitrary, so art cannot hope and should not try to mirror the existence of an objective reality. Art, Barth is saying again and again, assumes and affirms artifice."[11] Similar evaluations focusing on the textuality of Barth's vision and method abound in the by-now voluminous criticism of his fiction.

Barth's career cannot, I think, be understood from such a modernist perspective. Rather than a retreat from reality's downward gravitational drag to the high citadel of art, his fictions constitute an errant lover's explorative movement in the direction of the actual. His first two novels bring his own version of realistic fiction to the end of the road, as he becomes explicitly conscious of the obsolescence of that mode of representation and of its failure justly to reflect his existential themes. He discovers the inadequacies of Freitag's Triangle, whose severe geometry figures the Newtonian universe; such a mathematics cannot express—or allow—the free play of contingent beings. In his middle period, then, Barth finds, like Jacob Horner, that "when my mythoplastic razors were sharply honed, it was unparalleled sport to lay about with them, to have at reality."[12] With the "mythic method" Eliot praises in *Ulysses*, and with the tradition of the wandering hero articulated by Raglan and Campbell, Barth "has at reality." But his use of mythic patterns is, in that sense, radically different from that of Joyce and other modernists: while the latter invoke myth to create an alternative, timeless realm, Barth, like Coover in *Public Burning*, deconstructs the mythic method as he uses it, so that his protagonists are actually immersed in time. If their lives seem by the end to disclose an order typical of mythic heroes, the process of living those lives in *Sot-Weed Factor*, *Giles Goat-Boy*, "Menelaiad," "Anonymiad," and the three novellas of *Chimera* denies these figures the possibility of seeing from the end. They are lost in the midst, doomed to the uncertainty of the errant. Is Perseus estellated, or merely turned to stone? Is Menelaus home, or still on the beach with shape-shifting Proteus? Does George Giles get the "Answers" "right" and accomplish his tasks? The indeterminacy of these issues, and of the meaning or value of the very pattern he has invoked, is part of Barth's point. It was not part of Joyce's—or, at least, of the Joyce Eliot read.

I propose that Barth's affirmation of artifice ("A different way to come to terms with the discrepancy between art and the Real Thing is to *affirm* the artificial element in art")[13] should be understood as a rejection of antiquated modes of representation, but not of the idea that art refers to reality. "Imitations-of-novels," Barth writes in a seldom-quoted part of "The Literature of Exhaustion," "are no more removed from 'life' than Richardson's or Goethe's epistolary novels are: both imitate 'real' documents, and the subject of both, ultimately, is life, not the documents. A novel is as much a piece of the real world as a letter."[14] Since fiction is not the same as reality, affirming the artifice can express the actualist's perception of reality in art as readily as it can record the modernist's retreat from reality to art—depending on how artifice functions in the text. My own reading suggests that even the highly "artificial" fictions of Barth's middle period, like the self-conscious novels of Nabokov or Barthelme, address life as well as art.[15]

Barth's return as "errant lover" to a mistress "too long ignored" makes *LETTERS* his most explicitly actualistic text. The Author adumbrates a sense of reality akin to that of Pynchon or Gaddis: "I approach reality these days with more respect, if only because I find it less realistic and more mysterious than I'd supposed" (189–90). The novel bears out this understanding, setting in motion and correspondence seven subjective and uncertain observers in a world that is relative, energetic, discontinuous, and accidental. The mode of presentation is not, the Author insists, to be "naive literary realism," for the breakdown of old boundaries between art and life provides one "good argument for steering clear of traditional realism" (191, 342). In the elegant terms proposed by Thomas Carmichael, Barth attempts "to retain a place for mimesis in narrative while calling into question the traditional strategies of literary representation. . . Barth's interrogation of realistic strategies reflects a fundamental ambivalence in his attitude toward the legitimacy of fictional representation."[16] With its multiple points of view, its breaks in the continuity of time, its prodigal expansiveness, its exposure of authorial subjectivity, and its inconclusiveness, *LETTERS* presents an actualistic understanding of reality.

Like other actualists, Barth uses the terms of contemporary physics in his novel. He refers to a physics of transformation: "the tender physics by which paralyzing self-consciousness becomes enabling self-awareness," the "magic physics of the heart," the "metaphorical physics to turn stones into stars" (348, 436, 652). Such references demonstrate Barth's awareness of a new physics based, not on the static discovery of fixed laws, but on the exploration of dynamic changes among relative states. Other references reveal an acquaintance with the current phenomena of astrophysics—

"black hole" (359, 428), "dead sun" (561), "collapsing star" (333), and "white dwarf" (277). Others, such as to the notion of atomic half-life (257, 748), show at least a popular knowledge of particle physics. "Entropy" appears (108, 186), as does a rather sophisticated reference by Lady Amherst to Heisenberg's uncertainty principle. "Thus has chronicling transformed the chronicler, and I see that neither Werner Heisenberg nor your character Jacob Horner went far enough: not only is there no 'non-disturbing observation'; there is no non-disturbing historiography. Take warning, sir: to put things into words works changes, not only upon the events narrated, but upon their narrator" (80). Barth's awareness that major shifts in worldview have been occasioned by those in recent science emerges in Ambrose's remark that "in my student days [. . .] science had still not purged itself of 19th-Century pathos" (38); Ambrose echoes "The Literature of Replenishment":

> I deplore the artistic and critical cast of mind that repudiates the whole modernist enterprise . . . that rushes back into the arms of nineteenth-century middle-class realism as if the first half of the twentieth century hadn't happened. It *did* happen: Freud and Einstein and two world wars . . . and there's no going back to Tolstoy and Dickens & Co. except on nostalgia trips. As the Russian writer Yevgeny Zamyatin was already saying in the 1920s . . . : "Euclid's world is very simple, and Einstein's world is very difficult; nevertheless, it is now impossible to return to Euclid's."[17]

Clearly, Barth places his fiction in a world that has changed because of the new physics.

Like other actualistic texts, *LETTERS* is energized by the opposition between Newtonian science and contemporary physical theories. Specifically, a conflict between the pursuit of various absolutes, traceable to an assumption that the world contains Newton's absolute time, space, and motion, and the consciousness of relativity, of the implications (at least) of Einstein's work, provides one important organizing principle for *LETTERS*. Classical physics required an inertial frame of reference, a nonearthly locus where its laws were fully valid. Newton therefore felt compelled to define in his *Principia* absolute time, space, and motion: "Absolute, true, and mathematical time, of itself, and from its own nature, flows equably without relation to anything external. Absolute space, in its own nature, without relation to anything external remains always similar and immovable. Absolute motion is the translation of a body from one absolute space into another."[18] Physicists judged their experimental data against this fixed, unalterable background, as if the cosmos ticked out the measure of one universal clock.

Einstein, however, rejected these concepts as unobservable and therefore meaningless. After the Michelson-Morley experiment failed to disclose a stationary ether, which would enable the detection of absolute rest or absolute motion, Einstein leaped to the revolutionary conclusion that no absolute and privileged reference frame exists in the universe. The special theory of relativity (1905), confined to systems moving uniformly relative to each other, and the general theory (1916), which applies to all types of motion, postulate that two moving systems have their own proper times and spaces, which differ from each other according to their motion. Time cannot be imagined as absolute or universal, for Einstein discovered that moving clocks change their rhythm. Space, time, and matter are no longer imagined as separate, stable entities: space-time forms a continuum, and matter (which is also energy, since $E = mc^2$) curves this continuum. Asked to explain the essence of relativity in a few words, Einstein replied: "It was formerly believed that if all material things disappeared out of the universe, time and space would be left. According to the relativity theory, however, time and space disappear together with the things."[19]

Perhaps most devastating of all to the worldview of classical physics and to the parallel ontology of realistic fiction, now no inertial, accurate, or absolute frame of reference exists. According to historian of science P. C. W. Davies: "The special theory of relativity demands that there are no privileged reference frames, nobody has the special status to be 'right' and everybody else who is moving differently 'wrong.' The inescapable conclusion is that certain occurrences which are traditionally considered to happen objectively in a certain way are not objective at all, but merely *relative* to a particular state of motion."[20] The rejection of a privileged frame implies, for modern and postmodern artists, that narratives cannot "frame" or enclose reality in a static picture.[21] Unlike classical narratives and classical physics, they cannot provide a means for what Heidegger calls "enframing"—the way of revealing that makes beings available for *use*.[22] For postmodern fiction, the relativity of reference frames entails a consequent end to authorial omniscience and objectivity and, in broader terms, an end to the notion that a "proper" work of art is directed toward closure or framed by an eye privileged with complete and accurate knowledge.

LETTERS makes explicit references to Einstein and relativity. Jacob Horner describes his nameless black Doctor, who has white hair, a white mustache and goatee, as "a dapper negative of Albert Einstein" (109). The depiction is apt, for the Doctor inverts Einstein's world to recover something like Newton's; he envisions the world divided by paralysis and motion, which he takes as an absolute end regardless of its source, velocity, or direction. Taking to extremes the faith in absolute motion, against a fixed, inertial frame of reference, the Doctor dismisses as irrelevant all forms of history, narrative suspense, etiologies, "idle ontologies," literature—in short, any effort to shape stories about events related in time (100, 107–8). The Doctor dies while fishing in a storm, a victim of his own ignorance of the physical world.

The larger and more important influence Einstein and relativity theory exert in *LETTERS* appears in the contrast Barth employs between characters, institutions, and systems enacting a misguided Newtonian faith in privileged, inertial, and absolute frames of reference and others open to relative motions, interrelations, and correspondence among plural reference frames. As in other actualistic texts, public institutions commonly endorse the antiquated Newtonian view of reality—John Schott, for example, is as committed to classical assumptions as Gaddis's Whiteback, Coover's Eisenhower, Atwood's Miss Lumley, or Barthelme's doctor. Well schooled in Newton's laws, Barth's absolutists conceive of history as a formalist document straining for closure, for the circular return to origins measured in a time that is essentially spatial. For others, however, time is relative to the observer's motion and perspective, and history, while disclosing inevitable echoes between events, is more properly understood as an open spiral than a circle, and better understood without any spatial form at all. Ambrose observes that "history is a code which, laboriously and at ruinous cost, deciphers into *HISTORY*" (332).

The locus of the aesthetic debate in *LETTERS* expands beyond that—or better, makes explicit connections that remain latent—in other actualistic texts. Barth takes issue with traditional literary realism, which, authorized by a Newtonian physics, assumes an absolute frame of reference. "If, as the Kabbalists supposed, God was an Author and the world his book, I criticized Him for mundane realism," Barth writes in *LETTERS* (189), echoing a quip from the 1964 interview.[23] The realistic author typically constitutes a fixed and godlike reference frame with his detached, superior, and omniscient eye. Barth also directs a parodic mockery at romanticism in *LETTERS*, with multiple references, especially in the 1812 segments, to Mme. de Staël, Goethe, Byron, Poe, and others, and to their invented follower, Consuelo del Consulado, who repeats history as farce. Based on an idealistic metaphysics, romanticism—however adversary its relation to Newtonian realism—also posits an absolute frame, a realm of enduring truth and beauty beyond the deceptive and evanescent appearances of physical reality. Furthermore, and most especially, Barth interrogates formalism or modernism, as he variously calls the movement whose commitment to spatial form rests on the assumption of a timeless and inertial reference frame. Like Ambrose, Barth has felt the attractions of a form that distances the messiness of experience and makes the realm of art autonomous; but Ambrose, "Author," and Barth bid in *LETTERS* a "Farewell to formalism" (768).

"The Literature of Replenishment" explores these aesthetic modes: realism, or the "premodernist mode," and modernism, which Barth sees as heir to romantic assumptions about reality and art. He clarifies his relation to these traditions in a passage that deserves extended quotation for its illumination of *LETTERS*.

> It is no longer necessary, if it ever was, to repudiate *them*, either: the great premodernists. If the modernists, carrying the torch of romanticism, taught us that linearity, rationality, consciousness, cause and effect, naive illusionism, transparent language, innocent anecdote, and middle-class moral conventions are not the whole story, then from the closing decades of our century we may appreciate that the contraries of these things are not the whole story either. Disjunction, simultaneity, irrationalism, anti-illusionism, self-reflexiveness, medium-as-message, political olympianism, and a moral pluralism approaching moral entropy—these are not the whole story either.
>
> A worthy program for postmodernist fiction, I believe, is the synthesis or transcension of these antitheses, which may be summed up as premodernist and modernist modes of writing. My ideal postmodernist author neither merely repudiates nor merely imitates either his twentieth-century modernist parents or his nineteenth-century premodernist grandparents. . . . The ideal postmodernist novel will somehow rise above the quarrel between realism and irrealism, formalism and "contentism."[24]

This passage expresses Barth's version of actualism. Rejecting as the proper goal of art either the simple reflection of a Newtonian reality, with the linearity, causality, and objectivity that characterize realism, or the retreat from content to pure form, to the irreal, private, centered labyrinths of modernism, Barth projects a fiction expressing postmodern reality with a sophisticated awareness of the need to renew fictional conventions. As Charles Harris argues, "*LETTERS* strives to achieve this transcension by incorporating into its fictional process esthetic principles from both modernism and premodernism without repudiating or unselfconsciously imitating these principles."[25] In the terms Pynchon uses, Barth repudiates the binary logic that divides ideal and real, form and content, elect and preterite. Hoping to transcend these alternatives, both of which privilege one set of artistic values and techniques from different grounds in absolute systems, Barth will recover the excluded middle: the relative, the actual.

Framing the Absolute

Looming over Barth's fictional landscape in *LETTERS*, two towers symbolize these aesthetic traditions with their absolutist assumptions. The camera obscura at the Menschhaus suggests the premodernist mode, or realism. "A long-focus objective lens is mounted on the roof; the image it receives is mirrored down a shaft in the center of the tower [. . .] the dark chamber and luminous plate make the commonplace enchanting. What would scarcely merit notice if beheld firsthand—red brick hospital, weathered oysterdredger toiling to windward [. . .] are magically composed and represented; they shine serene by their inner lights and are intensely interesting" (155–56). As in realistic art, an objective lens with a comprehensive scope re-presents, or brings to self-revealing presence, the commonplace objects of reality; the camera obscura holds a literal mirror up to nature. The Author may be imagined as the objective lens on the roof, surveying his creation from above, and as the craftsman in the basement who turns the apparatus "by hand, full circle on its rollers" (155). Even more monumental, the Tower of Truth figures the modernist retreat from reality into the citadel of autotelic art. Those who bring about its construction reject the notion "that the university should be a little model of the *actual* world rather than a lofty counterexample: lighthouse to the future, ivory tower to the present, castle keep of the past!" (8, my emphasis). Like the well-wrought modernist text, the university should be self-contained, nonreferential, olympian, and timeless. To learn to read, in such a Tower of Truth, is to renounce time and differences and discontinuities in order to perceive from above—from the Author's privileged perspective in the belfry, as it were—the single, simple timelessness beneath apparent contingencies.

For all their superficial differences, both towers share an absolutist perspective, surveying reality metaphysically from the end of time. Both towers are erected by the same corporation, whose motto could serve equally well for modernist and realist versions of art's refutation of time: "Build not your house upon the shifting sand" (178). A. B. Cook, the doggerel laureate, voices the doctrine of art's atemporal permanence:

> The stoutest fort'll
> Fall; the final portal
> Open. Death's the key
> Of keys, the cure of cures.
> All passes. Art alone endures.
>
> (671)[26]

Understood as a retreat from the messiness of reality into a monumental order, traditional art, whether premodernist or modernist, realistic or symbolic, is aptly expressed in these towers.

In their structure and function, both towers are panoptic, suggesting a mechanics of absolute power aligned with seemingly innocuous aesthetic orders. Bentham's Panopticon prison, as Michel Foucault notes in *Discipline and Punish*, relies on a centrally located tower which serves as an inspection hall.

> The central inspection hall is the pivot of the system. Without a central point of inspection, surveillance ceases to be guaranteed, continuous and general; for it is impossible to have complete trust in the activity, zeal and intelligence of the warder who immediately supervises the cells. . . . But surveillance will be perfect if from a central hall the director or head-warder sees, without moving and without being seen, not only the entrances of all the cells and even the inside of most of them when the unglazed door is open, but also the warders guarding the prisoners on every floor.[27]

In immediately obvious ways, the university's Tower of Truth, designated from its conception as the seat of campus administration (7), enables surveillance and control over both students (docile bodies to be "reformed" in the image of society) and their warders, the faculty, pursuing "discipline" but not fully trustworthy. Indeed, MSUC's administration addresses its energies largely to the supervision (frequently hidden, as when unknown watchers search Lady Amherst's trash) and the punishment (suspension, firing, legal prosecution) of student and faculty "deviants." The retreat from reality to the order of modernist art is not, by extension, simply a way to distance the mess; it is also a way to coerce multiplicity into alignment with an absolute and monolithic Truth.

The camera obscura is less clearly disciplinary, since it is used by the Mensch family "merely" for entertainment and profit. Similarly, realistic art is less obviously coercive, since it appears to include some of the chancy and irrelevant details that constitute reality's messiness. But, we recall, the camera obscura turns "full circle" to survey the world panoptically, and its data are "magically composed and represented"—disciplined by the way they are enframed and brought to presence. To the "long-focus objective" eye of the realist, no detail is truly chancy or irrelevant, for all conspire to produce a causally complete picture. Like Pynchon's rocket, both the camera obscura and the Tower of Truth symbolize the Western will to power over the errant phenomena of existence. To erect towers, with all their phallocentric connotations, is to aspire to repress and conquer nature in the name of civilized power.

Not only are both towers built by the same corporation, but both reveal faulty "groundings" and inadequate "foundations" during the course of the novel. Both towers are built of the same mossy stones, more or less held together with similarly adulterated mortar, and both are erected on the sandy loam of the Eastern Shore. The Mensch tower is built from various sorts of fraud, and "the Tower of Truth is rising from a lie" (241–43). Since artists can build only on shifting sands—since, as Ambrose says, "Art passes too" (671)—these fraudulent constructions inevitably tilt, crack, and threaten to collapse. The camera obscura ceases to revolve; it no longer provides a complete view of reality but becomes clearly "one-sided," static and frozen. The tower foundation cracks, and the entire edifice may be prevented from collapse only by explosion.

Appropriately, then, LETTERS invokes its own monumental status ironically, on the very last page: "Time now to lay the cornerstone, run Old Glory up the pole, let off the fireworks, open doors to the public. This way, please. Mind your step: floors just waxed. Do read the guide markers as you go along. Here's one now [. . .] the end" (772). In monumental art, every "marker" points to the end; in Barth's ironic version, however, the tower becomes a funhouse, whose slippery floors may trip the reader and whose entrance turns into an exit. If this conclusion invites readers to consider the novel a newly completed Tower of Truth, it also ironically reminds us of the latest letter, Todd's, suggesting that the tower will be exploded at sunrise on the morning of its dedication. At the moment when its completion allows it to become a monument of letters, the text destroys that model.

Virtually every character in Barth's antimonumental epic is an artist in one medium or another, including letters. Many of these authors define Barth's own relative universe and actualist aesthetic by contrast: pursuing absolutist ends in art, many seek to become the Author, or to align themselves with his finalizing perspective, in order to create monuments of their own. As Jan Gorak observes, Barth "investigates the personal illusions of a cluster of artists, each of whom attempts to become a god of his own making" or "a self-elected deity."[28] These self-privileging writers mystify authorship; they deny its history and temporality, as well as its uncertainty and irresolution. Above all, they resist "correspondence," in the sense of relations among texts and authors that make writing dialogic, multiple, and relative. In Gorak's terms, they ignore the "interlocking mutualities" which Barth prefers over "privileged subjectivities." These authors become, then, as fully self-indulgent and narcissistic as some critics mistakenly accuse Barth of being.[29]

Among the faulty authors in Barth's text, none remain more clearly or more destructively committed to the old aesthetic and the old reality than the Cooks/Castines/Burlingames. As witnessed by the fact that their political, aesthetic, and personal goals and practices have not changed from their earliest recorded history, and as suggested by the fact that Burlingame III "had gone to school with Henry More & Isaac Newton" (129), these authors attempt always to recuperate antiquated fables of order.

Primarily authors of "action historiography," the Cooks and Burlingames pursue through Byzantine intricacies a single, simple end. Their goal appears consistently to be the reversal of time and the nullification of change: they seek revolution, conceived in its most purely circular and regressive form; they want to restore America to a lost (and never-existent) golden age. Each generation of Cooks and Burlingames tries to help the Indians to overthrow white, Western, imperialist powers, not to defend minority rights or to check the power of corrupt governments, but rather to achieve the return to a precivilized, static time, when their own "noble savage" forebears lived at peace in the wilderness. While achieving this increasingly anachronistic end takes on absolute importance, the means cease to matter, and various Cooks and Burlingames steal, swindle, traffic in drugs, betray, and murder. They abandon their wives and children through the centuries except at points when these relatives may be useful for their cause.

As authors of letters, the Cooks and Burlingames serve the same regressive, atemporal end. Their ventures into writing are never, after Eben Cooke, frivolously artistic. Though the writing of Eben's progeny is indeed artful, it serves purely utilitarian and didactic ends; it communicates always and only, if never simply or directly, in order to accomplish a return to a lost Origin. All of their letters seek essentially to bring their children home, back to the patriarchal fold, into alignment with their Author/Father. "The Barth protagonist is a wandering hero always looking for a way home to the father," writes Douglas Johnstone in a psychoanalytic reading of Barth's fiction that casts interesting light on the Cooks and Burlingames of *LETTERS*.[30] Their letters reevaluate history in the light of a single pattern of generational rebellion, which each author renounces. Cook IV vows to spend the second half of his life canceling out the first, effecting his own return to the father so that his offspring may remain from birth in a simple accord with theirs (323). Cook VI urges his son repeatedly to return to his presence and to his values, so that they might together return their country to a simpler and more orderly time. All of these Cook letters wage war against the complexities of actual history in the name of a suprahistorical telos and in behalf of an ahistorical harmony.

Given their "theistical" view of authorship as the creation of patterns of meaningful return, the Cooks fittingly trap themselves in a vicious circularity. Dedicated to exposing the pattern for their sons, none can break it—each son revolts against his father and returns quite directly to the values of his grandfather. All return to the same places, their motion through space fixed by an inertial and absolute end that draws them to the axes north (Castines Hundred) and south (Maryland) of their self-replicating family history. Underlining the egoism of these patriarchal Authors, who imagine themselves creators of dynastic permanence, Castines Hundred is named to echo Sutpens Hundred, scene of Thomas Sutpen's fatherly and authoritarian follies in Faulkner's *Absolom, Absolom!* Invited, then, to provide a model for one character in *LETTERS*, Cook VI replies to his own author—whom he ironically addresses, "Dear Professor"—that he accepts his "invitation to play the role of the Author who solicits and organizes communications from and between his characters, and embroils himself in their imbroglios!" (405). The latest reader of the family "line" chooses, of course, to find it fiction, so the final irony is the Cooks' double failure, as authors of history to affect real events, and as authors of letters to "correspond" with their readers.

Like the Cooks, Jerome Bray pursues an absolutist form of authorship, envisioning art as the creation of an inert and permanent end. Bray, too, serves the cause of a second revolution destined to bring a cyclic return to a lost golden age. While the Cooks foment political revolt, Bray works on an aesthetic, "an utterly Novel Revolution!" (32). For Bray, the single end of authorship is to stop time and motion; he sees his text as "The Complete and Final Fiction" (36), enabling "an end to letters! ZZZZZZZ!" (528). Bray's understanding of the "New Golden Age" includes "revelation of true identity. Rout of impostors and pretenders. Assumption of throne of France. . . . Reunion with parents" (37). Like the Cooks, Bray imagines a mythical return conferring identity, political ascendancy, and family harmony. It is, of course, no accident that Bray has been "raised" by the same father, "Ranger Burlingame VI," and may be an illegitimate offshoot of the Cook/Burlingame line (746).[31]

Bray's letters constitute one of Barth's wittiest critiques of modernist formalism. Bray privileges form in life and letters; his writing project changes from a Revolutionary Novel to NUMBERS, the first work of "numerature," whose form quite literally divorces the text from actual, worldly content. As their titles imply, while Barth's *LETTERS* let, Bray's NUMBERS numb. Bray does not complete his project; he invents only a drug, honey dust, itself a commentary on the modernist notion of art as withdrawal from reality. Far from a recovery of the aestheticized realm of Camelot, Bray founds instead Comalot, a scene of decadent sexuality become comatose.

Todd Andrews might seem strange company for Bray, given his commitment to humanism and his demonstrated will to protect bridges between various extremes—positions shared by characters, including the author, who reject absolutist approaches to life and art. As Jan Gorak says, Todd is "Barth's troubled custodian of common values."[32] Though he respects authorship, and though he writes, Todd does not envision himself as an Author: "I'm not an *homme de lettres*: my dealings are with the actual lives of actual people" (97). While Bray and Cook deny anyone's authorship but their own, so that Cook assumes he will take the role of Author in

LETTERS and Bray aspires to become King Author, Todd admits his status as creation. Though he gives Barth paternal advice, he realizes, "It's you who are in a sense *my* father, the engenderer of 'Todd Andrews' " (97).

Todd does, however, construct an imaginary Author plotting his life story, like a modernist narrative, in the form of a large, rapidly closing circle. When Jane Mack "re-seduces" him, Todd begins to posit a "ham-handed Formalist" shaping the apparent coincidences of his life. "I feel at least a grateful indulgence of that sentimental Formalist, our Author, for so sweetly, neatly—albeit improbably—tying up the loose ends of His plot" (256, 278). Onto this Author, Todd foists off his own freedom and responsibility and, like Cook and Bray, nullifies real (open-ended, indeterminate) time in place of a decadent nostalgia. It is not, as Charles Harris argues, that Todd "retreats from 'The Mystic Vision' that alone would have delivered him to the ontological, temporal world" and "avoids intimations of ultimate unity,"[33] but rather that Todd manufactures precisely such a fiction of ultimate unity in a text that denies its validity.

Todd too has his golden age—his lost past with Jane, which readers of *The Floating Opera* will recall as distinctly nonidyllic and which Jane herself seems scarcely to recall. Todd's entire activity becomes directed toward compelling a recurrence of this past. He thus ignores and manipulates actuality in the name of a formal pattern of recurrence that he himself constructs (256–59). He resigns Polly Lake, who loves him, to her fate; he allows Jeannine/Bea to join him on his final cruise only because she was present during his original tour of the Floating Opera (565). Then he uses her to bring his sexual story full circle, forcing Jeannine to reenact the role of Betty June Gunter, purely for the sake of form—"tying up the loose ends" (707).

In his authorship of letters, Todd coerces deviant present details into alignment with a rigid and regressive pattern. He writes to recapture and close off the past. His letters emphasize circularity, not only because Todd writes about events resembling previous ones, but also because he echoes refrainlike phrases and chooses insistently circular tropes. "Events recircle like turkey buzzards, from whose patient orbits—eccentric, even retrograde, but ever closing—we determine their dead sun" (561). He writes to his (dead) father and to the (absent) Author, revealing a drive as unquenchable as Bray's or Cook's to align himself with his progenitors and to recuperate a never-existent family harmony. Todd ends, appropriately enough, invoking a return of the "dead sun"/son to the father: "Good-bye, Polly; good-bye, Jane; good-bye, Drew. Hello, Author; hello, Dad. Here comes the sun" (738).

With his commitment to the priority of form and his choice of the letter *O* as his own formal imperative, Todd achieves as vicious a circularity as Cook or Bray. In identifying his fate with the *O* Jane moans in orgasm, Todd overlooks some obvious implications: the nil or zero of his hope to repeat the past, the nothing to come of a self-enclosed form. Todd also forgets that the pattern culminated the first time in his attempt to die; to repeat the past, as he himself sketches it, can only be to renew his suicidal despair. As he pursues formal completion, Todd's motion takes on fixed spatial poles; his last cruise on the Chesapeake, its itinerary designed to echo previous cruises, forms a large, erratic *O*.

Like Bray's and Cook's, Todd's letters implicitly reveal the inadequacy of formalism. The pattern proves so obviously unable to contain the detailed "messiness" of his existence that even Todd is moved to observe: "Okay, the correspondences aren't rigorous, and there are as many inversions as repetitions or ironical echoes. The past not only manures the future: it does an untidy job" (259). Subsequent letters bear out this observation; every invocation of a previous event actually emphasizes the difference between past and present. For all of Todd's efforts to tie up loose ends, complete his affairs, and close the circle, he achieves no resolution. In fact, though *LETTERS* is throughout committed to openness and uncertainty, nowhere do these qualities appear more forcefully than in Todd's contributions. Many of these letters break off in the midst; two are interrupted by phone calls (401, 566). Todd closes his inquiry and his last letter to his father without answering any of the questions he has raised or explaining his plans for a second suicide attempt. His last letter, the latest chronologically in the novel, ends quite literally up in the air. Will the tower blow up? Who is in it? How does Todd's last letter, the codicil to his will, survive? Todd's formal circle is broken by the content of his experience.

Like the writers who use words as means to an end—the return to a timeless, absolute space—Reg Prinz too would nullify temporal process in turning film to *Frames*. The inadequacies of realism meet the failures of modernism in Prinz, who began as "an avant-garde documentarist" (355), exploiting the realistic pretense to photograph and "capture" life; now, he endorses a formalist aesthetic, in which technique has priority over subject and form over content. Ostensibly filming Barth's texts, he neither reads nor re-creates them; he rejects and departs from much of Ambrose's screenplay, and during one typical shooting session on campus, Prinz "somehow made it clear to the students that he didn't care one way or the other how the scene ended" (225). Prinz's "frames" thus become content-less, empty containers, like Todd's hollow *O* or Bray's numbers. Freezing motion into permanence and reducing action to picture, frames define by contrast the enabling power of letters.

Like Barth's other faulty artists, Prinz hopes for a "revolutionary" return of time's circular wheel to a lost golden age. Prinz's version of return emphasizes a silence or wordlessness common to all the utopian dreams in *LETTERS*; Prinz plans to "revise the American revolution" and "return toward the visual purity of silent movies" (223). Prinz's regressive aesthetics would eliminate language—the signifiers that always defer the signified for beings striving in relative time—for a "visual purity" in which, aligned with atemporal, absolute meaning, things bespeak themselves utterly and eliminate the need for words.

Since he says nothing in a world of words, writes nothing in a universe of letters, Prinz has only minimal identity as a character and virtually none as an artist. He can only hover in the margins of those who do use letters. Lady Amherst appropriately wonders if he has an identity, "whether the man be not, after all, all surface: a clouded transparency, a . . . film" (218). Reg Prinz's names lend obvious credence to her suspicion, suggesting not only his place among those who aspire to royalty ("King George III," "King Author," "Arthur Morton King," etc.) but also the mechanical duplication of photographs, or prints. His death by explosion leaves little of a recognizable human identity, and since the fire destroys half of the *Frames* footage, Prinz leaves no artistic legacy, no work of art, either. No more, of course, do Bray, Todd, or Cook.

For all their yearning for monumental status, then, these formalists produce no towers of truth. None manages to complete the revolution he has envisioned or to finish his artistic project. None finds certainty or objectivity, either as writer of letters in Barth's text or as "camera eye" in his own production. These artists cannot bring things to self-revealing presence through words or pictures but, instead, leave them elusive, deferred, mysterious, and messy. Nor do Cook's "action historiography," Bray's "NUMBERS," Todd's *O* or Prinz's *Frames* achieve panoptic surveillance of or power over the recalcitrant world; instead, they strip their creators of vision and power. Least of all, perhaps, can these formalistic creations stop time, traced as they are in the relative, open temporal medium of *LETTERS*. The stories of these characters' futile efforts to achieve closure suggest that closure is death, but that death does not bring anything to completion; it only interrupts.

"Such Things Are Relative"

Not committed to what Bray terms complete and final fictions, Barth's actualists see themselves as amateurs and (re)beginners. While Cook and Bray become increasingly dedicated to the pursuit of *ends*—causes, revolutions, suicides, returns—these characters grow instead less certain about goals and more open to new beginnings, second chances. While Prinz and Todd achieve or verge on the traditional tragic closure of death, Germaine, Ambrose, and Jacob Horner undertake marriages which, resembling structurally the resolution of comedy, nonetheless withhold the finalizing reassurance that nullifies energy and uncertainty at the end of traditional comic plots. These characters look forward to no easy bliss, no equilibrium: every suggestion about their futures emphasizes instead ongoing possibilities for loss, death, and disaffection.

These characters embrace the relative temporality that enables rebeginning. Rather than yearning for the stability of a closed and already determined past, for recapitulation or reenactment, each of them seeks liberation from vicious circularity. While they see patterning in time, they reject the single unified pattern, whether that of linear causality or cyclic return, for multiple orderings that include accident and randomness. Like Pynchon's actualists, in other words, Barth's see history as connected, but loosely. Their openness to temporal process and their awareness that time—speeding, slowing, unending, changing—is life allow these figures to inhabit Einstein's relative universe.

Their progress toward an actualistic understanding of reality is no simpler in *LETTERS* than in other contemporary fiction, as Jacob Horner's story demonstrates. Jake has renounced time on the Remobilization Farm, where he has had no personal history for fifteen years (19). Far from nostalgia for a lost golden age, he regards the past with horror: "Who wants to replay *that* play, rewalk that road?" he asks his Author (279). Indeed, he sees the return to any form of temporality as a death sentence; invoking Heraclitus's image of stepping into the river of time, Jake imagines he would "step into the poisoned river" and be swept over Niagara Falls (20). He has, then, retreated from such a fate into something very like

Newton's "absolute time," unrelated to anything external. He has made himself nearly impervious to change, accident, and history.

Writing performs a crucial function in enabling Jake's return to time: as elsewhere in Barth's text, letters let. During the previous fifteen years, Jake has practiced forms of "scriptotherapy" solely in order to negate time. He has prepared an almanac card each day, listing events occurring on the anniversary of the date, and catalogued the cards by alphabetical priority. His "anniversary view of history," a truly antihistorical vision, replaces the development of events through time with the leveling juxtaposition of static states: "To Marlon Brando, Doris Day, Henry IV, George Herbert, Washington Irving, happy birthday. Dante has found himself lost in the Dark Wood. Napoleon is occupying Rome" (97). Similarly, Jake has compiled a "Hornbook," an alphabetical list of cuckolds. These exercises in cataloging consist of spatial orderings designed to deny the importance of time. But then, on the night Joe Morgan reappears, Jake is driven to write himself a letter that accounts for his experiences in time, including Joe's demand that he "Rewrite History" (20). In narrating the demand, Jake begins the process of complying. By his second letter, Jake is aware that he is neither merely listing events nor cataloging sources of unease but rather chronicling the complicated relations of various beings as these change in time. "You have Lapsed into Writing. Stop" he writes, and "But Stay: this is Writing" (100–101). He doesn't; he can't. His letters grow increasingly concerned with detailed accounts of present events as he rewrites history.

Jake does not resolve many important questions about his life but prepares to inhabit a relative temporality and a more or less cohesive self. His conquest of paralysis enables his commitment to Marsha and his willingness to raise her child in the "relative" relationship that *does* rewrite history. His future remains uncertain, though: his marriage appears doomed by Marsha's meanness and his own ineptitude, and his return to teach remedial English at Wicomico State College does not promise simple fulfillment. He retains the habit of capitalizing Significant Words in his last letter, as if for rapid alphabetical indexing. His story, then, resists traditional closure and leaves Jake in the midst of time. But he has gained a sense of the relativity of space, time, and motion that makes such open-endedness the only appropriate conclusion. Jake reflects that Joe "was perhaps correct about my Remobilization, though experience tempers my Optimism. In any case, such things are relative" (745).

Like Jake, Germaine Pitt comes to an actualistic stance slowly. As *LETTERS* begins, she subscribes to a premodernist ontology, believing in linear, causal connections and a stable, knowable reality. Her pen, bought in "Mr Pumblechook's premises," reflects her admiration of the realistic tradition. A belief in the singularity of phenomena prevents Lady Amherst from seeing patterns in history, and hence from seeing history at all. She begins, that is, on a "base-one" numerical pattern, in which everything is unique.[34] Where a modernist like Bray perceives only form, denying the complexity that muddies its clarity, a realist like Germaine sees only a densely woven mesh of experience, without pattern at all. In Ambrose's birthmark, she sees no bee; in the constellations, no initials— "Admittedly I can't see Perseus and company there either, only a blinking bunch of stars" (61). In the Mensch family Easter egg, "I could see nothing inside" (246). This blindness to patterns means, of course, that she fails to perceive repetitions in her own history and thus to understand herself. Like Jake, she must go backward in order to go forward, but she too prefers *not* to repeat the past: "I did not share what seemed all about me to be an epidemic rage for reenactment," she says to André, and "I do not particularly share his taste for reruns," she tells Ambrose (367, 545).

As a realist, Germaine posits an omniscient Author behind the evidently random plot, directing historical events toward preordained and absolute ends. Because she does not herself understand or take responsibility for patterns in her own experience, Germaine doubly relies on this external Author—much, in fact, like Todd's—to order the apparent accidents of her life. Her early history with André Castine, who claims to manipulate all of the supposed chances of history and who assures Germaine that she is personally "watched over" (74–75), confirms her predisposition to mystify the Author. André becomes for her the hidden solution to all of the seeming mysteries she encounters; she advises Ambrose that "there is no They, only a He: André" (359), whom she will later dub "the very god of Coincidence" (375). When André orders her to go to Maryland, she goes (205), and when she is offered the provostship at Marshyhope, she waits "to learn whether André wanted me elsewhere" (222). Though he is so committed to disguise that she never surely knows him after 1940, she would "no doubt" have married him as late as February 1969 (224). In Germaine's misreading of her experience as a realist text, André's authorship stifles her own.

Clearly, Germaine must discover the enabling power of letters as well as the relativity and multiplicity of authorship. With André in 1940, she was "happily letting life write *me* instead of vice versa" (73); she must turn that scriptural tide. She defines herself as a recipient of letters (from her father, when he dies, and from André, once a year) and as an editor of letters (those of Mme. de Staël and Heloise and Abelard), but not, until the novel begins, as a writer of letters. Furthermore, although she has been surrounded from birth by authors and had involvements with Wells, Hesse, Huxley, Waugh, Mann, and Joyce (among others), she has nonetheless seen André as the single Author of her plot. By becoming herself an author of letters, Germaine discovers with Pynchon's Leni that there are many authors, many plots. Writing her story also teaches Germaine that authorship is not omniscience but repeated and uncertain beginnings from a subjective point in time. Through letters, Germaine demystifies authorship.

Barth assists in this process, not only by inviting Germaine to write letters narrating her past and present experience, but also by enacting a version of authorship as absence. With the close of his letter asking her to be his "heroine," he vows to be, "as in better-lettered times gone by, your faithful Author" (53). He breaks this promise, failing to answer her repeated pleas for confirmation that he receives or reads her epistles. She drives to his cottage and finds "no one at home," her last letter unopened in the postbox: Barth is not even a faithful reader (362). Finally, of course, the pretense animating LETTERS is that Barth is not her author but her editor; *she* is the author of her own story. As she comes to perceive her other author's benign absence, Germaine, like Jake, realizes that she writes herself.

Writing makes Germaine a better reader because she learns to see and evaluate patterns. First, she gradually relinquishes her abiding hope for a return to André. When André gives her the letters by "A. B. Cook IV" to read and publish, she responds, "I perceive a pattern of my own, A. C. IV's and V's and VI's be damned: It is the *women* of the line who've been the losers" (254). Two weeks later, she returns these letters to "André," refusing to use her own writing further in his service. She writes to Barth, "Indeed, at this point I put an end not only to our interview, but to our remaining connexion" (367).

As she liberates herself from the past by repeating it in letters and in life, she gains an open relation to relative time. Scriptotherapy enables her to see similarities between past and present, André and Ambrose: "it was André (I suddenly understand, with a dark *frisson*, what would have been at once apparent to another: I *shall* profit, then, perhaps, from this 'scriptotherapy') who made me vulnerable, three decades later, to his pallid echo, Mr Mensch" (72). She and Ambrose become each other's echoes, assisting each other through a "purgation by reenactment" (544) to regain and transcend their pasts. Germaine stars in a "re-make" of Ambrose's previous five affairs, though she insists on her difference from any of his lovers (386–89); Ambrose, meanwhile, plays the modern novelist seducing and seeking to impregnate Germaine: a role he is approximately seventh in her life to fill. Through this process she learns to prize the echo that permits change and variation above the recollection that circles back on itself.

Germaine's last letter articulates an actualistic view much like Jacob Horner's. She acknowledges all of the troubles threatening her new marriage and still-unconfirmed pregnancy but faces them with reasonable hope. Knowing her "Seventh Stage" with Ambrose confined to temporality and thus doomed to end, she nonetheless wishes "that Stage Seven, like the outer arc of some grand spiral, will curve on and out at least beyond our sight. May it be so" (678). Germaine admits the inevitability of loss which, sooner or later, relative time entails. Yet she perceives in her own ongoing history an order that allows her to share Ambrose's vision on their wedding night: "Should Ambrose one day cease to love me; [. . .] should my dear friend come even to deny (God forfend!) that he *ever* loved me, even that he ever *knew* me . . . I should still (so I envision) remain serene, serene" (691). For her, the "vision" is not of timeless bliss or absolute identity or oneness; more complexly, it is of an achieved relation to herself that allows her to face an uncertain future with "negatively capable" tranquillity.

Her opposite and eventual mate, Ambrose, arrives at a similar position. His resistance to the relativity of time, life, and letters begins from opposite grounds: where Germaine has failed to see pattern, Ambrose has imposed elaborate design, and where she has celebrated content at the expense of form, he has privileged form over content. While she has come to seem (especially to him) an embodiment of the premodernist great tradition of realism in letters, he has become a "last-ditch provincial Modernist" (767).

But Germaine's premodernism and Ambrose's modernism are of course deeply aligned. As Harris observes, they are equally metaphysical. "The modern novel is less a reaction against premodernism than a fulfillment of the metaphysical possibilities inherent in the genre."[35] Barth will have a marriage of these aesthetic modes, transforming each through their correspondence and changing metaphysics into physics. So, for all their differences, Germaine and Ambrose do correspond. Both have mystified authorship, seeing the Author as metaphysical source and fount of objective truth. Ambrose has endorsed an exalted, "theistical" view of authorship (152). His use of the pen name "Arthur Morton King" reveals his objectification of an Author-self and his Bray-like projection of literary creation into the recuperative never-never land of King, Arthur. Like Germaine, Ambrose has also resisted the process of relative time. His life tilts like hers toward a repetition of the year 1940, when she gave birth to André's son and he received the water message whose blankness compelled him to write. If she has, since, danced to the tune André calls, he has equally complied with "Yours Truly," becoming "Whom It Still Concerns" and filling in with his own words that other Author's blanks.

A first, generally realistic phase in Ambrose's art expresses itself in "The Amateur, or, A Cure for Cancer." In this incomplete manuscript, Arthur Morton King makes "an early effort, abortive . . . to come to terms with conventional narrative and himself" (149). He begins by invoking sources: "Our story is *ab ovo*: nothing here but hatched from there" (153). The notion of a Platonic form preceding existence and containing its "seeds" (a locus for Newton's absolute time flowing without relation to anything external) receives some mockery, for Ambrose's *ovo* is a brummagem trinket from the Oberammergau Passion play; Ambrose, however, is at least half-serious in attempting to hatch himself from that artful egg. Barth has given this motif a special relevance for Ambrose by beginning *Lost in the Funhouse* with a sperm's account of his journey toward the egg that *will* hatch Ambrose. Yet while "Night Sea Journey" treats the quest for origins ironically, "The Amateur" exists, as a relic of Ambrose's "theistical" phase, unironically to recover familial, personal, and artistic origins.

The manuscript begins, too, with the alphabetic egg, A or Alpha, and continues in linear order. The alphabetic form imposed on the linear temporality of "The Amateur" anticipates Ambrose's modernist phase and suggests the close kinship between premodernist and modernist spatial forms. Unlike Barth's own alphabetic subtitle, in which letters scattered through time can be gathered so as to spell out a meaningful phrase ("An old time epistolary novel . . ."), Ambrose's alphabetics constitute a "pure" form, devoid of content. The manuscript breaks off, appropriately, by naming the O—invoking the omega in which alpha is supposed to culminate, but achieving only omicron, a leaving off without closure which, like Todd's O or zero, reflects the emptiness of such formal patterns.

A second, modernist phase fulfills the promise inherent in the first, to abandon "such traditional contaminants of fiction" as "characterization, description, dialogue, plot—even language, where I could dispense with it" (151). Though Ambrose believes he had left this phase by 1967, and though in 1969 he expresses contempt for the "Schwarzwald cuckoo clocks of Modernism" (151), he continues to employ a modernist aesthetic during *LETTERS*, especially in the screenplay for *Frames* and in his Perseus story. Adopting a classical and distanced subject and the mythic cycle of heroism, following Campbell and Raglan (646–47), his Perseid consists of an intricate outline—letters and numbers within letters and numbers (648–50).

Nowhere does Ambrose's formalism appear more abundantly or more destructively than in his major project, the "re-make" he acts out with Germaine. He stages his seduction to culminate precisely "as the sun entered Aries" (64). With its detailed recapitulation of his previous five affairs, its imposition of various roles and costumes on Germaine, and its preordained betrayals of her, the affair enacts formalism with a vengeance. It leads to a marriage proposal "dictated" by Ambrose and transcribed by Germaine—adopting, despite its sinister implications, the role of his first, ill-tempered and ill-fated wife, Marsha—and rehearsing the six series of sixes they have recapitulated. Ambrose proposes a series of seven conjoinings on their wedding day, "to peak, vindicate, purge, and be done with this obsession for reenactment!" (764). And "peak" he certainly does, managing to achieve, on the sixth stroke of the sixth coupling, an orgasm that leads to a "Vision" on the seventh stroke.

But does Ambrose "purge" his formal obsession? Does he transcend the antithetical positions of premodernism and modernism? Much in Barth's text suggests he does. Even during the planning of the Perseid in June, Ambrose has seen through its formal cycles to its thematic question: "How transcend mere reenactment?" (429). In August, Ambrose abandons the Perseus project, the correspondence with "Yours Truly" and the roles of Arthur Morton King and "Whom it Concerns." He recognizes at last that all patterns are incomplete and arbitrary, if "provisionally useful" (648). Most important, Ambrose reconciles his love of form and his wish to participate in the world; an artist who is more enamored of the formal arrangements of fiction than of the world might still be "enabled to love [. . .] the world" *through* his love of form (650–51). In his last letter, dated September 22, Ambrose thus bids "farewell to formalism" (768).

It would seem, then, that Ambrose has recovered through form his "original" commitment to the world. But the "expert amateurship" Ambrose imagines represents an origin transformed by temporality; it is not simply a recuperation of the timeless values of "The Amateur." Like the synthesis or transcension of antitheses Barth looks for in "The Literature of Replenishment," Ambrose's new program will neither imitate nor repudiate its predecessors but will somehow rise above the quarrel between them. It will attend to both form and content, fantasy and actuality, mind and heart: "Fire + algebra = art. Failing the algebra, heartfelt ineptitude; failing the fire, heartless virtuosity" (768).[36]

Ambrose does not, of course, enact his new insights in art. He does *not* write *LETTERS*. He does not, quite, leave off saying farewell to his past mistakes, former selves, or first cycle; his last two letters are (still) addressed to "the late Arthur Morton King" and to "Whom it may concern" (758, 765). For all his farewell to formalism, Ambrose does not abandon formal priorities or, indeed, replace the abstract alphabetic form that characterized "The Amateur" and his first letter (38–42). In a late letter, Ambrose delivers alphabetized (and numbered) instructions to the author (652). In his last letter, he ironically dismisses formalism in seven sections, each containing seven subparts, beginning with the first seven letters of the alphabet. If these "letters" contain notes toward *LETTERS*, they do not achieve what they call for, "a form that spells itself while spelling out much more and (one hopes) spellbinding along the way" (767). Ambrose does not, either, relinquish his old habit of reading form onto life, and while Germaine has suffered from his insistence on "re-casting" her as his former lovers, she will surely suffer more from his belief, now he has aligned himself with the author's base-seven, that a seventh love affair will follow her. She will suffer as well if he goes to the Tower of Truth at dawn and is exploded with those other formalists, Bray and Todd Andrews, who have monumentalized art.

Ambrose only arrives near, but not at, the point from which his author begins. This point requires some insistence because of the many important similarities between Ambrose and Barth: their personal histories have entwined so closely that, as Barth writes, "we served each as the other's alter ego and aesthetic conscience; eventually even as the other's fiction" (653). Both receive awards as honorary Doctors of Letters in 1969, in Maryland, and both are described as "doctors" and "doctorers" of letters (50, 85). Both characters are referred to as "the author," even as "the Author." While Ambrose becomes "an actor in his own script now, hired to play the role of Author," Barth also takes an unusual actor's role as Author in his own creation (224–25). The two authors share a similar aesthetic history: both began as realists but turned to irrealism and avant-garde experiments (151, 340). Now, both want to recover the origins of narrative—Ambrose imagines writing "an old-fashioned novel," and Barth one "regressively traditional in manner" (336, 341). Ambrose has produced a master's thesis on the epistolary novel; in mid-August, he begins writing "fiction in the form of a letter or letters to the Author from a Middle-aged English Gentlewoman" (556). But it is only after Barth sketchily describes the novel, with its seven correspondents from his previous fictions, with its eighty-eight letters dated over seven months, that Ambrose works out his own vision of the form of LETTERS (769). Ambrose has not, however, invented the idea of multiple correspondents or envisioned the "corresponding" stories of the rest of Barth's cast.

Although he resembles Barth, then, Ambrose does not serve as a mirror—nor, if "the Author" is a second self, can Ambrose be envisioned as "a third self" for Barth, as one reviewer suggests.[37] To understand the larger issues at stake, one might consider an authentic mirroring—"Marcel" for Proust, "Arthur Morton King" for Ambrose, or "Eugene Gant" for Wolfe. Such a mirror serves to objectify, to fix, and to stabilize the author in an invariably mystified form; one witnesses the origins of creation and locates the authority of the text, but these are fundamentally extratemporal, quasi-divine. The creation of author-characters who provide a stable reflection of their creator belongs to a group of logocentric assumptions: that language mirrors reality, that the text can or should be a mirror up to nature, that the artist is an earthly allotrope of God, that good narratives reflect the large cycle of fall and redemption that is, in the Western tradition, the story of human life. Such assumptions characterize the metaphysical tradition in literature in its various (realist and modernist) phases. Like other actualists, Barth focuses some of the energy of his text on the disruption of this heritage and therefore demolishes the tidy system for which one thing is the same as another. Ambrose, then, is no more exact a reflection of his author than, say, Bray, who works at a "Bellerophoniad" like the one in Chimera and whose obsessions with Phipoints, Fibonacci numbers, and second cycles provide "a mad and useful limiting case" of the other authors' formal concerns (382). Bray is a distorting mirror—a funhouse reflection, as it were, in which his author's ideas appear comically altered. So too is Ambrose, and since every character in LETTERS becomes an author, so too is every author of letters. These altered reflections exist to celebrate differences and to restore authorship—Ambrose's, Bray's, Barth's, Germaine's—to the actualistic realm of relative time.

Placing John Barth in the text as one of the "seven fictitious drolls & dreamers, each of which imagines himself actual," Barth demystifies his own authorship as he has that of his characters. He strips authorial originality of its traditional absolute status, emphasizing instead the multiplicity of origins and sources brought to intertextual relation in the novel. Like the author, he brings the text and the reader down from their traditionally exalted frames of reference atop the Tower of Truth and locates them in history; he explodes the inherited (premodernist and modernist) models of art as timeless truth ("Art alone endures"), created by an atemporal panoptic source and consumed by a reader who is uplifted by its omniscience to the same metaphysical perceptions. Text, reader, and author are instead thrown into relative time by an actualistic narrative form open to the various, changing "nows" of writing and reading.

Where the traditional author may be understood as an absent Presence, guiding events from a position above the text, Barth elects instead to become a present absence in *LETTERS*. He enters the text to correspond with the characters; he makes himself visible and assailable inside the fiction, rejecting the convention celebrated by Flaubert of the impersonal, objective, and invisible author. He appears, moreover, as a being with a history, one more actual than invented: he shares the biography, bibliography, mailing address, and artistic concerns of an identifiable John Barth. This historicizing of the author as an actual being who lives, imagines, and writes in time, as opposed to an omniscient voice speaking from some unidentified locus beyond the end, places Barth's text in relative temporality. But while he makes himself present, Barth refuses to become the traditional authorial Presence, exemplified by Fielding, who orders the world he has ordained with omniscience and omnipotence. Instead, Barth is functionally an absence in *LETTERS*: he is not at home when the others visit; he does not answer the letters they most wish answered; he does not claim to order their lives or to "embroil himself in their imbroglios"; indeed, he claims to have nothing to do with authoring their letters or their plots. As I have suggested, Barth intends this as a benign absence: it allows his correspondents the freedom to write themselves, while he, an ironic and earthly creator, chooses Sunday as his day to address them.

He presents his own authorship as relative, rather than absolute; by displacing the origins of his text onto the characters, Barth multiplies the sources of creation and insists on their interrelations. The novel is well underway when he admits to lacking "a story, a way to tell it, and a voice to tell it in!" (53). Characters who claim Barth has used (or stolen) a version of their histories in his previous works then provide their own way of telling through letters to him. Each also suggests some crucial part of the project—the idea of sequels, the Tragic View, the subject of reenactment, the Anniversary View of history, and so on. A reader of even average sophistication will of course see through these fictive pretenses to Barth's own originary invention. But his choice of pretenses remains significant, for they help make the larger point that a postmodern novel like *LETTERS* conceives of its origins as more multiple and less unitary than a premodernist or modernist text. In Woolf's *The Waves*, for example, plural streams of consciousness are captured and represented by the author, whose power extends to a surveillance of the mental processes of her characters. The multiplicity of their voices and perceptions is gathered into unity by the single omniscient author who must be posited as their point of origin. *LETTERS* does away with such a version of omniscience and with such a unitary origin. For Barth, originality is relative; with Borges, he "maintains that 'originality' is a delusion; that we writer chaps are all more or less faithful amanuenses of the human spirit" (656).

These strategies contribute, too, to Barth's construction of a historical and temporal version of authorship. Used differently, they might produce a quite opposite effect: the author's appearance inside the text could become a metafictional device to nullify the external world, to fictionalize the author and his actual historical milieu in an infinite regress of drolls and dreamers. But the encyclopedic wealth of accurate detail in *LETTERS* makes John Barth and the America of 1969 impossible to aestheticize into neutrality. Rather, they are immersed in history to show that authorial creation occurs only and always in relation to time and is therefore a process of multiple beginnings from the midst, rather than a single moment of divine inspiration or patriarchal fiat. In the useful terms of Harris's Heideggerian analysis, "*LETTERS* acknowledges the processional nature of all artistic creation as well as the temporal horizon within which literature must move."[38] If Barth does not actually draw his characters from life or simply edit their manuscripts, he does depend on many sources for his invention: on Borges, Beckett, Calvino, and other writers he admires, for his sense of what fiction might do; on his own previous writing, for an incremental awareness of what *his* fiction might do; and on the new and revived characters he creates, as they emerge with vivid dreams of their own. Barth's "ideal postmodernist author," we recall, brings an extensive knowledge of fictional traditions to bear on his own imagination. He "neither merely repudiates nor merely imitates either his twentieth-century modernist parents or his nineteenth-century premodernist grandparents."[39] His writing emerges from a historical occasion in Western culture.

Barth's use of multiple correspondents also creates an emphasis, common to actualist fiction, on the subjectivity and uncertainty of vision. Each author brings a unique perspective and personal concerns to bear on events they share in common; from their different angles of vision, they see and record different things. The July 4 filming appears, for example, in letters by Germaine and Jerome Bray. She was not present but reports what Magda told her, which focuses on Ambrose's writing of the "Unfilmable Sequence" (390–93). Bray, however, is so dazzled by what he terms the "Blank Illuminations"—a mumbled wish by Marsha Blank to "do a number on" Ambrose—that he notices very little of the filming or the "Unfilmable Sequence" (526–27). Though Germaine's letter is more detailed and her style more realistic, the contrast does not establish her reliability as against Bray's madness. Instead, her attention is as subjectively focused on Ambrose and what concerns him as Bray's is on Bea Golden and then Marsha. Their authorship is not so much unreliable, which presumes reliability were possible, as it is inescapably limited by and to the author's point of view. The collocation of two different records of the events of July 4 does not enable the reader to construct an "objective" and hence reliable final version but reinforces the relativity of all accounts.

No one viewer can occupy a privileged frame of reference. In relativity theory, we recall, motion changes a clock's rhythm, and neither the clock on a spacecraft nor the one on earth, both of which appear slow to the observer in the other reference frame, can be understood as "accurate" in any absolute sense. Similarly, the observers in Barth's text inhabit single, moving vantage points that cannot be declared "right" or "wrong." No one character in the text—not even Germaine, for all her attention to detail—is given to know truth from falsehood, illusion from reality. Nor does John Barth, for all his authorial status and his dual roles in and out of the text, present himself as a locus of certainty. For an instructive contrast, one might recall Faulkner's *The Sound and the Fury*, where three different first-person accounts, each limited and unreliable, find resolution in the final, third-person omniscient account. Faulkner's author thus has the last word, whose effect is to unify, clarify, and lift readers out of the subjective uncertainties that characterized other narrators' versions. While Barth manages to be both "first" (chronologically) and "last" (in textual ordering), his letters do not resolve the plot or restore fragmentation to wholeness. Appropriately, readers leave Barth's construction as they enter it, without having attained a privileged, panoptic view from above.

Barth's narrative form also places an important emphasis on the relations among authors. His correspondents echo each other, answer questions they have not yet received, express similar concerns both human and aesthetic, and develop increasingly complex webs of relationship. Barth thus develops the notion of correspondence in its widest sense: not merely as writing to or addressing, but as standing in a set of relations that modify the vision of each isolated author. *LETTERS* replaces the traditional view of authorship as olympian and absolute with an actualistic and relative view. In Smollett's *Humphry Clinker*, by contrast, five writers address a one-sided correspondence to various persons outside their traveling group; their authorship exists without relation to other letters in the text, so that each one writes from a monologic, independent, absolute vantage point—one called into question by the juxtapositions of the text at large but sustained in each writer's letters. For those of Barth's correspondents who read and write each other, authorship is instead multiple, dialogic, relational, and dependent: on other authors, on history, on the writings one "receives," on the discoveries one makes in the process of writing; as Germaine says, "to put things into words works changes" (80).

The epistolary form further insists on writing's relationships to multiple (fictive, possible, actual, intended, and unintended) readers. Regardless of their addressees, the correspondents' letters are most often written for themselves; Jacob Horner's memoranda to himself are simply a more forthright form of what Todd does with his letters to his dead father, Ambrose to his imaginary Yours Truly, the Cooks to their absent children, Germaine to her silent Author, Jerome Bray to his various, indifferent audiences, or the Author to his invented progeny. But the self they address is only one of plural readers they envision—for each retains the imagination of a willing, responsive, empathetic readership. As the Author puts it, "Never mind [. . .] that we capital-*A* Authors are ultimately, ineluctably, and forever talking to ourselves. If our correspondence is after all a fiction, we like, we *need* that fiction: it makes our job less lonely" (655). The necessary fiction of a larger, unknown readership leads each fictive correspondent to send letters to the Author, as it drives the Author to publish his invented correspondence. But, most important, the very plurality of writers and their imagined readers enables the text to make its "ends" as multiple and as indeterminate as its "sources." Wolfgang Iser has by contrast envisioned *one* "implied reader" for *Humphry Clinker* and privileged "him" with the ability to construct an implicit unity from Smollett's multiplicity: "different attitudes towards the whole correspondence are suggested to the reader. His knowledge surpasses that of the individual characters, and since the author has, to a large extent, withdrawn himself from the action, and no longer comments upon it, the reader himself becomes the agent that must combine all the different elements."[40] Barth implies dozens of readers in and for *LETTERS*; more important, he does not suggest readers can or should build a final, monolithic unity by combining elements, but rather an open multiplicity.

Barth's use of the epistolary form restores the text to the realm of historic and fluctuating time.[41] Time does not flow "equably without relation to anything external" in *LETTERS* but rather speeds and slows as characters perceive it in relation to events. For Todd, "Time itself has gone torpid in Maryland since the solstice; summer limps like one long day" (457). Similarly, for Ambrose, "Everything's suspended, held, arrested, as if Time had declared time out" (528). Since these letters are written from the midst of unfinished and ongoing histories, rather than from a narrator's secure foreknowledge of the chronicle's end, they explore their writers' changing and uncertain apprehensions of time. As Barth adapts it to his postmodern project, the epistolary narrative form becomes ideally suited to express a relative, varying temporality.

Placing the letters *in* time to create a meaningful structure, Barth's elaborate and unique calendrics further insists on the temporal ground of all writing. The arrangement of letters by days of the week enables each monthly panel to spell out one letter of the novel's title; by the end, the letters also spell out the subtitle (769). As letters of the alphabet join to form words and stories and *LETTERS* and literature, the combinative and intertextual qualities of Barth's project become apparent. But this strategy places its emphasis on the temporal process of writing, as letters gradually become *LETTERS*, piece by piece. The final diagram, furthermore, allows readers to see no more than the title page announces and the text all along enacts—*LETTERS* is an old-time epistolary novel. The calendric arrangement does not, then, serve as a climactic key to the treasure but rather, ironically, conducts readers back to the text, the treasure itself. Like Barth's concluding metaphorics, where the entrance to the completed monument becomes funhouse exit, the formal arrangement invokes traditional expectations of coded, acrostic revelation—like that Nabokov uses at the end of "The Vane Sisters," which Bray mentions (330)—in order to deconstruct the epiphanic convention and its metaphysical assumptions.

By locating the writing of each letter at a specified point in time, the calendrics also establishes a focus on the conflict, pervasive in fiction, between public (clock, calendar, objective, mechanical) and private (durational, subjective, psychological) time. The letters express their writers' private apprehensions of Bergsonian *durée*; their calendric ordering provides an objective framework. Like Fielding's *Tom Jones*, *LETTERS* makes accurate use of an almanac, which Ian Watt reminds us is "that symbol of the diffusion of an objective sense of time by the printing press."[42] But *LETTERS* does not objectify, spatialize, or stop time by "placing" events in correct almanac order. The calendrics grounds the text in what Barth calls "objective reality," but helps to define it, not as a realm one may fix and know, seeing it whole with a backward-looking certainty, but rather as the actualistic locus of relativity, uncertainty, and open-ended change. Barth's ironic use of almanac time accomplishes a similar end, by different means, to Gaddis's narration from durational time in *J R*. Both texts undermine the appeal to calendar time, in narratives like Fielding's, to stabilize reality: Barth's makes elaborate use of the calendar, while Gaddis's makes none, but both strategies enable the presentation of a relative temporality.

Each correspondent in *LETTERS* emphasizes the temporal occasion of writing. The insistence on various "nows" in Barth's text recalls, of course, Richardson's writing "to the Moment," whose comic potential, exploited in Fielding's *Shamela*, Barth also appreciates—like Shamela, Germaine writes in extremis and even in flagrante delicto on occasion. But beyond the parody of this epistolary convention, Barth uses it to make the serious point that writing is, like all human activities, defined by temporality; it is not eternal but written and read at a specific and finite series of "nows." It emerges in reaction to a background of current social and political events (the Vietnam War, for example) which influence authors and shape their artistic concerns. The author's first letter to the reader characterizes the state of the world on March 2, 1969, with a thoroughness of detail common to actualistic texts—one recalls especially Coover's *Public Burning* and Pynchon's *Gravity's Rainbow*. His commitment to the idea of "ongoing history" also leads Barth to remark on the finitude of characters, nations, and even authors. The "last of a letter's times" is that of its reading; Barth concludes his first letter to the reader by speculating, "Perhaps you're yet to have been conceived, and by the 'now' your eyes read *now*, every person now alive upon the earth will be no longer, most certainly not excepting / Yours truly" (45). Even the text itself must eventually succumb to time, since Barth holds, with Ambrose, that "art passes too." Noting that he shares an "apocalyptic concern" with the characters of *The Tidewater Tales*, Barth says in a recent interview that his concern is not with "the afterlife of individual characters but with the future life of the species on the planet, which is sufficient cause for anxiety, it seems to me."[43] His view of writing, indeed of human survival, as located in and subject to time contributes to Barth's larger refutation of any eternal or absolute frame of reference.

For all his belief in "ongoing history," however, Barth does not re-create in *LETTERS* the one-way chronological line that leads, in the Western tradition, to final revelation. Where Pynchon explodes the linear temporality of realistic fiction with the multiple gaps that create what I have called quantum discontinuity, Barth inverts the time-line and combines it with an open version of the mythic cycle to form a particularly appropriate spiral shape in *LETTERS*. By turning the calendric month on its side and ordering the letters top to bottom, Barth reenacts in the form of the text a concept central to its theme: one must go backward in order to go forward. The result, as he describes it with a tidal metaphor, is a plot that "will surge forward, recede, surge farther forward, recede less far" (49). The process of reading a plot constructed in this fashion reflects the letter writers' processes of writing, backing up to account for events that have happened since their previous letters, and also their processes of exploring their current situations, for they recall and recount the "first cycle" of their lives in order to understand their position in the second. For every character, these loosely self-repetitive cycles follow in a general way the heroic cycle articulated by Raglan and Campbell and cited by Ambrose. Barth opens up the cycle, though, by envisioning a second cycle "isomorphic with the '1st'" but never identical, even for characters who strain to make it so—for, as Ambrose sees, "Cycle II must not reenact its predecessor: echo, yes; repeat, no" (655, 767). The plot at large manages echoes in abundance, moving, for example, from the funeral of Harrison Mack to the funeral of Joe Morgan, but places its emphasis on the differences between recurring situations. The temporal form of the narrative thus breaks open the mythic circle as it breaks up the realistic line, achieving the "grand spiral" Germaine hopes for in her marriage, which "will curve on and out at least beyond our sight" (678).

Like other actualist texts, *LETTERS* withholds the closure traditionally granted at the end of time-lines, mythic cycles, and literary texts both premodern and modern. Narrative resolution appeals, after all, to a Newtonian faith that absolute motion culminates in absolute rest; in an Einsteinian cosmos, narratives must instead acknowledge ongoing changes of diffuse energies that never come to rest. So Barth's spiral remains open: the fate of each correspondent ends unresolved. None of them manages the recovery of origins or the reconciliation with the father they have sought—Andrea King Mensch dies without providing the key to Ambrose's paternity; Todd breaks off his lifelong correspondence with his dead father without reconciliation or revelation; in the silence of his parents, Bray turns further back, to his dead "granama," who is as silent as the others; Cook never recovers his lost son; Germaine finally gives up hope for a relationship with her lost son. No revolution is brought to culmination in the novel, but instead most of the revolutionaries embark near the end on new pursuits. No artistic project achieves completion— *Frames* is burned; NUMBERS is left, undecoded, to Lilyvac; Ambrose's various ideas, notes, and drafts are sent to the author; and the author is only beginning to draft *LETTERS*. Where it invokes the traditional closures of comic and tragic plots, *LETTERS* undermines their conventional status as the end of the story. The marriages of Jacob, Germaine, and Ambrose appear as complex rebeginnings that do not resolve difficulties or finish these characters' stories but rather change their directions. The deaths of Todd, Cook, and Bray are shrouded in uncertainty, and the possible inclusion of Ambrose in the Tower of Truth explosion muddies the traditional distinction between comic and tragic closure—he may have achieved both marriage and death.

When he declares, then, that "*LETTERS* reaches herewith and 'now' [. . .] the end" (771–72), the Author invokes the terms of the patriarchal fiat ironically, without providing the certainty and rest commonly conferred by such a patriarch—without, as he puts it in an interview, "lowering some god down on wires."[44] If we recall the end of a text like Dickens's *Hard Times*, where the omniscient narrator resolves the present action and foretells the futures of every central character, we can recognize the effects of such a god on wires to neutralize uncertainty and thereby bring his story to absolute rest. Barth's instincts are different. "Rightly or wrongly, I felt it critical that the reader remain in doubt, for example, about whether that tower Todd Andrews is last seen holed up in blows up or not."[45] It matters, too, that between "now" and "the end," Barth defines that moment in its historic temporality, locating the text one final time against its actual, sociopolitical grounds: "Further U.S. troop withdrawals from Southeast Asia scheduled for the fall" (772). Even at this conclusive moment, he emphasizes too the *processes*, rather than the *ends*, of writing: "the Author outlines this last on Tuesday, July 4, 1978 [. . .] drafts this in longhand at Chautauqua Lake, N.Y., on Monday, July 10, 1978 [. . .] types this on October 5, 1978" (771). This inconclusive conclusion reasserts that relative time, not eternity, is the medium of texts and lives, which reach their end but not their resolution.

SIX

MARGARET

ATWOOD

CAT'S EYE AND THE

SUBJECTIVE AUTHOR

Like other actualists, Margaret Atwood believes that art expresses a vision of reality. She argues that it intervenes in and modifies reality: like the new physicist, the writer does not simply report on a static external truth but rather changes the system she observes. Writing, in Atwood's view, acts as a moral agent. "I believe that fiction writing is the guardian of the moral and ethical sense of the community . . . fiction is one of the few forms left through which we may examine our society not in its particular but in its typical aspects; through which we can see ourselves." Writing also exposes the political use and abuse of power. "Traditionally the novel has been used not only as a vehicle for social commentary but as a vehicle for political commentary as well. The novelist, at any rate, still sees a connection between politics and the moral sense, even if politicians gave that up some time ago. By 'political' I mean having to do with power: who's got it, who wants it, how it operates."[1]

Unlike the other novelists I've discussed, Atwood has not been read as a writer of metafiction. Instead, she is often misread as an old-fashioned realist whose fiction is formally conservative. As Molly Hite argues persuasively in *The Other Side of the Story* (1989), Atwood is among a group of contemporary women writers who are seen as avoiding entirely the formal experimentation that distinguishes postmodernist fiction by men. While postmodern alternatives to realism have, Hite observes, "strong affinities with a specifically feminist interrogation of the assumptions encoded in realist conventions," contemporary women writers are nonetheless regarded as "conservative, upholders of tradition and thus to be found among the perpetuators of a realism that continues to flourish alongside the modes of writing that play off it."[2] Atwood is, therefore, excluded from the "rigorously masculinist" canon under construction: though by 1991 six monographs and three collections of essays, as well as scores of journal articles, have argued the importance of her writing; though she has published seven novels, two books of nonfiction prose, fifteen books of poems, and two collections of stories, Atwood is not listed among the hundred-odd writers of *Postmodern Fiction* in Larry McCaffery's extensive "Bio-Bibliographical Guide." As a Canadian, she is not mentioned in studies like those by Kuehl, LeClair, Klinkowitz, Caramello, Wilde, Gorak, Porush, and Hayles, most of which focus on fiction written in the United States.

Atwood's fiction deserves a place in the international company of experimental narratives; thematically important and formally interesting, it stands up to comparison with the fiction of Atwood's southern and eastern neighbors. A quick sketch here may indicate the kinship I see between Atwood's fiction and that of other actualists. A fundamental impulse to satirize societies gone over to greed, hypocrisy, and materialism appears through all of Atwood's texts, beginning with her first novel, *The Edible Woman* (1969); similar satire appears in *J R* and throughout Barthelme's fiction. A fascination with the neatness of finished plots, both fictive and historical, set against the sprawling accidental messiness of life, preoccupies Nixon in *The Public Burning* and Joan Foster in *Lady Oracle* (1976). A preterite-eye view of systems of power, with their origins in the lusts of insecure men and their ends in forms of sanctioned rape, appears in *The Handmaid's Tale* (1985) as in *Gravity's Rainbow*. The past, both historical and personal, returns to trouble and to fecundate the present vision of artists in *Cat's Eye* (1988) as in *LETTERS*.

Like other actualists, Atwood invokes some specific new physical theories in her fiction. *Cat's Eye*, her most recent and most actualistic novel, acknowledges its author's use of material from popularized versions of new physics: "The physics and cosmology sideswiped herein are indebted to Paul Davies, Carl Sagan, John Gribbin, and Stephen W. Hawking, for their entrancing books on these subjects, and to my nephew, David Atwood, for his enlightening remarks about strings." One of the novel's two epigraphs is from Hawking's *Brief History of Time* (1988): "Why do we remember the past, and not the future?"[3] The novel's beginning invokes relative theories of space-time: "Time is not a line but a dimension, like the dimensions of space. If you can bend space you can bend time also, and if you knew enough and could move faster than light you could travel backward in time and exist in two places at once" (3). Similarly, Hawking writes: "Imaginary time is indistinguishable from directions in space. . . . if one can go forward in imaginary time, one ought to be able to turn round and go backward."[4] Throughout the novel, new physical concepts are introduced by Elaine Risley's brother, Stephen (named, perhaps, for Hawking): he tells Elaine about the expanding universe and receding stars (110), about the curvature of space-time, about Einstein's thought-experiment in which one identical twin returns from a journey in space to find the other twin older, and about the intertwined nature of matter and energy (233). Become a famous physicist, Stephen delivers a lecture, "The First Picoseconds and the Quest for a Unified Field Theory," which echoes both Hawking and John Gribbin's *Genesis: The Origins of Man and the Universe* (1981). In his last months, Stephen explores string theory (408–9). Atwood makes, if anything, even more reference to the realm of physics than do Pynchon, Barth, or Coover. Like them, she sets her fiction in a world defined not by Newtonian certainty but by Hawkingian speculation upon an always uncertain ground.

In particular, Atwood focuses in *Cat's Eye* on the nature of subjectivity, as it is constructed in (and against) a traditional androcentric culture. For the humanist tradition, subject and object are absolutely separated; they are also gendered and arranged in a hierarchy of value. The subject, or self, is sovereign, transcendent, unitary—and male. The object, conversely, is passive, material, knowable—and female. Feminists have argued that this subject/object duality basic to humanist conceptions of self and world functions to devalue and exclude women. As Margaret Homans writes,

> For the same reason that women are identified with nature and matter in any traditional thematics of gender . . . women are also identified with the literal, the absent referent in our predominant myth of language. . . . A dualism of presence and absence, of subject and object, structures everything our culture considers thinkable; yet women cannot participate in it as subjects as easily as can men because of the powerful, persuasive way in which the feminine is again and again said to be on the object's side of that dyad. Women who do conceive of themselves as subjects—that is, as present, thinking women rather than as "woman"—must continually guard against fulfilling those imposed definitions by being returned to the position of the object.[5]

In the position of object, woman is silent; as part of the realm of nature and matter, she doesn't share in the process of thinking, knowing, and figuration that positions the masculine subject in the symbolic order for Freud, Lacan, and the Western tradition.

The subject/object dichotomy is as crucial to classical physics as it is to the humanist tradition. The scientific method of detached objectivity presumed an absolute separation of subject and object and a clear division within the subject. "Man" can "know" "nature"—leap across the gap—by virtue of the rational intelligence; abandoning all private and personal bias, desire, and feeling, the Newtonian scientist and the realist author/ narrator could forge secure connections between the knowing self and the material object. The subject of science is, then, a thinking but not a feeling self: the affective realm is gendered female and regarded as inferior. The highest form of subjectivity appears in scientific inquiry, where scientific reason, purified of baser attachments, solves the riddles of creation. But the subject of science is not, as Luce Irigaray observes, neutral, detached, unsexed. "He manipulates nature, utilizes it, exploits it, but forgets that he is also in nature, that he is still physical and not only in front of the phenomena whose physical nature he fails to recognize. Advancing according to an objective method that would shelter him from all instability, from all moods, from all emotions and affective fluctuations, from all intuitions that are not programed in science's name, from all interference by his desires, especially those that are sexed, he settles himself down, in his discoveries, in the systematic."[6] His syntax, Irigaray argues, privileges identity, noncontradiction, and binary oppositions (like the one between subject and object); it eliminates qualitative difference, reciprocity, exchange, permeability, and fluidity. His discourse is governed by a devaluation of his own affections, with the result that he is split within himself and alienated from his own desires. The division of subject and object has, then, been destructive for the transcendent male subject as well as for the manipulated female object.

Static binary dualities of all kinds have been discredited by contemporary theorists and replaced with forms of exchange and dynamic interaction. Subjectivity is radically redefined to include influences going both ways between subject and object: the subject can't erase parts of itself in order to achieve an unmediated confrontation with the object, and the object resists being grasped. Objectivity and omniscience are gone; in what may be the most dramatic shift between classical and new physics, scientists now perceive subjectivity permeating their relation to reality, an inescapable aspect of thinking about external states. Science cannot proceed with rational objectivity, nor is there any way to detach the observer from the observed. There can be no true and valid knowledge of the physical world into which the subjective knower doesn't enter from first to last. Einstein's theories began to move in this direction, though he continued to hope for objective confirmation; he wrote that "physical concepts are free creations of the human mind, and are not, however it may seem, uniquely determined by the objective world."[7] The work in subatomic theory of Bohr, de Broglie, Schrödinger, and Born led toward the conclusion Heisenberg reached with the uncertainty principle: that the observer does not issue a neutral report on external facts but rather changes the picture—even determines which parts of it are visible—in the act of observation. While this recognition limits physicists' power to know nature, to speak authoritatively, and to present "true facts," it also liberates them for a far more active use of the subjective imagination. Heisenberg focuses the dynamic quality of this role: "Science no longer confronts nature as an objective observer, but sees itself as an *actor* in this interplay between man and nature."[8]

We now imagine subject and object, not separated according to the conventional polarity, but rather interacting in "one inseparable process," as Raymond Williams suggests.[9] As a result, our notions of art, science, and thought itself are changing. Traditional models of the way subjectivity is gendered have been exposed as damaging and dangerous. Both the male subject who "transcends" his subjectivity to decode the external world and the female object whose nature is penetrated by his gaze reflect myths of conquest and colonization, rape and enslavement, dominance and submission. Responding to theoretical assumptions newly important in physics, as well as in political philosophy and feminism, the subject and object become permeable and open to reciprocity and exchange. Subjectivity extends to women as well as men; it is engaged, interested, and open to dialogue with other beings and with the world. The subject does not lose itself in inquiry, nor does it assert power over the objects of its study. Rather, the subject engages the object in an unfolding process of questioning, in which each modifies the other without combat, conquest, or loss to either side.

Such an engaged subjectivity animates Atwood's fiction, which portrays an interplay of subjects, who display a range of rational and emotional responses, and objects that cannot be known, grasped, or objectively represented. For Atwood, the artist's inescapable subjectivity leads from the subject to the world: "In writing, your attention is focused not on the self but on the thing being made, the thing being seen. . . . It is not 'expressing yourself.' It is opening yourself, discarding your *self*, so that the language and the world may be evoked through you."[10] At the same time, the world the artist evokes reveals its deep masculinist bias and thereby foregrounds the aberrant gender and subjectivity of the woman artist who calls it to account. In exploring this uneasy reciprocity, Atwood often focuses on the woman subject whose right to subjectivity, and especially *rational* subjectivity, is blandly denied by her culture. In her best-known novel, *The Handmaid's Tale*, a misogynist fundamentalism acts to strip women of subjectivity, in part with clothing that identifies them as objects categorized for use, in part with social proscriptions that deny them access to language. Rational architects of the social good, the commanders give themselves sovereign rights to subjectivity. The nameless handmaid, rendered a sexual object and maternal container for the seed of her commander, barred from the written word and ordered to speak only banal formulas, tells her story in a defiant act asserting the woman subject. Yet, in this dystopian satire, the broader social, economic, political, environmental, religious, and even biological conditions make women's subjectivity precarious.

Exploring an artist's education—the way her culture inscribes metaphysical and masculinist assumptions that would neutralize her voice, the way she learns to talk back—*Cat's Eye* probes the nature of actualistic subjectivity. Its features appear vividly in Elaine Risley's self-portrait, also called "Cat's Eye."

> My head is in the right foreground, though it's shown only from the middle of the nose up . . . I've put in the incipient wrinkles, the little chicken feet at the corners of the lids. A few gray hairs. This is cheating, as in reality I pull them out.
>
> Behind my half-head, in the center of the picture, in the empty sky, a pier glass is hanging, convex and encircled by an ornate frame. In it, a section of the back of my head is visible; but the hair is different, younger.
>
> At a distance, and condensed by the curved space of the mirror, there are three small figures, dressed in the winter clothing of the girls of forty years ago. They walk forward, their faces shadowed, against a field of snow (430).

Looking at herself, the painter sees images suggesting the distorted, personal, "framed," and enframing nature of vision. The painting is doubly mediated by mirrors: she looks in one mirror to paint the portrait of her present, external self. Informing this objective image is the other, subjective image, also seen in a mirror—the long-past, seen-from-behind, never-objectively-seen image of the back of her head. The distant, condensed figures of her three inexorable friends/tormentors reveal the memory that drives the painter: not of a particular event that occurred in objective space and time, but of a set of feelings (exclusion, shame, humiliation, worthlessness, fragmentation, emptiness) she subjectively suffered during several years. The reflection in the pier glass is not "there" in any objective space, either present or past, but is a painted image of the power—the luminous and disturbing presence—of the subjective.

Yet the subjective realm in the painting does not erase or replace the objective realm, nor does it "explain" or "solve" the riddle of the artist's vision. Conjoining both objective and subjective realms, the portrait suggests that the two meet in a necessary, limiting, and liberating interaction. This "self-portrait, of sorts" does not portray the conventional "self"—sovereign, universal, self-present, unitary. The objectively seen face in this painting is split and partial, neither wholly present nor forming a stable center for the painting: it is a half-circle, off-center, bisected through the nose. While clearly recognizable and detailed (with "incipient wrinkles"), this "objective" image falsifies reality, showing gray hairs that the painter pulls out. The subjectively recalled figure in the painting is similarly fractured; only "a section" of the back of her head appears. Nor is this subject transcendent, a creator of artistic or mnemonic order beyond the historical realm. Instead, she is driven by history, in the form of three figures who represent girlhood as the discourses of their culture construct it. Girlhood, in Toronto as in Gilead, means a style of clothing and acting and thinking; it means submerging the individual subject in a group identity.

The painting observes the rupture of Elaine's "self," which does not appear whole anywhere on the canvas. It shows the woman's and artist's eyes that emerge from the site of fracture, lower right, to see in a decentered way from a position at the margins. The painting sees inclusively, in nonbinary terms suggesting permeable double realms: it portrays both past and present, both artist and world, both history and feeling. It does not romanticize its own artistic vision, nor does the novel (unlike a modernist kunstlerroman) portray the artistic subject as the origin of meaning, controller of destiny, or locus of timeless truth. Though Elaine envies the cool glassy eternity of the "cat's eye," the spherical, complete, contained, sightless marble like "the eyes of something that isn't known but exists anyway . . . like the eyes of aliens from a distant planet" (67), her own eyes are not detached or transcendent but fully immersed in the conflicting, fragmentary details of this actual planet.

The Divided Woman Subject

Reviewers of Cat's Eye find it powerful as a story of girlhood friendship and cruelty but flawed, in degrees ranging from major to minor, by anticlimax and disunity. The reviewers object to the lack of a unitary self and plot in the novel, and their complaints reflect the novel's unusual (troubling) treatment of the woman subject. Elaine Risley's later life appears to have little to do with her intense battle, at nine, to assert her own worth in the face of severe criticism by her friends Cordelia, Grace Smeath, and Carol Campbell. In a favorable review, Alice McDermott notes that "inevitably, the emotional intensity of these early scenes makes the more familiar material of Elaine's later life seem somewhat anticlimactic."[11] In a negative review, Judith Thurman expresses grave reservations over the same issue. "But 'Cat's Eye' might best have ended when Elaine's ordeal ends, on page 206. A child has gambled and lost her self and recovered it, and from here on the tension dissipates. Atwood attempts to pump suspense back into the narrative and to restore its unity by insisting on Risley's unresolved obsession with Cordelia. . . . She kills off Stephen improbably long after he, too, has ceased to count in his sister's life or for the reader."[12] The novel fails to meet the old standards of unity and economy; it exceeds the boundaries of the conventional bildungsroman, whose proper fulfillment is the recovery of the lost self.

An even more revealing review praises *Cat's Eye* for its "return to form"; this reviewer locates the unity the others miss. Carole Angier's brief description of the plot performs miracles of selection in making the novel seem a single, well-orchestrated story, while suppressing the elements of discord and excess that trouble other reviewers. "It's the story of Elaine Risley, a middle-aged painter, who has lost herself for 40 years because she's forgotten the central experience of her childhood. . . . The book itself uncovers the mystery to us little by little, interleaved with Elaine's present, as she walks the streets of Toronto for the first time since the events she now remembers."[13] The desire reflected in this innocent summary— to peel away extraneous detail and to expose the essential coherence of Atwood's endeavor in its focus on the recovered self, the old metaphysical self of essences—appears frequently in the large body of criticism published on Atwood. Such a poetics eliminates change: forgetting is always followed by remembering, and the self one loses at nine reappears unchanged at forty-nine. This sovereign self has never really entered the differential matrix of the world outside; subject and object don't affect or alter each other. But Atwood hasn't written such a novel. Elaine doesn't immediately leave Toronto to abandon "the central experience" of her lost child-self; she lives in Toronto for twenty years after the events of her childhood. She completes high school, attends university and art school, has an affair with Josef, marries Jon, gives birth to Sarah, begins to show her paintings, and changes daily as she lives in Toronto. The novel does not focus on the illumination of the mystery of childhood torture; that stands fully revealed and resolved by page 206, leaving 240 pages that don't belong, at least according to the reviews.

Atwood chooses her inclusions and digressions, her own form of unity, to suit her novel's focus on a woman subject who is divided and scarred by her position in a culture that prefers to understand woman as object. The woman subject fails to triumph over or transcend her culture: *Cat's Eye* doesn't end on page 206 because it doesn't assume that a sovereign self can achieve victory over a threatening external world. Atwood's protagonists have never been unitary, transcendent selves seen in isolation; rather, they are gendered subjects struggling within and against cultural definitions and expectations. They don't lose and recover selves any more than they vanquish culture; culture helps to shape, though it doesn't determine, who they are. In *Cat's Eye*, a conservative patriarchal culture educates women, exerting its formative influence through schools, churches, parents, stores, fashions, toys, comic books, and friends. These authorities teach "femininity": what choices, allegiances, limitations, value, and identity girls and women may have, as distinct from boys and men. A double standard emerges on the first day of elementary school, when children learn they must go in by different doors. Boys and girls don't, later, have the same doors open to them.

The culture that positions women in Atwood's fiction is patriarchal, authoritarian, and misogynist; it places women at the bottom and on the margins. Elaine lives her first eight years in nature, with parents who reject many of Toronto's values and assumptions. When her family returns to the city, Elaine receives an accelerated course in culture from Carol and Grace, who teach her the devalued identity assigned to women. She learns at once to deprecate her own achievements; she learns that women don't achieve. The girls cut up *Eaton's Catalogues*, used up north as toilet paper, to make scrapbook collections depicting women and the domestic objects women "properly" consume. They praise each other's pages while denigrating their own: " 'Oh, yours is so good. Mine's no good. Mine's *awful.*' . . . Their voices are wheedling and false; I can tell they don't mean it, each one thinks her own lady on her own page is good. But it's the thing you have to say, so I begin to say it too" (56). To succeed as a girl, Elaine realizes, she doesn't have to make "any effort at all": "I don't have to think about whether I've done these things well, as well as a boy. All I have to do is sit on the floor and cut frying pans out of the *Eaton's Catalogue* with embroidery scissors, and say I've done it badly. Partly this is a relief" (57). While male worth like her brother's proves itself through active effort and accomplishment, female value comes in a humble passivity—in denigrating, muffling, and muting, rather than asserting, one's subjectivity.

The grown women in *Cat's Eye* fulfill the promise of these scrapbooks. The mothers of Elaine's three friends do very little, make very little, earn very little; none has an income aside from what their husbands give them. Passive, conventional, and concerned with appearances, each is squarely placed in the world of domestic objects, and each appears as a dependent object—for veneration, use, indulgence, control, consumption—to her husband's subject. Carol's mother buys, treasures, aspires to, owns, and consumes domestic objects. With less money, Grace's mother frantically conserves objects, washing the underwear to a dim grayness, restricting the supply of toilet paper to three squares per visit, guarding her own frail and meager heart with a daily rest. Cordelia's mother, the most wealthy of the three, decorates objects. She takes painting classes and produces "pretty" things to hang on the wall; she decorates and redecorates her houses and her daughters. Absentminded and frivolous, each of the three is as silent as her object-status would prescribe; in particular, each has no voice at all when her husband is present. These women are not much different from the wives in *The Handmaid's Tale*, who colluded with their husbands to produce a social system that erases women's freedom and, surrounding them with luxurious objects, makes them one of the properties of the house.

Woman as Abject: Cordelia

From the role of the silent and devalued object, the women of *Cat's Eye* find it easy to descend the small step to the role of the erased, canceled, abject object. In this state of pathological self-loathing, Julia Kristeva suggests, both subject and object disappear; a nullified, canceled subject can't find an erased, phantom object.[14] The woman becomes abject, cast away (from the Latin *abjectus*: *ab-*, "away," and *jacere*, "to throw"). The abject is contemptible, wretched, miserable, mean, vile. Split, worthless, and empty, the subject encounters no sustaining object; no exchange or engagement can occur, but only silence and fear. She becomes a nonobject, negated and denied. It is the next, logical transmutation of the woman who, in Homans's "traditional thematics of gender," not only bears the word of "her own status as a silent natural object" but also occupies the linguistic place of the *absent* object, the *absent* referent.[15] In the culture described by Atwood's fiction, women are made into nullified objects, rendered absent, cast away.

Throughout her fiction, Atwood takes for her focus the woman who is denied subjectivity. Taught to be submissive and passive, told by the authorities of her culture that she is worth less, and less worthy of subjectivity, that she contains filth and defilement, and that she *is* nothing but a container, woman finds that she is a precariously flawed object. Trained to listen to other voices, she hears contempt and loathing from paternal authorities in home, church, school, and state. For the daughters of patriarchal culture, as a result, acculturation has become synonymous with abjection. This culture makes women the abject, the outcast, the erased from history. For political reasons, then, women write the daughter's abjection, whose effects ricochet back through culture: the ritualized paternal rape of *The Handmaid's Tale*, the paternal desertion of *Life before Man*, the paternal beatings and rape of *Bodily Harm*—and elsewhere, the paternal abuse of Alice Walker's *Color Purple* and Joan Didion's *Democracy*.

Raised by a father who loathes women, Cordelia stands for the possibility of self-erasure; though sketchy, her story illustrates the reduction of the woman subject to objecthood, and eventually to the status of the canceled and nullified abject. Cordelia's fate stands as the complementary other half of Elaine's: she is not so much Elaine's nemesis as her reflection in a distorting mirror. Her story, itself as fragmented and partial as the painting of Elaine's head, makes Elaine's reinvention of her necessary, much as her active intervention helps create Elaine in her own image. The two appear in Elaine's narrative, not as subject and object, but as intertwined subjectivities creating each other in response to a father who would reduce them both to the abject.

Toronto, and the West more generally, orbit in *Cat's Eye* the dark power of the fathers, who have designed hierarchies of value that place women at the bottom and girls below them. The fathers of Atwood's girls resemble Broderick Slothrop, using their children as objects and selling them out; the difference is that Broderick appears affable and disinterested in his son, while Atwood's fathers display active contempt and fury toward their daughters. The fathers appear only by night: "Darkness brings home the fathers, with their real, unspeakable power" (175). Fathers rage and punish: Cordelia's father terrifies his household, and Carol Campbell's father whips her with the buckle end of the belt. Even the Smeath household, which appears to be run by the mother, actually obeys a grimly repressive father, for Mrs. Smeath rules in the name of a judgmental God. Her eyes are "heavy with unloved duty. The eyes of someone for whom God was a sadistic old man" (427). Behind all three girls' punishment of Elaine under the guise of reforming her lies the father's refusal of his daughter's subjectivity—his will to recast her as a silent, compliant object, or to cast her out as the repellent abject. Elaine has been exempt; her father is kindly and nonabusive. She must hear this fatherly voice, which reigns in Toronto, from others. Her best friend Cordelia, named for a daughter destroyed by the father, vocalizes the father's punitive contempt as she forces Elaine into abject silence. First, of course, she suffers the same process herself.

Although he is not the originator of the chain of abuse, which extends behind him into previous generations and above him to Mrs. Smeath's (and other Torontonians') God, Cordelia's father represents patriarchal power in *Cat's Eye* and thus speaks for his civilization. He is most often absent from his house and rarely seen in the novel, yet his presence looms over both. Vengeful and deceptive, he punishes in private but hides his destructive anger behind a facade of charm and affability in public. He is two-faced: "He is large, craggy, charming, but we have heard him shouting, upstairs" (77). He conveys a scarcely evolved, wild-animal roughness, "with his craggy eyebrows, his wolvish look," incongruously joined with a highly civilized charm: he "bends upon me the full force of his ponderous, ironic, terrifying charm" (263). His speech itself is duplicitous, ironic, mocking, especially when he disclaims power. " 'I'm hag-ridden,' he says, pretending to be mournful. 'The only man in a houseful of women. They won't let me into the bathroom in the morning to shave.' Mockingly, he invites my sympathy and collusion" (263). His charm is ponderous, as believable and terrifying as his fury. Both express his fear and loathing of the woman subject; both aim to control her.

This fatherly contempt for the woman produces (as elsewhere in Atwood's fiction) a deeply divided house.[16] Household functions have two different forms: when he is there, the women behave formally and suppress their voices; when he is not, they express ideas and desires and feelings. When he is absent, dinners are casual, loose; the women "jump up from the table, saunter into the kitchen for more butter. . . . They talk all at once, in a languid, amused way, and groan when it's their turn to clear the table" (263). When the father is home, flowers, pearls, candles, "neatly rolled" napkins, proper posture, and silence among the women appear by contrast. In the presence of their father, "None of the girls jokes or drawls" (77). He muzzles and muffles the women, which means they must pretend, in his presence, to be nonsubjects.

His wife is the perfect product of his fatherly conditioning: she almost never speaks. She has renounced aggression, practical competence, the production of marketable goods, and most forms of adult responsibility in order to remain childlike, a model of decorative (girlish) femininity. Her daughters "speak of her with affection and indulgence, as if she's a bright but willful child who has to be humored. She's tiny, fragile, absent-minded; she wears glasses on a silver chain around her neck and takes painting classes. Some of her paintings hang in the upstairs hall, greenish paintings of flowers, of lawns, of bottles and vases" (77). Her arts are decorative, designed to grace the domestic realm; these floral paintings are a trope for the identity (sweet, small, fragile, pluckable) she offers up to her husband's consumption. While she has some education (she attends the ballet, she names her daughters Perdita, Miranda, and Cordelia from Shakespeare), she cultivates the "absent-minded" air preferred in women, inept, vague, full of flowery feeling but without thought. In choosing the names of three daughters raised motherless, taught by their fathers and used as instruments of patriarchal will, Cordelia's "Mummie" acquiesces to a power structure in which she is effaced, erased, and mummi-fied—reduced to a female object.

Cordelia's older sisters are plagued by their own deep divisions between experiencing themselves as subjects and being returned by the way they are seen to the position of objects. As they mature, they inevitably take on the feminine identity endorsed by their parents and their culture, with its dual assertion that their value emerges from their status as beautiful objects, and that they are merely female objects, worthless and inadequate. Their greatest investments of time and art are devoted to bodily self-perfection. They file their nails, heat wax to remove the hair on their legs, anxiously "look into their mirrors" as they perform these rites of self-improvement (97). But, in a house where Daddy complains he is "hag-ridden," the sisters' mirror is haunted by this specter: the old, unmarried, useless, and unwanted woman-object. "Sometimes they say, 'I look like an absolute hag,' and sometimes, 'I look like Haggis McBaggis.' This is an ugly old woman they seem to have made up" (76), Elaine thinks, though Daddy more likely brought her into their discourse. Predictably, the girls find themselves most wanting, most flawed and failing, when they are menstruating: "I look like Haggis McBaggis! It's the curse!" (97). They earnestly polish and improve; they fail, again and again, to come up to the mark, because their arts are betrayed by nature—specifically, by their nature as women.

The figure most deeply split by her father's misogyny, Cordelia vacillates between insisting on her own subjectivity in passionate acts and gestures, which the adults around her can read only as signs of rebellion, and attempts to win adult approval by acting the polite, restrained female object. From her first appearance at age nine, she has one parentally approved side: she has "beautiful manners," a "voice for adults," and a "smile like a grown-up's" (123, 74). Sophisticated, she knows Giselle and

Swedish glass. But Cordelia is also rebellious, wild where Grace and Carol are tame, untidy in her room and sloppy in her personal habits, and inherently disrespectful of adults (138). This side of Cordelia expresses itself in "a defiant, almost belligerent stare," a "stubborn, defiant look" (239, 378). Feeling herself a subject, Cordelia refuses to play the *Eaton's Catalogue* game, draws mustaches on the models, invents, acts, and creates dramas. She not only refuses to repress abject and excremental substances but exposes and explores them in fascination—she shows the other girls menstrual blood, and her first remark to Elaine is, "There's dog poop on your shoe" (97, 75). Elaine understands this position as uncivilized, unfeminine, and inherently rebellious. Mr. Smeath and Stephen "are on the side of ox eyeballs, toe jam under the microscope, the outrageous, the subversive. Outrageous to whom, subversive of what? Of Grace and Mrs. Smeath, of tidy paper ladies pasted into scrapbooks. Cordelia ought to be on this side too. Sometimes she is, sometimes she isn't" (132–33). Cordelia swings between the poles of passive submission to, and energetic defiance of, the role of tidy paper lady-object. In her outrageous phase, she not only refuses the limits of cultural propriety, she also rejects the constraints of femininity: she plays the male role in the girls' dramas and draws mustaches on female models, as if to escape objecthood by renouncing her gender.

Cordelia's father reduces her to object and abject. He prevents her self-possession and punishes any expression of her subjectivity. He would like his daughters to be his own silent possessions, and Cordelia has always had a hard time pretending to comply. Cordelia tells Elaine that as a child, she wanted to dig a hole in the ground where she could sit by herself. "I wanted someplace that was all mine, where nobody could bug me. When I was little, I used to sit on a chair in the front hall. I used to think that if I kept very still and out of the way and didn't say anything, I would be safe. . . . When I was really little, I guess I used to get into trouble a lot, with Daddy. When he would lose his temper. You never knew when he was going to do it. 'Wipe that smirk off your face,' he would say. I used to stand up to him" (267–68). Cordelia's father instructs her in her own abject worthlessness. He teaches her to fear male anger and to avoid it by keeping still. Cordelia learns his contempt and disgust; these have evidently little to do with her actions ("You never knew when he was going to do it") but rather with her existence, her expression, her sex and age. She understands that she has the wrong face. She tries to efface herself, to put on masks and roles. She realizes that she has no place in Daddy's house, and foreshadowing her later life, she must dig a grave in order to make a room of her own.

At nine, Cordelia adopts Elaine as a double, twin, and alter ego: determined to preserve her own worthiness, Cordelia projects onto Elaine the role of the bad, rebellious, defiant child, the daughter Daddy rejects. Cordelia digs a hole to make her own space in the back yard; then she buries *Elaine* in it, as if to dramatize the transferal of her "bad" side and her will to punish and repress it. Cordelia plays the long-suffering parent teaching an abnormal, errant child proper behavior. "Wipe that smirk off your face," she says to Elaine on various occasions, aligning herself with her father's perspective on offensive girls (183, 205). In the viciousness of her cruelty to Elaine, Cordelia shows how bitterly hurt and angry she feels toward her own parent. Simultaneously, she demonstrates an earnest will to be the good daughter, not only by detaching herself from those "bad" traits that express the woman's forbidden subjectivity, but by condemning the daughterly badness she locates in Elaine.

After Elaine breaks away, Cordelia is left to struggle with the forbidden subject who comes home. She can no longer project her outward and disown her; neither can she reintegrate the defiance, aggression, desire, and anger she feels, or approve the subjective responses she has been condemned for having. Sent off to private school by Daddy, Cordelia rebels against male authority; she draws a penis on a bat and labels it with the teacher's name (217). Expelled, she returns to public high school, where she becomes a caricature of the female mindlessness and ineptitude that confirm her father's judgment. Cordelia loses combs and homework, fails tests and courses. As she becomes an object, progressively nullified by her inability to please her father, she grows sloppy and indifferent to grooming: a bleached strip of hair grows out "so it's disconcertingly two-toned. . . . Her lipstick doesn't seem to fit her mouth" (270). These two mouths and two shades of hair announce Cordelia's division and emptiness, while her face sometimes looks "as if she's not inside it" (234). Annulled, she cowers out of sight. Watching Cordelia and her father, Elaine understands that "her dithering, fumble-footed efforts to appease him" are doomed: "nothing she can do or say will ever be enough, because she is somehow the wrong person." Cordelia can only annihilate herself, while Elaine watches in angry disbelief: "How can she be so abject?" (264).

In her last appearance, about eight years after high school, Cordelia has become the woman-object, the powerless mummy. Confined in a "discreet private loony bin," she is plump, conservative, and muted. She wears her mother's colors, the "soft green tweeds and tailored blouses of her good-taste background," and her hair has been done in "tight little waves" (374–75). She cannot act; she can barely stand or walk. A mad-woman in the attic doubly trapped in the guise of an angel in the house, she is led by a motherly attendant, made docile by a chemically induced invalidism. Her voice has been "slowed-down," thickened and damaged by heavy doses of tranquilizers. Forced into the meek, dependent pas-sivity of the good daughter, Cordelia becomes by the same stroke a sadly reduced version of her mother: mindless, inept, irrelevant, neat, unsexed. Sparks of defiance remain—a fumbled profanity, an expressed determina-tion to get out. But Cordelia is now nullified, gone; she has thrown herself away. Her efforts to win approval from a patriarch who loathes women have culminated in a suicide attempt and, more broadly, in her having "let go of her idea of herself" (376). Though Cordelia disappears from the home, Elaine has no reason to suppose she can resurrect a subject from the abyss into which she has sunk.

Speaking the Woman Subject: Elaine

Cat's Eye expresses an original understanding of women's intertwined and responsive subjectivity, as well as of the politics that would keep it at bay. While the repression of her subjectivity leads both Cordelia and Elaine to art, Atwood focuses on the cost to both women and culture of its habitual translation of woman into object or abject; Atwood attempts to encourage a feminist art that quarrels with its own grim origins. Her fiction would be the way out; it would limit the patriarch's power and endorse repudiation rather than complicity in the daughter. It would reconceive the woman, neither as abject nor as object, but as subject. Out of her childhood experience as Cordelia's rejected half, the abhorrent female, Elaine Risley becomes an artist committed to disrupting her cul-ture's view of women. In the crucial second half of the novel, she chal-lenges the father's loathing. Atwood equips her to do so, not with a recovered, essential self, but with an acquired politics, an artistic voice, a woman's engaged subjectivity.

Elaine, like Cordelia, intuitively seeks approval; she appears from the outset as the good daughter who is obedient to parental authority. She learns to fight silently with her brother and never tattle, and her eagerness to please often dictates her response, as in the Eaton's Catalogue game. Her ready submission to the will of others makes her an easy prey to, and able colluder with, Cordelia. Like Cordelia, Elaine tries hard to succeed as a daughter, to win love by pleasing an implacable parent. Forced to play Cordelia's abject, unapproved side, Elaine responds with angelic submissiveness: she becomes the silent object, she stays in whatever place she is assigned, she makes herself small, invisible, and inoffensive. She becomes, in this role, the nullified object, and she embraces the role as Cordelia does, abjectly. For both women, silence—or the self-effacing repetition of the father's discourse—is the sign they have yielded up their subjectivity.

During two miserable years, Elaine suffers the pain of the canceled, the nonobject. Thrown away by Cordelia, she tries to cast out her own base qualities. She feels deeply shamed and nullified: "Cordelia, I think. You made me believe I was nothing" (211). She responds by dividing herself; she would distance and expel a defiled, bad side, as Cordelia did, to preserve a worthy side. Elaine literally rends herself: she peels the skin from her feet, shreds the skin on her fingers, bites her lips. Creating a dramatic metaphor for the subject/object split, she cultivates the ability to faint at will and leave her object-body below. She comes to see herself as visibly split and doubled, a transparent, forceless I-subject coupled with a numb object: "I feel blurred, as if there are two of me, one superimposed on the other, but imperfectly. There's an edge of transparency, and beside it a rim of solid flesh that's without feeling, like a scar" (184). When she reasserts herself on page 206, it is not the "self" she brought to Toronto but one shaped there by the contempt she has suffered. Elaine is no longer continuous or self-identical but mired in difference: from "herself," first, and then from Cordelia and all the other kin, friends, doubles, and partners she will later have.

Elaine walks away from Cordelia only when, making a literal descent into the abyss, she invents a new parent for herself—a powerful mother who approves the daughter's subjectivity. Her crisis occurs in the ravine, a symbolically apt place for renewed connection to the mother (though *Lady Oracle*'s protagonist is rescued there in a similar scene by a fairy god-father).[17] Having renounced the condemning patriarch, the Smeath's God (who is "on a side from which I'm excluded" [192]) and the father who expresses his loathing through Cordelia, Elaine prays to the Virgin Mary. Punished, sent into the ravine alone in the dark, she falls through the ice and is powerfully tempted by numbness, stasis, pure objecthood, the annihilation of death. She has a vision of Mary as the nurturing mother who walks to earth, speaks, warms, acts to preserve her daughter: *"You can go home now,* she says. *It will be all right. Go home"* (201). Her words stand in opposition to the father's will to estrange and banish the daughter; they affirm her right to life and warmth.[18]

As a first result of Elaine's vision of the powerful mother who accepts her, she regains voice. She speaks up; she rejects silent objecthood; she refuses any further punishment from Cordelia. Then, in adolescence, she neatly turns the tables—she adapts Cordelia's own biting irony to talk back to her. She terrifies Cordelia by telling a story about the dead returning to haunt the living; Cordelia invented a similar story, about the same graveyard, to scare Elaine at nine (246, 79). Elaine discovers a "mean mouth" in grade eleven: she has seized the boldly critical, even insulting verbal wit that characterized the young Cordelia and provided the basis for her power over the other girls in grade five. Elaine uses her "mean mouth" to insult Cordelia, achieving exact revenge: "The person I use my mean mouth on the most is Cordelia. She doesn't even have to provoke me, I use her as target practice" (248). Elaine's meanness verges on profanity and skirts bad taste, as did Cordelia's; her targets are always girls, as were Cordelia's; girls fear her and follow half a step behind, as they followed Cordelia. Illustrating what Mikhail Bakhtin calls "dialogic discourse," Elaine brings in the father's critical voice and turns it back on his minion, Cordelia.[19]

But the transformation goes beyond a will to punish Cordelia, for Elaine becomes what Cordelia throws away and learns to talk back to the father. She gradually becomes the "bad" Cordelia, the daughter Daddy can't tolerate, the inventive, defiant, mouthy, assertive female subject. Through Cordelia, Elaine takes in the discursive authority of her culture, with its condemning fatherly voice; unlike Cordelia, Elaine finds ways to give it back, to rework the father's objections and replies for her own purposes, and in the process to strip the father of his authority to speak for her. While Cordelia becomes progressively more silent in the face of the father's criticism, Elaine engages increasingly in "mean" rejoinders to the cultural positioning of daughters and to daughters who accept a meek and subordinate role. Her refusal, after high school, to play the good daughter; her rejection of all formulaic constructions of who she is or should be, as woman or artist; her recalcitrance with the journalist who wills her to be the "feminist artist": these and other acid retorts to others' versions of Elaine insist on her own authority.

Because she rejects a feminist label and because she emerges from her experience with Cordelia distrusting women, one reviewer sensed an "undercurrent of misogyny" in *Cat's Eye*.[20] Elaine remains through the rest of her life uneasy both with women and with feminism, and though her paintings are enthusiastically received by both women and feminists, she finds herself frozen, unable to trust and form friendships with other women. Some readers of the novel find it problematic, as a result, because the novel's clearly feminist critique of patriarchal culture does not lead to any evident criticism of its protagonist's distrust of and refusal to join the feminist community. In place of condemnation, the narrative appears to endorse pity for Elaine, a sorrowful recognition of what she has lost. Atwood remarks in an interview that "Cordelia really got around, and she had a profound influence on how the little girls who got run over by her were able to respond to other women when they grew up."[21] The father's refusal of the daughter's subjectivity ramifies outward. Daddy punishes Cordelia, who punishes Elaine, who loses the trust that makes women's friendship possible. Elaine refuses a feminist manifesto, and she is not particularly nice to the journalist who tries to make her subscribe to one. As well as mistrust of the women's agenda, Elaine's attitude reflects a refusal to be spoken for, an insistence on speaking for herself. Its real objective is resistance to the fatherly voice of culture that would return woman to her position as a silent object.

Many of Elaine's adult choices emerge from her fierce renunciation of the abject daughter's acquiescent propriety. She selects her first two lovers, for example, for the triangular relationships they offer and for the revolt they permit her against the proper behavior of the good daughter, Daddy's submissive possession. She does not feel romantic love for either Josef or Jon; when she first sleeps with Josef, she believes she has renounced marriage to anyone. She chooses Josef in part because of his involvement with Susie (a double and an echo of Cordelia) and Jon in part because of his various semiattached girls. Elaine is two entirely different half-objects to these men: Josef idealizes her, dresses her in Pre-Raphaelite gowns, and seeks an ethereal otherness in her; Jon calls her "pal" and offers her an escape from grown-up responsibilities (334). The relationships overlap and require concealment and deception, shielding Elaine from intimacy with either man. She enjoys the danger and finds that treachery makes her feel "safer. Two men are better than one, or at least they make me feel better. . . . having two means that I don't have to make up my mind about either of them" (332). She has chosen two for this reason; they are a "pair of bookends" allowing her to remain freestanding (340), her own bookish word kept quietly to herself between them.

Elaine also makes a choice to become a painter through a series of repudiations of fatherly authority. She has intended to study biology, and when she chooses art instead, she rejects her own father's profession—he is an entomologist. She also disappoints and worries both her parents, who "reacted with alarm" to her decision to paint (289). She takes courses in art history, where male professors teach the traditions of her artistic forefathers; these too she rejects. She observes a heavy concentration of paintings of naked women, who "are presented in the same manner as the plates of meat and dead lobsters, with the same attention to the play of candlelight on skin, the same lusciousness, the same sensuous and richly rendered detail. . . . They appear served up" (342). Her own paintings will refute and replace this view of women as objects for artistic representation. She also leaves behind her own personal guides, Josef and Jon, each a self-proclaimed authority on the proper direction for contemporary art. She abandons the favored medium, oil paint, and teaches herself to make and use egg tempera. She discards the current trend toward abstraction and paints human figures; "I'm aware that my tastes are not fashionable, so I pursue them in secret" (343–44).

Elaine's paintings talk back: they interrogate the cultural positioning of woman as empty surface, as container for the masculine word, as luscious "skin" and sensuous object. Woman as model and muse for art is the ultimate form of the abject/object daughter: she is the silent, passive space in which the fatherly "master" muses on beauty and finds it within his grasp. He re-presents it, brings it to fruition under his controlling gaze, turns woman to his own master "piece," and renders the female subject as erotic object. Atwood's reflections on the representation of women in Western art reveal a sophisticated awareness of the connection, important to feminist art historians and film theorists, between art forms that objectify women and political systems that oppress them. Kate Linker defines the relation clearly: "The apparatus works to constitute the subject as male, denying subjectivity to woman. Woman, within this structure, is unauthorized, illegitimate: she does not represent but is, rather, represented. Placed in a passive rather than active role, as object rather than subject, she is the constant point of masculine appropriation in a society in which representation is empowered to construct identity."[22] Atwood gives Elaine power to respond to this history in paintings that suggest the ungraspable, unrepresentable, layered, hidden, richly multiple nature of women. Elaine's paintings express a personally rooted political vision. They speak out about gender and culture, resisting simple formulas as vehemently as Elaine refuses others' agendas. She paints relationships that haunt her, in images that disclose (sometimes despite her expressed intention) unresolved questions, unmastered anxiety, turbulence. The power in her paintings derives from their lack of mastery over the subjects they show.[23]

Some of Elaine's paintings respond explicitly to the traditional artist's positioning of woman as abject object, appropriated by the masculine gaze. "Falling Women," for example, addresses a conventional idea about women's sexuality and its representation in art. Feminist art historian Linda Nochlin observes a "sexual asymmetry peculiar to the notion of falling"; fallen men have been killed in war, but fallen women have indulged in sexual activity outside of wedlock. The figure of the fallen woman "exerted a peculiar fascination on the imagination of nineteenth-century artists."[24] The fallen woman typifies abjection, and in the paintings Nochlin surveys she often cowers before an upright male figure. Elaine's "Falling Women" alters this spatial configuration and strips away the judgment against the women: three women are "falling as if by accident off a bridge," skirts belled by the wind, onto men who lie unseen below. The painting, she says, is "about men, the kind who caused women to fall"; it suggests the gravitational pull of those men, and the odd inappropriateness of the notion that "fallen" describes the women's relation to men who lie "jagged and dark and without volition" in wait for them (282). "Life Drawing" explores the way male artists create images of women—serve them up—on canvas. Josef and Jon stand on each side, painting a model seated at the center. The men are nude, seen from the rear, objectified and sensuously rendered to evoke the traditional rendering of women. Each paints the same model: Josef produces a voluptuous woman with a brooding, Pre-Raphaelite face, and Jon a series of "intestinal swirls" in red and purple. Her own painting of the model emphasizes her plainness—her bare feet are "flat on the floor," her hands are "folded neatly"—while insisting on the ungraspable mystery of her consciousness: "Her head is a sphere of bluish glass" (386). Not seen as a commodity, not given or brought to presence, woman exists in a different dimension from those in which she has been represented.

Elaine's paintings of the Virgin Mary revise the image of the sacred woman central to Western art, especially by rejecting the ethereal and passive qualities traditional artists have given Mary. Since divine quiescence and self-effacement endorse women's acceptance of objecthood, Elaine's sacred woman must have a subjectivity and an active role in the world. For her, Mary is not a vessel for the masculine word, a receptive container for the Other's power, or a calm spirituality meditating in repose above the secular realm. In one painting, Mary has the head of a lioness, Christ a cub in her lap: "My Virgin Mary is fierce, alert to danger, wild. She stares levely out at the viewer with her yellow lion's eyes. A gnawed bone lies at her feet" (361). She emanates her own fierce will, her own natural power, and she takes a position of alert watchfulness which, with the gnawed bone, suggests her readiness to act in the world. In another painting, Mary is descending to earth in a winter coat, a purse over one shoulder, carrying two bags of groceries. Things have fallen out. "She looks tired" (361). Mary takes an active place in a nonidealized secular world, amid the domestic activities of contemporary women. Far from being a replete container who passively awaits delivery, she carries her own load, even cold and tired and unable to control her goods, which spill into the snow and slush. What falls from her bags, moreover, is not the masculine word but symbols of mythic femininity: an egg, an onion, an apple. This painting, titled "Our Lady of Perpetual Help," suggests that help comes from Mary as woman.

Elaine's portraits of women refuse to make their subjects into objects, "served up," sensuous, or "richly rendered." They show women busy or thoughtful, not absorbed in being seen by the painter. They focus on women's consciousness and provide images for its layered complexity. Elaine's women are never simply beautiful or voluptuous; they are never grasped or graspable; they are often troubled, but never empty or abject. Her most fleshy paintings expose Mrs. Smeath, whose existence in flesh intrudes to undermine her hypocritical claims to a pure life of the spirit. Unwrapping Mrs. Smeath in the panels of "White Gift," one finds cheap underclothes and flabby, pallid flesh, and beneath that a diseased heart suggesting the failure of charity (369). Yet through her anger at the mother who saw the girls' punishment of Elaine as God's righteous judgment, Elaine also paints Mrs. Smeath with light, depth, and pity. Years later, looking at the painting, she sees "defeated eyes, uncertain and melancholy, heavy with unloved duty" (427).

When she paints Cordelia, Elaine produces a vivid image of double-sided and repressed consciousness. Titled "Half a Face," the painting shows Cordelia's entire face; behind her, hanging on the wall, is "another face, covered with a white cloth. The effect is of a theatrical mask. Perhaps" (239). Elaine chooses to paint Cordelia at thirteen, with her defiant look—but the eyes escape her and reveal fear instead. The fear freezes the defiance; the defiance reveals the fear emanating from an impossible, empty object. The shrouded second face hides its expression, suggesting the masked quality of the face turned toward the world and the depths it represses. These severed, shrouded, fearful twin halves of Cordelia suggest the deadliness for women of the binary logic of subject and object.

Elaine's latest painting is titled "Unified Field Theory," after the physicists' sought-after theory that can bridge dualities like particle and wave, quantum uncertainty and relativity, and make a universe full of seemingly irreconcilable oppositions one whole, interactive field. In the painting, a woman stands in air, above the railing of a bridge. "She is the Virgin of Lost Things. Between her hands, at the level of her heart, she holds a glass object: an oversized cat's eye marble, with a blue center" (430). The woman in the painting bridges different levels of past: she brings together the crisis point in Elaine's life when she had a vision of Mary on the bridge and the point years later when, going through a trunk in the cellar shortly before her mother's death, Elaine rediscovered her favorite blue cat's-eye marble. Both moments are significant for the recovery of a lost subjectivity. In the first, Elaine reasserts her right to be a subject in the face of a culture that, speaking through Cordelia, reduces women to objects. In the second, she recovers the talisman that has symbolized her subjectivity under duress: hard, impervious, glassy, with its richness buried inside. The marble replaces the traditional symbols associated with Mary—the red heart that signifies her sympathetic intercession for humankind and the Christ child who is the masculine word she bears. The cat's-eye marble is neither "feminine" affective feeling nor male seed of a masculine deity. It comes from the realm of children's play and is virtually the only play Elaine recalls from her school days in which girls and boys participate jointly, with equal enthusiasm and interest, without barriers or hierarchies based on gender.

Many details in the background of the painting reinforce its attempt to transcend traditional binary oppositions with a vision of the dynamic field. As Elaine describes it, the painting bridges disparate realms, including both the far distant space of interstellar night, with "star upon star, red, blue, yellow and white, swirling nebulae, galaxy upon galaxy: the universe, in its incandescence and darkness," and the close at hand, the microscopic "beetles and small roots" from underground (431). In its oddly conflated images, the painting combines darkness and light, small and large, earth and sky; even the black cloak worn by the woman contains "pinpoints of light." The light tone at the bottom of the painting is the "clear blue of water"—like the blue marble, the creek conjoins vitality and death, for it comes from "the land of the dead people." In setting up dialogues between different systems, scales, and values, the painting sets its vision resonating with the uncanny energy of a unified field.

Cat's Eye suggests, through the evident power of Elaine's paintings, that women contribute to changing the historical context by the way they define their problems surviving it. But the novel's emphasis is not on the consoling process through which great suffering produces great art, or great art better politics. The novel does not suggest that art can resolve the problems, change the culture, or give women positions of greater dignity. Rather, *Cat's Eye* measures the cost for both individuals and culture of the encoding of women as objects who may be rendered abject. For Elaine, this cost is large: she survives a suicide attempt, but she suffers ongoing bouts of depression, days when she lies on the floor in the dark (121). She remains divided, haunted by self-doubt and yearning to achieve the reunion with Cordelia that would reunify herself. But the reunion never occurs, and Elaine's recognition—"I've been prepared for almost anything; except absence, except silence" (435)—amounts to the realization of a loss as complete as death. Elaine never learns Cordelia's story. Surely, though, the story of Stephen's death extends outward to suggest Cordelia's. Stephen, the stranger, brother, double, and companion for Elaine in her youth, also doubles for her "sister" and best friend Cordelia. Like Cordelia, Stephen figures as Elaine's twin, in a series of references to doomed twins that runs through the novel and binds the three characters together.[25] Like Cordelia and Elaine, Stephen is alien to the culture of Toronto—unassimilable, different. Like Cordelia, he appears alone and isolated. Stephen is shot by terrorists in the Middle East; he dies five years before Elaine's return to Toronto, but she tells of his death very near the end. Stephen's death, bizarre, accidental, and unexplained, inhabits the blank in the text left by Cordelia's absence and suggests why the only trace of her Elaine can find in Toronto is a hungry ghost.

Elaine finds this ghost in the ravine, where the present meets the past at the novel's end. She has a strange vision there, not of unity and identity but of difference. She expects to see herself at nine in a blue knitted hat; instead, she sees Cordelia, and sees her as other. She feels an echo of the worthless objecthood she shared with Cordelia. "There is the same shame, the sick feeling in my body, the same knowledge of my own wrongness, awkwardness, weakness; the same wish to be loved; the same loneliness; the same fear. But these are not my own emotions any more. They are Cordelia's; as they always were" (443). In place of identification with Cordelia, Elaine now perceives their distance. She understands that the feeling of nonexistent emptiness emanated from Cordelia. Elaine becomes, then, the maternal figure she imagined for herself when she needed rescue, and she reaches out to Cordelia's ghost with forgiveness. But she takes back no ease or consolation. On her flight home to Vancouver, Elaine addresses Cordelia: "This is what I miss, Cordelia; not something that's gone, but something that will never happen. Two old women giggling over their tea" (446). The recognition of all she has lost and missed—an ability to mourn her losses—is what Elaine gathers in Toronto.

The Subjective Form of Cat's Eye

Cat's Eye measures the cost as well in its strangeness, its lack of climax and resolution, its diffuseness. The novel truly is as divided, anticlimactic, and disunified as most reviewers sensed; these elements are more important and more constructive than they realized. The "flaws" in the novel reflect its failures to conform to realist and modernist standards—Atwood departs by choice from traditions in which the artist's subjectivity is produced as a static object in and above the text, and in which the text itself becomes a closed, impermeable, and static object. She chooses not to write the story of the recovered, essential self or the reunion of girlhood friends; she can't explore the politics that strip the female subject in a good-daughterly novel, a bildungsroman or chronicle properly affiliated to patriarchal conventions, because these conventions have produced the dominant male subject and the passive female object/abject. Instead, she writes an actualist novel in which subjectivity exerts a reciprocal and relative influence. Memory brings its own discontinuities and gaps, like the narrative memory of *Gravity's Rainbow*. The subject—even the artist—can't find an absolute frame from which to validate its perspective but floats without attainable certainty in relative space-time.

In its form, Atwood's novel invokes the narrative model of the kunstlerroman, that most modernist of forms tracing the development of the artist's consciousness. Her protagonist, like Joyce's Stephen, receives an education that moves outward from family to church, state, and eventually art. Like Joyce's Stephen, Elaine chooses exile from the place where she learns her artistic vocation; she is perhaps most like Stephen in renouncing the aesthetic goals, values, and practices of her forebears and her contemporaries. But if her story resembles his in some ways, it departs from the serene chronology that produces Joyce's artist, abandons the secure stages that mark his growth, gives up on the epiphanic penetration of experience that leads him to increasing certainty, and rejects the production of the artist—or of Art—as a suitable end of narrative. Elaine Risley narrates her experiences but does not produce herself or her artistic vision as their culmination; nor does her narrative eventuate in stasis, certainty, or aesthetic comfort.

In the modernist hands of Joyce or Proust, the kunstlerroman arrives at the end back at its point of origination: with the artist's subjectivity cultivated to a degree empowering the creation of art. The artist is the object produced by the narrative, all of whose seemingly accidental circumstances find justification as they construct the artistic perspective necessary to its own creation. It, too, is a product, an objet d'art. At the point of closure, the modernist becomes the necessary deity in the private realm of art decreed by virtue of the artist's finally developed genius. This pattern persists in contemporary texts whose artists achieve an aesthetic liberation, whether earnest or ironic, at the narrative's end. In what I consider Nabokov's ironic critique of modernism behind his oblivious narrator's back, *Ada* "properly" begins with Van Veen's arrival at a writing "I" self in part 5; Van is the most modernist of Nabokov's protagonists, the most subjective of his narrators, and, I believe, the most distant from his creator. From a more genuinely modernist perspective, one lacking irony about the election to art, Marguerite Young's *Miss MacIntosh, My Darling* culminates in the protagonist's approaching marriage and achieved impregnation—symbolically, with the vision of reality she needs to produce the epic novel just reaching its conclusion. Similarly, Alice Adams's *Listening to Billie* concludes with its poet-protagonist's epiphanic moment of vision, in which she foresees her art arriving: "She closed her eyes, and in the dark space behind her vision she saw, or suddenly felt, an urgency of words, a kaleidoscope that stopped to form a pattern. Words, her own work. But stronger, somehow enlarged."

Elaine Risley has a vastly different relation to her own art at the end of *Cat's Eye*. The novel describes her return to Toronto for a retrospective showing of her paintings; in the narrative present, she prepares for the show, shops for a dress to wear, gives an interview to a journalist, and finally attends the show. Near the novel's end, she looks around at her paintings.

> I walk the room, surrounded by the time I've made; which is not a place, which is only a blur, the moving edge we live in; which is fluid, which turns back on itself, like a wave. I may have thought I was preserving something from time, salvaging something; like all those painters, centuries ago, who thought they were bringing Heaven to earth, the revelations of God, the eternal stars, only to have their slabs of wood and plaster stolen, mislaid, burnt. . . .
>
> I can no longer control these paintings, or tell them what to mean. Whatever energy they have came out of me. I'm what's left over. (431)

Alice Adams's protagonist, Eliza, sees words in a kaleidoscope "that stopped to form a pattern"; Elaine sees paintings that, finished years ago and hung around her, have never stopped. She sees that her paintings are time and therefore are moving. The artist does not stop time or its effects; indeed, she sees her own paintings differently now than when she painted them. Far from the necessary deity who produced the work of art and who therefore controls it, she is the by-product or husk, as much a spectator of this show as anyone else.

The temporal form of *Cat's Eye* helps its subjective narrator to fracture the illusion of Newtonian absolute time and to create, in its place, a sense of relativity. The narrative shifts between layers of time, folding back the present to evoke a glimpse of some obliquely corresponding part of the past, itself in multiple fragments that aren't rendered as continuous or whole. Section titles tend to refer both to a thing or image from Elaine's past and to a painting she has subsequently done in a more recent past; these paintings emerge in the present at the end, as they hang on the walls in the gallery show. "Deadly Nightshade," for example, refers both to the common weed that grew in the ravine and to the title of one of Elaine's early paintings. Most of the novel's fifteen sections begin in the present, with Elaine's activities as she prepares for the show, and shift without explanation or transition, at a chapter break, to the past. Both present and past narratives are very loosely chronological, but their combined effect is to disrupt both linear and cyclic time—to dispel any sense of firmly shaped time—while enabling past and present to float in relationship. The past clearly haunts the present with an uncanny energy, and *Cat's Eye* displays an "elegiac" impulse to recall lost things. "I wanted a literary home for all those vanished *things* from my own childhood—the marbles, the Eaton's catalogues, the Watchbird Watching You, the smells, sounds, colors," Atwood said in an interview.[26]

As she navigates various layers of time and memory, Elaine narrates everything in the present tense. "Today we hang," she says of the gallery's preparations for the retrospective show of her work, and "The school we are sent to is some distance away," she begins the next chapter, which moves back over forty years (44, 48). All of her experience remains equally present; nothing is finished, over, safely boxed in the preterite tense. Most actualist texts rely on present-tense narration, as Atwood's does, to invoke unfinished, relative time: "A screaming comes across the sky"; "On June 24, 1950, less than five years after the end of World War II, the Korean War begins"; "At the end of the current semester, Marshyhope State University will complete the seventh academic year since its founding." They commonly avoid the preterite, for reasons defined by Roland Barthes in *Writing Degree Zero*:

> Through the preterite, the verb implicitly belongs with a causal chain, it partakes of a set of related and orientated actions, it functions as the algebraic sign of an intention. . . . It presupposes a world which is constructed, elaborated, self-sufficient, reduced to significant lines, and not one which has been sent sprawling before us. . . . Behind the preterite there always lurks a demiurge, a God or a reciter. . . . So that finally the preterite is the expression of an order, and consequently of a euphoria. Thanks to it, reality is neither mysterious nor absurd; it is clear, almost familiar, repeatedly gathered up and contained in the hand of a creator.[27]

Looking back from the secure perspective of the end of the story, a conventional narrative in the preterite tense can detect causal connections, gather up threads, and highlight patterns of significance. Beginning with the premise that "time is not a line but a dimension, like the dimensions of space," *Cat's Eye* uses juxtaposed glimpses in the present tense to "bend time," without suggesting the closed and causal order that stops time. The narrator travels backward in time without superior knowledge; in effect, her past memories are "sent sprawling before us" in inexplicable mystery rather than coming clear and yielding up their secret meaning to the older Elaine.

For similar reasons, *Cat's Eye* chooses first-person narration rather than third, and everywhere denies omniscience. The first person admits and even celebrates the subjective; the third cloaks its subjective origin and bias in a feigned objectivity that confers dignity, authority, and certainty on the narrator. In third-person omniscient narrative, the subject becomes object, its uncertainties blotted out by a disciplinary and finalizing memory. For this reason, most actualist texts use either an openly subjective third person, like the narrators of *Gravity's Rainbow* and of half of *The Public Burning*, or a third person limited, like *Paradise* and Coover's "Charlie in the House of Rue," or first person(s), like *LETTERS* and *Cat's Eye*.

The most conspicuous feature of the first-person narrative in *Cat's Eye* is the lack of retrospective control exercised in an essentially retrospective narrative. Elaine "time travels" like Billy Pilgrim, in Vonnegut's *Slaughterhouse-Five*: without any evident control over the process, without a secure afterknowledge that would soften, explain, and neutralize events. As she recalls the past in vivid detail, her own intense anxiety returns: it is the anxiety of an uncertain subject before its own singular life, in which events are "sent sprawling" in painful ambiguity. Elaine does not reread her own life from the end; she does not take the insight that enables her final forgiveness of Cordelia as the starting point for a narrative designed to restore, resolve, and console. The properly affiliated novel—the one the reviewers wished for—would have done so: it would have used its culminating insight to order the fluctuations, to fill the gaps, to lead coherently toward the moment in the ravine when Elaine reaches out to Cordelia with understanding and pity. In this way, the novel's recurrent absences would be redeemed by the exposure of an underlying presence.

But Atwood chooses to end *Cat's Eye* with real and unmitigated absence. Cordelia is not there in the ravine. She is absent; she is the abiding absence throughout the novel. Her story has no closure: though Stephen's death reaches out suggestively to claim her, no rumor, anecdote, or fact—not the least scrap of narrative—surfaces from the abyss into which Cordelia disappears. Elaine, too, is more an absence than the novel's unifying presence. Just as she doesn't produce a static, final, and definitive oeuvre in the narrative, she isn't produced by the narrative as a static, final, and definitive "life." Her story has no end or resolution: she does not die or satisfy her abiding wish to see Cordelia or recuperate her own lost youth or achieve a vision of artistic certainty. She changes, but she remains in time, with its promise that she will continue to change. While Elaine achieves new understanding and forgiveness of Cordelia in the ravine, her story ends in midair, like so many other actualist texts. She flies back to her husband, her daughters, her future, with no clear sense of how her story will proceed. She never lands, the objective product of experience restored to ongoing time. As the novel ends, she looks out the plane window at the night sky, and her gaze disperses outward into relative space-time, moving toward infinity and absence, rather than finding its center in her own reflection contained in the window. Erasing Elaine and all other objects of vision, the novel concludes with old starlight offering the possibility of vision in the dark.

SEVEN

DONALD BARTHELME

PARADISE AND THE UNCERTAIN

PRINCIPLES OF ACTUALISM

An important figure in the American literary landscape, Donald Barthelme published four novels and ten collections of stories; before his death in 1989, he had earned distinguished status in the *New Yorker* and wide recognition from critics of contemporary fiction. Unlike other actualists, Barthelme did not produce an encyclopedic text— he wrote no *Gravity's Rainbow* or *LETTERS*, displayed none of the impulse to "render the full range of knowledge and beliefs of a national culture" which, according to Edward Mendelson, characterizes encyclopedic narratives.[1] Indeed, Barthelme's fiction is antiencyclopedic: his tales redefine the inner limits of the "short" story, and his brief novels provide glimpses, rather than compendia, of culture. Barthelme makes less use of contemporary history than other actualists, and he sets his fictions in more abstract realms. Much concerned with writing, language, art, his texts address the process of their own creation; whatever else they are, they are *also* self-reflexive.

No wonder, then, that Barthelme has been considered the arch-metafictionist by influential critics. He appears centrally in studies of metafiction, ranging from Robert Scholes's early essay "Metafiction" (1970) to Patricia Waugh's later book *Metafiction* (1984). Critical approaches to Barthelme's fiction often bring the metafictional paradigm to bear on it or, more subtly, ground their readings in an assumption that Barthelme is more interested in aesthetics than in actuality.[2] So, for example, John Domini traces Barthelme's "allusive games" to European Modernism and argues that Barthelme should be seen as "our replenisher of Modernism."[3] The useful study by Maurice Couturier and Régis Durand, on the one hand, recognizes that Barthelme's concern extends beyond forms to "the interaction between the real (its signs and its meaning) and the self (its imaginative power and its emotions)" but, on the other hand, places Barthelme as a metafictionist. "Barthelme, like Escher, paralyses our intelligence and lures us into entering his surrealistic world which has indeed very little to do with our own."[4]

But Barthelme's statements about fiction and aesthetics reveal a progressive insistence that art meditates on external reality. True, he felt an early faith in art's autonomy that gave critics license to read him as a metafictionist. "Twenty years ago," he wrote in 1985, "I was much more convinced of the autonomy of the literary object than I am now, and even wrote a rather persuasive defense of the proposition that I have just rejected: that the object is itself world."[5] His latest position, articulated consistently since 1981, amounted to a rejection of metafictive premises in favor of a set of actualistic assumptions about art and reality. He told Larry McCaffery that he "does not particularly fancy 'metafiction,' either as a word or as a fictional mode."[6] Asked by another interviewer in 1981, "Don't you write more about the mind than about the external world?", Barthelme responded that art depends on their collision: "In a common-sense way, you write about the impingement of one upon the other—my subjectivity bumping into other subjectivities, or into the Prime Rate. . . . That's what's curious when people say, of writers, this one's a realist, this one's a surrealist, this one's a super-realist, and so forth. In fact, everybody's a realist offering true accounts of the activity of mind. There are only realists."[7] Barthelme developed this quintessentially actualistic position at length in his important essay "Not-Knowing" (1985). "This is, I think, the relation of art to world. I suggest that art is always a meditation upon external reality rather than a representation of external reality or a jackleg attempt to 'be' external reality. . . . Art is a true account of the activity of mind. Because consciousness, in Husserl's formulation, is always consciousness *of* something, art thinks ever of the world, cannot not think of the world, could not turn its back on the world even if it wished to."[8]

The world on which Barthelme meditates surely differs from the stable, known one of realism. Barthelme is as aware as any actualist of the shifts in reality, for physicists, writers, and readers, over the past fifty years. His own particular fascination, and the focus of this chapter, lies in the shift from secure knowledge to uncertainty. The choice to title his essay on narrative "Not-Knowing" reveals Barthelme's sense of the liberating possibilities in uncertainty; so too do statements like "the not-knowing is crucial to art, is what permits art to be made" and the complaint that some criticism displays "a rage for final explanations, a refusal to allow a work that mystery which is essential to it."[9] Explicitly aware of the scientific grounds for the not-knowing or mystery that animates art, Barthelme identifies them memorably in the 1981 interview: "In this century there's been much stress placed not upon what we know but on knowing that our methods are themselves questionable—our Song of Songs is the Uncertainty Principle."[10]

Developed in 1926 by Werner Heisenberg, the uncertainty principle provides a dramatic locus of the difference between classical and quantum physics. According to this principle, a scientific observer cannot know both the position and the velocity of subatomic particles. Using light energy to measure the position alters the velocity of particles; in measuring velocity, without altering the energy level of the system, one cannot determine position. No improved technology can ever remove this fundamental uncertainty from scientific knowledge. Since classical physics had assumed that reality proceeded independently of its observers, and could be watched and predicted according to causal laws, Heisenberg's principle revolutionized physics. Not only does it undermine the notions of a causal universe, an objective observer, and a perfectible scientific grasp of the known world, but it also calls into question the concept of the identifiable "thing"—a particle—under study. It suggests that scientific activity turns back upon itself, or as Heisenberg puts it, "What we observe is not nature itself, but nature exposed to our method of questioning."[11] The uncertainty principle therefore implies all the terms I've used to characterize actualism: it enforces subjectivity on the observer, for example, and assumes the immaterial nature of observed reality.

To have the uncertainty principle become "our Song of Songs" is to meditate, in a posture of "not-knowing," on an indeterminate external world. For Barthelme, it is also and especially to invert the forms and formulas through which traditional narratives have affirmed certainty. Barthelme's fiction energetically subverts the bildungsroman, that most typical form of fiction, and particularly of realistic novels, with its assurance that the life experience of the protagonist leads, through continuous and causal stages, to a stable and certain identity. For Barthelme it doesn't—any life experience leads instead to increasing uncertainty, through a series of groping recognitions of the bankrupt promises made by Western culture. As a result, Barthelme typically writes stories of reeducation, in which protagonists discover the failure of patterns traditionally held to produce fulfillment and stability (marriage, career, education, etc.) and begin to learn how little they can trust the culturally constituted certainties on which they have built. Their experience opens them to uncertainty as an inevitable way of life.

"Me and Miss Mandible" provides an early, brief, and definitive paradigm for much of Barthelme's fiction. After a "ruined marriage, a ruined adjusting career, a grim interlude in the Army," thirty-five-year-old Joseph is returned to the sixth grade for reeducation. There he discovers that people are taught to read signs as promises of certainty, but "signs are signs, and some of them are lies." The culture guarantees that reality can be surely known through a linear reading of signs, and this pledge, which "cannot be redeemed . . . will confuse me later and make me feel I am not *getting anywhere*. Everything is presented as the result of some knowable process; if I wish to arrive at four I get there by way of two and two. . . . Who points out that arrangements sometimes slip, that errors are made, that signs are misread?" Nobody, of course. Future citizens are trained to believe in linear progress (the school is named Horace Greeley Elementary), secure interpretation (at the end, Sue Ann Brownly is "certain now," and Miss Mandible "knows now" how the narrator fits into their own narratives), and the stone determinacy of all phenomena. The school is not alone in endorsing certainty: the army, the insurance company, the "venal publishing industry" that produces widely read gossip magazines, the ironically named "Board of Estimate" that predicts the size of sixth graders, the writers and producers of a math text that claims to give students "confidence in their ability to take the right steps and obtain correct answers"—these institutions and agencies reinforce the promise of certainty.[12]

Only the narrator understands "that somehow a mistake has been made." Opened to this discovery by the failure of promises in the first half of his life, then placed in a classroom where his absurd presence is as blandly accepted as the promise of correct answers, he writes his way toward an understanding of his situation. His writing provides brief glimpses (not in linear order) of his past life; first person, private, subversively fragmentary, and ahistorical, his journal refuses in both form and content the secure spatial mapping of knowledge going on in the geography lessons during which Joseph writes. This process culminates, not in any epiphanic moment of certainty, but in Joseph's awareness that he cannot read the signs. Ironically enough, he has read accurately the signs of potential disaster in Miss Mandible's desire for him; caught in a sexual embrace with her, he is expelled and—in a sinister display of the scientific logic impelling his culture—"sent to a doctor, for observation." The doctor will surely produce a map of Joseph's mysterious behavior, but everything else about his fate remains uncertain.

As "Me and Miss Mandible" suggests, traditional authorities voice the promise of certainty in Barthelme's fiction. As in Coover's *Public Burning*, Barthelme's public sector endorses realistic certainty in order to stabilize, and finally to manipulate, the contingent forces of history. As in Atwood and Gaddis, these claims emerge, simplified and forceful, in elementary school. Barthelme's fiction addresses much of its satire to social institutions, including schools of various kinds and levels, that proclaim certain knowledge. These institutions include the military ("Engineer-Private Paul Klee Misplaces an Aircraft between Milbertshofen and Cambrai, March 1916," "The Game," "The Sergeant"), religions of various kinds ("A City of Churches," "The Catechist," "The Leap"), psychiatry ("The Sandman"), businesses and enterpreneurs ("Report," "I Bought a Little City"), systems of justice ("The Policemen's Ball," "Rebecca"), the press and publishing industries ("Robert Kennedy Saved from Drowning," "Our Work and Why We Do It"), and art institutes ("The Dolt," "On the Steps of the Conservatory," "The Farewell"). These institutions meet in the web of public life, and each story suggests their collusion in shaping, for their own authoritarian ends, an unredeemable pledge of certainty. Each story criticizes by implication *all* appeals to knowable processes and correct answers.

Barthelme's critique focuses especially on those true believers in the scientific method of knowing. The most powerful legacy of classical science, this method assumes that reality is material, stable, and graspable and that one can proceed through a logical series of steps (observation, measurement, analysis) to knowledge. The scientific method relies, also, on a faith that its own tools, including the language for formulating assertions about reality, are transparent and trustworthy. As a result, Barthelme's scientists speak a humorless and unironic language; they often bring materialist assumptions to bear, incongruously, on intangible actualities; they subscribe to the acquisitive doctrine of Gardner's dragon, that one's best policy is to "seek out gold and sit on it"; they approach human being—their own and others'—as a thing to know and grasp; they reify, control, and manipulate. Barthelme's criticism of the scientific investigator focuses on the comic inappropriateness (with potentially disastrous results) of the attempt to know the wrong things in the wrong way. So Paul, the inept prince of *Snow White*, responds to the challenge of mythic sexuality and love by constructing a bunker and a system for observation. "A lucky hit! the idea of installing this underground installation not far from the house. Now I can keep her under constant surveillance, through this system of mirrors and trained dogs."[13] Similar figures (the analyst in "The Sandman," Q in "Kierkegaard Unfair to Schlegel," the Dead Father, and dozens of others) reduce complex uncertainties to questions of money, systems, machines, and manipulable data throughout Barthelme's fiction.

Uncertainty, by contrast, is voiced ironically and indirectly by private individuals, often artists, who are detached from institutions, alienated from the culture, marginalized especially by their estrangement from the world of material production and consumption. With remarkable frequency, Barthelme's uncertain protagonists do nothing—the artists, like Peterson in "A Shower of Gold" or Simon in *Paradise* or Edgar in "The Dolt," cannot complete a project, and other protagonists, like Joseph in "Miss Mandible," the narrator in "See the Moon?," Snow White and King Arthur, simply watch and wait. In the absence of a "productive" relation to *things*, these figures recognize with Susan ("The Sandman") "that America has somehow got hold of the greed ethic and that the greed ethic has turned America into a tidy little hell." Yet even while they realize the emptiness of materialist definitions of value, these figures remain uncertain how to construct or express intangible values.

They speak ironically, obliquely, metaphorically—like Barthelme's fictions themselves—because saying the not-true is, for subscribers to the uncertainty principle, the closest approximation to cloudy "truth." Peterson, at the end of "A Shower of Gold," reconstructs his life in the metaphoric language of myth, "and although he was, in a sense, lying, in a sense he was not." As Pynchon puts it, "The act of metaphor then was a thrust at truth and a lie." In the same way, stories like "The Balloon" and

"The Glass Mountain" and novels like *Snow White, The Dead Father,* and *The King* come at actuality through the duplicitous lens of metaphor, substituting flagrant untruths for fiction's old impossible pretense to be the clear pane of glass or reflective mirror. Barthelme's linguistic irony makes a similar gesture and point: by rejecting the old impossible pretense that language could transparently fix and name, the ironic statement becomes an indeterminate supplement to, rather than a certain replacement for, external reality. "You've been pretty hard on our machines. You've withheld your enthusiasm, that's damaging," says Q in "Kierkegaard Unfair to Schlegel." A replies, ironically, "I'm sorry": between the speaking of the formulaic untruth and its invocation of implied alternatives ("Why should anyone invest enthusiasm in machines?" for example), Barthelme's narrator lies and suggests uncertain truths.

Barthelme takes a consistently ironic position, though it must be imagined as a peculiarly unlocatable one, in his fiction. His ironies are not "grounded" in stable certainties shared between "knowing" authors and readers but rather are "suspended" in uncertainty. Wayne Booth calls this form of irony "unstable" because it resists resolution into "some final point of clarity"; rather, it suggests "a possibly infinite series of further confusions." An irony that raises doubts and opens questions—"not so much because we don't know enough as because uncertainty is intrinsic, of the essence"—has engaged recent critics and theorists like D. J. Enright and Gary Handwerk. Alan Wilde sees postmodern irony as typically "suspensive" in its acceptance of fundamental uncertainty; among Barthelme's most perceptive readers, Wilde uses the notion of suspensive irony to focus the doubly ludic and assenting quality of Barthelme's texts.[14] All of these recent explorations of irony account similarly for the typical tone of actualism, for they focus on the relation between a hovering, unresolved ironic stance and the acceptance of a radical indeterminacy in the nature of things.

Barthelme and his protagonists resist the impulse to construct stable knowledge and certain meaning at every level. Assuming that actuality is not stable, material, or knowable, they reject the scientific method in favor of artistic imagination, provisional possibility, and openness. In place of "the right steps" and "the correct answers," they prefer resonant questions and rich, if arbitrary or whimsical, suggestions. In "The Sandman," Susan's lover writes a letter to her analyst, who has tried "to 'stabilize' Susan's behavior in reference to a state-of-affairs that you feel should obtain." The unnamed writer criticizes this scientific attempt to "know"

Susan, mocks its pedantry with learned and ironic footnotes, and answers its foolish assertions with questions: "Am I wandering too much for you?" "What do you do with a patient who finds the world unsatisfactory?" "Are you, Doctor dear, in a position to appreciate the beauty of this reply, in this context?" Against the doctor's attempts to improve Susan, the narrator sets his own perception that "Susan is wonderful. *As is*." Against the doctor's faith in the solutions to the puzzle of Susan's identity to be had through analysis, the narrator affirms Susan's ability to create herself, provisionally, with play and variation, through art—she wants to terminate the analysis and buy a piano, and the narrator concludes, "I can't help it, Doctor, I am voting for the piano."

Like other actualist texts, Barthelme's fiction typically defines its position tentatively, relatively, in response to the inherited certainties of classical science and realistic fiction: it always votes against analysis, for pianos. One well-known early story, "See the Moon?," focuses particularly on the failures of the scientific method, set off against the ambiguous, intangible values of "lunacy."[15] Like Joseph, the unnamed narrator of "See the Moon?" has stumbled through a first attempt to fulfill the promises made by his culture and fallen flat: education, marriage, military service, a son, a career—and then, at "no particular point," "I stopped being promising" to become "light-minded" instead. The narrator's early attempts at certainty occur, and express themselves, in the context of a scientific approach to experience and value, seen ironically through the narrator's current moonstruck eyes. In raising Gregory, for example, "we wanted to be scientific. Toys from Procreative Playthings of Princeton. . . . and that serious-minded co-op nursery, that was a mistake." As a result, Gregory "thinks science will save us" and rejects his father's joking-serious advice for a sober immersion in education, career, and success. "I said try the Vernacular Isles. Where fish are two for a penny and women two for a fish. But you wanted MIT and electron-spin-resonance spectroscopy. You didn't even crack a smile in your six-ply heather hopsacking."

These are, of course, the same premises that have guided the narrator, who has invested in the material values surrounding him. His friends measure concepts like "fidelity" in terms of "sixty watts' worth of bass," and his father measures success in terms of possessions and income. No wonder the narrator defines his worth in quantifiable terms: "My percentile was the percentile of choice." His first marriage is summed up in the Ant Farm, monument to the scientific observation of nature, he built with Sylvia, and his first career in the drive to "grab my spot at the top."

Now, however, the narrator's energies turn to the ironic deflation of scientific attempts to know by measuring. He invents two antisciences, lunar hostility studies and cardinology, both of which reflect on the failure of Western scientific methods for constructing certainty. He studies Cardinal Y (Why?) because "it seemed to me that cardinals could be known in the same way we know fishes or roses, by classification and enumeration." He asks questions, takes notes, and tests and measures the cardinal but finds "one can measure and measure and miss the most essential thing. I liked him." The cardinal's kindness, faith, playfulness, good will, and joy in life emerge in glimpses, and the narrator demonstrates that science cannot account for these qualities which give him value. Similarly, he studies the moon, graphing its seas on the screen wire of his porch, convinced "It hates us." Why should the moon be hostile? Because it represents all the ludic values repressed and excluded by the grave culture sketched in this story: dreaming rather than striving, imagining rather than fixing in the clear light of day, irrationality and intuition rather than reason and classification. The narrator's methods for studying the moon are, he admits, "a touch irregular. Have to do chiefly with folded paper airplanes at present": the study becomes as playfully "lunatic" as its object.

In place of a scientific method that controls and orders phenomena with a view to producing complete explanations, the narrator substitutes an artistic "method" that allows juxtaposed fragments to suggest various unresolved possibilities. He pins souvenirs on his wall, in the hope that they "will someday merge, blur—cohere is the word, maybe—into something meaningful. . . . A work of art, I'll not accept anything less." In an echo of the collage of disparate bits, left in unranked disorder on his wall, the story itself provides fragmentary, nonchronological glimpses of his past and present life. What does he know? Chaos and hope, and especially a hope in letting chaos be, rather than manipulating it into some falsely certain order. The story turns out to be a letter, written to warn the unborn child whose advent has left the narrator "drunk with possibility once more" of how little can be certainly known. "Here is the world and here are the knowledgeable knowers knowing. What can I tell you? What has been pieced together from the reports of travelers. Fragments are the only forms I trust."

He has little to give his unborn child or his reader by way of resolution to or affirmation in the face of the conditions he has presented. His story concludes with the unironic "hope you'll be very happy here," but as Alan

Wilde points out, "Barthelme's is a world of *Sadness*, sadness occasionally moderated . . . but never, especially in the stories of unmitigated acceptance, canceled."[16] An actualistic response to uncertainty liberates this narrator to see himself, his culture, his language, and his relationships more accurately but provides no escape or transcendence. His account, like Barthelme's art more generally, makes of indeterminacy both a subject and a form, but not a solution.

Serpent in Paradise: The Will to Know

Published a year after the essay "Not-Knowing," *Paradise* (1986) fictionalizes the uncertainty principle. As a late novel, it illuminates many of the patterns I've sketched in the early stories; it develops more extensively the actualistic point of view, even though it refuses the massive scale of all the other novels discussed in this book. And *Paradise* differs in important ways from *Snow White* (1967), *The Dead Father* (1975), and *The King* (1990): it sets the action in a recognizable, contemporary, urban realm, rather than in the tattered fabric of myth, and thereby manages a more direct meditation on actuality than the other novels. Formally, *Paradise* is less structured and conclusive than the earlier novels, because it lacks the traditional beginning-middle-end order conferred by the fairy tale in *Snow White* and by the epic journey in *The Dead Father*. Although Barthelme invokes those narrative structures ironically, and although the novels subvert with their content the formal ordering of experience, and although they achieve emphatically ironic resolutions (the apotheosis of Snow White, the burial of the Dead Father, the dream of Launcelot), the other novels build their actualistic vision on these bleached bones. By making a far more radical break with inherited narrative forms, *Paradise* gains in looseness, openness, and uncertainty. Its protagonist, Simon, lives with the text and texture of the uncertainty principle and learns to define himself by "not-knowing." He speaks in the most ironic voice Barthelme projected, and this amorphous novel of "ordinary conversations" becomes Barthelme's most important actualist text.

Paradise begins with paradise lost, as fifty-three-year-old Simon sorts out, cleans up, and "wonder[s] what to do next" after his beautiful young housemates depart.[17] His marriage has ended; his father has died; his daughter phones but won't visit; three models have shared his bare New York apartment for eight months—then they leave. No wonder he wonders what to make of his situation. What does he do? He dreams "with new intensity," returns after a long sabbatical to his work as an architect, and begins a series of conversations with a doctor. Presented in the divided, double-minded Q/A format Barthelme has used before (in "Margins," "Kierkegaard Unfair to Schlegel," "The New Music," etc.),[18] these dialogues compose ten of the novel's sixty brief sections.

It's important to begin, as the novel does, after the "end" that leaves Simon aware his life is all middle. He defines where and who he is in conversation with the doctor, who represents the scientific method, the materialist assumptions I've discussed above, and especially the quest for certainty through the manipulation of quantifiable data. Not a therapist or an analyst (he rejected that because "it's not medicine" [29]), this medical doctor speaks for the world Simon inherits after his ironic paradise falls to earthliness. The doctor also stands for the larger legacy of Western reason, linear purpose, moral formulas, death-oriented gravity, sexual voyeurism, reification, and control that Simon, as a Western man, must recognize as his own. He stands, appropriately, as Simon's interlocutor and foil; he represents everything to which Simon must answer—even though, ironically, he neither asks Simon the right questions nor listens to Simon's answers.

The novel itself apparently began with these dialogues, published as a story titled "Basil from Her Garden" in the *New Yorker* in October 1985.[19] A dialogue between unnamed (and only sketchily characterized) Q and A on the subject of marriage, values, and A's adulterous relations with Althea, this story returns in *Paradise*, reordered and slightly revised, as the series of ten dialogues between Simon and the doctor. New material added in the novel makes even clearer the doctor's commitment to scientific rationality, fact, order, and empirical method, though these preoccupations certainly appear in Q's comments in the story. A gains depth in becoming the novel's Simon, and Simon's situation differs from his prototype's: his marriage has ended, and in place of a single affair with Althea, who appears conventional, even "a little on the boring side," he has three housemates who model lingerie. Most dramatically, the contrast between Q's and A's perspectives appears in sharper relief in the novel, where Simon's playful, nonacquisitive, unsystematized values have scope to become clear and forceful as an alternative to the doctor's. In both texts, Q covets his neighbor's leaf blower, while A enjoys his neighbor's basil and helps her jump-start her car; in the novel, Q's ironically treated materialism contracts, against the expanding and more serious question of A's attempt to live generously in a materialistic culture. But Q remains important as a foil; an understanding of the satirically sketched doctor illuminates the deadly (but still vocal and powerful) certainties of classical science and realistic fiction against which the actualist speaks his oblique ironic discourse.

Guided by the primary assumption that one can know reality as *res*—thing, material fact—the doctor pushes Simon to define his situation in factual terms. He comes at Simon as a measurable quantity: "You're how tall?" he begins, and he goes on to inventory Simon's physical properties (14). He speculates that the sexual activity with the women must have left Simon physically tired (127); he asks for physical descriptions of the women, comments on Simon's clothes, and asks, "What's in your wallet?" (152–55). The material view of reality pervades the doctor's language, values, and assumptions. He recalls his own former wife only in terms of the things she left lying around (which he, compulsively tidy, picked up [29]). When Simon argues that coveting one's neighbor's wife is "a mental exercise," the doctor responds, "I covet my neighbor's leaf blower. It has this neat Vari-Flo deal that lets you—" (154). As the latest representative of Western science, then, the doctor sums up its essential materialism—its drive to grasp and manipulate reality.

Reduced to objects of the scientific gaze, Anne, Dore, and Veronica become fetishes for the doctor's voyeuristic desire. He slights all of the human, mental, emotional, and conversational aspects of Simon's complex relationship to his housemates; he seeks a detailed picture of the sexual experience in order to gratify his vicarious and prurient lust. He imagines and projects, revealingly enough, the power of the underclothes they model: "Bikini pants burning at eye level," "The white lacy *Büstenhalter* encompassing the golden breasts nudging your arm" (16). He asks, "Were they strident in bed?" and "Which one was the best?" (99, 152). His fantasies lead the doctor to conclude, "So you were pretty much in hog heaven, there, with the three women" (128). Hog heaven, connoting all gratifications of the flesh, is the only paradise imaginable by a materialist—even the excess implied by the presence of *three* women simply guarantees a large quantity of physical pleasure. Simon's story means to the doctor an indulgence in sexual pleasures, which the doctor seeks to assess by the scientific method.

The doctor's quest for clear data shapes the story he allows Simon to tell—it dictates the questions he asks, the interruptions he makes, and the information he hears. Eliciting the story of Simon's first encounter with the women, he rigorously pursues its material setting.

Q. . . . You acquired them, maybe that's not the word, in a bar.
A. At five o'clock in the afternoon. The day was quite beautiful. The light, afternoon light—
Q. This bar was where?
A. In a hotel on Lexington. I don't remember the name of the hotel.
Q. What kind of a hotel? Was it seedy, or was it—
A. Seemed to me quite okay (15).

In the doctor's view, the women are objects for Simon's acquisition, and Simon's response to the nuance of light only digresses from the need to establish a tangible location for this originating event. The doctor wants, in short, a realistic narrative, in which opening details reliably indicate the content and the outcome of the story. Since he knows the women have left, the doctor has already constructed a narrative shape from this end-point; he expects not a love story but a story of erotic adventure, announced in the bar, the hotel, and the seediness he envisions. Because he brings the erotic paradigm so rigidly to bear on Simon's identity, he elicits background details about Simon's adulterous affairs during his marriage to Carol (46) and returns, interrupting Simon's attempts to talk about other (mental, moral, spiritual) aspects of his identity, obsessively to the question of these affairs (76, 98, 154). He will not hear Simon's past in any but erotic terms; he will not admit his present except as a diagnosable exhaustion, satiation, and withdrawal from exotic pleasure that leaves shaky hands, bad dreams, and headaches. With his commitment to medical science and material remedies, the doctor offers Simon pills—Extra-Strength Tylenol, "little yellow guys," and "some of these little green ones" (15, 167, 207).

The deadliness of the doctor's scientific will to control (narrative, eros, pestiferous life) appears nowhere more clearly than in his fantasy of working in "Pest Control." This section, in which Simon has nothing to say, develops the doctor's humorless voice, his methodical purpose, his voyeurism, his identification with machines, and especially his will to order life by spreading death. The doctor, whose life-denying pleasures include watching his "video of the Tet offensive with Walter Cronkite" (47), has admitted that he worries about cancer, wonders what will kill him and when, and thinks these are "a proper set of things to worry about. Last things" (77). The doctor's fantasy life develops logically from this premise; he visits a "neat three-hundred-thousand-dollar home," smiles at the young wife, and moves methodically from room to room spraying deadly pesticide from a silver canister. The adventure concludes with "a properly-made-out receipt," a rising stench of poison, and a triumphant parting for the military conqueror: the wife "pins a silver medal on my chest and kisses me on both cheeks" (191). His pleasure comes in the controlled release of power/death from his canister, in the orderly sur- roundings, in the wife's chaste admiration for his services. He dwells on his linear progress toward its preordained end; controlling pests becomes a metaphor for repressing sexuality, eliminating mess, ordering chaos, and establishing scientific progress through death. This fantasy recapitu- lates that of Pynchon's Blicero in a farcical key—Blicero sends his lover off to fiery death in a silver rocket, while the doctor exterminates instead fleas and roaches. Both scientists, versions of Dr. Strangelove, lust after the certainty found in death.

Every other doctor in the novel, like the analyst in "The Sandman," plays variations on these sinister themes. Medicine, ideally born of the impulse to help, heal, and cure, becomes in Barthelme's fiction a will to "treat," to control, to establish certainties—and Barthelme's doctors typ- ically appear sicker themselves than their patients. By this logic, Veron- ica's father, who beat her with a rolled-up newspaper when she was a child, wanted to be a doctor (111). The obstetrician who delivers Simon's daughter Sarah uses "large dull-steel forceps" that leave "dark bruises" on the baby's head—the birth is dangerous and difficult, but he is "known for not doing Caesareans" (32–33). Most suggestive of all, Simon stops a doctor on the street when he finds a sick, bleeding, drunk, unconscious "semi-corpse" in the vestibule of his building. The doctor "looks an- noyed," follows Simon "with clear reluctance," and refuses to help the man; "Call the hospital," he advises (193–94). Like the doctor who ques- tions Simon, these physicians, indifferent to the "invalid" beings they treat, don't heal the visible sickness in the culture around them.

While the doctors most obviously pursue material certainty, other pub- lic institutions and professions collude in *Paradise*, as in Barthelme's short fiction, to promise that reality can be known. From the religious perspec- tive, knowledge comes from the end: "you know that in the end, you gonna be victorious," proclaims a preacher on the radio (31). A faith in guaranteed ends leads to hearty optimism about approaches; the Catholic priest tells Veronica, when she describes serious obstacles to her marrying a Catholic, "Well, we can work with you on that" (40). The president, "a hearty, optimistic American," brings this faith in reasonable approaches and secure ends to the realm of politics, though Simon wonders if the president is privately "a gloomy, obsessed man with a profound fear of the potentially disastrous processes in which he was enmeshed, no more sanguine than the Fisher King. He did not really believe this to be the case" (58). Simon can't imagine a private uncertainty in the public figure who represents the promise of sure and consistent progress. Education—Anne calls it "standing in lines" (56)—offers similar guarantees of linear and methodical illumination. While Simon believes in education, he recognizes that freshman English conspires to produce "one bright notion and four hundred and fifty words of hay. Or psychology: *Harlow, rhesus monkeys, raisins, reward*" (169). System and order—the right steps leading to the correct answers—promise control to the educated, who are in turn controlled by their faith in promised certainties.

Brief glimpses of city life suggest, in contrast, a vital and violent uncertainty. With its criminal aggression, craziness, conquest, and chaos, city life is digressive and uncontrolled. At six o'clock one morning, Simon sees a couple making ardent love in the garden, on the flagstones; then he sees two men beating a slender black policewoman (23–24). In the market, a man tells Veronica, "I'm a Vietnam Vet and I'm crazy"; he slaps her, she throws a cauliflower at him but hits an old lady, and the Korean grocer falls down in a fit (90–91). In the courtroom where Simon appears for jury duty, a defendant accused of rape stands and "takes a little bow" to the jury (140). A man called Hal, who sleeps on a grate in front of the hospital, wanders the streets at night screaming obscenities (169–70). In a bar, an armless man in a business suit sits holding a Gibson between mittened toes (126). With these urban grotesques, Barthelme sketches a fallen, distinctly unparadisiacal environment, full of random energy, destructiveness, violence, and yearning.

That so much of the city's violence occurs between the sexes is, of course, part of Barthelme's point in this novel about failed marriages and unfulfilling liaisons. Imagining the self as stable and the other as knowable, this culture projects sexual relationships as conquest and marriage as enduring certainty. One partner fixes the other: "I know you," Carol says to Simon, accusing him of a lust he does not in fact feel for the babysitter (52). And out of this presumption that the determinate subject can know a graspable object, men and women build relations based on acquisition, possession, and sometimes violent use. At the socially unsanctioned pole, Hal screams obscenities and the rapist conquers by force; in sanctioned marriages, however, Carol throws ice water at Simon, Dore's husband "cut me in the face one time with a linoleum knife. He was explaining himself" (19), and Tim's wife calls and "says that if the resident bitches and tarts don't keep their hands off her husband she will cause a tragic happenstance" (147). Neither Simon nor Barthelme holds out much hope for any enduring relationship: desire is pluralistic, unfixed; the self shifts and changes; the other also moves unpredictably. To know someone requires openness and listening, but the nature of language and communication make knowing approximate at best. To project attainable certainty onto human relations, as the institution of marriage does for many of Barthelme's characters, is to invite frustration and failure.

Frolic and Detour: The Not-Knowers

Simon knows this, and not much else. Defined by his awareness of what he doesn't know, what cannot be known, Simon *wonders*. While the women are with him, Simon wonders, "What was there to do with these women?" (101); after they leave, he "wondered what to do next" (10). Confronted with the details of daily life or with its larger meaning, Simon responds not with answers but with questions: he does not know. Among other things, he doesn't know why steel is pretty, why firemen seem decent, or what to do with a bra the women have left (36, 35, 10). He doesn't know how to interpret Veronica (112); he doesn't know if Tim is telling the truth (115); "Tarnation take it," he says to Anne, "if I get your drift" (162). "How do you know?" he often asks (162, 171), and "How does she know so much?" he thinks about Sarah (180). He questions everything and everyone, including himself, without arriving at clear answers. "When he asked himself what he was doing, living in a bare elegant almost unfurnished New York apartment with three young and beautiful women, Simon had to admit that he *did not know* what he was doing. He was, he supposed, listening" (59).

Part of Simon's ability to listen, wonder, and accept not knowing in a spirit of negative capability derives from his arbitrary, open, and fluctuating sense of self. He does not see his identity as stable or material or necessary—he remains a fluid and not-so-simple Simon, rather than seeking to become the rocklike Peter on which faith might be built. He has no grandiose self-image: "he identifies with the giraffe. An improbable design, a weird ensemble overall, no special reputation for wisdom, an uncle-figure at best" (71). He has no sense of destiny, no perception of necessity in his career as an architect; he takes no particular pride in his fame (39), and he thinks of himself as a person who "could have done something else, it doesn't matter what particularly." He thinks of "starting completely over in something completely new, changing the very sort of person I am" (75–76). He has no goal, no purpose, no plan demanding linearity of direction. He does not think of last things, as the doctor does; he plays instead with immediate things. "That's what my mind does. Wander," he says, and he embraces "frolic and detour" (188, 164). Like many of Barthelme's protagonists, Simon doesn't work—he's taken a sabbatical, bought little, "thought of no new projects" (41). Instead, he reads, thinks extravagantly, and plays with the women.

Simon's relations with his housemates suggest a model of digressive, frolicsome, and uncertain knowledge, coupled with generosity in the face of difference. While he listens carefully and sees their individual differences, and while he comes to know each (carnally, emotionally, mentally), he does not fix stable identities for the women. He recognizes the inadequacy of the generalizations he attempts about each (43). He does not dominate their conversation, which drifts and leaps at the whim of any participant. He admires and enjoys all three women; he shares—his apartment, his money, his body, his attention and concern—generously among them. He does not envision an "end" or future directing the present relations toward marriage and stability; when he projects forward, he sees ironic and impossible visions of all four living "happily ever after," having babies, playing football, growing old (100, 195). He doesn't attempt to control or possess the women (124); not possessed by them, he has an affair with a red-headed poet. While he appears most attached to Anne and asks her to stay when the others leave, he does not single her out for exclusive desire or commitment: "I love you guys," he tells her (95). Most revealing of all, he does not see his housemates as partners, as sex objects, as mistresses, or even primarily as women: "They were very good people" (30).

Futureless, useless, issue-less and end-less, sexuality becomes play rather than conquest in *Paradise*. It becomes what the French feminists have taught us to call *jouissance*—feminine pleasure that is supplementary, excessive rather than necessary, multiple rather than single, based on difference (or *différance*) rather than fusion into phallic unity.[20] Simon's phallic power, intermittent at best ("He's not potent more than forty-two percent of the time" [48]), loses its point and purpose in couplings (dual, triple, quadruple) directed at pleasure rather than possession or procreation. Simon does not initiate the sexual contacts, nor does he control the women during them; the women come to him, arouse him, direct his responses according to their moods and pleasures: "One night on his back in bed he'd had six breasts to suck, swaying above him, he was poor tattered Romulus. When they couldn't get a part of him they'd play with each other" (60). These woman-directed couplings emphasize play. "Play is what it's all about," Anne says (163). They include tactile and oral play, and in fact focus on these rather than more "end-oriented" penetration; the play goes on after Simon's orgasm (163, 182), sustains itself regardless of his ability to penetrate, and renders his phallic power—his phallus itself—irrelevant. In this way, Simon gets out of the traditional Western man's dilemma, in which "knowing" the woman leads to certain "death." Not-knowing, the actualist's open response, leads to vital, if uncertain joy.

In much the same way he refuses to "know" the women, Simon resists the impulse to fix certain meaning in language. Barthelme explains, in a passage from "Not-Knowing" that illuminates Simon's ironic mode of speech, why writers can't communicate straightforwardly with readers. "First, there is art's own project, since Mallarmé, of restoring freshness to a much-handled language. . . . Secondly, there is the political and social contamination of language by its use in manipulation of various kinds over time. . . . Finally, there is the pressure on language from contemporary culture in the broadest sense—I mean our devouring commercial culture."[21] What those problems leave most readily available is cliché and banality; everyone in *Paradise*, including the women and Simon, mouths dead formulas and dreadful clichés. To avoid this, to restore freshness, and to say approximately the unformulaic things he means, Simon often resorts to irony and metaphor—as if saying what he doesn't mean can obliquely express what he does. Sarah calls, having lost a boyfriend and miscarried a baby: "Probably there's something wrong with you," Simon says, "Some kind of character flaw, final and ineradicable" (88). He means something very different, something sayable only in trite terms that would undermine his wish to comfort. In a similar way, Simon's witty, ironic metaphors (Tim's Medlapse project has "crash-and-burn written all over it," and Dore's opportunity to be vice-president is "like being vice-president of a bag of popcorn" [177]) loosely supplement what Simon means, suggesting with playful excess what cannot be pinned down with rational precision.

For all his openness to uncertainty, Simon wins no triumph over it; he lives with it, speaks it, thinks it, and it's no paradise. He can't give the women solutions to their problems, the result of their dispossessed status in a material culture; he doesn't know what to do with them or for them. He can't solve his own problems; he doesn't know what to do next. When he returns to work after the women leave, he explores a problem of getting light into an office building, but he doesn't know how to solve it (184–85). His experience leads Simon to no epiphanic moment of sure insight, no heroic action, no burst of creative activity, no posture of what Alan Wilde calls assent.[22] While the novel's first sentence, "After the women had gone Simon began dreaming with new intensity" (9), suggests imaginative renewal, Simon's dreams express frustration, inadequacy, and dread (9, 36, 165, 176). He feels "that everything is being nibbled away, because I can't *get it right*" (98). And that sense of gradual loss to small erosive forces leads inevitably to the novel's conclusion, a last "dialogue" with the doctor in which noncommunication trails off into triviality and irresolution. "Q. Feels like Saturday today, I don't know why . . . / A. It does feel a bit like Saturday . . ." (208, Barthelme's ellipses). Not-knowing culminates in no sabbath of atonement and reconciliation, like the Easter Sunday at the end of *The Sound and the Fury*; it winds down instead into an uncertain feeling of loose and unredeemed ends.

While Simon at least knows his own uncertainty, the women experience theirs without understanding it. They are caught in a more radical form of not knowing, not only because they know still less than Simon does, but because they expect to be able to know and don't know that they can't, or why. As heirs of the Western tradition, they expect certainty and reason; as women, they find themselves excluded from these promises and re- duced to exploitable objects in the masculine quest for fulfillment. While their marginal status liberates the women to perceive the bankruptcy of cultural promises of certainty (so that they reject formal education, for example), their exclusion operates still more fundamentally to trap them.[23] As Simon puts it, "There was no place in the world for these women whom he loved, no good place. They could join the underem- ployed half-crazed demi-poor, or they could be wives, those were the choices" (168). Their entrapment is partly economic and social: they have no marketable skills, no acceptable fate outside of marriage. But it's also emotional and personal: they have no voice and no identity in a world that reduces them to "pure skin" (143).

These women don't know. Discussing men as an alien species, they "don't know how their minds work" (49). They don't know Keith Jarrett or modern jazz (61). They don't know the Marshall Plan or modern history (63). They don't know the natural world (130, 200). They don't know what "to do about this bozo" Simon (102), and they don't know if he cares about them as individuals: "How would we know?" "How do we find out?" (105–6). They especially don't know what to do with their own lives: "What are we going to do?" they ask (103), and when Simon asks what they want to do, "Something. But I don't know what" (182). In one of the dialogues among the women where the voices, unidentified, become interchangeable, one says to another, "You're like one of those people who don't know their ass from their elbow" (148).

But the women see this as their own fault. They don't know, as Simon does, that not-knowing is in the nature of things—or as Barthelme puts it, that "our Song of Songs is the Uncertainty Principle." So the women see themselves as dumb and believe they could know if they weren't so dumb. They come to live with Simon because they've sent a lot of money to Africa and arrived in New York without any: "This is dumber than necessary don't you think?" (12). They call each other dumb; they call themselves dumb; they accuse Simon of thinking they're "dumb bunnies" (142, 95, 187). Simon, who doesn't find them uninteresting or unintelligent, calls Dore "dummy" at the point where she rejects education (169)— and, as professional models, the women do serve as "dummies." In marketing their bodies, the women also render themselves "dumb," or voiceless. They accede to, in order to profit from, a cultural definition of woman as beautiful and silent object. They buy into the very model that traps them.

The women are, then, doubly victims of their culture, which both strips them of options from without and judges them by its faulty voice from within. Their internalization of the worst and most damaging assumptions of the phallocentric society appears especially in their sense of their own bodies as imperfect objects. Veronica, for example, "thinks she's got a problem with her rear," and Anne thinks, "my boobs are too small" (55, 94). All three women exercise to make their bodies conform to the ideal presented in magazines that market women to men, like *Playboy* or the lingerie trade journal whose editor Simon meets in court. All three cultivate their own bodies as objects and assess other bodies as objects. "I saw a beautiful ass. In a picture. It was white" (150).

Because the promises made by their culture don't square with—and aren't fulfilled in—their experience, these women are trapped in multiple contradictions. They know better than to believe in material goods as a solution to their problems, but they nonetheless want "the car of my dreams" (149). They know by experience that marriage creates more problems than it solves, but they wonder if Simon will "fall in love with one of us" (39), and they imagine marriage as a viable alternative. Certainty tempts them, even though they don't believe in it. They often invoke the quantifiable, statistical mode of knowing represented by the doctor; they measure Simon's age and potency and envision "some sort of a test" to measure his caring (106). They look to books for "scientific" knowledge: "Thirty-five percent of all American women aren't allowed to talk at dinner parties," Veronica reports (171). They recognize, however, the inadequacy of this formulaic approach to certainty, and they live with the powerful presence of all they don't—and seemingly can't—know.

In the face of uncertainty, the women adopt a generosity much like Simon's. They don't fix or control or possess him; they share him, with rare flashes of jealousy directed at each other. They share money and possessions, not only with each other but also with hungry Africans. Dore lends the others her books, and Veronica gives her OTB winnings to the group. They share labor, taking turns cooking and cleaning. Most important of all, they share talk: dialogue among these women does not focus on the assertion of self, but on the cooperative thrust toward approximate truth. While they have clear and distinct identities, backgrounds, habits, worries, and preoccupations, their voices merge in several dialogues whose speakers aren't identified, suggesting their rejection of the competitive model of talk. When Tim comes to dinner, he dominates and excludes the women; only Simon can break into Tim's self-centered monologue (114–18). The women, by contrast, exchange brief, sometimes formulaic, often playful volleys.

> "How can we leave him?"
> "How can we not leave him?"
> "He's gracious and good."
> "He's not the only pebble on the beach."
> "It's an impossible situation."
> "But I like it." (201)

Like the conversations between Julie and Emma in *The Dead Father*, the women's talk in *Paradise* is not fixed by the rules of male discursive practice, in which the voice insists on its identity and defines its certainties. The women share uncertainties instead, in a spirit of open and unselfish cooperation. "They were," Simon says, "very good to one another" (128).

They achieve no more accommodation to their uncertain condition than Simon. They experience similar forms of dread, apparent in their recurring talk about rabid skunks. They feel, like Simon, frustrated and inadequate. If Simon is not in paradise, the women are in limbo—the anteroom of hell. Unlike Simon, however, they feel angry—at Simon, each other, themselves, and more generally, the conditions that have left them so short of money, options, clarity, and joy. Their anger is necessary, Simon realizes, to "starting the engine" that will take them off on their own (177). When they leave, they accept an uncertainty even more extensive and threatening than Simon's. Simon can expect to read ongoing episodes, but not resolution, in the postcards they send.

At the novel's end, though, the women have left, for valid reasons and with active hope. Simon has returned to his work as an architect—or to his play with the question of bringing in the light. Rather than a passive or quiescent abdication before the power of uncertainty, these characters should be envisioned enjoying a generous hiatus in its midst, at the end of which they return to constructive and appropriate, if limited and approximate, activity. As Alan Wilde puts it, reading "Basil from Her Garden" in *Middle Grounds*, Simon's prototype "A (and Barthelme, on this reading) accept what follows from inhabiting a postlapsarian world," and in A's neighborly relation with Rachel, "there is imagined another, postlapsarian garden that celebrates . . . the *ordinary*."[24] Rachel's brief appearance as the good neighbor is supplemented, in *Paradise*, by the women's kindness with each other and with Simon, and his with them. Such a generous acceptance of less-than-ideal conditions does not amount to defeat at the hands of transcendent mystery. Rather, Simon and the women achieve a skepticism wise to the limits of human knowledge, alive to the plight of neighborly knowers, and engaged in the mysteries of ordinary experience.

Forms of Uncertainty

Like much modern and postmodern fiction, *Paradise* offers a vision of the wasteland, as the references to the Fisher King, the doctors who don't heal, and the unaccomplished Sabbath suggest. The novel's setting reinforces the notion of a wasted paradise: a barren, underfurnished, sublet apartment, with ceilings so high "you could hang yourself in here" (13), with a plastic smoke alarm whose batteries are wearing down, with no plants and with only one artwork on the wall, a print of "automobile bumpers smashed together into a sculptural block" (86), set in the anonymous urban sprawl of New York City where the gardens are mostly fence and flagstone—this is no Eden. Barthelme's contemporary wasteland differs from those of Eliot and his heirs, though, in that it lacks the range of references to myth, literature, the cultural tradition, the stabilizing forms of art. Barthelme is not allusive, in the modernist sense, nor do his fragments work to stave off ruin. He refers less to the eternal and exalted realm of art than to the present, trivial, energetic, and random forces of contemporary culture—to MTV, crack, off-road vehicles, Bloomingdale's, redeye gravy, Christian rock, Black Russians, and Lubriderm. Seeing tradition not as enriching but as damaging, because it offers false promises of certainty, Barthelme revises Eliot's wasteland.

Since the inhabitants of *Paradise* can neither know nor be known, Barthelme's novel inverts traditional narrative forms that imply a stable self and a determinate reality. Several fictive forms, each treated ironically, converge in the field of a text whose possibilities for irony increase exponentially. The private confession, whose maker achieves no illumination and whose auditor neither hears nor absolves, meets the public intruder story, whose aliens come to town with no power to challenge or change the social fabric. The romance or love story confronts the story of erotic adventure, but the actors are pluralized to the point of absurdity; eros is defused by its context in the trivial, the banal, and the material, and romance, stripped of the assumption of attainable certainty, becomes impossible. The individual quest for fulfillment, emotional or erotic, faces the social satire, in which glimpses of city life identify a culture that dooms individuals and their quests.

The most important form underlying *Paradise*—and much of Barthelme's short fiction, as I've suggested—is the story of reeducation, in which a character realizes at midlife the need for new premises and renewal. A postmodern version of the kunstlerroman whose protagonist is an aging artist, this form appears often in contemporary fiction: *Daniel Martin, Mickelsson's Ghosts, Herzog, The Blood Oranges, Good as Gold*, and *A Book of Common Prayer* all describe the later lives of figures—thinkers and artists—who come to the end of early certainties; *LETTERS* focuses on multiple variants of this protagonist. The traditional kunstlerroman typically culminates in regeneration for art and renewal for the artist, and some postmodern versions of the form fulfill these promises as well. But Barthelme treats this form as ironically as the others he invokes in *Paradise*. Unlike Peter Mickelsson and Daniel Martin, Simon finds no lodestone for love and art, no Jessica or Jane, no "one true marriage in the mind" of moral and human certitude that sends Peter and Daniel home in the end of their respective novels—and home to a richer mode of thought and art, as well as an enduring bond.[25] Simon remains homeless and mateless, tinkering with the unsolved question of how to bring in the light.

When these various forms join in the text of *Paradise*, they join in ironic battle. They undermine each other's premises and cancel out the stability such forms confer on fiction. The spiritual biography of the artist might sit happily at the same table with the confession and the love story, but the social satire, the intruder story, and the bawdy erotic adventure normally eat in a different diner. Placed together at Barthelme's banquet, they produce babel. Made plural, relative, incomplete, and discordant, forms that traditionally confer certainty operate instead to remove it.

Barthelme has, like other actualists, his attraction to that most distinctive Western narrative form: the epic. Like Pynchon, Barth, Gaddis, and others, Barthelme brings this originary form ironically to bear on contemporary actuality. But while Pynchon and Barth fulfill the formal imperative in part, producing vast and inclusive statements that also break down the epic assumption of wholeness, Barthelme opts instead for brevity and fragmentation. "Fragments are the only forms I trust," writes the narrator of "See the Moon?" in what may be Barthelme's most quoted (ironically complete) sentence. *The Dead Father* has obvious epic underpinnings, but it fractures conventions like the heroic quest, the journey, the book-within-the-epic, into brief segments.[26] In *Paradise*, written with the barest glance at Milton, Barthelme presents a culture so complex and diffuse that the possibility of epic summation is itself lost. Fragmentary episodes, not developed fully but left incomplete, make up a short novel in sixty pieces, averaging three pages each in length, about the impossibility of grand and comprehensive statements.

Its antiepic stance makes particular sense of the lists appearing throughout Barthelme's fiction. These lists—in *Paradise*, of drummers, of the ingredients of frozen pizza, of stores where the women apply for jobs, and so forth—echo against the epic catalogue, like that of ships in the *Iliad*. There, parts made up wholes, names suggested the larger systems, cultures, and values they represented, and the known world could appear suggestively ordered by entries in a list. In Barthelme, by contrast, the world resists order and refuses completeness. Things point beyond themselves only to the materialism of culture, and knowledge takes the form of amassing trivia rather than constructing plenitudes. Since hierarchical value and temporal causality lose force as structural principles, the impulse to order reduces itself to arranging static nouns side by side in a list.

Skeptical, then, about the validity of order, Barthelme stands at the opposite pole from a writer like John Barth, who delights in ornateness and intricacy. Yet both actualists share crucial assumptions about fictional form; they simply address form in different ways. Barth's play with formal convolution discloses the shaping hand of the artist, who gives artificial shape to the experience of fragmentation and relativity. Barthelme's artists, drifting in their own shapeless experience and not knowing what to do next, find they cannot impose order in art. They can never complete projects, so they can't see the structure that suggests itself from the end. Barth's highly wrought structures flaunt their made status and point to the contingent, chaotic world that makes such structures desirable; Barthelme, abandoning in *Paradise* the mediating structure of myth, writes a loose, fragmented text that points in the same direction.

Among the ordering devices jettisoned in *Paradise* is the beginning-middle-end structure of linear chronology. In traditional narratives, the chronological line implies causal connections and secure interpretations; experience, seen historically as the movement from beginning to end, leads toward resolution and certainty. *Paradise* inverts this structure: it begins after the women have left, moves to their arrival, and proceeds with interspersed glimpses of unplaced conversations with the women and the doctor, as well as unlocated memories from Simon's previous life. The novel does not gather time like traditional epics—it begins, not in medias res, but rather after the sack of Troy or the rout of the suitors. Nor does it suspend time like traditional accounts of paradise; it is mired in ordinary time, though it does not locate events on a time-line. The novel ends with anticlimax and irresolution—like *J R*, it trails off into ellipsis. The absence of definitive beginning and ending points leaves Simon's experience all unshaped middle; the lack of chronological locations for any of the middling events or conversations is more disruptive yet. One cannot trace changes or determine causes or anticipate outcomes; one cannot read Simon's experience with any more certainty than he has.

A mixture of past and present verb tenses assists in the disruption of linear time. The novel begins in the preterite, as Simon "dreamed" and "wondered" after the women "had gone." Moving back in time to their arrival, it switches to the present, as Dore "says" and Simon "says" and "thinks" and "doesn't understand." The rest of the novel follows this general pattern, describing conversations and actions during the women's finite past with Simon in the present tense and changing to the past tense for Simon's later ("present") actions and retrospective judgments on his experience with the women. The effect is a peculiar double vision, in which the women's past presence takes on an untimed, endless quality, a whiff of durational paradise, and their departure plunges Simon back into inexorable clock time, where preterite verbs mark the single, fallen, final quality of thoughts and actions. But that paradisiacal present makes, like everything else in this novel from its title to its final ellipsis, an ironic comment on the nonparadisiacal nature of experience—it serves more fundamentally to suggest stopped, uneventful, insignificant time, a time of waiting in limbo. It helps to dislocate conversations and to disrupt any historical view of events; unlike the closed and causal preterite that tells of the known past, it sets readers adrift in uncertainty.

The alternation between past and present produces one of the most disorienting treatments of time in fiction. The juxtaposed tenses imply different views of experience, and they reach no alignment in Barthelme's text. In *Daniel Martin*, by contrast, an early pattern alternating past and present tenses reflects Dan's failure to perceive the essential continuity in his history; as he recovers a right relation to his past, the novel moves to a univocal preterite that confers unity and coherence on his story. Coover's *Public Burning* also mixes preterite and present but confines them in separate sections assigned to different narrators—the "omniscient" third-person narrator uses only the present tense, while Nixon consistently uses the past. In *Paradise*, the tenses are neither coherently divided (the same narrator uses both, sometimes within the same section) nor finally united. Both completed action and ongoing state, both closed and open, finished and enduring, time slips and bumps in *Paradise*.

It also wheels repetitiously in circles, for one effect of Barthelme's dispersal of linear time is to replace progress with repetition. Wayne Stengel points out that many of the stories develop through repetition, particularly "in those dialogue stories which envision conversation as an endless echoing of stock phrases and responses."[27] So, in *Paradise*, the word "bad" echoes Beckett-like through a conversation in which Dore and Anne judge Veronica, without making any progress toward a definition of why she's "been bad" (134). Conversations between Simon and the women repeatedly explore the same topics, and the doctor returns often to the issue of adultery. Situations recur, like Simon listening to his radio late at night, in the midst of cultural conditions that don't change. Progress, the most important product of linear time, becomes impossible without chronology; so too do epiphany and growth, the whole model by which narratives move protagonists and readers toward interpretive certainty.

Closure and resolution disappear with the same stroke. Lacking linear time, one can't reach the end of the line; lacking progress, one can't achieve a crisis or denouement. Finished before the novel begins, Simon's time with the women changes nothing, so when the text returns at the end to their departure, what climactic "news" can this scene convey? Muttering comic banalities ("Time boogies on"), the women "lurch through the door" (206). Their destination, fate, and future remain obscure. Out of the eight months they've shared with Simon comes no gestation, and while the pregnant young German Simon meets late in the novel casts her "lucky" shadow over the conclusion (205), no rebirth occurs for Simon. He returns to work and throws out the bra, "not knowing what else to do with it" (10). Open-ended and irresolute, the novel leaves Simon and the reader in the midst of uncertainty.

Because it resists the traditional imperative to "fix" experience in time and space, *Paradise* is dominated not by vision but by voices. While vision, hard-edged and definitive, selects significant details and places them securely in a picture, voices produce a plural, loose, and nondefinitive impression. Heard in all their inconclusiveness and banality, with their hesitations and false starts and clichés and interruptions, the overlapping voices of *Paradise* suggest the actualist's world. As in *J R*, where voice more totally excludes vision, this world is energetic, immaterial, disjunctive, and fluctuating. Barthelme's heard speech makes a statement about the poverty of language, much handled and tainted by commercial culture; his dialogues suggest the broader failure of communication in these circumstances. But by privileging the audible over the seen, Barthelme more importantly rejects the discriminating gaze that "captures" things securely in realistic fiction, in favor of the open hearing of multiple voices, fallible guides to what can be said only approximately in language.

With the focus on spoken language, Barthelme also dismisses the significant to take up the ordinary. As the traditional subject and aim of fiction, the significant heightens narrative discourse, validates the narrator's voice over those of the characters, drives the plot through increasingly revealing moments toward a culmination in great themes, and confers unity, harmony, and wholeness on the text. Barthelme's novel, instead, amounts to "a series of ordinary conversations" (30). These appear in ordinary, domestic, and banal situations, as while Simon makes soup in the kitchen. They often address ordinary and trivial subjects—the new Honda design, for example (124); when they take on meaningful subjects, like life after death, they tend to place them in contexts that are immediate and banal: "An eternity of keeping the armpits tidy? No thank you" (84). Barthelme's speakers use ordinary language—common speech, full of fragments, colloquialisms, and clichés—rather than the elevated and edited discourse of traditional fiction. Like Gaddis's, Barthelme's speakers do not know what they mean; they don't see the end they're driving toward, and their language is not an innocuous vehicle. Barthelme himself, meanwhile, does not presume to know the end of his writing or its access to significance; he therefore chooses a narrative voice no more graceful, authoritative, or knowing than the voices of the characters.

Barthelme's explicit awareness of narrative uncertainty—the questionable nature of its elements and methods—has led critics to regard him as the dean of metafiction. He is concerned above all with structure and language, writes Jerome Klinkowitz, and "the key to Barthelme's new aesthetic for fiction is that the work may stand for itself, that it need not yield to complete explication of something else in the world but may exist as an individual object."[28] As an actualist, however, Barthelme believes instead that his own artistic uncertainty reflects on the state of the world as described by Heisenberg. While he doesn't try to explicate the world, Barthelme meditates on it—and believes we can change it. "We can quarrel with the world, constructively . . . if I have anything unorthodox to offer here, it's that I think art's project is fundamentally meliorative. The aim of meditating about the world is finally to change the world."[29] A novel like *Paradise* does not pretend to change the conditions of uncertainty, but it addresses and tries to modify some of the old assumptions— that one can *know* the self, the woman, the world, the meaning of life— that imprison contemporary beings. Addicts of the scientific method, chasers of the material and quantifiable, mongers of the complete explanation, those like the doctor trap themselves in a futile effort to locate the securely and fully known world of the previous century. Not-knowing, risky and unstable, challenges the imagination and vitalizes its meditation on the world. For those doomed to and liberated by uncertainty, not-knowing is not a solution or an end but rather a means of reading the text and living with the texture of an actualistic universe.

EIGHT

BEYOND THE BORDERS

ACTUALISM IN THE QUANTUM UNIVERSE

T he very nature of the literary movement I've discussed in this book invalidates any claim to absoluteness in critical discourse about it. My own terms, including the term "actualism," are not final or determinate; they scarcely "pin down" the subject and surely don't exhaust it. If terms like "discontinuous," "relative," "accidental," or "uncertain" begin to describe the external world as we know it in the later years of the twentieth century, these terms are no mantra whose repetition can give us serenity in the face of what are, out there, multiple evidences of our inability to master nature with language. I subscribe to John Barth's "Tragic View of Categories": "Terms like Romanticism, Modernism, Late-Modernism, and Postmodernism are more or less useful and necessary fictions: roughly approximate maps, more likely to lead us to something like a destination if we don't confuse them with what they're meant to be maps *of*."[1]

Liberated, then, by the irreducible roughness of terms, I want to add a few supplements to the list of six that have structured my essays on contemporary actualistic fiction. These new terms amplify implications present in the other six, while opening up new areas beyond the borders mapped in previous sections of this book. Actuality, seen through the kindred lenses of physics and fiction in our times, is *indeterminate*; its meaning cannot be singly or completely determined, because it contains a paradoxical *complementarity*, a doubled difference, within itself. Opposite and contradictory states—say, behavior as particles and as waves—coexist in potential and interfere with each other, making a single determinate meaning impossible to construct. Seen as definitive of the intersection of physics and literature in important recent essays, these intertwined concepts allow, in both physics and fiction, for a richness of possible meanings and for increased complexity in the models of actuality we can construct.[2] Where binary dualities assumed the absolute identity of terms and the absolute difference between opposites, complementarity assumes that each term is relative and contains some potential interference within itself. More important, complementary terms coexist in a both-and structure.

The external world, for both physics and fiction, is also highly *complex*, *patterned* with a wide variety of intricate structures. In one of the more dramatic recent developments in physics, chaos theory proclaims that these patterns—found in cloud movements, cotton prices, the eye movements of schizophrenics—are regular, obedient to discernible laws, and therefore meaningful. James Gleick writes that chaos theory has opened new territory for physics.

> The most passionate advocates of the new science go so far as to say that twentieth-century science will be remembered for just three things: relativity, quantum mechanics, and chaos. Chaos, they contend, has become the century's third great revolution in the physical sciences. Like the first two revolutions, chaos cuts away at the tenets of Newton's physics. As one physicist put it: "Relativity eliminated the Newtonian illusion of absolute space and time; quantum theory eliminated the Newtonian dream of a controllable measurement process; and chaos eliminates the Laplacian fantasy of deterministic predictability."[3]

While it has roused as much skepticism as fascination in the scientific community, chaos theory has applications in virtually every scientific discipline, from mathematics to chemistry to medicine; studying the nature and patterned motion of apparently random systems, it theorizes about the overarching order in highly complex data, including the human and physical universe.[4]

The set of chaotic patterns discernible in nature is *jagged* and *recursive*.

Developed as recently as 1975, Benoit Mandelbrot's fractal geometry explores rough, irregular shapes: the coastline of Britain, to take one example developed by Mandelbrot. Fractal geometry, says Gleick, "is a geometry of the pitted, pocked, and broken up, the twisted, tangled, and intertwined. The understanding of nature's complexity awaited a suspicion that the complexity was not just random, not just accident."[5] Mandelbrot found qualities of self-similarity, replication of jagged patterns in smaller and smaller scales, pattern within pattern. Studying nonlinear systems in the mid-1970s, Mitchell Feigenbaum found a similar recursive and self-referential quality, whereby patterns replicate themselves across various scales. Feigenbaum's universal theory describes the numerical recursion of patterns on varying scales in complex systems.

The theoretical unfolding in contemporary physics is an ongoing process certain to lead to striking new developments. Related efforts in string theory, four-dimensional interacting supersymmetric field theory, five-dimensional Kaluza-Klein theory, ten-dimensional superstring theories, and eleven-dimensional supergravity reflect attempts in particle physics to construct a unified description of nature.[6] Chaos theory proceeds in a different direction, concerned with the behavior of global systems rather than of discrete invisible particles; it too changes with every new conference and journal publication in the field. Itself a global system in a turbulent process of development, current science has its own jagged intricacy, its own complementarity of behaviors both particulate and systemic, its own indeterminacy of perspective.

The invention of fictive forms commensurate to this intricate, irregular, recursive, complex, and constantly evolving actuality extends well beyond the North American borders represented by the novels I've discussed in preceding chapters. Accurate translations of well-known authors appear very quickly, creating for the first time an international community of writers whose current work is known to each other. Beyond lines of direct influence between specific writers, the possibility now exists for a meaningful global grouping of novelists whose texts explore similar ideas, express similar views of art and actuality, and probe the limits of fictional forms in similar ways. The new physics shows its trace in the fiction of several countries: in the work of J. M. Coetzee (South Africa), Milan Kundera (Czechoslovakia), Gabriel García Márquez (Colombia), V. S. Naipaul (Trinidad), Nawal El Saadawi (Egypt), Manuel Puig (Argentina), Italo Calvino and Umberto Eco (Italy), Georges Perec (France), and Carlos Fuentes (Mexico), among others. These writers share a common fascination with intricate patterns whose meanings remain indeterminate; an immersion of their fiction, however fantastic or magical some of its qualities, in the details of class, race, and gender that constitute the social world in their countries; a sense of political urgency and an engagement with issues of power and exploitation; a thoroughgoing departure from Newtonian stabilities and from realistic causalities; an exploration of historical events and patterns characterized by discontinuity and accident, presented from angles subjective and uncertain, in fictional forms whose recursive intricacy points toward the actual world. Actualism, a radically new fictive way of reflecting on art and actuality, extends virtually around the world.

Contemporary fiction is an ongoing border-crossing, not only because the novel is always new, but also because the world is suddenly and recently new. With the alignment of these complementary novelties, fiction changes; it reconceives itself and its relation to actuality. It reinvents authorship: no longer a necessary deity, the actualistic author descends from the Tower of Truth and wanders, in earnest play, through an irregular, energized field. Actualistic fiction allows for both-and thinking in place of either-or; it creates new models of fictive complementarity where seemingly divergent possibilities, voices, plots, outcomes, and perspectives on reality come together in dialogue. Its version of artistic activity differs vastly from the two limiting and exclusive choices identified by Ortega y Gasset with the garden or the glass: one may represent the world, or one may reflect on the processes of artistic creation. Instead, actualism reflects both, in and through each other.

Actualistic texts refuse the privileged and absolute frame of reference associated with traditional authorship. In place of detachment and omniscience, actualist narrators and authors choose positions of involved uncertainty. The author becomes a character (an author named John Barth) in Barth's *LETTERS*, and he enters into relation and correspondence with the other authors in the text. Didion's *Democracy*, Auster's *City of Glass*, Fowles's *French Lieutenant's Woman*, and Gardner's *King's Indian* locate their specific, historically situated authors by name inside the texts. Nabokov brings his own factual and fictional universes together with intertextual allusions to his previous fiction, with biographical references to his passion for lepidoptera, and with sometimes cryptic citations of his name. Making the author visible, personal, and active inside the text removes the artist's mystified authority *over* it; single and limited, even openly biased, the author exposes the text's multiple and relative sources, rather than withdrawing to the unassailable—invisible, detached—absence that confers absolute authority on traditional authors.

Origins are plural rather than unitary in contemporary physics, and their meaning is indeterminate. The universe evidently originated in a Big Bang, before which neither time nor space, matter nor energy existed; as John Gribbin writes in *Genesis: The Origins of Man and the Universe*, "The very beginning would be at time zero, when the density of the Universe was infinite. But we can't cope with singularities and infinities," so we begin in the first picoseconds after creation.[7] Italo Calvino's *Cosmicomics* are parables of origins, fables of scientific and authorial creation; each is narrated by a character who experienced all origins, Qfwfq. Written fifteen years before Gribbin's book on the origins of galaxies, of earth, and of life, Calvino's interrelated stories are strikingly similar: they offer glimpses of the origins of light, signs, colors, species, and a whole series of stages in the cosmos. One story, "All at One Point," recalls the unimaginable era before the Big Bang, when "we were all there" because "where else could we have been? Nobody knew then that there could be space. Or time either: what use did we have for time, packed in there like sardines?"[8] Closed and petty, full of conflicts and narrow-mindedness, the originary "we" resent the family of immigrants, the Z'zus, who try to hang their laundry on the point, and the unpleasant Mr. Pbert Pberd. The Big Bang occurs when the generous Mrs. Ph(i)Nko imagines noodles: "Oh, if I only had some room, how I'd like to make some noodles for you boys!" and the others imagine the kitchen and flour and fields and sun and space and planets to fulfill her life-affirming wish.

The story is a remarkable account of origins. For one thing, though the universe originates in a recognizable act of "general love," it emanates from the amply female Mrs. Ph(i)Nko and from her seemingly trivial wish to make noodles. Rather than intending the entire human story, this creator can see no further than one meal; no goals or endings are implicit in this beginning, and no transcendent meanings. Furthermore, the force that generates time and space is *not* identified with the author/narrator of the story; here as elsewhere, Qfwfq is rather a dolt, easily confused, a watcher rather than an originator, one of the petty "we." His status as narrator derives from his surviving through millennia to tell tales (he is often called "old Qfwfq"), but he has no superior understanding or insight into the meaning of events. From before time begins, Qfwfq bears the subjective and uncertain perspective of one enmeshed in the midst of time.

While the narrators of actualistic fiction are inescapably subjective, their subjectivity does not withdraw from reality; critics sometimes call it narcissistic, but this fiction is neither self-involved nor self-limited. Though it sometimes invokes conventionally enclosed forms like the personal confession or the chronicle of the refinement of artistic sensibility to a point enabling the creation of the text at hand, actualistic fiction does not fulfill the self-directed imperatives of these forms. Rather, it places the subjective author in relation to other, different voices and forces. Milan Kundera enters *The Unbearable Lightness of Being* to meditate on his connection to his characters. "The characters in my novels are my own unrealized possibilities. . . . Each one has crossed a border that I myself have circumvented. It is that crossed border (the border beyond which my own "I" ends) which attracts me most. For beyond that border begins the secret the novel asks about. The novel is not the author's confession; it is an investigation of human life in the trap the world has become."[9] At this point of authorial self-exposure in the first person, Kundera reveals a will to engage what lies beyond the limits of his own subjectivity. The artist's identity is not a sufficient subject for art; as Margaret Atwood puts it, "Writing is self-less in the same way that skiing is, or making love. . . . your attention is focused not on the self but on the thing being made, the thing being seen."[10] To an actualist, subjectivity itself is no more stable or absolute than any other frame of reference in the quantum universe.

Actualistic fiction therefore narrates from the vantage of one or more unstable subjectivities. Where the author enters the text, she or he speaks with personal conviction and even passion—but with neither more eloquence nor more assurance than the characters. Where a third-person narrator describes characters and events, this narrator does not appear to control fates or to foresee outcomes. Third-person subjective voices, like the narrators' in Pynchon's *Gravity's Rainbow* and in García Márquez's *One Hundred Years of Solitude*, change inflection, tone, diction, distance from the material and response to it—and thus abandon the guiding certitude that characterizes third-person narrators in the realist tradition. Similarly, first-person narrators are unsure how to read their experience and unable to sum up its meaning at the conclusion. Adso in Eco's *The Name of the Rose*, Anna Blume in Auster's *In the Country of Last Things*, Noah's doomed brother in Coover's "The Brother," the author/narrator in Nawal El Saadawi's *Woman at Point Zero*, and Nixon in *The Public Burning* are all narrators who struggle unsuccessfully to construct personal and narrative sense but instead grow less sure as the telling progresses.[11] More often, actualistic texts do not foreground a single voice and vantage point but rather set plural voices in motion and conflict. Dialogues between two perspectives underscore each other's relativity in Puig's *Kiss of the Spider Woman*, Vernon's *La Salle*, Coover's *Public Burning*, and many of Barthelme's fictions. Barth's *LETTERS* sets seven writers in overlapping and sometimes contradictory correspondence; Calvino's *If on a Winter's Night a Traveler* sends two readers in pursuit of the continuations of ten different novels; Gaddis's *J R* virtually eliminates narrative guidance in favor of dozens of heard voices. In actualistic fiction, no voice has a vantage point outside or above the world of the text; each engages its experience without attainable certainty.

Actualistic perspectives on reality by no means dominate the texts in which they appear. In fact, Newtonian assumptions about reality far outnumber—and overpower—post-Newtonian intuitions of relativity and indeterminacy. The conflict with a still-authoritative Newtonian vision, sanctioned by public institutions and reinforced by popular art forms, energizes actualistic fiction: each of the texts I discuss in this book sets a public faith in Newton's laws, together with values constructed on Newtonian bases, against private experiences of the new physical universe. Governments, schools, news media, institutions and professions of various kinds, and virtually all public servants speak throughout postmodern fiction for causal continuities, absolute reference frames, objective detachment, and material certainty. The Newtonian legacy remains powerful in fact as well as in fiction, for reasons explained by Milič Čapek.

> Classical physics simply cannot be forgotten, even though its prestige no longer survives. It cannot be forgotten not only because it still remains valid at the macrophysical level . . . not only because it is being taught for that reason in high schools and in the basic undergraduate courses; but also because its principles are embodied in the present structure of the average human intellect or in what is usually called "common sense." Euclidean geometry and Newtonian mechanics are both based on deeply ingrained habits of imagination and thought whose strength is far greater than we are generally willing to concede.[12]

Because of its alliance with common sense rationality and even more because it so fulfills the human rage for graspable order and predictable clarity, classical physics persists to this day as a habit of thought inscribing the inquiry into and the discourse about reality in various disciplines and institutions—including those portrayed in contemporary fiction.

To counter the prevailing Newtonian imagination of reality, actualistic fiction does not introduce an authoritative voice speaking for the new physical reality, nor do characters arrive at an epiphanic moment of insight into relativity and indeterminacy. Rather, they struggle privately to account for their experience with the Newtonian logic upheld by the culture but find it inadequate. Promised causal order, they bump into accident; in a culture affirming clear certainty, they encounter their own inability to know. Marginalized from systems of production and consumption, deviant from social norms, isolated from each other, confused and erratic in their processes of evaluation, these witnesses to contingency speak— hesitantly and without authority—for the new physical reality. Even those who appear to share the author's perceptions or values—Zoyd in *Vineland*, Simon in *Paradise*, the cabdriver in *Public Burning*, Serge Valène in *Life: A User's Manual*, Gibbs or Bast in *J R*, Michael K in *Life and Times of Michael K*, for example—speak without the conviction, eloquence, or persuasive force that convey authorial sanction in traditional narratives. Powerless to convince others of intuitions they cannot articulate with clarity or force, they also doubt themselves. Amateurs, buffoons, cranks, and eccentrics, these preterite figures cannot translate their perceptions of reality into a set of normative values or a program of resistance; they form no counterforce.

The postmodern writer's assent to the new physical reality emerges less at the level of explicit statement (which would, of course, neutralize uncertainty in an appeal to the authoritative frame beyond the text) than implicitly, in the choice of stories and in the way they are told. And the most obvious formal quality of actualistic fiction is its length: these texts are massive, unrestrained, ponderously heavy in the hand. But they are not simply long, in the way of many traditional novels that unfold their material at length. They more strangely refuse the concept of novelistic economy to become prodigal or wasteful of their material—"loose, baggy monsters." Edward Mendelson has suggested a genre of "encyclopedic narrative" to describe *Gravity's Rainbow*: evolving out of epic, these attempt "to render the full range of knowledge and beliefs of a national culture" and its ideologies.[13] In my own view, actualistic fiction has less faith in comprehensive completeness than this genre Mendelson describes, and while it includes a detailed view of culture, it does not create an encyclopedic compendium. Nor does its "excess," usefully named by Tom LeClair, hold out the hope for readerly "mastery," or prove artistic "mastery" of the world or the reader.[14] It is, in my view, a form of unmasterable excess that explains why length becomes an issue in contemporary texts: Perec's extraordinary *Life: A User's Manual* begins by comparing itself to an unsolved jigsaw puzzle and ends with a map, an index, a chronology, a list of stories, and a postscript, demonstrating the multiplicity and fragmentation of the unassemblable puzzle. *Gravity's Rainbow*, *J R*, and *LETTERS* do not "come together" to produce a "big picture" at the end but rather, like *Life*, fall apart.

These texts' excessive size and scope derive in part from their detailed references to contemporary history and culture. Actualistic texts resemble historical novels with their immersion in the minute particulars, carefully researched and accurately cited, of recent events—World War II in *Gravity's Rainbow* and *Cat's Eye*, the Cold War in *Public Burning*, Vietnam in *LETTERS* and *Democracy*—or, more broadly, of contemporary cultures and their social, political, and historical roots. But their treatment of historical material differs profoundly from that in historical novels: actualistic texts do not trace causal lines through time, nor do they present events as logical and inevitable outcomes of previous conditions. They do not construct histories out of the fragmentary details they cite;[15] rather, they allow the individual detail its own uncanny energy, unassimilated to history's larger picture. They do not miniaturize events in order to contain them in a domesticated version of temporality; they point outward to collocations of loosely related minor and major events. As I have argued in the discussion of Coover, actualistic texts immerse themselves in historicity without being historical at all; they narrate past events in a mode Foucault terms, after Nietzsche, genealogy. Unlike history, which tries "to restore an unbroken continuity" and "to compose the finally reduced diversity of time into a totality fully closed upon itself," genealogy operates through "patience and a knowledge of details and . . . a vast accumulation of source material" in order "to discover that truth or being do not lie at the root of what we are, but the exteriority of accident."[16] Their accumulation of discontinuous and uncomposed accidents accounts for the sense of excessiveness and waste in actualistic novels; at the same time, it places them in the quantum universe.

So too does their lack of closure. Actualistic novels treat events inconclusively, without resolving meaning into graspable forms. Individual sequences and whole novels substitute anticlimax and irresolution for the cathartic end that enables, in conventional narrative, the reader's final detachment from the textual field. Where they invoke traditional structures for closure, like marriage and death, actualistic novels subvert the finality attached to these structures: Ethel Rosenberg's extended death in *Public Burning*, the death of Mr Biswas in V. S. Naipaul's *A House for Mr Biswas*, Germaine Pitt's achieved marriage in *LETTERS*, and the marriage of readers at the end of Calvino's *If on a Winter's Night a Traveler* do not "finish" these characters' stories. Nor do actualistic texts fulfill the spatial imperatives, identified by Marianna Torgovnick in *Closure in the Novel*, of circularity or parallelism, where the ending recalls and completes the beginning. Instead, actualism favors the antipatterns Torgovnick calls incompletion, where echoes fail to achieve a return, or the tangential ending, where the end introduces a new direction. In *Gravity's Rainbow*, the rocket launched at the beginning receives its echo, but not its completion, in the rocket suspended over the Western theater at the end; *J R* and *Public Burning, Democracy* and *Life and Times of Michael K*, end with tangential new beginnings for their protagonists.

Actualistic endings remain open, indeterminate, and unsatisfying to the readerly wish for fulfilled promises and completed patterns. *Gravity's Rainbow* ends, not with a definitive period, but with a suspensive dash; *J R* and *Paradise* trail off in anticlimactic ellipses. These novels remain, to the end, closely involved in the time, place, and events of the text. Actualistic authors and narrators do not rise above the novel's field to provide an overview or epilogue or afterhistory, as many traditional novelists do in order to provide a conclusive view of the novel's action and meaning. Where the last chapter is an epilogue, as in *Public Burning*, or an envoi, as in *LETTERS*, it does not depart from the temporal field of the novel to summarize its meaning or to trace characters' lives forward to their conclusion. Barth's envoi to the reader announces no more than that "*LETTERS* reaches herewith . . . the end";[17] the end of *The Tidewater Tales* suggests "A whole / New ball game! Maybe a whole new tale in verse."[18] The last section of Atwood's *Handmaid's Tale* presents "Historical Notes" on the text, an ironic satire on retrospective analysis and particularly on academic interpretation.[19] In contrast, a more traditional ending, like that in Stanley Elkin's "Making of Ashenden," departs from the limited first-person perspective the story has maintained in order to buttonhole the reader—"it was not outside as you and I know it"—and to provide information and understanding that lifts readers to a position superior to Ashenden: "Ashenden did not know this."[20] Similarly, John Fowles departs from the scene of his text in his epilogue to *A Maggot*, where he explains the characters, history, and meaning of his novel to the reader. In actualistic fiction, even the author speaks from a relative frame of reference, making superior or conclusive knowledge impossible.

Actualistic inconclusiveness frustrates the will to extract retrospective meaning that is, Torgovnick says, basic to readers' expectations of completed stories. "We value endings because the retrospective patterning used to make sense of texts corresponds to one process used to make sense of life: the process of looking back over events and interpreting them in light of 'how things turned out.' "[21] This wish for a final perspective is, of course, a wish to attain Newton's absolute frame, from which causal laws can be objectively identified with clear certainty. It is, equally, a wish to achieve the perspective of history as Foucault defines it, where the "finally reduced diversity of time" becomes "a totality fully closed upon itself." And it is, furthermore, a wish to recover the stable Newtonian/ historical values of traditional texts, both realist and modernist, whose endings settle apparent accident and fortuitousness into reassuring meaning. From the vantage point of the new physical universe, completion or closure is arbitrary: where does an interconnected field conclude? And where do the energetic processes of space-time crystallize into determinate shape?

For related reasons, actualistic texts cannot achieve, and do not aspire to, the unified continuity of traditional narratives. The serial clarity of conventional plot derives, as Robert Nadeau observes, from its Newtonian treatment of time and space. "Motion in the map space of the novel . . . resembles motion as it was conceptualized in classical physics in two important respects: the movement of the character-substance is linear and causally connected, and tends to culminate, like the classical experiment, in arrival at some fixed, preordained location where results of interactions are fully known."[22] In actualistic fiction, events do not follow in a serial order that expresses underlying causal laws; where texts follow chronological order, they fracture the continuity it normally bestows on plot. Narratives leap unpredictably from one subject or scene to the next without placing the action and without providing the retrospective summary that normally justifies such shifts. In *J R*, the narrator's attention to heard voices leads to changes of scene and speakers across telephone and television lines; in *Gravity's Rainbow*, the narrator shifts focus and scene without mapping relations between disconnected events; in *Paradise*, fragmentary glimpses of unplaced conversations and temporally unlocated memories occur in nonlinear order. Actualistic time does not tick regularly at the beat of a universal clock but speeds and slows as it encounters the durational field of the characters' perceptions. In *Cat's Eye*, "time is not a line but a dimension," so Elaine can bend it backward to recall different parts of her past in nonlinear order and at different lengths. Even the most "calendric" of texts, like *LETTERS*, *Public Burning*, or *The Name of the Rose*, disrupt the stable, progressive, and essentially spatial view of time conveyed by calendar order.

In the same way they deregulate time, actualistic novels also energize space. While realistic narratives typically construct solid, believable, particularized environments, full of plausible but suggestive physical objects, located in or around cities of the World We Know, actualistic texts depict less confident relations between people and places. The world we thought we knew, with a recognizable Berkeley campus or an Ithaca-like New Wye, has suburbs we've never seen, like San Narciso or Zembla. Even more disorienting, fictional qualities invade factual places, so that Coover's Times Square, Slothrop's Europe, and Gaddis's Long Island take on some of the fantastic qualities of Van's Antiterra, García Márquez's Macondo, and Coetzee's Empire. Instead of creating clear relationships between solid characters and a solid world, these novels displace characters and readers, making both experience an uncanny loss of bearings—like Oedipa Maas, who "did not know where she was."[23] Because space is not detached from time but part of the same energized field, and because matter does not occupy sites in a void but curves space and alters time, spatial setting cannot serve its conventional ends, shaping and revealing character in more or less subtle ways, like the closed, dark office whose every detail signals Rosa Coldfield's character and fate. Instead, characters, objects, and places take on ambiguous and indeterminate relations.

As relativistic space-time displaces the conventional map-space of the novel, the preterite tense, which mapped closed and causal actions in time, disappears. The preterite was the operative mode of nineteenth-century realism—and remains operative for historical writing as well—because it affirms finality, certainty, and causality. Roland Barthes writes that "through the preterite, the verb implicitly belongs with a causal chain, it partakes of a set of related and orientated actions, it functions as the algebraic sign of an intention. . . . It presupposes a world which is constructed, elaborated, self-sufficient, reduced to significant lines, and not one which has been sent sprawling before us."[24] Preterite events occurred once, in a past time now closed and retrospectively ordered by the omniscient creator; the past can be re-presented with a clarity accessible only from a point after the conclusion. In this way, the preterite casts traditional novels into what Mikhail Bakhtin calls the "absolute epic past," whose world "is an utterly finished thing. . . . It is completed, conclusive and immutable," walled off from contemporary time; the preterite does not lead these narratives to "the spontaneity of the inconclusive present" he sees as characteristic of the novel genre.[25] While Bakhtin argues that novels differ from epics precisely in their open inconclusiveness and their immersion in the incomplete processes of the present time, the reverse is in fact true for most conventional novels, both realist and modernist. The preterite tense identifies utterly finished actions, however recent, set in an absolute past; even yesterday's appearance in preterite dress makes it as completed and detached from the present as King Tut's tomb.

Actualistic fiction therefore breaks out of the preterite enclosure, either by narrating in the present tense or by undermining the completeness of preterite actions. Many actualist novels choose the present ("A screaming comes across the sky") to create a sense of open, relative time that is engaged in the field of space and matter. J. M. Coetzee's *Waiting for the Barbarians*, Italo Calvino's *If on a Winter's Night a Traveler*, Jay McInerney's *Bright Lights, Big City*, Perec's *Life*, and most of the stories in Alice Munro's *Friend of My Youth* occur, like *Gravity's Rainbow*, in the present tense. Others mix past and present: in *Public Burning*, Nixon narrates his first-person sections in the preterite, which appropriately suggests his efforts to achieve a closed and causal perspective, while Coover's third-person narrator uses the present tense to suggest that nothing is finished, and in the process disrupts Nixon's attempts at closure. Nabokov's Van Veen uses a resolute preterite in *Ada* to stop time and to preserve his past, but intrusions in the present tense demolish the artfully constructed finality he intends. Barthelme's *Paradise* mixes present and preterite tenses to produce one of the most disorienting treatments of time in contemporary fiction: neither coherently divided by sections or different narrators, nor finally brought into alignment, their juxtaposition dislocates events and allows no certain perspective on time. Gaddis uses the preterite but brings it alive with gerunds, suspended from each other in mobile fashion and implying imminent and ongoing action. In these and related ways, actualistic fiction opens up the past. It presents actions, not as the products of causality, but as processes in a larger field.

Actualistic fiction chooses an ironic and often parodic relation to traditional narrative forms. Where it invokes the forms that have most fully characterized the novel genre, it fails to fulfill their imperatives. It suspends the process by which these forms have granted stability and order—narrative certainty of one kind or another—to fiction. Though many actualistic texts can be seen as bildungsroman or kunstlerroman narratives, including each of the novels I discuss in this book, none of them achieves a harmonious accord with those forms, and in fact they become interesting, instead, for their divergence from the pattern as they use it. Pynchon's Slothrop, for example, draws upon the prototypical Jamesian figure, the American losing his innocence in Europe. But how different Slothrop proves from Lambert Strether: he does not come to know himself or his world; his consciousness is not enriched by his immersion in European culture; blasted rather than redeemed by his experience, he ends by renouncing consciousness altogether. Similarly, Atwood's Elaine, Barthelme's Simon, Gaddis's Bast, Coover's Nixon, and Barth's Germaine do not come to self-identical harmony, nor do their educations suggest the proper order in the world. None of these protagonists is truly "educable," nor does their environment provide the series of clear "lessons" that would lead to "illumination" and alignment with "truth."

Part of the method by which actualistic fiction loosens the secure grip these narrative forms have had on fictional experience involves the peculiar and incongruous blend of various forms. Each of the texts I discuss invokes the epic, with its summation of national culture and its monumental scope—but each subverts the epic's belief in heroism and wholeness and fractures the epic's elegiac mood. Each text also invokes the social satire, which adopts a perspective on history and culture that is incompatible with epic: witty, critical, dubious about the values the culture attaches to itself, and scathing in its measurement of how far short of these values particular instances fall, the satiric elements of the text pull against its epic impulse. Similarly, each text conjoins elements of the romance or love story, with an appeal to various myths suggesting love's transforming power, and stories of bawdy and grotesque erotic adventure that conflict with and undermine the romance in their version of human identity and contact. Lacking faith in a predictable and self-present identity, romance becomes impossible; love cannot transform in a context where no core of self exists and no union or homegoing can occur. Instead, actualistic texts either leave this narrative promise unfulfilled, as in *Paradise*, or fulfill it in bizarre and ironic ways, as in Nixon's final mating with Uncle Sam at the end of *Public Burning*. By yoking together forms with these inherent and unresolvable conflicts, actualistic fiction cancels out the stability such forms confer on fiction. Each formal ground becomes relative, incomplete; together, they produce a plural and discordant discourse, a paradoxical complementarity, that energizes the text.

Actualistic fiction is moved by a spirit of play that ranges from darker irony to lighter wit, from theoretical experiment with narrative form to broad slapstick and simple pun. John Kuehl identifies a "ludic impulse" emerging in various forms in the fiction of Sorrentino, Abish, Gass, Theroux, Barthelme, and Hawkes; it "involves more than artistic strategies structured through games" (Coover, Nabokov, and DeLillo have made specific games central in fiction) and extends "to make the ordinary seem strange, one hallmark of alternate worlds designed by cosmic jokers."[26] Because actualistic reality is not necessary, single, or absolute but multiple and uncertain, play is no longer the affair of children: scientists, artists, and philosophers play in order to understand. Playing with the pieces, putting them together, suggests a common metaphor for both literature and life in actualistic fiction; reading and living resemble the process of constructing a jigsaw puzzle, to Perec. The magistrate in Coetzee's *Waiting for the Barbarians* assembles a puzzle when he reads ancient wooden slips into a narrative political allegory—a satire directed at Colonel Joll's brutality. The handmaid spells out words in a game of Scrabble with the commander: "Larynx, I spell. Valance. . . . The feeling is voluptuous. This is freedom, an eyeblink of it."[27] The mah-jongg table, with its four corners and its inscribed ivory tiles, becomes a metaphor for life in Amy Tan's *Joy Luck Club*: "You must play using your head, very tricky. You must watch what everybody else throws away and keep that in your head as well."[28] These ludic moments in contemporary actualistic novels suggest that meaning is not already written, waiting to be read; rather, one spells it out and puts it together in play.

The other face of the ludic is the eerie, the uncanny: in the random fall of Scrabble tiles or puzzle pieces, a chaostician might discover an odd, intricate pattern. Actualistic fiction has its own fractal measure, its sense of the jagged, the recursive, the strangely patterned. References to fractals appear in some recent texts, reflecting again the pervasive awareness among writers of developments in scientific thinking. Fractals, intricate pattern within pattern, would appeal to a writer convinced that accidents contain their own complex design, that randomness has its own potential for interesting meaning.

One central use of fractals appears in "Buried Lives," a story by the Indian-American writer Bharati Mukherjee. As the story begins, Mr. Venkatesan recalls "talking about fractals with Dr. Pillai," a mathematics teacher at the college in Sri Lanka. "Fractals claimed to predict, mathematically, chaos and apparent randomness. Such an endeavor, if possible, struck Mr. Venkatesan as a virtually holy quest, closer to the spirit of religion than of science."[29] Yet for all his initial skepticism, Mr. Venkatesan discovers, in the multiple accidents that drive him out of Sri Lanka and into Germany, the marks of destiny. He finds his own fate in Queenie, the sensuous Sinhalese landlady who takes him in and saves him from a blond, racist German who resents the influx of darker-skinned foreigners. Mr. Venkatesan had never married—the astrologer had recommended against it; now he thinks it was "fate's way of reserving him" for Queenie. The events that have propelled him to Hamburg begin with his sister's defiant act, joining her rebel-boyfriend in a demonstration; they end with Queenie's parallel, public act of sudden defiance, moved by her dramatic choice to marry Mr. Venkatesan. As the story ends, Mr. Venkatesan recalls "Fractals. Nothing was random, the math teacher used to say. Nothing, not even the curliness of a coastline and the fluffiness of a cloud." The story demonstrates that the curls and twists may be labyrinthine and difficult to read; still, accidents have in this story their recursive patterns and may eventuate in joy.

Cumulative accidents unfurling in baroque patterns that lead to order, surprise, and the peculiar triumph of a long-delayed return also structure *Love in the Time of Cholera*, by Gabriel García Márquez. Florentino Ariza waits over fifty-one years for Fermina Daza, who eventually fulfills and returns his love. Cholera, sickness, and death do indeed surround them, from the opening death by cyanide to the accidental death of Dr. Juvenal Urbino to the suicide of América Vicuña, the news of which reaches Florentino as he is onboard the ship *New Fidelity* with Fermina. At last, to gain privacy on the ship, they hoist the yellow flag signaling cholera, and their love is consummated against this background. The endurance of attachment and hope through a half-century of accidents that appear to make them futile lead the ship's captain to sense, with Florentino, "that it is life, more than death, that has no limits."[30]

In *Vineland*, Pynchon defines his own sense of a possible return, however complex and incomplete, through the random motions of history. Where it oppressed in the first three, accident liberates the preterite folk in his fourth novel; in *Vineland*, chance works in favor of life and community. Most of the evil and oppression is visited on the novel's central characters by the U.S. government, especially the Drug Enforcement Agency branch of the justice department. Archvillain and DEA agent Brock Vond exerts a sadistic control over most characters in the novel: he exercises a mesmeric sexual control over Frenesi Gates; he intervenes in the lives of her former husband Zoyd Wheeler and daughter Prairie; he runs a military/spy operation designed to rid the nation of drugs, and through it he manages murder, blackmail, surveillance, and a fanatical campaign to destroy each season's marijuana crop. Though there are others behind him, even glimpses of others higher in the agency and repeated references to the Nixon and Reagan presidencies manipulating and directing the agency, Brock Vond represents the sexual energy, the personal magnetism and motivation behind oppression in *Vineland*. Frenesi "would have hated to admit how much of this came down to Brock's penis, straightforwardly erect."[31] To Prairie, "the heart of creep-out, lay back down the road behind her, in, but not limited to, the person, hard and nearly invisible, like quartz, of her pursuer, Brock Vond" (108). His colleagues, more simply, call Brock "Death from Slightly Above" (375).

Yet accident intrudes in its most comic form to restore order and to liberate the folk from tyranny—at least one face of it, at least temporarily. Using agent Hector Zuñiga and the appeal of an antidrug film, Brock has manipulated Frenesi's return to Vineland with her second husband, Flash, and son Justin; everyone gathers (including Prairie and Zoyd) at the annual Becker-Traverse family reunion. Brock comes in the night, by helicopter, intending to kidnap Prairie, who would give him renewed control over all the others. Prairie rejects and insults him, breaking the magic spell he appears to have exerted on her mother. Then Brock is abruptly pulled up. "Suddenly, some white male far away must have wakened from a dream, and just like that, the clambake was over. The message had just been relayed by radio. . . . Reagan had officially ended the 'exercise' known as REX 84, and what had lain silent, undocumented, forever deniable, embedded inside. . . Brock, his authorizations withdrawn, [was] now being winched back up, protesting all the way" (376). By accident, rushing back later in a stolen helicopter, Brock dies. By a series of further accidents, Prairie's extended family, itself shaped by the accidents of history, comes together in the private, communal celebration of the reunion. And by a last, happy accident, the dog Desmond, driven from its home in the early pages and since "roughened by the miles," finds Prairie as the novel ends, "smiling out of his eyes, wagging his tail, thinking he must be home" (385).

The story of the family reunion is set beside the equally complex and comic story of Takeshi and D L (Darryl Louise), an international pair whose acquaintance begins with mistaken identity and attempted murder (thinking he is Brock Vond, she gives him the deadly Vibrating Palm in a Japanese whorehouse) and ends with a peculiar but plausible love. D L stands near the window at sunset, watching Takeshi: "her light-bearing hair, against the simplicity out the window, a fractal halo of complications that might go on forever" (381). Measured by the fractal geometry of complex recursive repetitions, the relationships in *Vineland* show up a baroque jaggedness, a response to minute and distant accidents, and also an order within chaos that allows for comic resolution.

The stakes extend beyond these personal relationships, made possible by the fortuitous accidents at the novel's end; everywhere in Pynchon's fiction, the personal opens out on the political. The oppressors, as always, are opponents of the folk, elitist exploiters of the people's own energies. In the wake of the Vietnam-era "people's miracle," America is riddled with forces attempting to betray, co-opt, and use that energy: the film and television industries that drug viewers with mass fantasies (much like the movies in *Gravity's Rainbow*), the rock music industry that exploits popular music for profit, the government agencies that seize marijuana and attempt to control every other innocent pleasure. The "Nixonian Reaction continued to penetrate and compromise further what may only in some fading memories ever have been a people's miracle, an army of loving friends, as betrayal became routine, government procedures for it . . . simple and greased" (239). As in *Gravity's Rainbow*, sexuality has nothing to do with Their real motivation; Brock's lust is only an afterthought. Frenesi's role in the drama, suggests D L, is "to make it look normal and human so the boys can go on discreetly porkin' each other" (266).

But for all the power centered in "the boys," the people haven't lost their own potent magic. Frank Kermode misses part of Pynchon's point, I believe, in finding a "fairly simple nostalgia, or rather a rage for the lost innocence of America," that "childhood of pastoral innocence so often celebrated by this author," driving the mood of *Vineland*.[32] I find more optimism, more justified faith that the "people's miracle" was in fact real and can be counted on, despite the betrayals, to tip the scales its way again. Frenesi, double agent, betrayer of the movement, bringer of death to Weed, retains a strange innocence and a conscience. Prairie, named for a faith in natural openness, has her own courage and innocence; in rejecting Brock's mesmeric magic, she proves stronger and more self-confident than her mother. Zoyd, as eccentric and baffled as any of Pynchon's protagonists, as driven by others' plots as Slothrop, remains responsible, tries to the end to do the right thing for Prairie, Frenesi, and Flash. Though the eighties are much different than the sixties, the people have an unbroken community and an undimmed vitality which may, in fact, make their alliances better than those in the sixties. Natural community appears especially in the family reunion, but also in glimpses of the ninjettes, in groups of Prairie's friends, in the picketers who encourage Frenesi to go through, in the not-quite-dead Thanatoids. The destruction of Brock Vond opens up new territory for the quirky, humble, dope-smoking, irreverent, creative, and hope-filled preterite.

Pynchon's faith, however, goes even further than the people; at least some characters in *Vineland* express faith in "divine justice" guiding random events. At "the heart of this gathering meant to honor the bond between Eula Becker and Jess Traverse, that lay beneath, defined, and made sense of them all," is the annual reading of a passage from Emerson. "Secret retributions are always restoring the level, when disturbed, of the divine justice. It is impossible to tilt the beam. All the tyrants and proprietors and monopolists of the world in vain set their shoulders to heave the bar. Settles forever more the ponderous equator to its line, and man and mote, and star and sun, must range to it, or be pulverized by the recoil" (369). The faith in divine justice lies at the heart of the union of Eula and Jess, at the heart of their family and its young, at the heart of the annual return to celebrate their community. For a reader, it's impossible to tell whether divine justice or random accident kills Brock, reunites Prairie and her mother, and brings Desmond to the very glade where Prairie lies sleeping. It may not matter: new possibilities for life emerge either way.

C. P. Snow argued in 1959 that science and literature had diverged—with irreconcilable worldviews, they "had almost ceased to communicate at all."[33] Now, some thirty years later, science and literature sup at the same table (on noodles, no doubt) and talk long into the night. Sometimes they argue; they have trouble with each other's dialects, and they don't agree on what they see or what it means. Beside this strange intimacy hangs a glass, with a garden beyond. Science not only watches both the garden and the glass but watches them alter each other, sees its own reflection in the windowpane, and considers how its vision is framed by the window's square aperture. Literature breaks the glass, steps out, picks a flower from the garden: it turns out to be a glass narcissus. Literature hands the flower to science. Science breaks the glass, and inside is an identically shaped and colored smaller narcissus: it's alive. The pattern of glass shards remaining in the wooden frame looks, from a certain angle, oddly like a flower.

What began as "a very simple optical problem" yielding an equally simple aesthetic choice has become, by now, far more complex. Both science and literature bring complementary interests in the process of vision and creation and in the world on which those processes operate. Their dialogue appears in what I've called actualism: fiction in the quantum universe.

NOTES

1. Ortega y Gasset, *Dehumanization of Art*, 10–11; the quotations following are from 11–12.

2. Rother, "Parafiction," 38; Klinkowitz, *Literary Disruptions*, 32; Federman, "Surfiction," 7.

3. Kiernan, *American Writing since 1945*, 55.

4. Klinkowitz, *Life of Fiction*, 149.

5. Sukenick, in ibid., 18, 25.

6. Pynchon, *Slow Learner*, 21.

7. Patricia Waugh, for example, extends metafiction in the direction of actualism when she argues that some metafictionists accept a "substantial real world" outside of fiction and language (*Metafiction*, 53).

8. Williams, *Long Revolution*, 20.

9. Barth, "Literature of Replenishment," 70.

10. Wilde, *Middle Grounds*, 23–24. I find Wilde's phenomenological approach entirely congenial, and I agree with him in valuing the contemporary fiction that is neither realistic nor metafictional. I admire the wit and grace of Wilde's writing, and I share his interest in the process by which consciousness meets and reinvents actuality—or as Wilde puts it, "The world offers itself not as a fully realized datum but as a potential to be activated by human beings situated directly in its midst" (21).

11. Actualism is my own term, discussed in the latter half of this chapter. Like Heisenberg, others (including Arthur Schopenhauer, Robert Duncan, and Robert Creeley) have seen "actual" in opposition not to "ideal" but to

"real." "Actualism" does not appear in the *OED*, though "actualist" refers there to "one who aims at actuality or realism." A small group of contemporary poets belong to an unrelated actualist movement, represented in Sklar and Gray, *Actualist Anthology*. These poets gather for "happening"-style conventions in Iowa City and Berkeley; their poems emphasize spontaneity and play.

12. Čapek, *Philosophical Impact of Contemporary Physics*, xi.

13. Morris, *Dismantling the Universe*.

14. Munro, *Friend of My Youth*, 23.

15. Mellard, *Exploded Form*, 30. See also Sypher, *Loss of the Self*, 79–86.

16. Among the books addressing physics and fiction, see especially Hayles, *Cosmic Web*; Nadeau, *Readings from the New Book on Nature*; and Craige, *Literary Relativity*. Among the recent articles exploring the connection between physics and literature, I particularly admire Bohnenkamp, "Post-Einsteinian Physics and Literature"; and De Beaugrande, "Quantum Aspects of Perceived Reality."

17. See Čapek, *Philosophical Impact of Contemporary Physics*; Morris, *Dismantling the Universe*; Hawking, *Brief History of Time*; Gribbin, *Genesis*; Davies, *God and the New Physics*; Stableford, *Mysteries of Modern Science*; Bernstein, *Einstein*; Zukav, *Dancing Wu Li Masters*; Heisenberg, *Physicist's Conception of Nature*, *Physics and Beyond*, and *Physics and Philosophy*; Bohr, *Atomic Theory*; and Jammer, *Philosophy of Quantum Mechanics*.

18. Čapek, *Philosophical Impact of Contemporary Physics*, 140.

19. Ibid., 384.

20. Heisenberg, *Physicist's Conception of Nature*, 29.

21. Zukav, *Dancing Wu Li Masters*, 135; see also Bohr, *Atomic Theory*, 53–57.

22. Bohr, *Atomic Theory*, 54.

23. Mailer, "Man Who Studied Yoga," in *Short Fiction of Norman Mailer*, 279.

24. Heisenberg, *Physics and Beyond*, 14.

25. Watt, *Rise of the Novel*, 12.

26. Nadeau, *Readings from the New Book on Nature*, 187.

27. Flaubert, "On Realism," 90–95.

28. See Jan Gorak's fine study of this topos in *God the Artist*.

29. Joyce, *Portrait of the Artist*, 252.

30. Alter, *Partial Magic*, 129. Alter includes Melville in the self-conscious tradition, though the romance appears different in some important ways from the eighteenth-century novels of self-consciousness he discusses.

31. Mellard, *Exploded Form*, xii.

32. McHale, *Postmodernist Fiction*, 38.

33. Waugh, *Metafiction*, 18, 53.

34. Kuehl, *Alternate Worlds*, 293.

35. Siegle, *Politics of Reflexivity*, 2–4.

36. Indeed, Siegle argues that "self-conscious," the term used by both

Robert Alter and Brian Stonehill, preserves traditional notions of the self, which are misleading when applied to a literary text rather than a subject, and which imply a transcendental model of the self as "savior of truth": "A self that is coherent, stable, and knowable provides a center of fixed truth" (ibid., 7).

37. Hayles, *Cosmic Web*, 41.

38. Porush, *Soft Machine*, 70.

39. LeClair, *Art of Excess*, 7–8.

40. At a conference in April 1988, whose proceedings have appeared in *Critique*, LeClair raised the issue of mastery. Richard Feldstein objected to the exclusion of women from the "all-male circle" of postmodernism; speaking from the floor in response to the conference, he raised "the question of the word 'mastery,' which is circulating around here, unironically, which I find appalling." See "Postmodernism," 272.

41. Barth, "Literature of Replenishment," 65.

42. See my essay "Actualism" on Pynchon's education at Cornell.

43. T. Moore, *Style of Connectedness*, 14. See also Schaub, *Pynchon*, 149.

44. Ames, "Power and the Obscene Word"; Russell, "Pynchon's Language"; Quilligan, "Thomas Pynchon"; Hume, *Pynchon's Mythography*; Clark, *Reflections of Fantasy*; Cooper, *Signs and Symptoms*; Van Delden, "Modernism"; McHale, "Modernist Reading"; Morgan, "*Gravity's Rainbow*"; Seidel, "Satiric Plots"; and Mendelson, "Gravity's Encyclopedia."

45. Cooper, *Signs and Symptoms*; T. Moore, *Style of Connectedness*; Schwartz, "Thomas Pynchon"; Hayles, *Cosmic Web*; Friedman, "Science and Technology"; Friedman and Puetz, "Science as Metaphor"; Pearce, "Introduction," in Pearce, *Critical Essays*, 1–11; Henkle, "Morning and the Evening Funnies"; Schaub, *Pynchon*; and Hume, *Pynchon's Mythography*.

46. McHale, "Modernist Reading," 107.

47. See Quilligan, "Thomas Pynchon," 200; Schaub, *Pynchon*, 149; and T. Moore, *Style of Connectedness*, 14–15.

CHAPTER TWO

1. The definitive essay on Pynchon's self-reflexivity is Russell, "Pynchon's Language." See the discussion of Pynchon criticism above in chapter 1.

2. Pynchon, *Gravity's Rainbow*, 385. Citations of this novel, hereafter *GR*, appear in the text. All ellipses in quotations are Pynchon's, except those in brackets, which are mine.

3. Kevles, *Physicists*, 162.

4. Pynchon's unique strategy of narrative connection is discussed by many critics; I found especially important readings in Hite, *Ideas of Order*; T. Moore, *Style of Connectedness*; and Cooper, *Signs and Symptoms*. James Perrin Warren

treats the narrative discontinuities of *GR* from a linguistic perspective in "Ritual Reluctance." Steven Weisenburger argues that episodes in *GR* "are composed according to a complex, circular motion," a "heterocyclic" looping together of cycles based on the Christian liturgical calendar (*"Gravity's Rainbow" Companion*, 9–10).

5. Pynchon, *V.*, 286.

6. On mothers and other women in *GR*, see Kaufman, "Brünnhilde and the Chemists."

7. Notable exceptions include Mendelson, "Gravity's Encyclopedia," 182–83; Schaub, *Pynchon*, 46; Simmon, "Beyond the Theater of War," 127; these critics observe the falseness, control, or "spurious continuity" of films in *GR*. See also Clerc, "Film in *Gravity's Rainbow*."

8. Stark, *Pynchon's Fictions*, 142.

9. Cowart, *Thomas Pynchon*, 32.

10. For a related assessment of von Göll, see Hayles, *Cosmic Web*, 183–84.

11. Pynchon writes in the introduction to *Slow Learner* that he remains "a dedicated sucker" of chase scenes: "it is one piece of puerility I am unable to let go of" (19).

12. Siegel, *Pynchon*, 70.

13. Fowler, *Reader's Guide to "Gravity's Rainbow,"* 55. Similar positions are taken in Hayles, *Cosmic Web*, 183–88; and Hume, *Pynchon's Mythography*, 217–21.

14. Plater, *Grim Phoenix*, 214–15.

15. Mendelson, "Gravity's Encyclopedia," 176, 183. Similar readings appear in Slade, *Thomas Pynchon*, 200–210; and Weisenburger, "End of History?," 140–56.

16. Hite, *Ideas of Order*, 119–20.

17. Hayles, *Cosmic Web*, 188.

18. See Hite, *Ideas of Order*, 18; Quilligan, "Thomas Pynchon," 195–97; on Pynchon's own active reading of historical sources, see Weisenburger, "End of History?."

19. Hite, *Ideas of Order*, 127.

20. Quilligan, "Thomas Pynchon," 209–10.

21. Surrealism means as many different things as realism does to its various definers and practitioners. For my purposes here, what principally matters is the common agreement to see realism and surrealism as opposites and hence to define surrealism as an inversion of some aspects of realism. When Slothrop turns from the pursuit of linear order characteristic of realistic systems to the conviction that *no* order exists, he becomes what Pynchon will call a "sentimental surrealist": "There's nothing so loathsome as a sentimental surrealist" (696). See also *Slow Learner*: "I could also with an easy mind see axed much of the story's less responsible Surrealism" (22).

22. Pynchon, *Crying of Lot 49*, 136.

23. See George Levine's useful early discussion of Pynchon's catalogs in "V-2."

24. William Plater argues that Slothrop evolves beyond his early "map-consciousness" toward a perception of interior space (*Grim Phoenix*, 60–61). In the resonant terms provided by John Vernon, Slothrop should be understood, according to Plater, as leaving the map, a locus of discrete spaces often structured as opposites, for the garden, a place uniting opposites and making all areas of experience accessible to each other; see Vernon, *Garden and the Map*. I see Slothrop's abandonment of mapmaking, not as a liberation, but as a capitulation to precisely the schizophrenia Vernon describes. "The either-or structure of isolation from the world and merging with it represents such a polarization that the two are the same; both represent an alienation and deadening of consciousness, a total surrender to objectivity" (28).

25. This common assumption appears, for example, in Fowler, *Reader's Guide to "Gravity's Rainbow,"* 96; Mackey, *Rainbow Quest of Thomas Pynchon*, 37; and Simmon, "*Gravity's Rainbow* Described," 58.

26. Wolfley, "Repression's Rainbow," 883.

27. Wolfley argues convincingly that Pynchon presents "no totally healthy sex" in *GR*, but rather various sexual oddities, each "traceable to some peculiarly Western social perversion" (ibid., 882–83).

28. Seed, *Fictional Labyrinths of Thomas Pynchon*, 163.

29. Douglas Fowler, for example, believes that "Rilke's romanticism is always apropos in reading Pynchon" (*Reader's Guide to "Gravity's Rainbow,"* 284). See also Ozier, "Calculus of Transformation." Ozier argues that "the dissolution of Slothrop's persona is not a diminution but part of a transformation into the timeless Being of Rilke's angels" (197). Thomas Schaub reads the Rilkean references as more ambiguous (*Pynchon*, 72–73).

30. Fowler, *Reader's Guide to "Gravity's Rainbow,"* 80–85.

31. Ibid., 80–81.

32. Ibid., 14–15.

33. Hite, *Ideas of Order*, 40.

34. Kathryn Hume proposes that the novel is unified by a recurrent image-complex involving "an aerial force of destruction, the targeted city, and the cowering creature awaiting annihilation. Significantly, the image-complex is not rendered from the sidelines, from the distanced perspective of bystander or artist," but rather from above and below ("Views from Above," 625).

35. Pynchon, *Crying of Lot 49*, 10.

36. Cowart, *Thomas Pynchon*, 8.

37. Insightful discussions of Pynchon's subjective narrative voice appear in Schaub, *Pynchon*, 103–38; and Hite, *Ideas of Order*, 131–57.

CHAPTER THREE

1. Watkins, "W. S. Merwin," 189.

2. Mazurek, "Metafiction," 31, 41. On Coover as metafictionist, see also Schmitz, "Robert Coover"; Scholes, "Metafiction"; and Heckard, "Robert Coover." For an allied reading of Coover's games as strategies for disruption of literary reference, see Wilczyński, "Game of Response."

3. Coover, *Pricksongs and Descants*, 77–79.

4. McCaffery, "Interview," 69.

5. Ibid., 67.

6. Gado, *First Person*, 142.

7. McCaffery, "Interview," 66.

8. Coover, *Public Burning*; page citations of this novel appear in the text.

9. For Heisenberg's account of Einstein's response to quantum physics, see *Physics and Beyond*, 79–81. On the statistical, acausal base of quantum theory, see Zukav, *Dancing Wu Li Masters*, 58–62; and McKenzie, *Major Achievements of Science*, 324–26, 342–44.

10. Born, *Atomic Physics*, 102.

11. Coover, *Universal Baseball Association, Inc.*, 40. On Coover's use of physics in this novel, see Hansen, "Dice of God." For compatible approaches, see Hertzel, "What's Wrong with the Christians?"; Shelton, "Humor and Balance"; Berman, "Coover's UBA"; and Gorak, *God the Artist*, 101–2.

12. Coover, *Pricksongs and Descants*, 183. On this collection of stories, see Wineapple, "Robert Coover's Playing Fields"; and McCaffery, "Magic of Fiction Making."

13. See Ames, "Coover's Comedy."

14. For these two examples, see Wills, *Nixon Agonistes*, 24, 91–138. Coover has read Wills carefully, as demonstrated by his use of a remark Nixon made to Wills in an interview: "I'm an introvert in an extrovert profession" (32); it reappears in *Public Burning*, 348. Coover also relies on a range of biographies of Nixon; on the *New York Times*, *Time*, and other journalistic accounts of events, people, and culture; and on Nixon's own writings: *Six Crises* and *Almanack of Poor Richard Nixon*.

15. Groden, "Construct of Fictions." For a survey of other reviews, as well as a general introduction to all of Coover's early fiction, see Hume, "Robert Coover's Fiction."

16. Kuehl, *Alternate Worlds*, 225. Kuehl's insightful comparisons of Coover and Doctorow appear on 224–31.

17. Foucault, "Nietzsche, Genealogy, History," 146, 152.

18. Kevles, *Physicists*, 336–37.

19. Balitas, "Historical Consciousness."

20. LeClair, *Art of Excess*, 107.

21. Foucault, "Nietzsche, Genealogy, History," 153, 140.

22. Durand, "Exemplary Fictions of Robert Coover," 133–34.

23. Sartre, *Nausea*, 39–40, my ellipses.

24. Mazurek, "Metafiction," 34.

25. LeClair, *Art of Excess*, 117.

26. See also Gallo, "Nixon"; and LeClair, *Art of Excess*, 116–17.

27. The language of detection and causality permeates the reading of Nixon through R. D. Laing in John Z. Guzlowski's "Coover's *The Public Burning*," 60, 61, 70.

28. Kuehl, *Alternate Worlds*, 226.

29. LeClair, *Art of Excess*, 127.

30. See Coover's observations about Nixon in McCaffery, "Interview," 75.

31. Gado, *First Person*, 148.

32. Eliot, "*Ulysses*, Order, and Myth," 123.

33. Coover, *Pricksongs and Descants*, 77.

34. Gado, *First Person*, 152; Coover's discussion of myth extends to 157.

35. Ibid., 156. See Durkheim, *Elementary Forms*, 336–37.

36. For an approach to Coover's use of myth focused mainly on echoes of Eliade's *Myth of the Eternal Return*, see Ramage, "Myth and Monomyth."

37. Campbell, *Hero with a Thousand Faces*, 51; and Coover, *Public Burning*, 87.

38. Campbell, *Hero with a Thousand Faces*, 60.

39. Ibid., 79; Coover, *Public Burning*, 463.

40. Campbell, *Hero with a Thousand Faces*, 90.

41. Ibid., 120.

42. Kuehl sketches some of the novel's mixed genres (*Alternate Worlds*, 229).

CHAPTER FOUR

1. See Matanle, "Love and Strife"; and Thielemans, "Art as Redemption of Trash."

2. Black, "Paper Empires," 28–30.

3. Malmgren, "William Gaddis's *J R*," 10.

4. Kiernan, *American Writing since 1945*, 57.

5. LeClair, "William Gaddis," 588.

6. Weisenburger, "Paper Currencies," 20.

7. Kuehl and Moore, "Interview," 4–5.

8. Kuehl and Moore, "Introduction," in Kuehl and Moore, *In Recognition*, 12–13.

9. Gaddis, *J R*, 70. Subsequent references to this novel will be cited in the text. All ellipses in quotations are Gaddis's, except those in brackets, which are

mine. Except in long quotations, quotation marks replace the dash Gaddis uses for dialogue.

10. Gaddis, "Rush for Second Place," 35. See also Abádi-Nagy, "William Gaddis," 67.

11. Wiener, *Human Use of Human Beings*, 10. Gaddis cites Wiener in "Rush for Second Place," 35. Accounts of Gibbs's life and accomplishments can be found in Seeger, *J. Willard Gibbs*; and Crowther, *Famous American Men of Science*, 227–97. Jack Gibbs not only refers to Wiener's book (403) but steals some lines from it (498). See my "Disclosing Time," 5; reprinted in Kuehl and Moore, *In Recognition*.

12. Einstein and Infeld, *Evolution of Physics*, 208.

13. For a discussion of *J R* focusing on usury, see Weisenburger, "Contra Naturam?."

14. I discuss recurrent patterns of spilling, falling, and scattering in "For a Very Small Audience."

15. I discuss patterns of repetition in "Disclosing Time."

16. Karl suggests that *J R* could be seen "as an antipastoral. . . . J R denies pastoral—that is, natural truth—in every scene where he appears" ("Gaddis," 194).

17. Gaddis's interest in the player piano, and some of his research on the subject, appears in his brief essay "Stop Player. Joke No. 4."

18. Matanle, "Love and Strife," 117.

19. See Strehle, "Disclosing Time."

20. Gaddis, "Rush for Second Place," especially 32–35.

21. Weber, *Protestant Ethic*, 181. Gaddis refers to Weber in "Rush for Second Place," 36.

22. Weber, *Protestant Ethic*, 157–58.

23. Steven Weisenburger interprets the family heritage differently, arguing that Bast's "legacy from Thomas is one of technology, the rational separation of the musical flux into bits; from James, a devotion to art and an alienation from monetary culture" ("Paper Currencies," 15). As I will show, I find Bast's legacy more mixed on both sides.

24. For a review of some negative evaluations of Odysseus in the post-Homeric tradition, see Stanford, "Untypical Hero."

25. This wish is eventually realized, ironically, when the Bast sisters are placed in just such a mansion, now coverted to a nursing home (713).

26. McCandless has an affair with Elizabeth, who is an heiress like Amy; he betrays her and walks away from the hope for love. "You despise their . . . hopes because you haven't any," she says; "it was all your despair locked away in that room" (Gaddis, *Carpenter's Gothic*, 244). See John Kuehl's reading of this novel in his *Alternate Worlds*, 258–62.

27. Johan Thielemans reads Bast's progress differently; the recognition of

the futility of action "comes as a relief," but Bast takes up his compositional work "still pursuing that dream of communicating his inner vision" ("Art as Redemption," 141).

28. Tennyson's "Locksley Hall" serves as an apt measure of Bast's Newtonian perceptions, with its sense of end-ordered, progressive time ("Yet I doubt not thro' the ages one increasing purpose runs"), of linearity ("Let the great world spin for ever down the ringing grooves of change"), and of the superior reality of matter ("But the jingling of the guinea helps the hurt that Honor feels").

29. Beaton undergoes a similar purgation when he vomits in the same hospital men's room after destroying Cates's control of the corporation. Though Beaton's fate is as ambiguous as Bast's (Beaton will evidently go on working for the same company, now run by Amy Joubert Cutler), his last words are also promising: "I'm, I'll be all right" (713).

30. In his notes, Gaddis wrote of the end of *The Recognitions*, "I don't want the end to seem trite, an easy way out; because I don't want it to sound as though Wyatt has finally found his place. . . . I simply want the intimation that, in starting a drawing of his daughter, Wyatt, seeing her in her trust and faith (love), is *beginning*." But his revisions of the manuscript left only hints of this hope; see Koenig, "Recognizing Gaddis' *Recognitions*," 70. A similar, guarded faith that Bast has been prepared by his experience to begin, tempered by an awareness of everything in his environment that dooms most beginnings, characterizes the end of *J R*. By contrast, the end of *Carpenter's Gothic* is much bleaker; with Liz dead and Paul courting her wealthy friend's money, while McCandless has fled to Haiti, no new beginning or hope for one remains.

31. Thielemans, "Energy of an Absence," 115.

32. See Strehle, "Disclosing Time."

33. Watt, *Rise of the Novel*, 25.

34. S. Moore, "Chronological Difficulties," 90.

35. James, "Preface," x.

36. See Tom LeClair's essay on the "recursive form" of *J R* as an expression of various meanings of waste (*The Art of Excess*, 87–105).

37. Barthelme, *Snow White*, 106, 97–98.

38. Kuehl, *Alternate Worlds*, 256.

39. Gaddis has said that "in approaching *J R* as a novel, I was at pains to remove the author's presence from the start as must be obvious," and his paring down of narrative transitions is indeed a clear and characteristic feature of the text. But the novel does contain narrative as well as dialogue, and the narration emphasizes a single, subjective presence—one very different from the traditional author's, to be sure. See Kuehl and Moore, "Interview," 5.

CHAPTER FIVE

1. Barth, *LETTERS*, 52. Page citations of this work appear in the text. All ellipses in quotations are Barth's, except those in brackets, which are mine.

2. Reilly, "Interview with John Barth," 4.

3. Enck, "John Barth," 11.

4. Barth, "Literature of Exhaustion," 33.

5. See Rovit, "Novel as Parody."

6. Trachtenberg, "Barth and Hawkes," 18.

7. See Guerard, "Notes."

8. See Alter, "Self-Conscious Moment."

9. See Graff, "Babbitt at the Abyss," 322.

10. Said, "Contemporary Fiction and Criticism," 237.

11. Tatham, "John Barth," 71.

12. Barth, *End of the Road*, 119.

13. Enck, "John Barth," 6.

14. Barth, "Literature of Exhaustion," 33.

15. David Majdiak says of *The End of the Road*, "Though Barth's purpose is to discredit the norms which the novel assumes he does this to render a more credible picture of reality through a more viable fictional form" ("Barth," reprinted in *Critical Essays on John Barth*, 103).

16. Carmichael, "John Barth's *Letters*," 66.

17. Barth, "Literature of Replenishment," 70, my ellipses.

18. Cited in McKenzie, *Major Achievements of Science*, 300. See also Zukav, *Dancing Wu Li Masters*, 146–49; and Davies, *Space and Time*, 11–19.

19. Cited in McKenzie, *Major Achievements of Science*, 310.

20. Davies, *Space and Time*, 34–35. Relativity must not, however, be misconstrued to imply a relativistic equality in all outlooks and values. As a physical theory, it actually describes what is *in*variant or *un*changing in reality—the velocity of light, the laws of nature in uniformly moving systems, and the equivalence of gravity and acceleration. According to Gary Zukav, relativity theory "describes in what way the relative aspects of physical reality appear to vary, depending upon the point of view of different observers . . . but, in the process, it defines the non-changing, absolute aspect of physical reality as well" (*Dancing Wu Li Masters*, 143). Since one can derive valid propositions about systems in relative motion, relativism is not a necessary conclusion of Einstein's theories. Einstein himself rejected any connection between his work and relativism in religion, art, or moral values; see Holton, "Introduction," in Holton and Elkana, *Albert Einstein*, xiii–xiv. Nor can relativity be held to imply ethical relativism. "The theory of relativity does not lead to a relativistic interpretation of structures, and . . . it is patent that this theory

is utterly noncommittal concerning the thesis of ethical relativism" (Roten-streich, "Relativity and Relativism," 194).

21. Modernist artists also responded, quickly and enthusiastically, to relativity theory. Jean-Paul Sartre wrote in 1939, "The theory of relativity applies in full to the universe of fiction. . . . there is no more place for a privileged observer in a real novel than in the world of Einstein, and . . . it is no more possible to conduct an experiment in a fictional system in order to determine whether the system is in motion or at rest than there is in a physical system" ("François Mauriac and Freedom," 23). Williams, Frost, Pound, Eliot, Mann, Broch, Durrell, and other modern writers make direct, if occasionally faulty, references to Einstein's work. For a discussion of the influence of relativity theory on modern literature, with special emphasis on its appearance in Quentin's section of *The Sound and the Fury*, see Holton, "Introduction," vii–xxxii. A similar treatment of the topic appears in Johnson, "Theory of Relativity." Traces of these same physical theories appear differently in postmodern fiction.

22. Heidegger, "Question concerning Technology."

23. "God wasn't too bad a novelist, except he was a Realist" (Enck, "John Barth," 8).

24. Barth, "Literature of Replenishment," 70, my ellipses.

25. Harris, *Passionate Virtuosity*, 176. Max F. Schultz similarly notes that Barth combines premodernist and modernist modes from his own earlier fiction ("Barth, *LETTERS*," 104–5).

26. In a workshop session at SUNY-Binghamton on September 23, 1983, Barth said that the last line of this poem was carved on the proscenium of a theater he attended in Chautauqua, New York. Beneath it, ironically, he recalled mediocre plays being performed unmemorably; yet more ironically, the inscription itself had cracked as the proscenium decayed. Barth concluded his story by agreeing with Ambrose, who mutters after Cook reads his poem, "Art passes too" (671).

27. Foucault quotes this passage from the minister of the interior in 1841 (*Discipline and Punish*, 250, my ellipsis).

28. Gorak, *God the Artist*, 181–82, 186. Charles Caramello makes a similar point about Barth's project in *Lost in the Funhouse*: "Barth effects a loosening of authority that may signal a losing of the author-as-modernist-god/hero: the decentering of the origin of the work by the work's entering a multimedia and, more important, an intertextual field" (*Silverless Mirrors*, 115–16).

29. In Frederick Karl's judgment, *LETTERS* "is self-enclosed, not moral, ethical, or even social. It is the ultimate narcissistic artifact" (*American Fictions 1940–1980*, 457). Marjorie Godlin Roemer also finds in *LETTERS* "self-reflexivity carried to its limit. . . . Barth does not shy away from the ultimate

arrogance of the author playing God in the universe of his creation," and the text becomes "a peculiarly self-indulgent exercise in literary narcissism" ("Paradigmatic Mind," 42–43).

30. Johnstone, "John Barth," 68.

31. Bray also resembles the Cooks in his use of women as means to a dynastic end. He claims to have "5 females (variously) fecundated" (756), including Bea Golden, Merope Bernstein, Marsha Blank, probably Angie Mensch, and possibly Germaine Pitt Mensch or—since "females" does not restrict the field to humans—the nanny goat he resorts to in a pinch; when Todd visits Lily Dale, he sees "two mixed-beed nans, one pregnant" (731). Whether Bray truly fathers any offspring with his "greenish" fluid is questionable, but his commitment to authorship as self-perpetuating conquest is not.

32. Gorak, *God the Artist*, 188.

33. Harris, *Passionate Virtuosity*, 192.

34. As part of the intricate formal pattern in *LETTERS*, each character begins with a numerical "fix" corresponding to her or his position in the text. Todd begins on a base two, in which, as in *Catch-22*, everything happens twice; Jake on a base three, in which his triangular relationship to the Morgans can be resolved only with a triangular atonement; Cook on a base four, beginning with the four "prenatal" letters of Cook IV, followed by eight letters from Cook VI, though "four would be a more appropriate number" (408); with his pentagonal bed and his five-year plan for the "NOVEL" project, Bray begins on a base five; Ambrose, whose six love affairs lead him to perceive six patterns of sixes, begins on base six (763). Gradually, however, these characters come to perceive their relationship to their author's numerical patterning, and thus to make increasing use of sevens.

35. Harris, *Passionate Virtuosity*, 174.

36. See Barth's lecture "Algebra and Fire." Gorak reads Ambrose differently (*God the Artist*, 183–86).

37. Schultz, "Barth, *LETTERS*," 95.

38. Harris, *Passionate Virtuosity*, 176.

39. Barth, "Literature of Replenishment," 70.

40. Iser, *Implied Reader*, 71.

41. Carmichael observes the importance of history in *LETTERS*: it is "not only the exemplary text; it is also a signifier pointing to the immense weight of actuality" ("John Barth's *Letters*," 71).

42. Watt, *Rise of the Novel*, 25.

43. Lampkin, "Interview with John Barth," 486.

44. Reilly, "Interview with John Barth," 20.

45. Ibid.

CHAPTER SIX

1. Atwood, "End to Audience?," 346, 353.

2. Hite, *Other Side of the Story*, 11, 13. Raymond Mazurek surveyed college and university teaching of contemporary fiction to learn what novels are most frequently taught. He observes, "The most definite conclusion that can be drawn directly from the surveys seems to be that the contemporary canon tends to exclude or devalue novels by women" ("Courses and Canons," 152).

3. Atwood quotes from Hawking, *Brief History of Time*, 144.

4. Ibid., 143.

5. Homans, *Bearing the Word*, 4–5.

6. Irigaray, "Is the Subject of Science Sexed?," 64.

7. Einstein and Infeld, *Evolution of Physics*, 31. For a general discussion of the increasingly subjective role of the physicist, see also Zukav, *Dancing Wu Li Masters*, 114–36.

8. Heisenberg, *Physicist's Conception of Nature*, 29, my emphasis.

9. Williams, *Long Revolution*, 20.

10. Atwood, "End to Audience?," 344, 347–48.

11. McDermott, "Little Girls," 35. Stefan Kanfer makes a similar point: "Elaine's emotional life is effectively over at puberty. . . . Elaine's family members, from her doomed brother to her devoted husband, seem mere walk-ons compared with Elaine's nemesis Cordelia" ("Time Arrested," 70).

12. Thurman, "When You Wish," 110.

13. Angier, "Genesis of Cruelty," 37.

14. Rereading Freud and Lacan, Kristeva develops the notion of abjection in her writings after 1980: in *Pouvoirs de l'horreur* (1980), translated as *Powers of Horror* (1982), and then in "L'abjet d'amour" (1982), revised to become the first part of *Histoires d'amour* (1983), translated as *Tales of Love* (1987). For Kristeva, the abject is the gap (the hole in the mirror, the aporia between signifier and signified, the non-object) that challenges and enables the symbolic, makes narcissism necessary and precarious as a defense and propels the distressed subject toward signification, love, and art. Kristeva's meditation on abjection's pathological power in *Powers of Horror* would be closely relevant to *Cat's Eye* but for the fact that Kristeva identifies both abjection and art with the male subject and minimizes women's relation to the abject (*Powers*, 54). Kristeva's abjection becomes, in my view, an aesthetic category, a semiotic event outside of history that catapults the (male) subject into an uneasy relation to the world of signs. In this way it closely resembles the transcendent and timeless epiphany that leads the modernist to art. In contrast, Atwood's version of abjection focuses on women's experience of political oppression. While abjection originates in the paternal function for both Kristeva and Atwood, Atwood sees the

paternal function not as the neutral sign of discourse but as a political institution with its own repressive traditions and agendas.

15. Homans, *Bearing the Word*, 4, 32, 38.

16. Several important critics explore division, duality, difference, and inconsistency in Atwood's fiction. Sherrill Grace finds a violent duality of subject/object, self/other, male/female inescapable and potentially energizing for those characters in Atwood's fiction who learn to accept duality and to see double. From a New Critical perspective, her *Violent Duality* sees these dualities as static poles creating tension for the characters. Robert Lecker focuses on doubles, duplicity, and mirror reflections, which express Atwood's interest in the failed romance ("Janus through the Looking Glass"). Ildikó de Papp Carrington argues that characters in *Life before Man* internalize the demons of an ironically diminished spirit world as destructive doubles; the novel "is not about the discovery of identity as a permanently defined construct," but rather the experiencing of identity as "a constantly shifting pattern of alteration, attrition, and inevitable loss" ("Demons, Doubles, and Dinosaurs"). Lorna Irvine reads *Bodily Harm* as an ambiguously doubled text "replete with secrets that pull against straightforward interpretation" ("Here and Now").

17. *Cat's Eye* returns to the material Atwood used in *Lady Oracle*, chap. 6, pp. 53–67. Three slightly older female friends torment Joan Foster during their walks through the ravine on the way to and from Brownies. The two versions differ in many ways; most important, Joan is rescued by a man, while Elaine saves herself with the vision of Mary. The man in *Lady Oracle* may be the exhibitionist who appeared in the ravine earlier. In *Cat's Eye*, though rumors of such men haunt the ravine, no man appears—the ravine is an entirely female domain.

18. Margaret Homans sees the figure of the Virgin Mary as a recurrent literary image expressing ambivalence about "bearing the word." Since she carries the child "who is the Word, the embodiment of the Logos," she is the female bearer of the male word, the word of women's exclusion from linguistic practice (*Bearing the Word*, 29–33). Atwood's Mary is not visibly pregnant, but rather the bearer of heart, warmth, acceptance.

19. Bakhtin's description of double-voiced discourse in Dostoyevsky has important implications for Atwood, and particularly for the split and doubled consciousness in *Cat's Eye*. Reading *The Double*, Bakhtin finds "a double-voiced, interruption-prone construction" whose "field of action" is "a single self-consciousness. Authority in that consciousness, however, has been seized by the other's discourse, which has made its home in it" (*Problems of Dostoyevsky's Poetics*, 219). Cordelia, similarly, falls silent in favor of the father, as do her sisters and mother. Elaine, however, turns the father's ironic discourse back on him—even over his own dinner table, when he invokes a monoglossic, authorized discourse: "And what does the atom have to say for itself these days?" Elaine responds with heteroglossia, multiple atoms speaking in

many tongues: "Which one?" (264). That his atom reveals itself singly, while hers have no single speech, places his atom in classical physics, hers in the relativistic physics of Einstein.

20. McDermott, "Little Girls," 35.

21. Atwood notes that *"Cat's Eye* is partly about being haunted" by the experience of Cordelia's abuse. See Ingersoll, "Waltzing Again," 237, 236.

22. Linker, "Representation and Sexuality," 393. See also Mulvey, "Visual Pleasure"; Nochlin, *Women, Art, and Power*; and Chadwick, "Women Artists."

23. Elaine's painting and Atwood's writing would not earn membership in Tom LeClair's "art of excess," despite the reviewers' repeated objections to the excessive and disunified qualities of the novel's second half. LeClair's excess comes in "works of mastery, novels that represent and intellectually master the power systems they exist within and are about" (*Art of Excess*, 6). With Elaine's descriptions of the Western tradition in art, Atwood clearly identifies mastery with male domination of a woman-object. Her own paintings, as Elaine describes them, replace mastery with a more feminist and actualist mode of vision, one that explores contrasts and doubleness without choosing, one that does not master its own uncertainties, and one that praises woman's subjectivity in the absence of any master/slave dialectic.

24. Nochlin, *Women, Art, and Power*, 57.

25. In the zoology building where Stephen, Elaine, and Cordelia visit, "there's a jar of twins, real dead identical human twins" (180). In a horror comic that Cordelia steals (Elaine takes it home and stores it in Stephen's room), twin sisters compete over a boyfriend; the dead, disfigured sister steals the pretty sister's body (233). In the cemetery, Elaine tells Cordelia she is a long-dead vampire, "one of a twins. Identical ones, you can't tell us apart" (245). Elaine says that she and Cordelia are "like twins in old fables, each of whom has been given half a key" (434). Stephen's first girlfriend turns him into "a stupider, more nervous identical twin of himself" (109), and his references to Einstein's thought experiment place him as Elaine's twin. To show relative time, one twin travels in space and the other stays behind on earth (233), a prophecy fulfilled when Stephen dies and Elaine thinks he has, like the space twin, gone on a long journey (412). These references align the three characters, preparing for the extension of Stephen's death into the silence left by Cordelia.

26. Ingersoll, "Waltzing Again," 236.

27. Barthes, *Writing Degree Zero*, 30–31.

CHAPTER SEVEN

1. Mendelson, "Gravity's Encyclopedia," 162.

2. See especially Klinkowitz, *Literary Disruptions*; McCaffery, "Barthelme's *Snow White*"; and Stengel, *Shape of Art*.

3. Domini, "Donald Barthelme," 109.

4. Couturier and Durand, *Donald Barthelme*, 26, 60.

5. Barthelme, "Not-Knowing," 521.

6. Couturier and Durand, *Donald Barthelme*, 9.

7. O'Hara, "Donald Barthelme," 200–201.

8. Barthelme, "Not-Knowing," 521–22.

9. Ibid., 509–10, 517.

10. O'Hara, "Donald Barthelme," 200.

11. Heisenberg, *Physics and Philosophy*, 58. For general discussions of the uncertainty principle, see Zukav, *Dancing Wu Li Masters*, 132–36; and McKenzie, *Major Achievements of Science*, 321–25.

12. Because the stories are so brief and are available in both the original collections and *Sixty Stories*, I have chosen not to identify page numbers for quotations.

13. Barthelme, *Snow White*, 156–57.

14. For discussions of irony helpful in reading Barthelme, see Booth, *Rhetoric of Irony*, 241; Enright, *Alluring Problem*, 6; Handwerk, *Irony and Ethics*; and Wilde, *Horizons of Assent*.

15. For a helpful discussion of this story, which comes to similar conclusions about its emphasis on "the futility of knowing," see Stengel, *Shape of Art*, 23–29.

16. Wilde, *Horizons*, 170.

17. Barthelme, *Paradise*, 10. Citations of this novel appear in the text. Except as noted, all ellipses in quotations are mine; all emphases are Barthelme's.

18. Stengel discusses these and other "dialogue stories" in *Shape of Art*, 63–107. He argues that the stories involve "power relationships pitting an authoritative questioner against a consciously weaker, more vulnerable respondent. . . . The stories involve battles of will between scientific and humanistic sensibilities" (63). These conversations, failing as dialogue, suggest the division of self into scientific rationality and artistic play.

19. Barthelme, "Basil from Her Garden," 37. See Alan Wilde's fine essay focused on this story in *Middle Grounds*, 161–72.

20. Important in the writing of Hélène Cixous, Julia Kristeva, and Luce Irigaray, *jouissance* appears in the terms I've used here especially in Irigaray, "This Sex."

21. Barthelme, "Not-Knowing," 513.

22. Barthelme's early story "A Shower of Gold" provides a useful contrast as well as a source for *Paradise*. When three unknown girls move into the bare New York loft of the sculptor Peterson, joining other intrusive absurdities, he concludes by affirming: "Possibilities nevertheless proliferate and escalate all around us and there are opportunities for beginning again. . . . Don't be reconciled. Turn off your television sets . . . cash in your life insurance,

indulge in a mindless optimism." No similar resolution or assent appears in *Paradise*.

23. Elizabeth Jolley suggests that *Paradise* "is a fantasy of freedom in a world where there is no freedom" ("Is Simon in Hog Heaven?," 7).

24. Wilde, *Middle Grounds*, 164, 170.

25. Fowles, *Daniel Martin*, 629.

26. For an astute discussion of Barthelme's ironic use of traditional structures, see R. Davis, "Post-Modern Paternity."

27. Stengel, *Shape of Art*, 11.

28. Klinkowitz, *Literary Disruptions*, 80.

29. Barthelme, "Not-Knowing," 522.

CHAPTER EIGHT

1. Barth, "Postmodernism Revisited," 17.

2. Robert De Beaugrande writes that "if science and art are to interact, the new physics seems to be a splendid opportunity. Both domains would become more liberating if the professionals would acknowledge the key role of indeterminacy" ("Quantum Aspects of Perceived Reality," 32). Dennis Bohnenkamp observes that both quantum mechanics and modern literature describe worlds that defy common sense; a "post-Einsteinian literary criticism," he argues, would "operate on the principle of complementarity and admit that a text can be or say two or more things at the same time" ("Post-Einsteinian Physics and Literature," 29).

3. Gleick, *Chaos*, 5–6.

4. See also Hayles, *Chaos Bound*.

5. Gleick, *Chaos*, 94. See his chapter entitled "A Geometry of Nature," 83–118.

6. See Gibbons, Hawking, and Townsend, *Supersymmetry and Its Applications*.

7. Gribbin, *Genesis*, 32.

8. Calvino, *Cosmicomics*, 43.

9. Kundera, *Unbearable Lightness of Being*, 221.

10. Atwood, "End to Audience?," 344.

11. Some narrators claim to discover identity and certainty: Cyril in Hawkes's *Blood Oranges*, for example, or Humbert in Nabokov's *Lolita* and Van in *Ada*. I see these novels demolishing their narrators' certainties behind their backs. In actualistic texts, any narrator or character is unreliable who interprets experience with the belief in secure and certain knowledge.

12. Čapek, *Philosophical Impact of Contemporary Physics*, xii–xiii.

13. Mendelson, "Gravity's Encyclopedia," 162.

14. LeClair, *Art of Excess*, 20.

15. David Cowart makes a different assumption in *History and the Contemporary Novel*; he believes that fictions seek "to capture" the past or the future or "to pinpoint" the moment when the modern age came into existence. His language places contemporary fiction in an unrevised realist mode, for which representing historical reality is possible.

16. Foucault, "Nietzsche, Genealogy, History."

17. Barth, *LETTERS*, 771–72.

18. Barth, *Tidewater Tales*, 655.

19. See Davidson, "Future Tense."

20. Elkin, *Stanley Elkin's Greatest Hits*, 47, 56. For a different reading of "Ashenden," see Wilde, *Middle Grounds*, 30–34.

21. Torgovnick, *Closure in the Novel*, 5; I've drawn on her introduction (3–19).

22. Nadeau, *Readings*, 186.

23. Pynchon, *Crying of Lot 49*, 95.

24. Barthes, *Writing Degree Zero*, 30–31.

25. Bakhtin, "Epic and Novel," 17, 27.

26. Kuehl, *Alternate Worlds*, 103.

27. Atwood, *Handmaid's Tale*, 180.

28. Tan, *Joy Luck Club*, 22–23.

29. Mukherjee, *The Middleman and Other Stories*, 146–47.

30. García Márquez, *Love in the Time of Cholera*, 348.

31. Pynchon, *Vineland*, 241. Citations in the text refer to this novel.

32. Kermode, "That Was Another Planet," 3–4. Kermode finds it "a disappointing book," though "this judgment may depend on a measure of incomprehension."

33. Snow, *Two Cultures*, 2.

BIBLIOGRAPHY

Abádi-Nagy, Zoltán. "William Gaddis: The Art of Fiction CI." *Paris Review* 105 (1987): 54–89.

Adams, Alice. *Listening to Billie*. New York: Penguin, 1978.

Alter, Robert. *Partial Magic: The Novel as a Self-Conscious Genre*. Berkeley: University of California Press, 1975.

———. "The Self-Conscious Moment: Reflections on the Aftermath of Modernism." *TriQuarterly*, no. 33 (1975): 209–30.

Ames, Christopher. "Coover's Comedy of Conflicting Fictional Codes." *Critique* 31, no. 2 (1990): 85–100.

———. "Power and the Obscene Word: Discourses of Extremity in Thomas Pynchon's *Gravity's Rainbow*." *Contemporary Literature* 31 (1990): 191–207.

Angier, Carole. "The Genesis of Cruelty." Review of *Cat's Eye*, by Margaret Atwood. *New Statesman and Society*, January 27, 1989, 37.

Atwood, Margaret. *Cat's Eye*. New York: Doubleday, 1989.

———. *The Handmaid's Tale*. New York: Fawcett Crest, 1985.

———. *Lady Oracle*. New York: Fawcett Crest, 1976.

———. *Second Words: Selected Critical Prose*. Boston: Beacon, 1982.

Bakhtin, Mikhail. *The Dialogic Imagination*. Edited by Michael Holquist. Translated by Caryl Emerson and Michael Holquist. Austin: University of Texas Press, 1981.

———. *Problems of Dostoyevsky's Poetics*. Edited and translated by Caryl Emerson. Minneapolis: University of Minnesota Press, 1984.

Balitas, Vincent D. "Historical Consciousness in the Novels of Robert Coover." *Kwartalnik Neofilologiczny* 28 (1981): 369–79.

Barth, John. "Algebra and Fire." In *The Friday Book: Essays and Other Nonfiction*, 166–71. New York: Putnam's, 1984.

———. *The End of the Road*. New York: Bantam, 1958.

———. *LETTERS*. New York: Putnam's, 1979.

———. "The Literature of Exhaustion." *Atlantic Monthly* 220 (August 1967): 29–34.

———. "The Literature of Replenishment." *Atlantic Monthly* 245 (1980): 65–71.

———. "Postmodernism Revisited." *Review of Contemporary Fiction* 8 (1988): 16–24.

———. *The Tidewater Tales: A Novel*. New York: Putnam's, 1987.

Barthelme, Donald. "Basil from Her Garden." *New Yorker*, October 21, 1985, 36–39.

———. "Not-Knowing." *Georgia Review* 39 (Fall 1985): 509–22.

———. *Paradise*. New York: Putnam's, 1986.

———. *Sixty Stories*. New York: Dutton, 1982.

———. *Snow White*. New York: Bantam, 1967.

Barthes, Roland. *Writing Degree Zero*. Translated by Annette Lavers and Colin Smith. Boston: Beacon Press, 1967.

Berman, Neil. "Coover's *Universal Baseball Association*: Play as Personalized Myth." *Modern Fiction Studies* 24 (1978): 209–22.

Bernstein, Jeremy. *Einstein*. New York: Viking, 1973.

Black, Joel Dana. "The Paper Empires and Empirical Fictions of William Gaddis." *Review of Contemporary Fiction* 2, no. 2 (1982): 22–31.

Bohnenkamp, Dennis. "Post-Einsteinian Physics and Literature: Toward a New Poetics." *Mosaic* 22 (1989): 19–30.

Bohr, Niels. *Atomic Theory and the Description of Nature*. Cambridge: Cambridge University Press, 1934.

Booth, Wayne. *A Rhetoric of Irony*. Chicago: University of Chicago Press, 1974.

Born, Max. *Atomic Physics*. New York: Hafner, 1957.

Calvino, Italo. *Cosmicomics*. Translated by William Weaver. New York: Harcourt Brace Jovanovich, 1965.

Campbell, Joseph. *The Hero with a Thousand Faces*. Princeton, N.J.: Princeton University Press, 1949.

Čapek, Milič. *The Philosophical Impact of Contemporary Physics*. Princeton, N.J.: Van Nostrand, 1961.

Caramello, Charles. *Silverless Mirrors: Book, Self and Postmodern American Fiction*. Tallahassee: University Press of Florida, 1983.

Carmichael, Thomas. "John Barth's *Letters*: History, Representation, and Postmodernism." *Mosaic* 21 (1988): 65–72.

Carrington, Ildikó de Papp. "Demons, Doubles, and Dinosaurs: *Life before*

Man, *The Origin of Consciousness*, and 'The Icicle.' " In *Critical Essays on Margaret Atwood*, edited by Judith McCombs, 229–45. Boston: G. K. Hall, 1988.

Chadwick, Whitney. "Women Artists and the Politics of Representation." In *Feminist Art Criticism: An Anthology*, edited by Arlene Raven, Cassandra Langer, and Joanna Frueh, 167–85. Ann Arbor, Mich.: UMI Research Press, 1988.

Clark, Beverly Lyon. *Reflections of Fantasy: The Mirror-Worlds of Carroll, Nabokov, and Pynchon*. New York: Peter Lang, 1986.

Clerc, Charles. "Film in *Gravity's Rainbow*." In *Approaches to "Gravity's Rainbow,"* edited by Charles Clerc, 103–52. Columbus: Ohio State University Press, 1983.

———, ed. *Approaches to "Gravity's Rainbow."* Columbus: Ohio State University Press, 1983.

Cooper, Peter L. *Signs and Symptoms: Thomas Pynchon and the Contemporary World*. Berkeley: University of California Press, 1983.

Coover, Robert. *Pricksongs and Descants*. New York: Plume, 1969.

———. *The Public Burning*. New York: Viking, 1977.

———. *The Universal Baseball Association, Inc.* New York: Plume, 1968.

Couturier, Maurice, and Régis Durand. *Donald Barthelme*. London: Methuen, 1982.

Cowart, David. *History and the Contemporary Novel*. Carbondale: Southern Illinois University Press, 1989.

———. *Thomas Pynchon: The Art of Allusion*. Carbondale: Southern Illinois University Press, 1980.

Craige, Betty Jean. *Literary Relativity: An Essay on Twentieth-Century Narrative*. Lewisburg, Pa.: Bucknell University Press, 1982.

Crowther, J. G. *Famous American Men of Science*. New York: Norton, 1937.

Davidson, Arnold E. "Future Tense: Making History in *The Handmaid's Tale*." In *Margaret Atwood: Vision and Forms*, edited by Kathryn VanSpanckeren and Jan Garden Castro, 113–21. Carbondale: Southern Illinois University Press, 1988.

Davidson, Arnold E., and Cathy N. Davidson, eds. *The Art of Margaret Atwood: Essays in Criticism*. Toronto: Anansi Press, 1981.

Davies, Paul. *God and the New Physics*. London: J. M. Dent & Sons, 1983.

Davis, P. C. W. *Space and Time in the Modern Universe*. Cambridge: Cambridge University Press, 1977.

Davis, Robert Con. "Post-Modern Paternity: Donald Barthelme's *The Dead Father*." In *The Fictional Father: Lacanian Readings of the Text*, edited by Robert Con Davis, 169–82. Amherst: University of Massachusetts Press, 1981.

———, ed. *The Fictional Father: Lacanian Readings of the Text*. Amherst: University of Massachusetts Press, 1981.

De Beaugrande, Robert. "Quantum Aspects of Perceived Reality: A New Engagement of Science and Art." *Journal of Literary Semantics* 18 (1989): 1–49.

Domini, John. "Donald Barthelme: The Modernist Uprising." *South-West Review* 75, no. 1 (1990): 95–112.

Durand, Régis. "The Exemplary Fictions of Robert Coover." In *Les Américanistes: New French Criticism on Modern American Fiction*, edited by Ira D. Johnson and Christiane Johnson, 130–37. Port Washington, N.Y.: Kennikat Press, 1978.

Durkheim, Emile. *The Elementary Forms of the Religious Life*. Translated by Joseph Ward Swain. London: George Allen & Unwin, 1915.

Einstein, Albert, and Leopold Infeld. *The Evolution of Physics*. New York: Simon & Schuster, 1942.

Eliade, Mircea. *The Myth of Eternal Return; or, Cosmos and History*. Translated by Willard R. Trask. Princeton, N.J.: Princeton University Press, Bollingen, 1954.

Eliot, T. S. "*Ulysses*, Order, and Myth." In *Forms of Modern Fiction*, edited by William Van O'Connor, 120–24. Bloomington: Indiana University Press, 1948.

Elkin, Stanley. *Stanley Elkin's Greatest Hits*. New York: Warner, 1980.

Enck, John J. "John Barth: An Interview." *Wisconsin Studies in Contemporary Literature* 6 (Winter–Spring 1965): 3–14.

Enright, D. J. *The Alluring Problem: An Essay on Irony*. Oxford: Oxford University Press, 1986.

Federman, Raymond. "Surfiction—Four Propositions in Form of an Introduction." In *Surfiction: Fiction Now . . . and Tomorrow*, edited by Raymond Federman, 5–15. Chicago: Swallow Press, 1975.

———, ed. *Surfiction: Fiction Now . . . and Tomorrow*. Chicago: Swallow Press, 1975.

Flaubert, Gustave. "On Realism." In *Documents of Modern Literary Realism*, edited by George J. Becker, 90–96. Princeton, N.J.: Princeton University Press, 1963.

Foucault, Michel. *Discipline and Punish: The Birth of the Prison*. Translated by Alan Sheridan. New York: Vintage Books, 1977.

———. "Nietzsche, Genealogy, History." In *Language, Counter-Memory, Practice*, edited by Donald Bouchard, translated by Donald Bouchard and Sherry Simon, 140–53. Ithaca, N.Y.: Cornell University Press, 1977.

Fowler, Douglas. *A Reader's Guide to "Gravity's Rainbow."* Ann Arbor, Mich.: Ardis, 1980.

Fowles, John. *Daniel Martin*. Boston: Little, Brown, 1977.

Friedman, Alan. "Science and Technology." In *Approaches to "Gravity's Rainbow,"* edited by Charles Clerc, 69–102. Columbus: Ohio State University Press, 1983.

Friedman, Alan, and Manfred Puetz. "Science as Metaphor: Thomas Pynchon and *Gravity's Rainbow.*" *Contemporary Literature* 15 (1974): 345–59.

Gaddis, William. *Carpenter's Gothic.* New York: Viking, 1985.

———. *J R.* New York: Knopf, 1975.

———. "The Rush for Second Place." *Harper's,* April 1981, 31–39.

———. "Stop Player. Joke No. 4." *Atlantic Monthly,* July 1951, 92–93. Reprinted in *A Reader's Guide to William Gaddis's "The Recognitions,"* edited by Steven Moore, 299–301. Lincoln: University of Nebraska Press, 1982.

Gado, Frank, ed. *First Person: Conversations on Writers and Writing.* Schenectady, N.Y.: Union College Press, 1973.

Gallo, Louis. "Nixon and the 'House of Wax': An Emblematic Episode in Coover's *The Public Burning.*" *Critique* 23, no. 3 (1982): 43–51.

García Márquez, Gabriel. *Love in the Time of Cholera.* Translated by Edith Grossman. New York: Knopf, 1988.

Gibbons, G. W., S. W. Hawking, and P. K. Townsend. *Supersymmetry and Its Applications: Superstrings, Anomalies, and Supergravity.* Cambridge: Cambridge University Press, 1986.

Gleick, James. *Chaos: Making a New Science.* New York: Penguin, 1987.

Gorak, Jan. *God the Artist: American Novelists in a Post-Realist Age.* Urbana: University of Illinois Press, 1987.

Grace, Sherrill. *Violent Duality: A Study of Margaret Atwood.* Montreal: Véhicule Press, 1980.

Graff, Gerald. "Babbitt at the Abyss: The Social Context of Postmodern American Fiction." *TriQuarterly,* no. 33 (1975): 305–37.

Gribbin, John. *Genesis: The Origins of Man and the Universe.* New York: Delacorte, Eleanor Friede, 1981.

Groden, Michael. "Construct of Fictions." Review of *The Public Burning,* by Robert Coover. *Brick: A Journal of Reviews,* no. 6 (1979): 43–46.

Guerard, Albert J. "Notes on the Rhetoric of Anti-Realist Fiction." *TriQuarterly,* no. 30 (1974): 3–50.

Guzlowski, John Z. "Coover's *The Public Burning*: Richard Nixon and the Politics of Experience." *Critique* 29 (1987): 57–71.

Handwerk, Gary J. *Irony and Ethics in Narrative.* New Haven, Conn.: Yale University Press, 1985.

Hansen, Arlen J. "The Dice of God: Einstein, Heisenberg, and Robert Coover." *Novel* 10 (1976): 49–58.

Harris, Charles. *Passionate Virtuosity: The Fiction of John Barth.* Urbana: University of Illinois Press, 1983.

Hawking, Stephen W. *A Brief History of Time: From the Big Bang to Black Holes.* New York: Bantam, 1988.

Hayles, N. Katherine. *Chaos Bound: Orderly Disorder in Contemporary Literature and Science.* Ithaca, N.Y.: Cornell University Press, 1990.

———. *The Cosmic Web: Scientific Field Models and Literary Strategies in the Twentieth Century*. Ithaca, N.Y.: Cornell University Press, 1984.

Heckard, Margaret. "Robert Coover, Metafiction, and Freedom." *Twentieth Century Literature* 22 (1976): 210–27.

Heidegger, Martin. "The Question concerning Technology." In *Basic Writings*, edited by David Farrell Krell, translated by William Lovitt, 287–317. New York: Harper & Row, 1971.

Heisenberg, Werner. *The Physicist's Conception of Nature*. Translated by Arnold J. Pomerans. New York: Harcourt, 1955.

———. *Physics and Beyond*. Translated by Arnold J. Pomerans. New York: Harper, 1971.

———. *Physics and Philosophy*. New York: Harper, 1958.

Henkle, Roger B. "The Morning and the Evening Funnies: Comedy in *Gravity's Rainbow*." In *Approaches to "Gravity's Rainbow,"* edited by Charles Clerc, 273–90. Columbus: Ohio State University Press, 1983.

Hertzel, Leo. "What's Wrong with the Christians?" *Critique* 11, no. 3 (1969): 11–24.

Hite, Molly. *Ideas of Order in the Novels of Thomas Pynchon*. Columbus: Ohio State University Press, 1983.

———. *The Other Side of the Story: Structures and Strategies of Contemporary Feminist Narratives*. Ithaca, N.Y.: Cornell University Press, 1989.

Holton, Gerald, and Yehuda Elkana, eds. *Albert Einstein: Historical and Cultural Perspectives*. Princeton, N.J.: Princeton University Press, 1982.

Homans, Margaret. *Bearing the Word: Language and Female Experience in Nineteenth-Century Women's Writing*. Chicago: University of Chicago Press, 1986.

Hume, Kathryn. *Pynchon's Mythography: An Approach to "Gravity's Rainbow."* Carbondale: Southern Illinois University Press, 1987.

———. "Robert Coover's Fiction: The Naked and the Mythic." *Novel* 12 (1979): 127–48.

———. "Views from Above, Views from Below: The Perspectival Subtext in *Gravity's Rainbow*." *American Literature* 60 (1988): 625–42.

Ingersoll, Earl G. "Waltzing Again." In *Margaret Atwood: Conversations*, edited by Earl G. Ingersoll, 234–38. Princeton, N.J.: Ontario Review Press, 1990.

Irigaray, Luce. "Is the Subject of Science Sexed?" Translated by Carol Mastrangelo Bové. In *Feminism and Science*, edited by Nancy Tuana, 58–68. Bloomington: Indiana University Press, 1989.

———. "This Sex Which Is Not One." Translated by Claudia Reeder. In *New French Feminisms: An Anthology*, edited by Elaine Marks and Isabelle de Courtivron, 99–106. New York: Schocken Books, 1981.

Irvine, Lorna. "The Here and Now of *Bodily Harm*." In *Margaret Atwood: Vi-*

sion and Forms, edited by Kathryn VanSpanckeren and Jan Garden Castro, 85–100. Carbondale: Southern Illinois University Press, 1988.

Iser, Wolfgang. *The Implied Reader: Patterns of Communication in Prose Fiction from Bunyan to Beckett*. Baltimore: Johns Hopkins University Press, 1974.

James, Henry. "Preface to the New York Edition." In *The Tragic Muse*, v–xxii. New York: Scribners, 1908.

Jammer, Max. *The Philosophy of Quantum Mechanics*. New York: John Wiley & Sons, 1974.

Johnson, Julie M. "The Theory of Relativity in Modern Literature: An Overview and *The Sound and the Fury*." *Journal of Modern Literature* 10 (1983): 217–30.

Johnstone, Douglas. "John Barth and the Healing of the Self." *Mosaic* 21 (1988): 67–78.

Jolley, Elizabeth. "Is Simon in Hog Heaven?" Review of *Paradise*, by Donald Barthelme. *New York Times Book Review*, October 26, 1986, 7.

Joyce, James. *A Portrait of the Artist as a Young Man*. New York: Modern Library, 1916.

Kanfer, Stefan. "Time Arrested." Review of *Cat's Eye*, by Margaret Atwood. *Time*, February 6, 1989, 70.

Karl, Frederick. *American Fictions, 1940–1980: A Comprehensive History and Critical Evaluation*. New York: Harper & Row, 1983.

———. "Gaddis: A Tribune of the Fifties." In *In Recognition of William Gaddis*, edited by John Kuehl and Steven Moore, 174–98. Syracuse, N.Y.: Syracuse University Press, 1984.

Kaufman, Marjorie. "Brünnhilde and the Chemists: Women in *Gravity's Rainbow*." In *Mindless Pleasures*, edited by George Levine and David Leverenz, 197–227. Boston: Little, Brown, 1976.

Kermode, Frank. "That Was Another Planet." Review of *Vineland*, by Thomas Pynchon. *London Review of Books*, February 8, 1990, 3–4.

Kevles, Daniel J. *The Physicists: The History of a Scientific Community in Modern America*. New York: Random House, 1977.

Kiernan, Robert. *American Writing since 1945: A Critical Survey*. New York: Frederick Ungar, 1983.

Klinkowitz, Jerome. *The Life of Fiction*. Urbana: University of Illinois Press, 1977.

———. *Literary Disruptions: The Making of a Post-Contemporary American Fiction*. Urbana: University of Illinois Press, 1975.

Koenig, Peter William. "Recognizing Gaddis' *Recognitions*." *Contemporary Literature* 16 (Winter 1975): 61–72.

Kristeva, Julia. *Histoires d'amour*. Paris: Denoel, 1983.

———. "L'abjet d'amour." *Tel Quel* 91 (1982): 17–31.

———. *Pouvoirs de l'horreur: essai sur l'abjection*. Paris: Editions du Seuil, 1980.

———. *Powers of Horror: An Essay on Abjection.* Translated by Leon S. Roudiez. New York: Columbia University Press, 1982.

———. *Tales of Love.* Translated by Leon S. Roudiez. New York: Columbia
University Press, 1987.

Kuehl, John. *Alternate Worlds: A Study of Postmodern Antirealistic American Fiction.* New York: New York University Press, 1989.

Kuehl, John, and Steven Moore. "An Interview with William Gaddis." *Review of Contemporary Fiction* 2, no. 2 (1982): 4–6.

———, eds. *In Recognition of William Gaddis.* Syracuse, N.Y.: Syracuse University Press, 1984.

Kundera, Milan. *The Unbearable Lightness of Being.* Translated by Michael
Henry Heim. New York: Harper & Row, 1984.

Lampkin, Loretta M. "An Interview with John Barth." *Contemporary Literature* 29 (1988): 485–97.

Lecker, Robert. "Janus through the Looking Glass: Atwood's First Three
Novels." In *The Art of Margaret Atwood: Essays in Criticism,* edited by Ar-
nold E. Davidson and Cathy N. Davidson, 177–204. Toronto: Anansi
Press, 1981.

LeClair, Tom. *The Art of Excess: Mastery in Contemporary American Fiction.* Urbana: University of Illinois Press, 1989.

———. "William Gaddis, *J R,* and the Art of Excess." *Modern Fiction Studies*
27 (Winter 1981–82): 587–600.

LeClair, Tom, and Larry McCaffery, eds. *Anything Can Happen: Interviews
with Contemporary American Novelists.* Urbana: University of Illinois Press,
1983.

Levine, George. "V-2." Review of *Gravity's Rainbow,* by Thomas Pynchon.
Partisan Review 40 (1973): 517–29.

Levine, George, and David Leverenz, eds. *Mindless Pleasures.* Boston: Little,
Brown, 1976.

Linker, Kate. "Representation and Sexuality." In *Art after Modernism: Rethinking Representation,* edited by Brian Wallis, 389–417. New York: New Museum of Contemporary Art, 1984.

McCaffery, Larry. "Barthelme's *Snow White*: The Aesthetics of Trash." *Critique* 16 (1975): 19–32.

———. "An Interview with Robert Coover." In *Anything Can Happen: Interviews with Contemporary American Novelists,* edited by Tom LeClair and
Larry McCaffery, 63–78. Urbana: University of Illinois Press, 1983.

———. "The Magic of Fiction Making." *Fiction International,* no. 4/5 (1975):
147–53.

McCombs, Judith, ed. *Critical Essays on Margaret Atwood.* Boston: G. K. Hall,
1988.

McDermott, Alice. "What Little Girls Are Really Made Of." Review of *Cat's*

Eye, by Margaret Atwood. *New York Times Book Review*, February 5, 1989, 1, 35.

McHale, Brian. "Modernist Reading, Post-Modernist Text: The Case of *Gravity's Rainbow*." *Poetics Today* 1 (1979): 85–110.

———. *Postmodernist Fiction*. New York: Methuen, 1987.

McKenzie, A. E. E. *The Major Achievements of Science*. New York: Simon & Schuster, 1960.

Mackey, Douglas. *The Rainbow Quest of Thomas Pynchon*. San Bernardino, Calif.: Borgo Press, 1980.

Mailer, Norman. *Short Fiction of Norman Mailer*. New York: Dell, 1967.

Majdiak, David. "Barth and the Representation of Life." *Criticism* 12 (Winter 1970): 51–67. Reprinted in *Critical Essays on John Barth*, edited by Joseph J. Waldmeir, 96–109. Boston: G. K. Hall, 1980.

Malmgren, Carl D. "William Gaddis's *J R*: The Novel of Babel." *Review of Contemporary Fiction* 2, no. 2 (1982): 7–12.

Marks, Elaine, and Isabelle de Courtivron, eds. *New French Feminisms: An Anthology*. New York: Schocken Books, 1981.

Matanle, Stephen. "Love and Strife in William Gaddis' *J R*." In *In Recognition of William Gaddis*, edited by John Kuehl and Steven Moore, 106–18. Syracuse, N.Y.: Syracuse University Press, 1984.

Mazurek, Raymond A. "Courses and Canons: The Post-1945 U.S. Novel." *Critique* 31 (1990): 143–56.

———. "Metafiction, the Historical Novel, and Coover's *The Public Burning*." *Critique* 23, no. 3 (1982): 29–42.

Mellard, James. *The Exploded Form: The Modernist Novel in America*. Urbana: University of Illinois Press, 1980.

Mendelson, Edward. "Gravity's Encyclopedia." In *Mindless Pleasures*, edited by George Levine and David Leverenz, 161–96. Boston: Little, Brown, 1976.

———, ed. *Pynchon: A Collection of Critical Essays*. Englewood Cliffs, N.J.: Prentice-Hall, 1978.

Moore, Steven. "Chronological Difficulties in the Novels of William Gaddis." *Critique* 22, no. 1 (1980): 79–91.

———. *A Reader's Guide to William Gaddis's "The Recognitions."* Lincoln: University of Nebraska Press, 1982.

Moore, Thomas. *The Style of Connectedness: "Gravity's Rainbow" and Thomas Pynchon*. Columbia: University of Missouri Press, 1987.

Morgan, Speer. "*Gravity's Rainbow*: What's the Big Idea?" In *Critical Essays on Thomas Pynchon*, edited by Richard Pearce, 82–98. Boston: G. K. Hall, 1981.

Morris, Richard. *Dismantling the Universe: The Nature of Scientific Discovery*. New York: Simon & Schuster, 1983.

Mukherjee, Bharati. *The Middleman and Other Stories*. New York: Fawcett Crest, 1988.

Mulvey, Laura. *Visual and Other Pleasures*. London: Macmillan, 1989.

Munro, Alice. *Friend of My Youth*. New York: Knopf, 1990.

Nadeau, Robert. *Readings from the New Book on Nature: Physics and Metaphysics in the Modern Novel*. Amherst: University of Massachusetts Press, 1981.

Nixon, Richard. *The Almanack of Poor Richard Nixon*. Cleveland: World, 1968.

―――. *Six Crises*. Garden City, N.Y.: Doubleday, 1962.

Nochlin, Linda. *Women, Art, and Power and Other Essays*. New York: Harper & Row, 1988.

O'Hara, J. D. "Donald Barthelme: The Art of Fiction LXVI." *Paris Review* 80 (Summer 1981): 181–210.

Ortega y Gasset, José. *The Dehumanization of Art*. Translated by Helene Weyl. Princeton, N.J.: Princeton University Press, 1948.

Ozier, Lance W. "The Calculus of Transformation: More Mathematical Imagery in *Gravity's Rainbow*." *Twentieth Century Literature* 21 (1975): 193–210.

Pearce, Richard, ed. *Critical Essays on Thomas Pynchon*. Boston: G. K. Hall, 1981.

Plater, William. *The Grim Phoenix: Reconstructing Thomas Pynchon*. Bloomington: Indiana University Press, 1978.

Porush, David. *The Soft Machine: Cybernetic Fiction*. New York: Methuen, 1985.

"Postmodernism: The Uninhabited Word, Critics' Symposium." *Critique* 31, no. 4 (1990): 256–75.

Pynchon, Thomas. *The Crying of Lot 49*. New York: Bantam, 1966.

―――. *Gravity's Rainbow*. New York: Viking, 1973.

―――. *Slow Learner*. Boston: Little, Brown, 1984.

―――. *V*. New York: Bantam, 1963.

―――. *Vineland*. Boston: Little, Brown, 1990.

Quilligan, Maureen. "Thomas Pynchon and the Language of Allegory." In *Critical Essays on Thomas Pynchon*, edited by Richard Pearce, 187–212. Boston: G. K. Hall, 1981.

Ramage, John. "Myth and Monomyth in Coover's *The Public Burning*." *Critique* 23, no. 3 (1982): 52–68.

Raven, Arlene, Cassandra Langer, and Joanna Frueh, eds. *Feminist Art Criticism: An Anthology*. Ann Arbor, Mich.: UMI Research Press, 1988.

Reilly, Charlie. "An Interview with John Barth." *Contemporary Literature* 22 (Winter 1981): 1–23.

Roemer, Marjorie Godlin. "The Paradigmatic Mind: John Barth's *LETTERS*." *Twentieth Century Literature* 33 (1987): 38–50.

Rotenstreich, Nathan. "Relativity and Relativism." In *Albert Einstein: Histor-*

ical and Cultural Perspectives, edited by Gerald Holton and Yehuda Elkana, 175–204. Princeton, N.J.: Princeton University Press, 1982.

Rother, James. "Parafiction: The Adjacent Universe of Barth, Barthelme, Pynchon, and Nabokov." *boundary 2*, no. 5 (1976): 21–43.

Rovit, Earl. "The Novel as Parody: John Barth." *Critique* 6, no. 2 (1963): 77–85.

Russell, Charles. "Pynchon's Language: Signs, Systems, and Subversion." In *Approaches to "Gravity's Rainbow,"* edited by Charles Clerc, 251–72. Columbus: Ohio State University Press, 1983.

Said, Edward W. "Contemporary Fiction and Criticism." *TriQuarterly*, no. 33 (1975): 231–56.

Sartre, Jean-Paul. "François Mauriac and Freedom." In *Literary Essays*, translated by Annette Michelson, 7–23. New York: Philosophical Library, 1957.

———. *Nausea*. Translated by Lloyd Alexander. New York: New Directions, 1964.

Schaub, Thomas. *Pynchon: The Voice of Ambiguity*. Urbana: University of Illinois Press, 1981.

Schmitz, Neil. "Robert Coover and the Hazards of Metafiction." *Novel* 7 (1974): 210–19.

Scholes, Robert. "Metafiction." *Iowa Review* 1 (1970): 100–115.

Schultz, Max F. "Barth, *LETTERS*, and the Great Tradition." In *Novel vs. Fiction: The Contemporary Reformation*, edited by Jackson I. Cope and Geoffrey Green, 95–115. Norman, Okla.: Pilgrim Books, 1981.

Schwartz, Richard Alan. "Thomas Pynchon and the Evolution of Fiction." *Science-Fiction Studies* 8 (1981): 165–72.

Seed, David. *The Fictional Labyrinths of Thomas Pynchon*. Iowa City: University of Iowa Press, 1988.

Seeger, Raymond J. *J. Willard Gibbs*. Oxford: Pergamon, 1974.

Seidel, Michael. "The Satiric Plots of *Gravity's Rainbow*." In *Pynchon: A Collection of Critical Essays*, edited by Edward Mendelson, 198–212. Englewood Cliffs, N.J.: Prentice-Hall, 1978.

Shelton, Frank W. "Humor and Balance in Coover's *Universal Baseball Association, Inc.*" *Critique* 17, no. 1 (1975): 78–90.

Siegel, Mark. *Pynchon: Creative Paranoia in "Gravity's Rainbow."* Port Washington, N.Y.: Kennikat Press, 1978.

Siegle, Robert. *The Politics of Reflexivity: Narrative and the Constitutive Poetics of Culture*. Baltimore: Johns Hopkins University Press, 1986.

Simmon, Scott. "Beyond the Theater of War: *Gravity's Rainbow* as Film." In *Critical Essays on Thomas Pynchon*, edited by Richard Pearce, 124–39. Boston: G. K. Hall, 1981.

———. "*Gravity's Rainbow* Described." *Critique* 16, no. 2 (1974): 54–67.

Sklar, Morty, and Darrell Gray, eds. *The Actualist Anthology*. Iowa City: The Spirit That Moves Us Press, 1977.

Slade, Joseph. *Thomas Pynchon*. New York: Warner, 1974.

Snow, C. P. *The Two Cultures and the Scientific Revolution*. Cambridge: Cambridge University Press, 1959.

Stableford, Brian M. *The Mysteries of Modern Science*. London: Routledge & Kegan Paul, 1977.

Stanford, W. B. "The Untypical Hero." In *Homer: A Collection of Critical Essays*, 122–38. Englewood Cliffs, N.J.: Prentice-Hall, 1962.

Stark, John. *Pynchon's Fictions: Thomas Pynchon and the Literature of Information*. Athens: Ohio University Press, 1980.

Stengel, Wayne B. *The Shape of Art in the Short Stories of Donald Barthelme*. Baton Rouge: Louisiana State University Press, 1985.

Strehle, Susan. "Actualism: Pynchon's Debt to Nabokov." *Contemporary Literature* 24 (1983): 30–50.

———. "Disclosing Time: William Gaddis's *J R*." *Journal of Narrative Technique* 12, no. 1 (1982): 1–14. Reprinted in *In Recognition of William Gaddis*, edited by John Kuehl and Steven Moore, 119–34. Syracuse, N.Y.: Syracuse University Press, 1984.

———. " 'For a Very Small Audience': The Fiction of William Gaddis." *Critique* 19, no. 3 (1978): 61–73.

Sypher, Wylie. *Loss of the Self in Modern Literature and Art*. New York: Vintage, 1962.

Tan, Amy. *The Joy Luck Club*. New York: Ivy Books, 1989.

Tatham, Campbell. "John Barth and the Aesthetics of Artifice." *Contemporary Literature* 12 (Winter 1971): 60–73.

Thielemans, Johan. "Art as Redemption of Trash: Bast and Friends in Gaddis' *J R*." In *In Recognition of William Gaddis*, edited by John Kuehl and Steven Moore, 135–46. Syracuse, N.Y.: Syracuse University Press, 1984.

———. "The Energy of an Absence: Perfection as Useful Fiction in the Novels of Gaddis and Sorrentino." In *Critical Angles: European Views of Contemporary American Literature*, edited by Marc Chénetier, 105–24. Carbondale: Southern Illinois University Press, 1986.

Thurman, Judith. "When You Wish upon a Star." Review of *Cat's Eye*, by Margaret Atwood. *New Yorker*, May 29, 1989, 108–10.

Torgovnick, Marianna. *Closure in the Novel*. Princeton, N.J.: Princeton University Press, 1981.

Trachtenberg, Alan. "Barth and Hawkes: Two Fabulists." *Critique* 6, no. 2 (1963): 4–18.

Tuana, Nancy, ed. *Feminism and Science*. Bloomington: Indiana University Press, 1989.

Van Delden, Maarten. "Modernism, the New Criticism, and Thomas Pynchon's *V.*" *Novel* 23 (1990): 117–36.

VanSpanckeren, Kathryn, and Jan Garden Castro, eds. *Margaret Atwood: Vision and Forms*. Carbondale: Southern Illinois University Press, 1988.

Vernon, John. *The Garden and the Map: Schizophrenia in Twentieth-Century Literature and Culture*. Urbana: University of Illinois Press, 1973.

Wallis, Brian, ed. *Art after Modernism: Rethinking Representation*. New York: New Museum of Contemporary Art, 1984.

Warren, James Perrin. "Ritual Reluctance: The Poetics of Discontinuity in *Gravity's Rainbow.*" *Pynchon Notes* 18–19 (1986): 55–65.

Watkins, Evan. "W. S. Merwin: A Critical Accompaniment." *boundary 2*, no. 4 (1975): 187–99.

Watt, Ian. *The Rise of the Novel*. Berkeley: University of California Press, 1957.

Waugh, Patricia. *Metafiction: The Theory and Practice of Self-Conscious Fiction*. London: Methuen, 1984.

Weber, Max. *The Protestant Ethic and the Spirit of Capitalism*. New York: Scribners, 1958.

Weisenburger, Steven. "Contra Naturam?: Usury in William Gaddis's *J R.*" *Genre* 13 (Spring 1980): 93–109.

———. "The End of History?: Thomas Pynchon and the Uses of the Past." In *Critical Essays on Thomas Pynchon*, edited by Richard Pearce, 140–56. Boston: G. K. Hall, 1981.

———. *A "Gravity's Rainbow" Companion: Sources and Contexts for Pynchon's Novel*. Athens: University of Georgia Press, 1988.

———. "Paper Currencies: Reading William Gaddis." *Review of Contemporary Fiction* 2, no. 2 (1982): 12–22.

Wiener, Norbert. *The Human Use of Human Beings*. Rev. 1950. Reprint. Garden City, N.Y.: Doubleday, 1954.

Wilczyński, Marek. "The Game of Response in Robert Coover's Fictions." *Kwartalnik Neofilologiczny* 33 (1986): 513–23.

Wilde, Alan. *Horizons of Assent: Modernism, Postmodernism, and the Ironic Imagination*. Baltimore: Johns Hopkins University Press, 1981.

———. *Middle Grounds: Studies in Contemporary American Fiction*. Philadelphia: University of Pennsylvania Press, 1987.

Williams, Raymond. *The Long Revolution*. New York: Columbia University Press, 1961.

Wills, Garry. *Nixon Agonistes: The Crisis of the Self-Made Man*. Boston: Houghton Mifflin, 1970.

Wineapple, Brenda. "Robert Coover's Playing Fields." *Iowa Review* 10, no. 3 (1979): 66–74.

Wolfley, Lawrence C. "Repression's Rainbow: The Presence of Norman O. Brown in Pynchon's Big Novel." *PMLA* 92 (1977): 873–89.

Young, Marguerite. *Miss MacIntosh, My Darling*. New York: Scribner's, 1965.

Zukav, Gary. *The Dancing Wu Li Masters: An Overview of the New Physics*. New York: William Morrow, 1979.

INDEX

16–17; Coover on, 67; in *J R*, 102–3, 115–16; represented by towers in *LETTERS*, 133–34; monumental status in *LETTERS*, 134–35; in *Cat's Eye*, 183; Barthelme on, 191–92. *See also* Paintings

Artistic activity: scientific model of, 16–18

Artists: in Gaddis's novels, 94–95; in *LETTERS*, 135–41; in *Cat's Eye*, 179–83

Atwood, Margaret, 2, 23; on writing, 154, 159–60, 223; as realist, 160; Hite on, 160; relationship to other actualists, 160–61; reviewers on, 166–67; interviews with, 178, 186–87

—Characters (in *Cat's Eye*): Elaine Risley, 168–69, 174–84; Cordelia, 169–75

—Works: *Bodily Harm*, 170, 252 (n. 16); *Cat's Eye*, 4, 161–89, 226, 229; *The Edible Woman*, 160; *The Handmaid's Tale*, 160, 164, 169–70, 227; *Lady Oracle*, 160, 252 (n. 17); *Life before Man*, 252 (n. 16)

Auster, Paul, 221, 223

Author-characters: in *LETTERS*, 149

Authorial presence: in *J R*, 122, 247 (n. 39); in *LETTERS*, 150–51; in actualistic fiction, 221–22

Authors: in *LETTERS*, 135–49

Authorship: in *LETTERS*, 143–44, 146, 150–53

Bakhtin, Mikhail: on epic past, 230; on double-voiced discourse, 252 (n. 19)

Balitas, Vincent, on Coover, 72–73

Banks, Russell, as metafictionist, 4

Barth, John, 2, 23; on postmodern fiction, 6; Nadeau on, 21; inter-

viewed, 124–25; on reality and realistic fiction, 125; critics on, 125–26; middle period of, 125–27; similarities with Ambrose (in *LETTERS*), 148–49; presence as Author in *LETTERS*, 150–52; compared with Barthelme, 214; on literary categories, 218

—Characters (in *LETTERS*): Ambrose, 128, 145–49; Cooks and Burlingames, 135–38; Jerome Bray, 137–38, 250 (n. 31); Todd Andrews, 137–38; Reg Prinz, 139–40; Jacob Horner, 141–42; Germaine Pitt, 142–45

—Works: "Anonymaid," 126; "Autobiography," 4; *Chimera*, 125–26; *The End of the Road*, 125; *The Floating Opera*, 125; *Giles Goat-Boy*, 125–26; *LETTERS*, 4, 124–58, 161, 221, 226–27, 229; "The Literature of Exhaustion," 125, 127; "The Literature of Replenishment," 131; *Lost in the Funhouse*, 125; "Menelaiad," 126; *The Sot-Weed Factor*, 125–26; *The Tidewater Tales*, 156, 227; "Tragic View of Categories," 218

Barthelme, Donald, 2, 23, 160; critics on, 190–91; interviews with, 191–92; on fiction and aesthetics, 191; compared with Barth, 214

—Characters: Joseph (in "Me and Miss Mandible"), 193–94; Simon (in *Paradise*), 199–211; the women (in *Paradise*), 208–11

—Works: "The Balloon," 195–96; "Basil from Her Garden," 200–201; "The Catechist," 194; "A City of Churches," 194; *The Dead Father*, 196, 199, 213; "The Dolt," 194–95; "Engineer-Private Paul Klee Misplaces an Aircraft between Mi-

Endings: in *Gravity's Rainbow*, 37–38, 50, 62–63; in *The Public Burning*, 85; in *J R*, 110, 115; in *Paradise*, 208, 211; in actualistic fiction, 227–28. *See also* Closure

Energetic form: in *J R*, 116–23

Energy: in Gaddis's fiction, 93; in *J R*, 108–16

Enright, D. J., on irony, 196

Entropy: in Pynchon's fiction, 23; in Gaddis's fiction, 95; in *LETTERS*, 128

Epic form: and Barthelme's fiction, 213–14; in actualistic fiction, 231

Epiphany: in *Gravity's Rainbow*, 62; in *J R*, 120

Fathers: and continuity in *Gravity's Rainbow*, 32; in *Gravity's Rainbow*, 45, 51; in *J R*, 108, 115–16; in *LETTERS*, 136, 138–39; in *Cat's Eye*, 170–74 passim, 176–79. *See also* Men; Mothers

Federman, Raymond, as metafictionist, 4

Feigenbaum, Mitchell: universal theory of, 220

Feminism: in *Cat's Eye*, 178. *See also* Women

Fielding, Henry, 118, 150, 155; as ancestor to actualists, 18

Film: in *Gravity's Rainbow*, 33–36, 55; in Coover's fiction, 69–70; in *LETTERS*, 139–40. *See also* Television

Flaubert, Gustave, on art and scientific method, 16

Form: of realism, 14–17; of fiction and actualism, 14–26; of modernism, 17–18; of actualism, 18–26; in *Gravity's Rainbow*, 57–65; in *The Public Burning*, 85–92; in *J R*, 116–23; in *LETTERS*, 131, 150–58; in *Cat's Eye*, 184–89; in *Paradise*, 211–17. *See also* Narrative form

Formalism: in *LETTERS*, 139, 147–48. *See also* Modernism

Foucault, Michel, 78–79, 228; on genealogy, 71–73; on Panopticon prison, 133

Fowler, Douglas: on Tyrone Slothrop (in *Gravity's Rainbow*), 37; on end of *Gravity's Rainbow*, 50

Fowles, John, 2, 212, 215, 221, 227–28; Nadeau on, 21

Fractal geometry: of Mandelbrot, 220

Fractals: in actualistic fiction, 232–33

Frames of reference: and special theory of relativity, 9–10, 129; in modernism, 17; in *LETTERS*, 130–31, 152–53; in actualistic fiction, 221–23

Frank, Joseph, on modern literature, 17

Gaddis, William, 2; reference to reality, 93–94; critics on, 94, 117; interview with, 94
—Characters (in *J R*): Jack Gibbs, 95, 111–12; Bast family, 107–8; Dan DeCephalis, 109–10; J R, 109–10; Norman Angel, 110–11; Amy Joubert, 111–12; Edward Bast, 112–16, 123
—Works: *Carpenter's Gothic*, 93; *J R*, 4, 93–123, 160, 226, 228, 277; *The Recognitions*, 93; "The Rush for Second Place," 95, 105

García Márquez, Gabriel, 223, 233

Gardner, John, 23, 212–13, 221

Gass, William, as metafictionist, 4

Genealogy: and history in *The Public Burning*, 71–73, 82; and form in *The Public Burning*, 85–92; in actualistic fiction, 226

Gibbs, Josiah Willard, 95

Gleick, James: on chaos theory, 219; on fractal geometry, 220

Gorak, Jan, on Barth, 135, 137, 250 (n. 36)

Grace, Sherrill, on duality in Atwood's fiction, 252 (n. 16)

Gravity: and relativity theory, 10

Gribbin, John, 161, 222

Handwerk, Gary, on irony, 196

Harris, Charles: on *LETTERS*, 132; on Barth, 138

Hawkes, John, 2, 23, 212

Hawking, Stephen, 161

Hawthorne, Nathaniel, as ancestor to actualists, 18

Hayles, N. Katherine, 21–22; on Tyrone Slothrop (in *Gravity's Rainbow*), 38

Heisenberg, Werner: on distinction between actual and real, 7, 14; and matrix mechanics, 12; reference to in *LETTERS*, 128; uncertainty principle of, 192–93

Heller, Joseph, 2, 212

Heroic adventure: in *The Public Burning*, 88–90. *See also* Campbell, Joseph

Hierarchical categories: in *Gravity's Rainbow*, 66, 243 (n. 34)

Historical detail: in contemporary fiction, 4; in *Gravity's Rainbow*, 27–28; in *The Public Burning*, 70–71; in *LETTERS*, 124–25; in actualistic fiction, 155–56, 226; in contemporary fiction, 256 (n. 15)

Historicizing of author: in *LETTERS*, 150

History: and genealogy in *The Public Burning*, 71–73, 82; in *The Public Burning*, 74–78, 80–84; in *LETTERS*, 142

Hite, Molly, 160; on Tyrone Slothrop (in *Gravity's Rainbow*), 38

Hoarding: in *J R*, 99

Homans, Margaret: on subject/object duality, 162; on Virgin Mary, 252 (n. 18)

Image of success: in *J R*, 109–10

Insignificant events: in *Gravity's Rainbow*, 60–61; in *J R*, 122; in *Paradise*, 216–17

International writers: new physics in works of, 220–21

Irigaray, Luce: on subject of science, 162–63; on jouissance, 254 (n. 20)

Irony: in Barthelme's fiction, 196; in *Paradise*, 207

Irvine, Lorna, on duality in Atwood's fiction, 252 (n. 16)

Iser, Wolfgang, on "implied reader," 154

James, Henry, 58, 119

Johnson, B. S., as metafictionist, 4

Johnstone, Douglas, on Barth, 136

Joyce, James, 17–18, 64, 117, 184–85

Karl, Frederick, on *LETTERS*, 249 (n. 29)

Katz, Steve, as metafictionist, 4

Kermode, Frank, on *Vineland*, 235

Kesey, Ken, 2

Kevles, Daniel, on shift from classical to quantum physics, 29

Kiernan, Robert, on metafiction, 3

Klinkowitz, Jerome: on metafiction, 4; on Barthelme, 217

Kristeva, Julia, on abjection, 169, 251 (n. 14)

Kuehl, John: on antirealistic poetics of contemporary fiction, 20; on Doctorow's *The Book of Daniel*, 70;

Movies. *See* Film

Mukherjee, Bharati, 232–33

Munro, Alice, 230; on individuals' acceptance of progressive ideas, 8

Mythic patterns: in *The Public Burning*, 87–91; in *LETTERS*, 126, 147, 156. *See also* Campbell, Joseph

Nabokov, Vladimir, 3, 23, 185, 230; appearance as author in fiction, 221

Nadeau, Robert: on realistic fiction, 15–16; on new physics and fiction, 21; on motion in the novel, 228

Naipaul, V. S., 227

Narrative form: in *Gravity's Rainbow*, 63–64; in *J R*, 96, 116–17, 121–23; in *LETTERS*, 153–55; in *Cat's Eye*, 184–86; in *Paradise*, 212–13; in actualistic fiction, 230–32. *See also* Form

Narrative voice: in *Gravity's Rainbow*, 58–59; in *The Public Burning*, 86–87; in *Cat's Eye*, 187–88; in actualistic fiction, 223–24, 255 (n. 11)

Natural world: in *J R*, 101–2

New physics: impact on literature, 6–9; and actualism, 7–14; terms for traits shared with actualistic fiction, 8; and Newtonian science, 9–10; and criticism of contemporary fiction, 21, 24; in Pynchon's fiction, 24; in *Gravity's Rainbow*, 28–29; in Coover, 68; in *J R*, 95; in *LETTERS*, 127–28; in *Cat's Eye*, 161–63; in Barthelme, 192–93; complexity of, 219–21. *See also* Chaos theory; Fractals; Newtonian science; Physics; Quantum theory; Relativity theory; Uncertainty principle

Newton, Isaac, on absolute time, space, and motion, 128

Newtonian science: reality in, 8–9; and new physics, 9–10; and realistic fiction, 15–17; and modernism, 17–18; and public sector in *Gravity's Rainbow*, 28; and causality, 68; in *J R*, 95–96; absolutes in, 128–29; in *LETTERS*, 130; in actualistic fiction, 224–25

Nochlin, Linda, on fallen women in art, 180

Not-knowing, 80–81; in *Paradise*, 205–11. *See also* Barthelme, Donald; Uncertainty

Oates, Joyce Carol, 2

Objectivity: in modernism, 17–18; in *The Public Burning*, 75–76, 79. *See also* Frames of reference; Subjectivity

Objects: women as, in *Cat's Eye*, 168–75 passim; women as, in *Paradise*, 208–11. *See also* Subject/object duality

Observation. *See* Scientific method

Origins: in *LETTERS*, 146, 150–51; in Calvino, 222; in contemporary physics, 222

Ortega y Gasset, José, on perception, 1–2

Paintings: in *Cat's Eye*, 165–66, 180–83. *See also* Art

Parallels: in *Gravity's Rainbow*, 29–30, 41–42, 52–58, 241–42 (n. 4)

Paranoia: in *Gravity's Rainbow*, 28, 54–55; in *The Public Burning*, 73–74. *See also* Antiparanoia

Patriarchal culture: in *Cat's Eye*, 167–68, 170, 178

Patterns: in *LETTERS*, 143–44

Perception: metaphor for, 1–2, 18; new facts about, 5

15; perception by precursors of actualism, 18; clash between old and new in *Gravity's Rainbow*, 28; and film in Pynchon's works, 33–35; for Tyrone Slothrop (in *Gravity's Rainbow*), 38–39; Coover's approach to, 68; in media, 78–79; public and private in *The Public Burning*, 80–81, 84–85; in *J R*, 94; in Newtonian physics, 96; in *LETTERS*, 124–25, 127. *See also* Historical detail

Reality (new): and postmodern fiction, 7, 14, 225; terms describing, 8, 13, 218–19; and Pynchon, 25; in *Gravity's Rainbow*, 28

Reed, Ishmael, as metafictionist, 4

Reeducation: in Barthelme's fiction, 193–94; in *Paradise*, 212–13. *See also* Education

Referential nature of contemporary fiction, 19. *See also* Actualism; Art

Reflexivity: in contemporary fiction, 3, 20–21, 240–41 (n. 36)

Relativity: in *Gravity's Rainbow*, 28; in *LETTERS*, 128–29, 141–49; and absolutes in *LETTERS*, 128–29

Relativity theory: and concepts of reality, 7; special, 9–10, 129; general, 10–11, 129; and matter and energy, 96; and relativism, 248–49 (n. 20); and modernists, 249 (n. 21). *See also* Einstein, Albert

Religious institutions: in *Cat's Eye*, 176; in *Paradise*, 203. *See also* Public institutions

Repetition: in *Paradise*, 215–16

Rilke, Rainer Maria: Pynchon's view of, 48

Roemer, Marjorie Godlin, on *LETTERS*, 249–50 (n. 29)

Romance, unfulfilled: in actualistic fiction, 231

Roth, Philip, 2

Said, Edward, on Barth, 125–26

Sartre, Jean-Paul, 75, 249 (n. 21)

Scholes, Robert, 3, 191; and fabulation, 17

Schrödinger, Erwin: and wave mechanics, 12

Scientific method: in Newtonian cosmos, 15; in Barthelme's fiction, 194–98; in *Paradise*, 200–201

Scientists: and Newtonian continuity in *Gravity's Rainbow*, 32–33; in Barthelme's fiction, 195

Seed, David, on Tyrone Slothrop (in *Gravity's Rainbow*), 47

Seigle, Mark, on Tyrone Slothrop (in *Gravity's Rainbow*), 37

Self-referentiality: Hayles on, 21–22

Self-reflexivity. *See* Reflexivity

Setting: in *Gravity's Rainbow*, 27–28; in *J R*, 120–21; in *Paradise*, 211–12

Sexuality: in *Gravity's Rainbow*, 42; in *J R*, 101; in *Paradise*, 206–7

Siegle, Robert, 20; on reflexivity in fiction, 20

Simultaneity: in special theory of relativity, 10

Smollett, Tobias, 153–54

Snow, C. P., on science and literature, 236

Social satire: in actualistic fiction, 231

Song: in *Gravity's Rainbow*, 55–56

Sorrentino, Gilbert, as metafictionist, 4

Space: in actualistic fiction, 229. *See also* Setting

Space-time continuum: in relativity theory, 10–11

Stark, John, on film in Pynchon's works, 33

Stengel, Wayne, 254 (n. 18); on repetition in fiction, 215

Sterne, Laurence, as ancestor to actualists, 18

Structure: of *The Public Burning*, 86; of *Paradise*, 214. *See also* Form; Narrative form

Subject: women as, in *Cat's Eye*, 173, 175–84. *See also* Objects; Subject/object duality

Subjectivity: and uncertainty principle, 13; of actualism, 18–19; and feminism, 161, 164; in *Cat's Eye*, 161–62, 164–66, 181; in Atwood's fiction, 164; in form of *Cat's Eye*, 184; in actualistic fiction, 223

Subject/object duality: in *Cat's Eye*, 161–62, 165–66, 176; in classical physics, 162–63

Sukenick, Ronald: as metafictionist, 4; on fiction, 4

Surrealism. *See* Realism: and surrealism

Symmetry: in *The Public Burning*, 74, 86

Tan, Amy, 232

Tatham, Campbell, on Barth, 126

Television: in *Vineland*, 33; in *The Public Burning*, 79. *See also* Film

Temporality: and relativity theory, 10; in *LETTERS*, 141–42, 146–48, 155–56

Tense: in *Cat's Eye*, 187; in *Paradise*, 214–15; in actualistic fiction, 229–30

Terms describing actualistic fiction, 8–9, 218–19

Thielemans, Johan, on Gaddis's fiction, 117, 246–47 (n. 27)

Thurman, Judith, on *Cat's Eye*, 166–67

Time: in *Gravity's Rainbow*, 54; in *The Public Burning*, 74–75, 78, 81–82, 85–87; in *J R*, 105–6, 117–18, 155; in *LETTERS*, 141–42, 144–46, 154–56; Atwood quoting Hawking on, 161; in *Cat's Eye*, 186–87; in *Paradise*, 214–16; in actualistic fiction, 229

Time and space: in relativity theory, 10

Torgovnick, Marianna, 227; on endings, 228

Uncertainty: in *Gravity's Rainbow*, 28. *See also* Certainty/uncertainty

Uncertainty principle: in new physics, 9; of Heisenberg, 12–13; and disruption of Newtonian worldview, 13; and accident, 68; and matter and energy, 96–97; in *LETTERS*, 128; Barthelme on, 192; in actualism, 192

Universal theory: of Feigenbaum, 220

Updike, John, 2

Vernon, John, 224, 243 (n. 24)

Virgin Mary: in *Cat's Eye*, 176–77, 252 (n. 18)

Vision: in *LETTERS*, 152; in *Cat's Eye*, 165; in *Paradise*, 216

Voices: in *Paradise*, 216–17. *See also* Dialogue; Language; Narrative voice

Walker, Alice, 170

Waste: in *J R*, 119–20

Watt, Ian: on fiction, 15; on time in *Tom Jones*, 118

Waugh, Patricia, 191; on antirealistic poetics of contemporary fiction, 20